These seminal essays introduce the reader to the interdisciplinary approach of recent New Testament scholarship which is affecting the way the Book of Acts is studied and interpreted. Insights from the social sciences, narratological studies, Greek and Roman rhetoric and history, and classical studies set the Acts of the Apostles in its original historical, literary, and social context. These methods of interpretation have only recently been applied to biblical study in a systematic way, and the discussions from a shared general perspective range over genre and method, historical and theological problems, and issues of literary criticism. *History, literature, and society in the Book of Acts* is an interesting and valuable overview of new work being undertaken on some of the chief preoccupations of current biblical studies with contributions from leading scholars in the Old Testament, the New Testament, and the history of antiquity.

HISTORY, LITERATURE, AND SOCIETY IN THE BOOK OF ACTS

HISTORY LITERATURE, AND SOCIETY IN THE BOOK OF ACTS

EDITED BY

BEN WITHERINGTON, III

Professor of New Testament Interpretation,
Asbury Theological Seminary, Wilmore, Kentucky

CAMBRIDGE
UNIVERSITY PRESS

Published by the Press Syndicate of the University of Cambridge
The Pitt Building, Trumpington Street, Cambridge CB2 1RP
40 West 20th Street, New York, NY 10011-4211 USA
10 Stamford Road, Oakleigh, Melbourne 3166, Australia

First published 1996

Printed in Great Britain by Athenæum Press Ltd, Gateshead, Tyne & Wear

A catalogue record for this book is available from the British Library

Library of Congress cataloguing in publication data

History, literature, and society in the Book of Acts /
edited by Ben Witherington, III
p.   cm.
ISBN 0 521 49520 2
1. Bible. N.T. Acts – criticism, interpretation, etc.
1. Witherington, Ben, 1951–
BS2625.2.H57   1996
226.6'06 – dc20   95–3394   CIP

ISBN 0 521 49520 2 hardback

CE

This collection of essays is dedicated to the memory
of F. F. Bruce and C. J. Hemer

Contents

ix

Preface

It is a strange, but nonetheless true, fact that the only chronicle we have of the life of the early church from about AD 30–AD 60 has gone through long periods of relative neglect in twentieth century NT scholarship, especially in the English-speaking world. A testimony to this fact is that there has been no major commentary on Acts written in English since the work of F. F. Bruce a generation ago, and before that one must go back to the seminal contributions of H. J. Cadbury and his collaborators in *The Beginnings of Christianity*. All of this, however, is now changing. As I write, the first volume of what is likely to be a landmark study by C. K. Barrett on the Acts is about to appear in the prestigious ICC commentary series. One may add to this the recent helpful commentaries of L. T. Johnson and J. B. Polhill,[1] several important studies in the SNTS monograph series,[2] the detailed work of C. J. Hemer, *The Book of Acts in the Setting of Hellenistic History*,[3] a crucial monograph by C. C. Hill,[4] and finally a projected series of volumes emanating from Cambridge including *The Book of Acts in its Literary and Regional Settings*, *The Book of Acts in its Diaspora Setting*, *The Book of Acts in its Prison Settings*, *The Book of Acts in its Theological Setting*, *The*

---

[1] L. T. Johnson, *The Acts of the Apostles* (Collegeville, 1992); J. B. Polhill, *Acts* (Nashville, 1992).

[2] See J. C. Lentz, *Luke's Portrait of Paul* (Cambridge, 1993), and the forthcoming monograph by Prof. L. Alexander on the prologue in Lk. 1.1–4 (cf. her chapter below, pp. 73–103).

[3] Published in the US by Eisenbrauns (Winona Lake, IL, 1990).

[4] C. C. Hill, *Hellenists and Hebrews: Reappraising Division within the Earliest Church* (Minneapolis, 1992). This volume, while achieving its main aim of putting Baur to rest once and for all, nonetheless has some problems. See my review in the *Journal of Ecclesiastical History* 44, 2 (1993), 289–291.

Book of Acts in its Graeco-Roman Setting, *The Book of Acts in its Palestinian Setting*, and finally a commentary on the Greek text of Acts.[5]

This book, however, seeks to do something none of the above volumes will do – *introduce* the reader to a sample of some of the major and recent trends of NT scholarship that are affecting and in some cases changing the way we study the Acts of the Apostles. All the scholars contributing to this volume are concerned to help us understand and set the Acts of the Apostles in one way or another in its original historical setting. The book is deliberately eclectic by nature, intending not to argue for the validity of one particular point of view but to give the reader exposure to the variety of the pertinent current discussion, with sufficient bibliographic resources that one may pursue further study in an area of interest.

In part I chapters by W. J. McCoy, C. K. Barrett, C. H. Talbert, L. C. A. Alexander, and J. Jervell help the reader begin to assess Acts in the context of other ancient historical, biographical, and scientific works. Barrett and Talbert need no introduction to this audience, but it needs to be pointed out that Professor McCoy is a historian specializing in ancient Greek history, particularly in Thucydides, while Dr. Alexander comes to the study of the NT by way of a background in classics. It is my own conviction that progress in understanding the Acts as a historical document can be made only as NT scholarship takes more account of the long history of work by ancient historians and classicists on the Greek and Roman historians, biographers, and other ancient writers. Too often statements by NT scholars have been made, for example about Thucydides and the composition of speeches, in an attempt to draw analogies with Luke's practice, without an adequate knowledge of either the primary classical sources or the detailed research done upon them by classicists and Greek and Roman historians.

Dr. McCoy's chapter provides the reader with the proper

---

[5] This is all undertaken under the editorship of B. W. Winter, a disciple of E. A. Judge, and his collaborators in Cambridge, and will be published by Eerdmans. The first two volumes have already appeared, and the third is in the press.

introduction to Thucydides and the relevant secondary literature. He offers a basis for meaningful discussion of the bearing
the writings of Thucydides have on the assessment of historical
methodology and the use of speeches in ancient Greek historical works. In addition, he provides a sampling of both the
ancient and modern critique of Thucydides. Of especial
importance is the way this chapter stresses how much later
Hellenistic historians, and indeed Roman and later western
ones as well, stood in the shadow of Thucydides. Thucydides
set a standard and provided a model for many if not most later
historians writing in Greek, who sought either to follow in his
footsteps or to set out on their own path, but not without one
eye either on the master or on later disciples of his such as
Polybius.

Professor Barrett's chapter offers us clear evidence that at
least some of the ancients, such as Lucian, knew what critical
historiography *ought* to look like, however far short the attempt
to achieve the ideal might fall. At the same time he shows how
two highly influential nineteenth-century scholars (F. C. Baur
and J. B. Lightfoot) have shaped the contours of the modern
discussion of early Christianity in both its diversity and its
unity. This chapter is a crucial one and we reprint it here with
minor emendations because the scholarly discussion of Acts
today is often still concerned with the issues raised by Baur and
Lightfoot, especially in regard to the tensions between Jewish
and Gentile Christians in the early church. One need look no
further than Dr. C. C. Hill's chapter in this volume, which
strongly critiques the viability of the old Baur hypothesis about
the radical divisions between the "Hebrews" and the
"Hellenists", and between James and Paul, to see how the
history of the interpretation of Acts still strongly affects how we
view the text (see below).

C. H. Talbert has spent many years studying Luke–Acts
from a variety of angles, and in his clear and helpful chapter he
provides us with a further argument for his view that both
Luke and Acts should be seen as biographies rather than
historical monographs, if one is asking about the genre of this
material. This conclusion is not unimportant because in

antiquity there could be a considerable difference in method and character between historical and biographical works. The latter focused mainly on issues of character and characterization of the major figure(s) in the narrative, while historical monographs were concerned with matters of historical causation and dwelt especially on crucial events and deeds. The biographer might record a trivial incident that was nonetheless revealing of the character of the subject of the narrative, whereas the historian concentrated on "historical" events that caused important social changes. Then, too, ancient biographical literature tended to use historical examples for certain clear moralistic aims, as is certainly the case in Plutarch's famous *Lives*, while historical monographs tended to be more concerned with informing the audience about things that had transpired and their historical significance. Obviously, if Acts is some kind of *bios*, this must affect the way we view the historical data in this text.

Dr. L. Alexander's chapter seeks to help us better evaluate the preface to Acts as a means of getting a handle on the genre classification of the Book of Acts as a whole. She points out that the preface to Acts does not make clear whether Luke intended from the outset to write a two-volume unified composition, or whether Acts should be seen as an independent monograph which begins by simply reminding the reader that it is a sequel to the Gospel. She also points out that dedication of a work in its preface does not necessarily signal to the reader that this is a work of ancient historiography, though there are certainly examples of dedications in historical works. The reference back to the content of the first volume in the preface in Acts at least suggests that the reader should expect what follows to be a continuation of what has been offered in the Gospel. The lack of a prospective remark in the Acts preface means that one cannot say that this preface itself clearly suggests that some sort of history writing will follow. Dr. Alexander finally suggests that perhaps the genre of Acts may be seen as residing somewhere on the border between certain kinds of ancient history writing (archaeology? ethnography? apologetic historiography?) and the ancient scientific tradition.

Another related area of interest is the study of the Acts in light of what may be called a salvation historical perspective informed by OT historiography and Hellenistic Jewish literature such as the LXX, the Maccabean corpus, and even Luke's contemporary Josephus. Many scholars are convinced that this is the primary matrix out of which Acts should be interpreted. J. Jervell reprises and advances the discussion of these matters in his chapter on Luke's view of salvation history. He even goes so far as to suggest that Luke may have seen himself as writing Scripture, seeing not merely the content but the form of what he was a writing as a continuation of what we find in the LXX. He demonstrates the considerable thematic links between Luke and Acts, centering on the revelation and enactment of God's βουλή (plan or counsel) for the people of God. For Luke, the sort of history that was worth recording was the record of God's intervention and saving actions in space and time for Jew and Gentile alike. There is a certain similarity of approach to and discussion of the plan of God to be found in D. P. Moessner's chapter in this volume, and the reader will do well to compare the two discussions carefully.

While the first few chapters in this collection deal with questions of genre and historical method, in part II the reader will find several chapters dealing with particular historical and theological problems in Acts. The first of these is by Dr. C. C. Hill and deals with Luke's portrayal of early Christianity and early Judaism in the crucial material found in Acts 6.1–8.4. Through a careful and probing argument Dr. Hill shows that on the one hand, Luke portrays the Jewish authorities as being at odds with both the Hebrews and Hellenists among the early Christians, and on the other hand, Luke does not portray early Christianity, including even Stephen, as being anti-Law or anti-Temple. Rather the gist of the Lucan critique is leveled against the Jewish people, perhaps in particular their authorities, not merely because they had not lived up to the requirements of the Law, but because they had not seen that it pointed forward to a particular messianic figure, namely Jesus of Nazareth. Hill's essential argument is that both early Judaism

and early Christianity were complex, not the least in the way
they related to each other. Furthermore, the theory that tries
to pit early Jewish (conservative) Christianity over against
early Hellenistic (more liberal and universalistic) Christianity,
in the persons of James and Stephen and their supposed
"parties," does justice neither to Luke nor to the historical data
that lie behind his account.

R. Bauckham is well known for his careful and persuasive
work on early Jewish Christianity. In this volume he tackles
the thorny problems of the speech of James found in Acts 15, a
speech regularly assumed to be composed by Luke since it cites
the LXX and is clearly a speech composed in Greek. Prof.
Bauckham shows that the evidence is considerably more
complex than this, that in fact the citation involves the conflation of the Hebrew text with elements of the LXX, and that
a pesher technique of handling the text is used. These and other
factors lead him to the conclusion that while Luke is surely
responsible for the final form of this text, he likely had a source
or sources for both the event and the speech given by James.
This conclusion is significant, as the speech material in Acts 15
is widely thought to provide the clearest evidence that Luke
engaged in the invention and free composition of his speeches.
His conclusions comport with my own as they are presented in
my chapter on Luke's editorial techniques (see below). In a
further chapter, Prof. Bauckham deals with the problem of the
speeches in general. He argues at length that these speeches are
neither transcripts of speeches nor free compositions of Luke,
but rather that Luke follows a form which may be called a
kerygmatic summary of early Christian preaching. Bauckham's work is distinguishable from the earlier work by C. H.
Dodd and others along this line in that he draws not merely on
patterns found in Paul (e.g. 1 Cor. 15.1–7), but on kerygmatic
summaries in the *Ascension of Isaiah*, a much-neglected early
Christian work, in the writings of Ignatius of Antioch, and in
other early Christian sources. The net effect of this argument is
to reveal a kerygmatic summary pattern that was adopted and
adapted with some flexibility by Luke and others.

The fourth chapter in the second part of this volume is by a scholar who is a specialist on Luke–Acts. Dr. D. P. Moessner deals with one of the thornier historical problems confronting the reader of Acts, namely where and what is Luke's theology of the cross? It has not infrequently been argued that Luke has no such theology, and this is thought to count strongly against his having any personal knowledge of Paul, his preaching, or his letters. Moessner shows that such a caricature of Luke's theology will not do, for in fact Luke has a good deal to say about Jesus' death, tying it closely to one of his major themes, the plan of God, while drawing on the Suffering Servant material to interpret Jesus' death. For Luke the basis of release from sins and forgiveness is Christ's death, which stands at the heart of God's salvation plan, as the fulcrum of salvation history. Moessner in fact argues that the death, resurrection, and proclamation of these events by the early church are seen as providing the basis and key to "release from sins," as was foretold by the prophets (see Acts 10.43). This benefit, which is appropriated through faith in the kerygmatic message and its content, is accompanied by purification of the heart of the one responding in faith (see Acts 15.9). By paying attention to the echoes of the Hebrew Scriptures, especially Isaiah in Acts, one discovers that Luke has more of a theology of the cross than is often thought.

Increasing attention in all of biblical studies is being paid to the light that the disciplines of sociology and cultural anthropology can shed on the biblical texts. This is sometimes coupled with broader studies by classicists and Roman historians about the shape of the Greco-Roman world.[6] Prof. J. H. Neyrey has been a leader in discussing sociological, anthropological, and rhetorical matters as they have a bearing on the Acts of the Apostles.[7] In his chapter he focuses on the issue of portrayal of the social location of Paul in Acts. His conclusion, that Paul is

[6] See, for example, the older study by A. N. Sherwin-White, *Roman Society and Roman Law in the New Testament* (Oxford, 1963). On Roman social relations see the important work by R. MacMullen, *Roman Social Relations 50 B.C. to A.D. 284* (New Haven, 1974).

[7] See the volume he edited and contributed to *The Social World of Luke–Acts* (Peabody, 1991).

portrayed as being in the company of the elite of the Greco-
Roman world as one of their retainers, has considerable
importance for the discussion of whether or not Luke portrays
the "historical Paul," or one who is at variance with the
portrait we find in Paul's letters. Neyrey argues at length that
one must attend to Luke's rhetorical strategy in presenting
Paul in this fashion. I would suggest that Paul's letters must *also*
be evaluated in terms of their rhetorical strategy, and when this
is done the portrait that Luke gives us of a Paul who is a Roman
citizen, rhetorically adept, in contact with patrons, and a
person of considerable honor is not significantly different from
the Paul one finds in the capital Paulines, even though from
time to time Paul chooses to portray himself as a weak enslaved
sage for rhetorical purposes.[8]

The various forms of literary criticism, including redaction
criticism, of Acts continue apace, spurred on by detailed and
comprehensive works such as R. Tannehill's *The Narrative
Unity of Luke–Acts*.[9] The last four chapters in this volume can be
grouped together under this heading. The first is by Dr. J. B.
Green, a specialist in Luke–Acts who deals with the issues of
intertexuality and narratology as they impact our understanding of Acts. He shows that the internal repetitions in the text, as
well as the echoes in Luke–Acts of the Hebrew Scriptures,
point to Luke's historical purposes. Like other historians such
as Thucydides, Luke seems to have believed that while history
did not simply repeat itself, nevertheless there were persons
and events in the past that bore striking similarities to persons
and events in the present. It could be said that there were
certain patterns that recurred in history. Hence there was a
good deal to learn about the present from studying the past,
and Luke was convinced that the present was in fact the
continuation, indeed even the fulfillment, of the past. As Green
sees it, the story of the church is inscribed into the story of

---

[8] See my discussion in *Conflict and Community in Corinth: A Socio-Rhetorical Commentary on 1
and 2 Corinthians* (Grand Rapids, 1994), and also in my socio-rhetorical commentary
on Philippians entitled *Friendship and Finances in Philippi* (Valley Forge, 1994).
[9] Published by Fortress Press (Minneapolis, 1986).

Jesus, which in turn is inscribed into the story of Israel found in the Scriptures.

The second chapter in part III, by Dr. B. T. Arnold, a scholar of the OT with a special interest in its use in the NT, works through a series of passages where the OT is alluded to in speech material. This work shows the subtle ways in which certain major figures such as Stephen, Peter, and Paul are portrayed as speaking Scripture, or speaking with the voice of God by using biblical language to suggest that what was now happening was like, and in some cases a fulfillment of, things God had spoken or done before. Of importance for the purposes of this volume is his conclusion that this approach reveals that Luke, like other ancient historians, used the technique of *imitatio*, which has as one of its basic assumptions the continuity of the present with the past so that the former can be expressed in terms of the latter. This conclusion comports well with some of those that arise from J. Jervell's chapter in this volume. Dr. Arnold also makes clear that the use of the LXX in this way shows that the earliest Jewish Christians are being depicted as standing in the Old Testament tradition, critiquing Israel by drawing on the earlier Mosaic and prophetic critiques of Israel. Salvation history goes on, but its advocates draw on earlier stages in that history to illuminate the present. Dr. Arnold is not optimistic that we shall soon discern which version or versions of the Greek OT Luke used, since the issue is exceedingly complex.

The third chapter in part III of the volume deals with the matters of source and redaction criticism as it sheds light on Luke's composition of Acts. I have sought to show in this piece that we can learn a great deal about the character and nature of Luke as an editor in general by looking specifically at the way he handles Mark and Q, and then also the way he handles the three different accounts of Saul's conversion in Acts. What we learn from such an exercise is that Luke did not likely engage in free composition of his material, even the speech material, but rather drew on and edited sources according to his various purposes and agendas.

This volume concludes with the intriguing study of canonical books that are apparently without endings (Mark and Acts) by Dr. W. F. Brosend. Here we come full circle back to some of the concerns discussed in several of the first few chapters in the volume – namely the issues of the genre and purpose of Acts. Brosend ably shows how scholars' readings of Acts 28 have often been determined by their views of the purpose(s) and genre of the book. For example, if one sees this work as an *apologia* for the Gospel then the ending is seen as appropriate, for the book concludes with the Good News being proclaimed unabated for two years at the heart of the Empire. There might also be the further implication that it was to be seen as a legitimate part of the life of the Roman world for it was not proscribed by Roman authorities.

Brosend also points out some of the difficulties in explaining the ending of Acts if one reads it as an ancient biography, a romance, or a biographical or romantic novel. In Acts the main character's end is not reported – indeed his fate is left unresolved. This is quite different from what happens in the aforementioned works, especially since it was a widespread belief in antiquity that the end of one's life revealed much about one's true character and its divine evaluation. Furthermore, as Brosend stresses, ancient romances were characterized by sex, romance, and happy endings for the main character with loose ends all tied up, all of which are in short supply in Acts. Brosend goes on to suggest that the abrupt ending of Mark's Gospel may have suggested to Luke a way to resolve his narrative, or rather a way to force the reader back to the text, even to its beginning to look for clues to explain such an ending. Whether one finds this last proposal convincing or not, it is hoped that all these chapters will force the reader back to the text of Luke–Acts once more to see how it can and ought to be read in its own day as well as in ours. The Acts of the Apostles should not merely be subject to the acts of the historians, whether ancient or modern.

BEN WITHERINGTON, III
Christmas 1995

PART I

Issues of genre and historical method

CHAPTER I

In the shadow of Thucydides

W. J. McCoy

The Athenian Thucydides has cast such a giant shadow over
the domain of Klio that he cannot be ignored. Indeed so
magisterial is his *History of the Peloponnesian War* that comparison with other historians is inevitable. It matters not
whether the latter preceded him or followed in his wake; nor is
their familiarity with the nature and methods of his work
necessarily taken into account. In simple terms Thucydides has
become a barometer by which to gauge the writing of history
both past and present.[1]

Born the son of Oloros of the deme Halimous in c. 454 BC,[2]
Thucydides lived during the most significant and exciting
period in the history of ancient Athens, for among other things
he was able to witness first hand the consolidation of the
Athenian Empire, the emergence of radical democracy, the
cultural effervescence of the "Golden Age of Pericles," and the
grueling civil war between Athens and Sparta. The total effect
of these developments must have been overwhelming on any
contemporary, especially one of Thucydides' intelligence and

---

[1] For a concise yet informative discussion of Thucydides, his work and his times, see
W. R. Connor, "Thucydides," in T. J. Luce, (ed.), *Ancient Writers*, vol. I (New York,
1982), pp. 267–289, and P. A. Brunt, "Introduction to Thucydides," rev., in *Studies
in Greek History and Thought* (Oxford, 1993), pp. 137–180; for an in-depth presentation, see O. Lushnat, s.v. "Thukydides," *Paulys Realencyclopädie der classischen
Altertumswissenschaft*, Suppl. 12 (Stuttgart, 1970), cols. 1085–1354 (= *Thukydides der
Historiker* [Stuttgart, 1970]).

[2] 4.104.4. I have used the Oxford Classical Text of Thucydides throughout: H. S.
Jones (ed.), *Thucydidis Historiae*, rev. J. E. Powell (2 vols., Oxford, 1942). For a brief
yet informative prosopographical sketch, see J. K. Davies, *Athenian Propertied Families*
(Oxford, 1971), pp. 233–237.

station.[3] Given his education at the hands of sophists, he was probably all the more alert to the rapidly changing world around him and became determined to be a principal player in perpetuating the issue of events. We are quite uninformed about the details of his personal life and public career save for what he himself tells us,[4] namely that he was an aspiring author (as early as 431, if not before),[5] that he contracted and survived the plague in 429,[6] and that he was a member of the *strategia* in 425/4, during which time he was held responsible for the loss of Amphipolis and was exiled from Athens until 404.[7] In retrospect, we should be thankful for his misfortune, for had he remained an active public servant on campaign, we might not possess his *History*, which is certainly to be numbered among the most important literary works of the ancient Mediterranean world.

In the pages that follow, it is my intention to focus on three things: (1) what Thucydides tells us about his methods and the composition of his *History*; (2) how Greco-Roman historians and critics evaluated his work; and (3) how modern scholars assess his worth and impact. My purpose is not to be argumentative, but rather to identify a wide range of opinion and interpretation.

WHAT THUCYDIDES HIMSELF SAYS . . .

Thucydides appends two prefaces to his *History* (1.1–23 and 5.26). In the first, he says that he began to write about the war

---

[3] It is almost certain that Thucydides was related to the Philiadai (see E. Cavaignac, "Miltiade et Thucydide," *Revue de Philologie*, ser. 3, 3 [1929], 281–285; and more recently Davies) and enjoyed the fruits of family affluence. For one thing, he possessed gold mines in western Thrace (4.105.1; see also Plutarch, *Cimon* 4.1).

[4] Some scholars (e.g. Davies, *Athenian Propertied Families*, pp. 233–234) are more skeptical than others about the validity of biographical information about Thucydides as found in Plutarch and three ancient *Lives*, in particular that of a certain Marcellinus of the sixth century AD. Marcellinus asserts that Thucydides was a pupil of Anaxagoras and Antiphon, that he was born of a Thracian (Hegesipyle) and married a Thracian, that he fathered a daughter and perhaps a son, and that he was over fifty at the time of his death.

[5] 1.1.1.   [6] 2.48.3.   [7] 4.104.4 and 5.26.5.

from its very beginning, believing that it would prove a great war worthy of account.[8] In the second, he contends that he witnessed the whole war as a mature adult and followed its course with careful attention.[9] Would that the terminus of his narrative were coincidental with the last years of his life, or at least extended down to 404/3; as it is, the final Book 8 breaks off abruptly in the midst of events in late 411. In short, Thucydides never finished his *History*.[10] It is apparent from the outset, however, that he was not content with describing just a "great war," for by the second sentence in Book 1 he is referring to this clash of arms as "the greatest disturbance in the history of the Hellenes,"[11] an assessment that is re-echoed again and again.[12] Thucydides bases this judgment on his own research into the past, both near and remote. Exactly what sources he consulted is not entirely clear,[13] although he says it was impossible to recover clear information owing to the lapse of time.[14] Nevertheless, he proceeds with an abbreviated review of ancient times, emphasizing that earlier populations and communities were so hard pressed when it came to waging war, or even defending themselves, that they were incapable of bringing about peace and stability.[15] He deplores their lack of revenue and underscores the debilitating impact of continuing political strife (including tyranny) and the general tendency to abstain from alliances of any sort.[16] On the positive side, he recognizes a progressive trend in the making, particularly on the part of those naval states which accumulated capital and began to rule

---

[8] 1.1.1.   [9] 5.26.5.

[10] Since Thucydides apparently died before finishing his work (perhaps at sea, or so says Marcellinus), scholars postulate an editor, redactor, or literary executor as responsible for the ultimate edition of the *History* and its division into books and chapters. It has also been argued that there were nine or even thirteen books instead of the conventional eight that appear in all extant manuscripts; see R. J. Bonner, "The Book Divisions of Thucydides," *Classical Philology* 15 (1920), 73–82. Diogenes Laertius (2.57) attributes the publication to Xenophon.

[11] 1.1.2.   [12] 1.21.2; 1.23.1; 7.87.5.

[13] Although Thucydides would have us believe that he consulted a wide range of evidence, he mentions only Homer and Hellanicus by name. See nn. 18–20 below.

[14] 1.1.3 – τὰ ἔτι παλαίτερα σαφῶς μὲν εὑρεῖν διὰ χρόνου πλῆθος ἀδύνατα ἦν.

[15] 1.12.

[16] 1.15.2.

over others.[17] It is here that Thucydides finds the seeds of naval hegemony, which, by way of the Athenian experience, will constitute a central ingredient in his work.

More than once during this superficial (and self-serving) history lesson, Thucydides challenges the reliability of Homer and the poets[18] as well as traditional hearsay stories.[19] He also decries the chroniclers (λογογράφοι) who ξυνέθεσαν ἐπὶ τὸ προσαγωγότερον τῇ ἀκροάσει ἢ ἀληθέστερον, ὄντα ἀνεξελέγκτα καὶ τὰ πολλὰ ὑπὸ χρόνου αὐτῶν ἀπίστως ἐπὶ τὸ μυθῶδες ἐκνενικηκότα.[20] Thucydides will have none of this. He is not about to pen a fable (καὶ ἐς μὲν ἀκρόασιν ἴσως τὸ μὴ μυθῶδες αὐτῶν ἀτερπέστερον φανεῖται), or a declamation devised for a moment of listening pleasure (ἀγώνισμα ἐς τὸ παραχρῆμα ἀκούειν ξύγκειται).[21] Nor will he allow the divine to adulterate his narrative.[22] On the contrary, he will focus exclusively on the human element and offer a factual, season-by-season[23] account of the great Peloponnesian War designed to last for all

[17] 1.15.1. Thucydides (1.18.1) applauds the power and stability of the Spartan system of government – καὶ δι' αὐτὸ δυνάμενοι καὶ τὰ ἐν ταῖς ἄλλαις πόλεσι καθίστασαν, even though the Spartan league was not a true empire.

[18] 1.9.4: ὡς Ὅμηρος τοῦτο δεδήλωκεν εἴ τῳ ἱκανός, τεκμηριῶσαι; 1.10.3: τῇ Ὁμήρου αὖ ποιήσει εἴ τι χρὴ κανιαῦθα πιστεύειν, ἣν εἰκὸς ἐπὶ τὸ μεῖζον μὲν ποιητὴν ὄντα κοσμῆσαι; 1.11.2: καὶ αὐτά γε δὴ ταῦτα, ὀνομαστότατα τῶν πρὶν γενόμενα, δηλοῦται τοῖς ἔργοις ὑποδεέστερα ὄντα τῆς φήμης καὶ τοῦ νῦν περὶ αὐτῶν διὰ τοὺς ποιητὰς λόγου κατεσχηκότος; and 1.21.1: καὶ οὔτε ὡς, ποιηταὶ ὑμνήκασι περὶ αὐτῶν ἐπὶ τὸ μεῖζον κοσμοῦντες μᾶλλον πιστεύων.

[19] 1.20.1: Τὰ μὲν οὖν παλαιὰ τοιαῦτα, ηὗρον, χαλεπὰ ὄντα παντὶ ἐξῆς τεκμηρίῳ πιρτεῦσαι, οἱ γὰρ ἄνθρωποι τὰς ἀκοὰς τῶν προγεγενημένων, καὶ ἢν ἐπιχώρια σφίσιν ἦ, ὁμοίως ἀβασαθίστως παρ' ἀλλήλων δέχονται. Perhaps Thucydides is chiding Herodotus, among others, for perpetuating such misinformation. C. W. Fornara and L. J. Samons, II (Athens from Cleisthenes to Pericles [Berkeley, 1991], p. 6) call this the vanity of Thucydides, who "willingly seized the opportunity to illustrate how uninformed the Athenians were about their own history." Others argue that Thucydides owed an enormous debt to both Homer and Herodotus: e.g. J. L. Moles, "Truth and Untruth in Herodotus and Thucydides," in C. Gill and T. P. Wiseman (eds.), Lies and Fiction in the Ancient World (Austin, TX, 1993), pp. 88–121.

[20] 1.21.1. Later in 1.97.2 Thucydides seems almost exasperated at having to include an excursus on the Pentekontaetia.

[21] 1.22.4.

[22] In 5.26.4, Thucydides admits to the reliability of a lone oracle which prophesied that the war would last twenty-seven years. Still N. Marinatos (Thucydides and Religion [Königstein/TS, 1981]) contends that Thucydides genuinely accepted the traditional beliefs of Greek religion; see also B. Jordan, "Religion in Thucydides," Transactions of the American Philological Association 116 (1986), 119–147.

[23] 5.26.1.

time (κτῆμα τε ες αιει).[24] With this in mind, he takes special pains to elucidate the nature of his data base: τα δ' ἔργα τῶν πραχθέντων ἐν τῷ πολέμῳ οὐκ ἐκ τοῦ παρατυχόντος πυνθανόμενος ἠξίωσα γράφειν, οὐδ' ὡς ἐμοὶ ἐδόκει, ἀλλ' οἷς τε αὐτὸς παρῆν καὶ παρὰ τῶν ἄλλων ὅσον δυνατὸν ἀκριβείᾳ περὶ ἑκάστου ἐπεξελθών.[25] And yet in the end his censorship became so discriminating that he gave his readers no opportunity to judge controversial evidence for themselves. Instead he judged it for them.[26]

Thucydides also makes bold to embellish his narrative with speeches, but once again he countermands his apparent passion for objectivity. Indeed by his own admission, he took liberties in presenting what a speaker reputedly said and even how he said it,[27] claiming that, χαλεπὸν τὴν ἀκρίβειαν αὐτὴν τῶν λεχθέντων διαμνημονεῦσαι ἦν ἐμοί τε ὧν αὐτὸς ἤκουσα καὶ τοῖς ἀλλοθέν ποθεν ἐμοὶ ἀπαγγέλλουσιν.[28] This is perhaps the most provocative statement in the entire *History*, for in effect Thucydides is testing the willingness of his readers to accept on his authority the content of these crucial passages.

All in all, the various acknowledgments of purpose and methodology are remarkable revelations, especially for a historian from antiquity. They also set a precedent, whether Thucydides willed it or not, for the future writing of history. It remains to examine how readers and critics past and present hold him accountable.

IN THE OPINION OF THE ANCIENTS . . .

Whereas Thucydides was quick to carp at the deficiencies of his predecessors, his successors as late as the second century AD treated him with much greater respect and at times with

---

[24] 1.22.4.   [25] 1.22.2.

[26] Thucydides tells of his troubles in dealing with eyewitnesses, 1.22.3: ἐπιπόνως δὲ ηὑρίσκετο διότι οἱ παρόντες τοῖς ἔργοις ἑκάστοις οὐ ταὐτὰ περὶ τῶν αὐτῶν ἔλεγον, ἀλλ' ὡς ἑκαστέρων τις εὐνοίας ἢ μνήμης ἔχοι – yet he never tires of emphasizing the accuracy of his account: e.g. 1.21.1: ἐκ δὲ τῶν εἰρημένων τεκμηρίων ὅμως τοιαῦτα ἄν τις νομίζων μάλιστα ἃ διῆλθον οὐχ ἁμαρτάνοι . . . ηὑρῆσθαι δὲ ἡγησάμενος ἐκ τῶν ἐπιφανεστάτων σημείων ὡς παλαιὰ εἶναι ἀποχρώντως; 1.22.4: ὅσοι δὲ βουλήσονται τῶν τε γενομένων τὸ σαφὲς σκοπεῖν; and 5.26.5: ἐπεβίων δὲ διὰ παντὸς αὐτοῦ αἰσθανόμενός τε τῇ ἡλικίᾳ καὶ προσέχων τὴν γνώμην ὅπως ἀκριβές τι εἴσομαι.

[27] 1.22.1.   [28] Ibid.

considerable awe. Contemporary *Hellenica*-minded historians, such as P (or the Oxyrhynchus historian), Xenophon of Athens (c. 428/7–c. 354 BC) and Theopompus of Chios (c. 378–after 323 BC), deliberately began their narratives where Thucydides left off as if to concede that any rehash of the Peloponnesian War through the fall of 411 was both frivolous and foolhardy;[29] P, for one, even took Thucydides as his model and inspiration.[30] Ephorus of Cyme (c. 405–330 BC), who wrote a universal history of the Greeks, relied on and borrowed from Thucydides' work,[31] as did the author (Aristotle?) of the *Athenaion Politeia*[32] and the corps of Atthidographers from

[29] The identity of P is yet unknown. His *Hellenica* deals with the years 411–386; Xenophon's, 411–362; and Theopompus', 411–394.

[30] I. A. F. Bruce, *An Historical Commentary on the "Hellenica Oxyrhynchia"* (Cambridge, 1967), especially pp. 3–27, comments: "The nature of P's history . . . gives the impression that his choice of source material has much in common with that expressed by Thucydides (1.22.2–3)."

Re Xenophon's *Hellenica*, cf. V. Gray, *The Character of Xenophon's Hellenica* (Baltimore, 1989). Re Theopompus' *Hellenica*, G. S. Shrimpton (*Theopompus the Historian* [London and Buffalo, 1991], pp. 37–39) concludes that there is no way of determining how and if Theopompus followed the "Thucydidean model," but suggests that he "devoted the first book to tying up 'loose ends' from Thucydides" by recapitulating the events of 412–411; W. R. Connor (*Theopompus and Fifth Century Athens* [Washington, DC, 1968], p. 106) is more forceful: "Theopompus' familiarity with Thucydides' history is not likely to be disputed. His own *Hellenica* is a continuation of Thucydides' work, and many parts of the *Philippica* indicate an acquaintance with his predecessor's history. But, Theopompus did not always choose to accept Thucydides' views . . . Indeed, Theopompus' account of fifth-century Athens seems not so much a rejection of Thucydides' as a caricature of him. Thucydides' impartiality becomes Theopompus' anti-Athenian bias; Thucydides' skepticism becomes Theopompus' cynicism. Thucydides' avoidance of the pretentious, the pious, the sentimental becomes Theopompus' insistence on the vanity of human efforts and the depravity of human motives. The lofty reserve and balance of Thucydides often seems missing in Theopompus. Instead one finds the enthusiasm, the virulence, the intense contemporaneity of the political tract."

[31] The history of Ephorus is best mirrored in the pages of the *Historical Library* of Diodorus of Sicily (fl. to at least 21 BC), who used Ephorus as his principal authority for books 11–16 (which recount the history of the Greeks from 480 to 336/5 BC). G. L. Barber (*The Historian Ephorus* [Cambridge, 1935], p. 113) says that "the close connection between the narratives of Diodorus and Thucydides for the period 433–411 has been accepted as evidence of Ephorus' use of the latter," yet T. S. Brown (*The Greek Historians* [Lexington, MA, 1973], p. 114) is careful to point out that Ephorus (via Diodorus) preserves evidence about the Peloponnesian War that "we should otherwise lack and which Thucydides does not give."

[32] J. J. Keaney (*The Composition of Aristotle's "Athenaion Politeia"* [Oxford, 1992], p. 4) says, "On one level, he used Herodotus and Thucydides directly. He also used Atthidographers who themselves will have drawn their accounts from Herodotus and Thucydides." See also P. J. Rhodes, *A Commentary on the Aristotelian "Athenaion Politeia"* (Oxford, 1981), pp. 15–30.

Cleidemus (fl. c. 350 BC) to Philochorus (before 340–after 261/0 BC).[33] Theophrastus of Eresos (c. 370–288/5 BC) praised Thucydides for his rich and ornate diction,[34] and the Alexandrians listed him first in their canon of historians.[35] Polybius of Megalopolis (c. 200–after 118 BC) seems to have ignored Thucydides in his own *Histories*, but, in the words of one scholar, he "stands for a return to his [Thucydides'] aims and methods."[36] Cicero (106–43 BC) praised him with some ebullience;[37] Plutarch of Chaeronea (before AD 50–after 120) deemed his account of the Sicilian expedition (Books 6 and 7) ἀμιμήτως;[38] and Lucan of Samosata (c. AD 120–after 180) promoted him above all others as the paradigm of what a historian should be.[39]

---

[33] L. Pearson (*The Local Historians of Attica* [Philadelphia, 1942], especially pp. 27–48) argues that Thucydides, despite his innovations, was a vital link in the continuum of *Atthides* from Hellanicus on; F. Jacoby (*Atthis: The Local Chronicles of Ancient Athens* [Oxford, 1949], pp. 95, 103, 138–140, and 165) notes his probable influence on Philochorus, to whom he refers as the "last and greatest Atthidographer."

[34] Cicero, *Orator* 39: "primisque ad his [Herodotus and Thucydides], ut ait Theophrastus, historia commota est, ut auderet uberius quam superiores et ornatius dicere." Theophrastus was Aristotle's successor at the Lyceum and the author of many works, among them a Περὶ ἱστορίας (Diogenes Laertius 5.47).

[35] J. E. Sandys (*A History of Classical Scholarship*, vol. 1, 3rd ed. [London, 1921], p. 131) provides the following list: Thucydides, Herodotus, Xenophon, Philistus, Theopompus, Ephorus, Anaximenes, Callisthenes, Hellanicus, and Polybius. Cicero (*De Oratore* 2.57) says of Philistus of Syracuse: "otium suum consumpsit in historia scribenda, maximeque Thucydidem est, sicut mihi videtur, imitatus."

[36] F. W. Walbank, *Polybius* (Berkeley, 1972), p. 40. Walbank goes on (pp. 41–43) to enumerate the many similarities between the two historians and concludes "that though he [Polybius] did not agree in all things with Thucydides, he regarded him as an ally on the main issue of what history should be about. He had no immediate occasion to refer to him with praise (and in any case did not find praising a very congenial activity); but significantly he nowhere speaks against him, but devotes his polemic to those who regarded historical composition as a rhetorical exercise or as an occasion for emotional indulgence."

[37] Cicero, *De Oratore* 2.56: "Et post illum Thucydides omnes dicendi artificio, mea sententia, facile vicit: qui ita creber est rerum frequentia, ut verborum prope numerum sententiarum numero consequatur, ita porro verbis est aptus et pressus, ut nescias, utrum res oratione, an verba sententiis illustrentur." In *Brutus* 83. 287, however, he stops short of fully endorsing Thucydides' speeches: "Orationes autem quas interposuit – multae enim sunt – eas ego laudare soleo; imitari neque possim si velim, nec velim fortasse si possum."

[38] Plutarch, *Nicias* 1.1. P. A. Stadter (*A Commentary on Plutarch's "Pericles"* [Chapel Hill, NC, 1989], p. lx) comments: "Plutarch knew Thucydides' history well . . . He cites specific passages of Thucydides 23 times in the *Lives* and 30 times in the *Moralia*, not including general references."

[39] Lucian, Πῶς δεῖ ἱστορίαν συγγράφειν, especially 41–42.

The lone yet signal voice of censure throughout this entire
period belongs to the rhetorician Dionysius of Halicarnassus
(fl. 30–8 BC), who, in his Περὶ Θουκυδίδου, dared to find fault
with Thucydides' choice and arrangement of subject material
as well as the content and appropriateness of his speeches.[40] He
also took exception to Thucydides' individual style (ἰδιόν τινα
χαρακτῆρα), especially in passages that were overworked and
superfluous,[41] or marked by a poor choice of words.[42] If this
verdict strikes a dissonant chord in an otherwise harmonious
chorus of approval on the part of the ancients,[43] the courage of
Dionysius to criticize Thucydides would eventually inspire
many a modern scholar to follow in his footsteps and be
less daunted by the lofty reputation of the man and his
work.

MODERN VOICES SPEAK OUT . . .

Modern readers and critics have been less reverent and more
controversial in assessing Thucydides' methods and the worth
of his narrative. Indeed, scrutiny and debate have identified a
variety of "problems" and "questions" ranging from the composition of the *History* and the authenticity of the speeches to
such matters as style, the meaning of key words and phrases,
the intrusion of set themes, the author's biases and credibility,
and the like. Since space does not allow for an in-depth
examination of any one of these topics, I will limit myself to a
broad summary of recent discussion and debate.

The composition of the "History"

If it was once reasonable to hold that Thucydides conceived of
his *History* as a unity or wrote it as a consecutive whole, either

---

[40] See, in general, W. K. Pritchett, *Dionysius of Halicarnassus: "On Thucydides"*
(Berkeley, 1975).

[41] See Περὶ Θουκυδίδου 28.   [42] See Περὶ Θουκυδίδου 24.

[43] Although Dionysius was ready to admit that Thucydides was the greatest of
historians (2) and possessed admirable narrative powers (55), he chided others for
being too gullible in their veneration (e.g. 34). At the same time he admits that his
is a lonely and unpopular tack (2).

as a continuing project over many years or a single undertaking at or near the war's end, the overwhelming consensus of
modern scholarship has virtually determined that the composition was both piecemeal and subject to random revising
and re-editing. Current thought would have us believe that
Thucydides not only produced his narrative in distinct sections, but took the liberty of altering the content of the early
books in light of his changing thoughts about the war.[44] Scholars speculate, for example, that the extant manuscript contains
too many rough edges: that Books 1–5.24 (the Archidamian or
Ten Years War, 431–421) and Books 6 and 7 (the Sicilian
Campaign) were composed as separate and self-contained
items; that Books 5.25–end and 8 stand, deliberately or otherwise, unpolished and incomplete (particularly Book 8, which
breaks off abruptly in the midst of the events of late 411); that
digressions such as the abbreviated account of the Pentekontaetia (1.89–117) and the speech-making and policy role of
Pericles (Books 1 and 2, *passim*) were inserted after the fact; and
that passages such as 2.65 and 5.26 (the so-called second
preface) betray obvious signs of forecasting and late adjust-
ment. And yet, despite the many autopsies and revelations,
there is no unanimity amid this barrage of second-guessing.
Whereas the voices of unitarians in whatever guise have been
somewhat muted,[45] the corps of "separatists," "analyzers,"
and "revisionists" are far from resolving what has long been

---

[44] See, e.g., V. Hunter, "The Composition of Thucydides' History, A New Answer to
the Problem," *Historia* 26 (1977), 269–94; and E. Badian, *From Plataea to Potidaea,
Studies in the History and Historiography of the Pentecontaetia* (Baltimore and London,
1993), especially "Thucydides and the Outbreak of the Peloponnesian War: A
Historian's Brief," pp. 125–62 with notes. D. Proctor (*The Experience of Thucydides*
[Warminster, 1980], pp. 11–12) cautions against overconfidence in discerning the
changing pattern of Thucydides' thinking: "There are some daunting complexities
. . . in attempting to trace the path of Thucydides' thoughts through these dubieties
of early and late, especially as the difficulties are at their most acute in those parts of
the History, such as the speeches and one or two passages of sustained reflexion by
the historian, which are richest in thought-content."

[45] For the extreme view see J. H. Finley, Jr. "The Unity of Thucydides' History,"
Harvard Studies in Classical Philology (1940), Suppl. 1, 255–297. Cf. D. Kagan (*The
Outbreak of the Peloponnesian War* [Ithaca, NY, 1969], pp. viii–ix), and G. E. M. de
Ste. Croix (*The Origins of the Peloponnesian War* [London, 1972], pp. 51–52), who
accept the work "essentially" as a unity.

referred to as the "Thucydidean Question."[46] Perhaps we should all heed the cogent words of Mme. de Romilly: "Exhausted by the immense bibliography which it offers, completely negative in its results, the question of the composition of the work can at present be considered as the perfect example of a vain and insoluble problem."[47]

The speeches

The inclusion of speeches presents another crux, especially in light of the revelations in 1.22.1.[48] Claiming that he and his informants found it difficult to remember precisely what they had heard, Thucydides goes on to explain how he has accommodated the "λόγοι" portions of his narrative – ὡς δ' ἂν ἐδόκουν ἐμοὶ ἕκαστοι περὶ τῶν αἰεὶ παρόντων τὰ δέοντα μάλιστ' εἰπεῖν, ἐχομένῳ ὅτι ἐγγύτατα τῆς ξυμπάσης γνώμης τῶν ἀληθῶς λεχθέντων, οὕτως εἴρηται. At first glance this approach seems quite sensible, and we are inclined to be grateful for even a brief declaration of methodology. But we soon come to realize that the statement is altogether too succinct and too inadequate as it stands, for Thucydides neither identifies his informants by name nor discloses here or elsewhere the extent and accuracy of his and their recall. Instead he assumes sole discretion for both context and content (ἐμοὶ and ἐχομένῳ). As a result, we are faced with the predicament of accepting all the speeches on faith or judging each on its own merits (whether it is more or less genuine, or a product of invention and impulse, fashioned to reinforce the author's

---

[46] F. W. Ullrich (*Beiträge zur Erklärung des Thukydides* [Hamburg, 1846]) became the first "separatist" when he proposed that the account of the Ten Years War (431–421) constituted a distinct aggregate of the whole *History*; see also Luschnat, "Thukydides," cols. 1183–1229.

[47] J. de Romilly, *Thucydides and Athenian Imperialism*, trans. P. Thody (Oxford, 1963), p. 6.

[48] See in general A. W. Gomme, "The Speeches in Thucydides," in *Essays in Greek History and Literature* (Oxford, 1937), pp. 156–189; Luschnat, "Thukydides," cols. 1146–1183; P. A. Stadter (ed.), *The Speeches in Thucydides* (Chapel Hill, 1973), especially W. C. West, "A Bibliography of Scholarship on the Speeches in Thucydides 1873–1970," pp. 124–165; and S. Hornblower, *Thucydides* (Baltimore, 1987), pp. 45–72.

personal notions of what the war was all about).[49] Another pitfall of this passage is the challenge of interpreting such enigmatic expressions as τὰ δέοντα, τῆς ξυμπάσης γνώμης and τῶν ἀληθῶς λεχθέντων the way Thucydides intended.[50]

However we choose to resolve these dilemmas, it should be noted that Thucydides had a tendency to employ "paired"

[49] The question of the authenticity of the speeches is inextricably interrelated with Thucydides' credibility as a historian. M. Cogan (*The Human Thing: The Speeches and Principles of Thucydides' History* [Chicago, 1981], p. xi) sums up the situation: "Not to accept the speeches at face value would obscure Thucydides' interpretation of the war, for in that interpretation the speeches play their parts as speeches. This alone would compel us to deal with them as genuine speeches, since operationally it is only thus that we can securely recover Thucydides' view of this war, and understand what in fact the text of his history is saying. Again, this is no blind leap of faith or speculative hypothesis, for the alternative, denying the authenticity of the speeches (or Thucydides' accuracy in reporting them), has extensive and destructive consequences which I believe ultimately outweigh any benefits (for the understanding of either Thucydides or the Peloponnesian War) that might come from the apparent independence of such skepticism . . . To question the veracity of the speeches has the ultimate consequence of undermining – if not utterly destroying – the credibility of all of Thucydides' history."

[50] Translators and commentators are far from unanimous about the meaning of these words and how the complete statement should be construed. See, e.g., Walbank, "Speeches in Greek Historians," Third Myres Memorial Lecture, Oxford 1965 (= F. W. Walbank, *Selected Papers* [Cambridge, 1985], pp. 244–245): "Passing over τὰ δέοντα, which may mean either what the various occasions demanded or what the speakers had to say (and so *did* say), the crux of the matter is the meaning of τῆς ξυμπάσας γνωμης, for it is of course self-evident that the style and actual flavour of the argumentation, with their unmistakable Thucydidean stamp, whoever is speaking, are imposed on the material by the historian. If ἡ ξυμπᾶσα γνώμη is simply 'the general intention' of the speech, as deduced from Thucydides' knowledge of the potential color of the speaker and the historical situation in which the speech was delivered or was supposed to have been delivered, then Thucydides' speeches are in effect no more than free composition . . . But Thucydides also used the phrase τῶν ἀληθῶς λεχθέντων, 'what in truth was said', and it is surely hard to reconcile these three words with any theory which envisages that Thucydides simply composed his speeches without reference to the original words. True, the *ipsissima verba* are qualified . . . by the reference to Thucydides' opinion and by the limitation implied in ἡ ξυμπᾶσα γνώμη – which will mean 'the overall purport of what was said.' But they remain the foundations of the speech, if modified by the historian's opinion of what the situation demanded and by his giving the general purport rather than the words themselves." Hornblower (*Thucydides*) comments: "The speeches offer further evidence that two hearts beat in Thucydides' breast. In particular, the famous programmatic statement about the speeches in Book 1 contains another unresolved contradiction between the criteria of subjectivity and objectivity"(p. 45); and "Thucydides' aim in speeches, as in narrative, was to record truthfully – to give 'what was really said'; but again there was present an opposite and inconsistent aim, to omit, select and concentrate, giving instead 'what was appropriate'" (p. 71). A. Andrewes ("The Mytilene Debate: Thucydides 3.36–49," *Phoenix* 16 [1962], 65) believes, "Thucydides' practice altered with time

speeches (side by side or separated), or "complementary" speeches if this better suited his needs.[51] Many speakers are named individuals; others are anonymous groups. Although *oratio recta* predominates,[52] there are numerous instances of *oratio obliqua* particularly in Book 8.[53] Whereas such diversity enhances the presentation of material, it also complicates any assessment of Thucydides' accountability.

and came in the end to diverge widely from the principle he had enunciated in 1.22.1.1." Cf. D. Kagan ("The Speeches in Thucydides and the Mytilene Debate," *Yale Classical Studies* 24 [1975], 74–75): "Without recording devices or shorthand stenographers memory alone could not hope to achieve an accurate record, and Thucydides acknowledges the need to reconstruct rather than record. Thus the statement may be taken to refer to the form rather than the content of the speeches. It is also likely that Thucydides received reports of some speeches that were less complete than others. He may have been told of the general line of argument and given a few quotations and details and supplied the rest of the speech from what seemed to him τὰ δέοντα. That, however, is as far as his words will permit us to go. Seen in this light there is no contradiction between the two clauses." So, too, R. Develin ("Thucydides on Speeches," *The Ancient History Bulletin* 4 [1990], 58–59): "in itself this [1.22.1] is a perfectly straightforward statement. Readers had to be apprised of the fact that there was truth in the speeches: they were actually made and the intent of what was said has been faithfully communicated as far as was possible in the state of whatever knowledge was to hand in particular cases. And yet Thucydides is not disguising the fact, to which his audience would not object, that his historical imagination has composed for his speakers the words which seemed necessary to their intent. He cannot be taken as claiming to do what he has just said he could not do and stylistic considerations alone would show that, even if he has retained phrases and arguments from the original, he has composed in a free manner. What has concerned scholars is whether the speeches do in fact correspond to the principles here enunciated, but that is a separate question, the conclusion of which should not be allowed to complicate interpretation of 1.22.1." For further discussion, see J. Wilson, "What does Thucydides Claim for his Speeches?" *Phoenix* 36 (1982), 95–103, and D. Rokeah, "Τὰ δέοντα περὶ τῶν αἰεὶ παρόντων: Speeches in Thucydides: Factual Reporting or Creative Thinking?," *Athenaeum* 60 (1982), 386–401.

51 For a concise discussion of the various types of speeches, see W. C. West, "The Speeches in Thucydides: A Description and Listing," in Stadter, *Speeches*, pp. 3–15.

52 The speeches have been variously categorized as deliberative, judicial, and epideictic; there are also several battlefield harangues and a few dialogues. On the military speeches, see O. Luschnat, *Die Feldherrnreden im Geschichtswerk des Thukydides, Philologus*, Suppl. 34 (Leipzig, 1942); R. Leimbach, *Militarische Musterrhetorik: Eine Untersuchung zu den Feldherrnreden des Thukydides* (Weisbaden, 1985), and M. H. Hansen, "The Battle Exhortation in Ancient Historiography: Fact or Fiction?," *Historia* 42 (1993), 161–180.

53 Many would argue that the absence of *oratio recta* in this unfinished book is an indication that Thucydides inserted first-person speeches in his *History* only after he had drafted an entire unit of narrative and/or was engaged in a late stage of editing. Of the near forty occasions of reported speech in *oratio obliqua* in Book 8, none are more appropriate for conversion than Pisander's speeches to the Athenian assembly in 412/11 (specifically 8.53 and 8.67.1), for which see W. J. McCoy, "The 'Non-Speeches' of Pisander in Thucydides, Book Eight," in Stadter, *Speeches*, pp. 78–89.

Apart from discoursing upon the merits and deficiencies of 1.22.1, scholars have queried and examined the speeches in a variety of other ways. For example, why did Thucydides utilize speeches where he did, and when did he compose them?[54] Why do the speeches in the later books have a stronger ring of verisimilitude?[55] Do the speeches conform to contemporary theories of Greek rhetoric?[56] Why is the Greek more difficult in the speeches than in the narrative?[57] Granted their unique Thucydidean style, are the speeches also the mouthpieces of Thucydides?[58] Are there "universal" as well as "particular"

---

[54] Such discussions often overlap with the problem of composition.

[55] See, e.g., Proctor, *The Experience of Thucydides*, pp. 154–159.

[56] See, e.g., C. Macleod, "Rhetoric and History (Thucydides 6.16–18)," in *Collected Essays* (Oxford, 1983), pp. 68–87; and P. E. Arnold, "The Persuasive Style of Debates in Direct Speech in Thucydides," *Hermes* 120 (1992), 44–57.

[57] See, e.g., W. Jaeger, *Paideia*, vol. 1, 2nd ed., trans. G. Highet (Oxford, 1945), p. 392: "To do as some have done and search these speeches for the relics of what was actually said on any occasion, is a task as hopeless as to try to recognize the features of particular models in the gods sculptured by Phidias. And even though Thucydides tried to obtain true information about the course of each debate he described, it is certain that many of the speeches in his book were never delivered, and that most of them were substantially different from his version of them . . . As a language for these imaginary speeches he constructed a style which was the same for them all, which was always far loftier than the spoken Greek of his time, filled with antitheses that seem artificial to modern taste. With their excessively difficult language striving to express equally difficult thoughts, contrasting strangely with a figurative style borrowed from sophistical rhetoricians, these speeches are the most direct expression of Thucydides' thought, which rivals the work of the greatest Greek philosophers both in obscurity and profundity."

[58] See, e.g., Michael Grant, *The Ancient Historians* (New York, 1970), pp. 90–91: "His speeches make little attempt to reproduce speakers' individual characteristics or probable styles . . . the speakers talk the language not of themselves but of their author . . . In his view the speakers are not just there in their own right. To a certain extent they are mouthpieces of the historian, in that they provide the medium for a substantial part of his huge contribution to the development of abstract and rational thinking. But they are much more than merely his mouthpieces. They are there to reveal underlying causes; to display the characters and tempers and motives of individuals and nations; to penetrate to general truths which might not have emerged from the details of the narrative; to get the participants in events, political or military, to speak for themselves; and to bring out, by methods impossible for a mere chronicle, subjective elements that are indispensable to our understanding." See also de Romilly (*Thucydides and Athenian Imperialism*, p. 111), who regards the three speeches of Pericles as expressions of Thucydides' own views. Cf. D. P. Tompkins ("Stylistic characterization in Thucydides: Nicias and Alcibiades," *Yale Classical Studies* 22 [1972], 181–214) and H. P. Stahl ("Speeches and Course of Events in Books Six and Seven of Thucydides," in Stadter, *Speeches*, pp. 60–63), who disavow the "mouthpiece" theory in favor of a more individualized approach.

statements to be found in the speeches?[59] and what is the relationship between speeches and narrative?[60] We continue to ask these and other questions as if the answers were lurking somewhere in the pages of the *History*, but this is wishful thinking. It is more prudent to bow to necessity and accept the sobering fact that for all our ingenuity and devices we will never be able to disentangle the mystery of the speeches.[61] Maybe, then, we can find a degree of humor in the words of Simon Hornblower:[62] "there would be no problem at all if Thucydides, unlike all other writers in antiquity, had not pledged himself to give in some sense a truthful version of his speeches."[63]

---

[59] See, e.g., N. G. L. Hammond, "The Particular and the Universal in the Speeches of Thucydides," in Stadter, *Speeches*, pp. 49–59.

[60] Countering the once fashionable opinion that the real meaning of the *History* is contained in the speeches, Stahl ("Speeches and Course of Events," in Stadter, *Speeches*, pp. 60–77) argues that we should rely more on the narrative. H. D. Westlake ("The Setting of Thucydidean Speeches," in Stadter, *Speeches*, pp. 90–108) examines the close coordination between what he calls the "preambles" and "postscripts" and the speeches that they frame.

[61] See K. J. Dover, *Thucydides* (Oxford, 1973), p. 26: "Our predicament in almost every aspect of Thucydidean studies is that most arguments offered by most people on any one problem are rationally founded; but the evidence is hardly ever sufficient to reveal the relative importance of conflicting considerations."

[62] *Thucydides*, p. 71.

[63] New Testament scholars have often turned to Thucydides to assess what impact, if any, his use of speeches may have had on the author of *Acts* – see, e.g., G. H. R. Horsley, "Speeches and Dialogue in Acts," *New Testament Studies* 32 (1986), 609: "It is almost *de rigueur* for those commenting upon the speeches as a distinctive element in Acts to refer to Thucydides 1.22, that memorable programmatic statement in which the greatest of the historians from antiquity revealed part of his hand, at least, about his creative technique." It should come as no surprise that the ultimate dividing line rests on the interpretation of 1.22.1. Those who are convinced (either by way of their own analyses or leaning on prevailing translations and opinions among classicists) detect the same process at work in Acts (F. F. Bruce, A. W. Moseley, C. J. Hemer, et al.), or vice versa (M. Dibelius, H. J. Cadbury, B. Gärtner, et al.). For a brief review of this scholarship, see S. E. Porter, "Thucydides 1.22.1 and Speeches in Acts: Is There a Thucydidean View?," *Novum Testamentum* 32 (1990), 121–124 and nn. 1–11. Porter's own critique of Thucydides 1.22.1 (127–142) concludes: "any invocation of the Thucydidean view of speeches must argue for and defend a position rather than assume one. The attempt to formulate a position may prove profitable, although it may prove to be perpetually frustrating . . . future work with the Thucydidean view of speeches needs to rely less upon a troublesome programmatic statement than upon what Thucydides appears to be doing within the speeches themselves." These sentiments are echoed by C. Gempf, "Public Speaking and Published Accounts," in B. W. Winter and A. D. Clarke (eds.), *The Book of Acts in its Ancient Literary Setting* (Grand Rapids, 1993), pp. 260–303. On the popularity of the methodological statements in 1.22.1, K. S.

Influences and themes

Scholars presume a variety of stimuli to explain the way Thucydides wrote and thought. C. N. Cochrane,[64] for example, would have Thucydides a scientist, who was intellectually and spiritually inspired by Hippocrates and his school of medicine. R. G. Collingwood agrees and further avows that Thucydides was more interested in propounding psychological laws than narrating fact for its own sake.[65] J. H. Finley, Jr. insists on a broader base of inspiration, concluding that Thucydides' style, ideas, and the forms of arguments which he attributes to speakers are fully consistent with and representative of the general sophistic and political climate of contemporary Athens, especially the 430s and 420s prior to his exile.[66] M. I. Finley dubs Thucydides a moralist.[67]

Sacks ("Rhetorical Approaches to Greek History Writing in the Hellenistic Period," in *Society of Biblical Literature 1984 Seminar Papers*, ed. K. H. Richards, Society of Biblical Literature Seminar Paper Series 23 (Chico, CA, 1984), pp. 123–133) argues convincingly that Hellenistic writers (including Thucydides' most vocal critic, Dionysius of Halicarnassus), took him as their model for the use of speeches in historical narrative.

[64] *Thucydides and the Science of History* (London, 1929): "*The Histories of Thucydides* represent an attempt to apply to the study of social life the methods which Hippocrates employed in the art of healing"(p. 3); and "the power and originality of Thucydides lies in his having attempted to adapt the principles and methods of that science [medicine] to the study of society" (p. 15). See K. Weidauer, *Thukydides und die Hippokratischen Schriften. Der Einfluss der Medizin auf Zielsetzung und Darstellungsweise des Geschichtswerks* (Heidelberg, 1954); and G. Rechenauer, *Thukydides und die hippokratische Medizin: naturwissenchaftliche Methodik als Modell für Geschichtsdeutung*, Spudasmata 47 (Hildesheim, Zurich, and New York, 1991). Of related interest, see D. Page, "Thucydides' Description of the Great Plague at Athens," *Classical Quarterly* NS 3, 47 (1953), 97–119; and A. M. Parry, "The Language of Thucydides' Description of the Plague," *Bulletin of the Institute of Classical Studies of the University of London* 16 (1969), 106–118.

[65] *The Idea of History* (Oxford, 1946), p. 29: "The style of Thucydides is harsh, artificial, repellent. In reading Thucydides I ask myself, What is the matter with the man, that he writes like that? I answer: he has a bad conscience. He is trying to justify himself for writing history at all by turning it into something that is not history . . . Thucydides is the father of psychological history." See also P. Huart, *Le Vocabulaire de l'analyse psychologique dans l'œuvre de Thucydide* (Paris, 1968).

[66] See "Euripides and Thucydides," *Harvard Studies in Classical Philology* 49 (1938), 23–68; and "The Origins of Thucydides' Style," *Harvard Studies in Classical Philology* 50 (1939), 35–84.

[67] "Thucydides the Moralist," in *Aspects of Antiquity*, 2nd ed. (Harmondsworth, 1977), pp. 48–59. Cf. de Ste. Croix (*The Origins of the Peloponnesian War*, pp. 18–19), who points to the "amorality of Thucydides, which is very thorough-going in almost

On a different tack, there has been considerable clamor of late that there is more to Thucydides beyond the objective – in other words, that he has been less than candid in describing how he sorted and sifted through the evidence, that he manipulated content to accommodate or accent a particular theme or themes central to the way he presented material, and even more accusatory, that he deliberately programmed the flow of events to lure his readers into thinking what he wants them to think, namely that his account of the war is complete and truthful.[68] Thematic, conceptual, philological, and structural

everything that pertains to what we call 'international affairs' . . . When he deals with the relations of individuals inside the State he is quite prepared to make moral judgments, of a sensible if conventional kind, in his own person"; and Proctor (*The Experience of Thucydides*, p. 175): "Thucydides simply gives his account of the quarrels and the state of feeling which produced the war itself without entering into any question of morality . . . The 'judgement of history' was not a concept which Thucydides would ever have entertained." P. R. Pouncey (*The Necessities of War: A Study of Thucydides' Pessimism* [New York, 1980], p. xiii) contends that Thucydides was preoccupied instead with the progress of pessimism – "the conviction that human nature carries within itself drives that are destructive of its own achievements . . . This is a conviction that was borne in on Thucydides with increasing bitterness as the war and his exile dragged on, and he involves his readers in the process of formulation, to bring them to his own disillusionment"; see also A. M. Parry ("Thucydides' Historical Perspective," *Yale Classical Studies* 22 [1972], 50): "Thucydides' vision of history is of greatness measured by war, and greatness of war measured by destruction, or πάθος. This vision is a product of Thucydides' own experience."

68 See, e.g., J. de Romilly, *Histoire et raison chez Thucydide* (Paris, 1956) and *La Construction de la vérité chez Thucydide* (Paris, 1990); W. P. Wallace, "Thucydides," *Phoenix* 18 (1964), 251–261; H. P. Stahl, *Thukydides: Die Stellung des Menschen im geschichtlichen Prozess* (Munich, 1966), especially pp. 12–35, and "Speeches and Course of Events in Books Six and Seven of Thucydides," in Stadter, *Speeches*, p. 61: "mere narration of any set of historical facts already implies a subjective element (because presentation includes judgment, evaluation, selection, arrangement, in short: interpretation) – to recognize, I say, the inherent subjective character of any historical narration at the same time allows us, in this field too, to rediscover and appreciate more fully the categories which Thucydides applied for selecting and presenting events"; V. J. Hunter, *Thucydides, the Artful Reporter* (Toronto, 1973), p. 177: "Thucydides' 'facts' cannot be considered in isolation from the schema or pattern which informs them"; Hornblower, *Thucydides* p. 155: "Every sentence of Thucydides' narrative represents one of his opinions. But to an unusual degree this most magisterial of writers conveys the impression that all his pronouncements have the absolute authority of hard fact"; W. R. Connor, "A Post-Modernist Thucydides?," *Classical Journal* 72 (1976–1977), 298: "As we open our eyes wider it may be possible to behold in Thucydides the fusion of an historian of integrity with an artist of profound intensity"; D. M. Lewis, *Cambridge Ancient History*. vol. v, 2nd ed. (Cambridge, 1992), p. 370: "It is not an unreasonable attitude to be interested in the Peloponnesian War for what Thucydides made of it and not for its own sake,

approaches to the *History*, which are also adduced in connection with the problems of composition and unity, include such diverse foci as power,[69] Athenian imperialism,[70] γνώμη,[71] τύχη,[72] σωφροσύνη,[73] ἀνάγκη,[74] the use or meaning of certain words,[75] mirroring or "double vision,"[76] and divergences in

and few episodes in history are so closely associated with their chronicler"; and Badian, *From Plataea to Potidaea*, p. 127: "It might be said that, in modern terms, Thucydides' method of presentation is much more like that of a journalist than like that of the historian. He allows only 'edited' material to reach the reader, the facts that he regards as 'fit to print' and that will leave the reader no choice but to accept his own conclusions implied in the presentation. Like the journalist working for a paper that regards advocacy as an integral part of its business, he will at times give evidence that might contradict the conclusion to which he has been leading us." Such assertions, of course, run counter to the views of "positivists" (e.g., J. B. Bury, A. W. Gomme, and F. E. Adcock), who see Thucydides as purely an objective observer.

[69] See, e.g., A. G. Woodhead, *Thucydides on the Nature of Power*, Martin Classical Lectures 24 (Cambridge, MA 1970); H. R. Immerwahr, "Pathology of Power and the Speeches in Thucydides," in Stadter, *Speeches*, pp. 16–31; A. Rengakos, *Form und Wandel des Machtdenkens der Athener bei Thukydides*, Einzelschriften 48 (Stuttgart, 1984); and J. W. Allison, *Power and Preparedness in Thucydides* (Baltimore, 1989).

[70] See, e.g., de Romilly, *Thucydides and Athenian Imperialism*. Of related interest are assessments of the character and popularity of the Athenian Empire based in part or in whole on Thucydides' *History*. See, e.g., de Ste. Croix, "The Character of the Athenian Empire," *Historia* 3 (1954–1955), 1–41; D. W. Bradeen, "The Popularity of the Athenian Empire," *Historia* 9 (1960), 257–269; T. J. Quinn, "Thucydides and the Unpopularity of the Athenian Empire," *Historia* 13 (1964), 257–266.

[71] See, e.g., P. Huart, ΓΝΩΜΗ *chez Thucydide et ses contemporains* (Paris, 1973).

[72] See, e.g., Stahl, *Thukydides: Die Stellung des Menschen im geschichtlichen Prozess, passim*; and V. Hunter, *Past and Process in Herodotus and Thucydides* (Princeton, 1982), pp. 333–335.

[73] See, e.g., H. North, *Sophrosyne, Self-knowledge and Self-restraint in Greek Literature*, Cornell Studies in Classical Philology 35 (Ithaca, NY, 1966), especially pp. 85–120; and J. R. Wilson, "Sophrosyne in Thucydides," *The Ancient History Bulletin* 4 (1990), 51–57.

[74] See, e.g., M. Ostwald, ΑΝΑΓΚΗ *in Thucydides*, American Classical Studies 18 (Atlanta, 1988).

[75] See, e.g., F. Solmsen, "Thucydides' Treatment of Words and Concepts," *Hermes* 99 (1971), 385–408; and G. Kirkwood, "Thucydides' Words for Cause," *American Journal of Philology* 73 (1952), 37–61.

[76] See H. R. Rawlings, III (*The Structure of Thucydides' History* [Princeton 1981], pp. 5–6): "that while Thucydides considers the Peloponnesian War to be one great war, he also saw it as comprising two distinct wars; that these two wars were almost identical in length; that they presented similar problems and similar opportunities to the combatants; that the combatants reacted to them in different, sometimes opposite ways. It is the contention of this study that this double vision, this constant comparison and contrast of the events in the two wars, is the principal thematic regular of Thucydides' work, indeed that it controls to a very great extent the structure of Thucydides' *History*. In addition, it is responsible for much of the tragic irony in the work and shapes nearly every episode in it. It may not be an exaggeration to say that this double vision is the wellspring of Thucydides' *History*."

the treatment of leading individuals in different sections of his work.[77] Often the accent is on the antitheses in Thucydides' text.[78] W. R. Connor, on the other hand, defends a straight objective reading of the extant text "as a legitimate means by which the reader can be helped to an understanding of the events narrated."[79] While such autopsies of dissection and bisection expose the *History* to more intensive scrutiny and perhaps guide us to understand its intended meaning better, they are stark evidence of how complex any serious reading of this work has become – even more, of how successfully and effectively its author has managed to confound posterity.

Omissions and biases

In addition to charges that he doctored material to suit his purpose, Thucydides has been accused of deliberate omissions and bias on several counts. A. W. Gomme, for one, begins his compendious commentary with a litany of missing items under the disarming headings: "What Thucydides Takes for Granted" and "Thucydides' Self-imposed Limitations."[80] And although he bemoans the fact that Thucydides fails to provide a detailed spreadsheet of the finances of the Athenians[81] and has come up short in describing their fifth-century military (especially naval) and constitutional practices, to say nothing of the organization of their empire,[82] he politely forgives such

---

[77] See H. D. Westlake, *Individuals in Thucydides* (Cambridge 1968).

[78] See, e.g., L. Pearson, "Prophasis and Aitia," *Transactions of the American Philological Association* 83 (1952), 205–223; S. Schüller, "About Thucydides' Use of ΑΙΤΙΑ and ΠΡΟΦΑΣΙΣ," *Revue Belge* 34 (1956), 971–984; L. Edmonds, *Chance and Intelligence in Thucydides* (Cambridge, MA, 1975); and A. M. Parry, *Logos and Ergon in Thucydides*, Diss. Harvard, 1957 (New York, 1981).

[79] *Thucydides* (Princeton, 1984), p. 8.

[80] *A Historical Commentary on Thucydides I* (Oxford, 1959), pp. 1–29.

[81] Cf., however, L. Kallet-Marx (*Money, Expense, and Naval Power in Thucydides' History 1–5.24* [Berkeley, 1993]), who argues convincingly that "Thucydides' treatment of the role of financial resources in his *History* through the end of the Archidamian War constitutes, in its breaking away from a long and venerable tradition of ideas about wealth and power, a central aspect of his originality as a historical analyst" (p. 205).

[82] On the deficiencies in Thucydides' account of the Pentecontaetia (478–433 BC), see R. Meiggs, *The Athenian Empire* (Oxford, 1972), pp. 444–446. Proctor (*The Experience of Thucydides*, p. 185) likens the Pentecontaetia to "a badly loaded shopping-basket from which a number of sorely needed articles are missing."

exclusions.[83] Other critics are less relenting and add "contra-
dictions, inconsistencies and repetitions" to an ever expanding
list of miscues and oversights.[84] One, after christening
Thucydides "the artful reporter," calls him "the least objective
of historians";[85] another impugns him for disseminating "misinformation and misleading interpretations."[86]

Arguably the most flagrant strokes of bias surface in the way
Thucydides portrays characters and depicts their roles. Even a
cursory examination of the *History* reveals his obvious admir-
ation for the likes of Pericles, Nicias, Alcibiades, Brasidas, and
Hermocrates[87] as well as his great disdain for Cleon[88] and other
post-Periclean demagogues.[89] If we add to this his outspoken,
albeit enigmatic statement about the shortlived government of
the Five Thousand in Athens (411–410),[90] it is easy to explain

---

[83] "He confined himself to the war. We may regret this, and wish that he had written
of the glory that was Athens or some such noble theme; but we must recognize it.
More than this: he interpreted his task as one with narrow limits. He not only
omitted the cultural and economic history which would be proper to a *History
of Athens* or *of Greece*, but also political history where it did not seem to him to have
a direct bearing on the war . . . Owing to his austerity we have lost much"
(p. 25).

[84] See, e.g., Luschnat, "Thukydides," cols. 1112–1132.

[85] Hunter, *Thucydides, the Artful Reporter*, p. 184.

[86] Badian, *From Plataea to Potidaea*, p. 155.

[87] He certainly had some degree of respect for Themistocles (1.138.3), Antiphon
(8.68.1), and perhaps Theramenes (8.68.4). Such favoritism prompts the questions:
How well did Thucydides know his characters? Did he ever talk with them about
the war? And if so, did these personal conversations flavor his work? Whereas he
certainly had the opportunity to become acquainted with or befriend Pericles,
Nicias, and Antiphon while still in Athens, he could conceivably have conversed
with the others during the years of residence at Skapte Hyle, his Thracian Elba. On
Thucydides' personal contacts (including Democritus and Hippocrates), see
Proctor, *The Experience of Thucydides*, pp. 40–45 and 58–67; on his relationship with
Alcibiades, see also E. Delebecque, *Thucydide et Alcibiade* (Aix-en-Provence, 1965).

[88] 3.36.6 and 4.21.3. Over a century ago, G. Grote (*A History of Greece*, 4th ed., vol. v
[London, 1872], pp. 247–266 and 381–395) initiated the opposition against Thucy-
dides' judgment of Cleon; see also A. G. Woodhead, "Thucydides' Portrait of
Cleon," *Mnemosyne*, ser. 4, 13 (1960), 289–317, and D. Kagan, *The Archidamian War*
(Ithaca, NY, 1974), *passim*. Hornblower (*Thucydides*, pp. 5–6) complains that
Thucydides holds back on Cleon and denies him "a full say" in Books 1 and 4 to
avoid casting him in a more favorable light. See also A. S. Vlachos, *Partialités chez
Thucydide* (Athens, 1970); and on Cleon's family, F. Bourriot, "La Famille et le
milieu social de Cleon," *Historia* 31 (1982), 404–435.

[89] 2.65.10. On Androcles see 8.65.1 and on Hyperbolus 8.73.3.

[90] 8.97.2. See G. Donini, *La posizione di Tucidide verso il governo dei cinquemila*
(Turin, 1969); on the ambiguities of this particular passage, see G. Kirkwood,

the many efforts to discern the nature of Thucydides' personal
politics and what impact this might have had on his writing.[91]

Once more we are faced with the inevitable puzzler: were
these various and sundry "defects" sins of omission or commission? Whatever the answer, Thucydides' credibility as a
historian and the worth of his account of the war are at stake.[92]
And if we are resigned to admitting that no history is completely impartial, how much latitude do we allow for the *peccata*
of the author? And in the case of outright rejection, what are
our alternatives?

A possession for all times

It almost goes without saying that Thucydidean studies are
alive and well in the twentieth century. At least five complete
English translations of the *History* are currently in circulation[93]
as well as a new commentary[94] and scores of editions, monographs, dissertations, articles, and reviews which continue to
multiply annually.[95] Of special note is a recent volume of
essays, which confirms that the *History* is far from an anachronism when it comes to formulating the theories and assessing

"Thucydides' Judgment of the Constitution of the Five Thousand (VIII, 97, 2),"
American Journal of Philology 93 (1972), 92–103.

[91] See, e.g., M. F. McGregor, "The Politics of the Historian Thucydides," *Phoenix* 10
(1956), 93–102; M. Pope, "Thucydides and Democracy," *Historia* 37 (1988),
276–296; and V. Tejera, *The City-State Foundations of Western Political Thought*, rev.
ed. (Lanham, NY and London, 1993), pp. 39–46.

[92] See W. R. Connor, "Narrative Discourse in Thucydides," in *The Greek Historians:
Literature and History. Papers presented to A. E. Raubitschek* (Saratoga, CA, 1985),
pp. 1–17.

[93] Books in print include translations by Thomas Hobbes (1629), Richard Crawley
(1874), Benjamin Jowett (1881), Charles F. Smith (1919–1923), and Rex Warner
(1954).

[94] S. Hornblower, *A Commentary on Thucydides* vol. 1 (Oxford, 1991); a second and final
volume is forthcoming. This set is not meant to replace A. W. Gomme,
A. Andrewes and K. J. Dover, *A Historical Commentary on Thucydides* (5 vols., Oxford,
1950–1981), but rather to be "helpful to those students who are interested in the
detail of Thucydides' thought and subject-matter, but have little or no
Greek"(p. v). It also provides a valuable update of bibliography.

[95] Recent volumes of *L'Année philologique* (Paris) cite at least fifty Thucydides or
Thucydides-related titles per year. As Tejera remarks (*The City-State Foundations*,
p. 46): "a great work prevails even when it is misused or not fully understood or still
in need of editorial revision."

the actualities of war, strategy, politics and human relations in the modern world.[96]

Doubtless Thucydides would have been pleased with all the attention he has received and at the same time gratified that his words have inspired such serious thought and reflection. But then he planned it that way. More than a mere story of war between Greek city-states, the *History* is an in-depth study of human behavior that keeps us off balance and forever guessing about the ambiguities and exigencies of life as they are forecast in its extant pages. And so we are goaded to read and reread, analyze and reanalyze, suggest new meanings and interpretations or retreat to old ones – all in an effort to cope with this magnificent yet tantalizing opus and the man who wrote it.

Few would deny that Thucydides was the boldest of innovators, but perhaps his most outstanding accomplishment was the way he orchestrated his own survival. As if by legerdemain, this son of Oloros gambled with destiny . . . and won, apparently confident in the belief that future generations would accept his work as informative, authoritative, stimulating, and challenging to the intellect. And we have not disappointed him.

EDITOR'S ADDENDUM

Prof. McCoy's splendid chapter introduces the student to many facets of the discussion of Thucydides, but it will be helpful at this point to bring to light some further related material that will aid those who wish to understand the relevance of the discussion of Thucydides and other ancient historians to the study of Acts.

I should say at the outset that it is my own conclusion that Luke intends to be seen as a serious Hellenistic historian of contemporary events, rather like a Polybius or a Thucydides.

---

[96] R. N. Lebow and B. S. Strauss (eds.), *Hegemonic Rivalry: From Thucydides to the Nuclear Age* (Boulder, CO, 1991), which incorporates the papers and discussions of a 1988 conference in Cadenabbia, Italy, on the theme "Hegemonic Rivalry: Athens and Sparta, the United States and the Soviet Union"; participants included classicists and ancient historians as well as professors of modern politics, government, war studies, intelligence and international affairs.

Thus it is relevant to ask how his handling of the crucial speech material compares to what we find in Thucydides' or Polybius' works.[97] Firstly, we note that though there is a great deal of speech material in Acts, Luke's speeches are considerably *shorter* than many found in Hellenistic historical works, nor in general do Luke's speeches function to present a variety of viewpoints, though the speeches in Acts 15 may be said to represent something of an exception.[98] Furthermore, Luke gives more space and obviously more importance to the narrative settings of his speeches in Acts than does Thucydides.[99] Also the speeches function somewhat differently in the work of Thucydides and that of Luke: "In Thucydides speeches function as a commentary on events. In Luke–Acts, speeches are an essential feature of the action itself, which is the spread of the word of God."[100] There are thus some differences in the way Luke *uses* speeches from what we find in Thucydides or Polybius, but this does not mean that Luke had a different philosophy from Thucydides or Polybius about whether one should take the liberty of simply composing purely fictitious speeches as they were required or eschew such a practice. A closer look at what Thucydides and Polybius actually say about speeches should lead to caution before one concludes that Luke's speeches are simply his own creation, especially since, as C. W. Fornara has pointed out, *there was no convention in antiquity that a historian should compose speeches for a historical work* (see below).

We turn now briefly to the crucial Thucydidean text in 1.22.1–2 which has been analyzed endlessly by classics scholars, ancient historians, and biblical scholars.[101] If one takes this passage in its larger context, it seems clear enough that

---

[97] I intend to give full evidence for this conclusion in my forthcoming socio-rhetorical commentary on Acts.

[98] See now M. Soards, *The Speeches in Acts: Their Content, Context, and Concerns* (Louisville, 1994), p. 141.

[99] See D. Aune, *The New Testament in its Literary Environment* (Philadelphia, 1987), p. 125.

[100] Ibid.

[101] See. e.g., Grant, *Ancient Historians*, pp. 88ff.; J. Wilson, "What Does Thucydides Claim for his Speeches?," *Phoenix* 36 (1982), 95–103; S. Porter, "Thucydides 1.22.1 and Speeches in Acts: Is There a Thucydidean View?," *Nov. T.* 2 (1990), 121–42 and n. 50 above.

Thucydides is trying to say that he has been as accurate as he can be (cf. 1.22.3–4, where he disclaims interest in romance or myth).

As Prof. McCoy has pointed out, much of the debate has centered around whether Thucydides was contradicting himself in this passage by on the one hand claiming to adhere as closely as possible to what was actually said, and on the other claiming to make his speakers say what in his view they *ought* to have said. Though this view of the matter has both been popular and led to much puzzlement, it is probably incorrect. The ἐδοκοῦν in the key passage should be compared to the use of ἐδόκει in 22.2, where it means "seemed likely." It follows from this that Thucydides was claiming that he presented his speech-makers as saying what it seemed likely that they *did* say (not what they ought to have said), adhering as closely as he could to what he knew of what they actually spoke.[102]

The second semantic conundrum in the key Thucydidean quote centers around the word ξυμπάσης. There are various places in Thucydides where this word is used with an accompanying noun to mean the complete amount of something or something taken all together (for example 6.43.1). When coupled with the word γνώμης, it surely *cannot* mean "the main thesis." It is far more likely that it means something like taking into account all the ideas, thoughts, points behind or expressed in the speech.

What Thucydides claims here is not to *give* us all the γνώμη: he claims that what he gives is consonant with, indeed partly the result of, his keeping all the γνώμη in mind and sticking to it as closely as possible . . . Such a procedure is very different from the attempt to summarise a "main thesis," though in brief reportage it may amount to the same thing.[103]

This, of course, does not mean that Thucydides claimed to offer a verbatim of a speech.

J. Wilson concludes, after evaluating Thucydides' claims in light of what we can know of his actual practice, that his limits or rules of literary license in dealing with speeches were that he

[102] See Wilson, "What Does Thucydides Claim?," p. 97.   [103] Ibid., p. 99.

offered: (1) reportage in his own style, not that of the speaker; (2) a selection from a number of speeches actually made; (3) a selection of the ideas or thoughts (γνώμη) expressed in the speech, not all; (4) a reporting which contains nothing that does not count as γνώμη; (5) the adding of words to make the γνώμη clearer; (6) an abbreviating or expanding so long as the γνώμη is clear; (7) a casting of the γνώμη in terms which might serve his particular purposes (for example the pairing of remarks in two different speeches, for instance 1.69 and 144, or the arrangement into a formal dialogue 5.84–133).[104] In other words, Thucydides does not handle speeches in a radically different fashion than he handles the reporting of events. Both are subject to close scrutiny, analysis, and then a presentation in Thucydides' own style and way, with some concern for literary and rhetorical considerations. In the case of both Thucydides and Luke one must neither under- nor overplay the rhetorical dimensions of the text.

The very reason someone like Dionysius of Halicarnassus so severely criticizes Thucydides in his famous *Letter to Pompey* 3 is precisely that Thucydides does *not* treat history as an exercise in epideictic rhetoric, the writing of encomiums for great men and about great events. Thucydides does not see it as an occasion for free invention of speeches, and saying whatever is likely to please one's audience best. Hermogenes recognized that this did not mean that Thucydides did not use rhetoric; rather "he is as much forensic and deliberative as panegyrical" (*De Ideis* 422.10). I suspect that the limitations listed above for Thucydides in handling speeches come close to the practice of Luke who means to write accurately on a serious subject without neglecting certain concerns for style and rhetorical conventions.[105] This conclusion is also supported by the closeness of Luke at various points to Polybius, in view of what Polybius *also* says about speeches (see below).

---

[104] Ibid., p. 103. This view is much more convincing than that of various scholars who follow the "main gist" theory of G. E. M. de Ste. Croix.

[105] That Luke is style-conscious is shown by the very fact that in Luke 1–2 and in the first few chapters of Acts we find more Semitisms. Luke tries to suit the style of his narrative and speeches to the Jewish subject matter, just as in Acts 17.16ff. we find

One must not underestimate the influence of Thucydides and Polybius in establishing the conventions in regard to the *use* of speeches in historiographical works. Leaving aside the Declaimers during the Empire, who ignored traditional conventions and cannot be ranked among serious historians, we should bear in mind the warnings of Fornara:

conventions set the parameters of conduct; we are not entitled to proceed on the assumption that the historians considered themselves at liberty to write up speeches out of their own heads. That some or many or most actually did so is perhaps hypothetically conceivable. We must recognize, however, that such a procedure would have been contrary to convention and *not, as all too many moderns seem to suppose, a convention in its own right.*[106]

Diodorus Siculus in the first century BC warned against some writers who "by excessive use of rhetorical passages have made their entire historical work into an appendage of oratory" (20.1–2.2), because there was both the less rhetorical and the more rhetorical approach to history writing already extant in his day, and he is arguing for the more traditional, Thucydidean approach. "The principle was established that speeches were to be recorded accurately, though in the words of the historian, and always with the reservation that the historian could 'clarify.'"[107]

Polybius is quite clear about the conventions of handling speeches, and the function they should have in a historical narrative. The "whole *genus* of orations . . . may be regarded as summaries of events and *as the unifying element in historical writing*" (12.25a–b; cf. 36.1). He then goes on to castigate another writer who had the pretensions to write history, Timaeus, for inventing speeches when

it is the function of history in the first place to ascertain the exact words spoken, whatever they may be, and in the second place to

---

a much more Hellenized style, suiting the occasion of a speech before the Areopagus.

[106] C. W. Fornara, *The Nature of History in Ancient Greece and Rome* (Berkeley, 1983), pp. 154–155 (my italics).

[107] Ibid., p. 145.

inquire into the cause which crowned the action taken or the words spoken with success or failure . . . A historian . . . who suppresses both the words spoken and their cause and replaces them by fictitious expositions and verbosities destroys, in so doing, the characteristic quality of history. (12.25a–b)

As Fornara has stressed, there was no *convention* of inventing speeches for Greek historical works, though some armchair and highly encomiastic historians, who did not bother to investigate their subject matter closely or inquire of the eyewitnesses what was said, did so. The portion of Polybius italicized above is especially striking because of the recent work of M. Soards which makes very plain that perhaps the major function of the speeches in Acts is to unify the narrative through a repetition of the major themes of the Good News proclamation.[108] It appears that Luke is carefully following the methodology enunciated by Polybius in his handling of speeches in this regard.

Yet it is very striking to me that *even* some of the Roman historians who took a far more rhetorical approach to writing history nonetheless exercised *some* restraint in handling speech material. For example, Livy, who saw the transition from the Roman Republic to the Empire, was steeped "in Ciceronian rhetorical theory, and profoundly influenced by that orator's style." He "probably spent more time upon the literary composition of his history, which included many full-length speeches, than upon the study and comparison of his source material."[109] Yet even a Livy, whose use of sources can be checked when he draws on a speech from Polybius, does not seem to have engaged in the free invention of speeches; rather "he substantially reproduced the source-content of the speeches he inherited from others."[110] If one cannot assume with a highly rhetorical writer like Livy that the free composition of speeches was engaged in, it would be even less warranted to do so with someone like Luke, especially in the

---

[108] Soards, *The Speeches in Acts*, pp. 199ff.
[109] S. Usher, *The Ancient Historians of Greece and Rome* (London, 1985), pp. 180–181.
[110] Fornara, *History*, p. 161.

absence of a *convention* of free composition of speeches by historians.[111]

Well before the Empire there was an internal debate among historians about how much concession should be given to rhetorical concerns in the writing of history, with continuators of Thucydides like Cratippus disapproving of the inclusions of speeches in history *at all* since it gave too much freedom for rhetorical invention, while at the other end of the scale Theopompus was so obsessed with the literary qualities of his history writing that it may be said that he never saw a rhetorical device that he did not like and use.[112] It was not a matter, however, of the non-rhetorical historians vs. the rhetorical ones; the debate was over whether distortion or free invention was allowable in a historical work in the service of higher rhetorical aims.

No one was seriously arguing that composers of written history should eschew all literary considerations. As H. F. North says, "there were two essential elements in the ancient concept of history: fidelity to truth and perfection of style – *narratio* and *exornatio*."[113] We must speak of a sliding scale

---

[111] It is difficult to get the balance right in evaluating the influence of rhetoric on historians. Even a more sober, cynical, and cautious historian like Tacitus can be shown to have taken considerable rhetorical liberties in the presentation of a famous speech by Claudius for which we have an independent record. See the discussion in E. G. Hardy, "The Speech of Claudius on the Adlection of Gallic Senators," *Camb. J. Phil.* 32 (1913), 79–95 and K. Wellesley, "Can you Trust Tacitus?," *Greece and Rome* 1 (1951), 13–37. Some ancients even considered history and history writing a subset or part of the science of rhetoric. See Sacks, "Rhetorical Approaches to Greek History Writing," *SBL 1984 Seminar Papers*, ed. Richards, pp. 123–133.

[112] See Usher, *The Ancient Historians*, pp. 100–101.

[113] H. F. North, "Rhetoric and Historiography," *Quart. J. Speech* 42 (1956), 234–242, here p. 242. On the subject of whether the influence of rhetoric on history writing was a bane or a blessing, she rightly concludes that much depends on the period and on the person. How much freedom did the writer have to tell the truth during the period in which he wrote and about the subject he addressed? Secondly, how much personal and moral commitment did the person have to telling the truth, even if the work suffered somewhat from an aesthetic point of view? In view of the rough spots, even in some of the speeches in Acts, it seems clear that Luke's concern for style was subordinated to his concern for conveying truthful and accurate substance. Relating the Good News required a considerable standard of fidelity to the truth about one's sources. Luke also does not seem to be laboring with any imposed external constraints in the telling of his tale. Sometimes he records things

between those historians like Livy who are more dominated
by rhetorical considerations and those like Cratippus who are
less so.[114] Even so serious a historian as Tacitus gave full
attention to rhetorical considerations, especially in his speech
material and vivid descriptions of battles and other events told
in ways meant to evoke *pathos*. As Mellor says, Tacitus
"regarded rhetorical training not merely as a bag of oratorical
tricks but as the acquisition of a profound literary culture."[115]
I would suggest that the same seems to have been true of
Luke.

For example, the prologue or *exordium* in Lk. 1.1–4 reflects
Luke's rhetorical interests. This sentence has been rightly
called the best Greek period in the NT. Not only does Luke use
a variety of words not found elsewhere in Luke–Acts or the NT,
showing his concern to impress immediately upon Theophilus
by the style of his composition that this was an important
subject worthy of careful listening,[116] but he writes in a clear
and direct manner in this sentence, as Quintilian required in
an *exordium* (*Inst. Or.* 4.1.34).[117] In general, the places where
Luke's use of rhetoric becomes most apparent are in the pro-
logues, in the speech material, in his summaries, and in his own
travelogue at the end of Acts.

A variety of the speeches in Acts reflect the clear use of
forensic and deliberative rhetoric.[118] One may consider, for
example, the forensic rhetoric of the defense speeches in Acts

that were embarrassing to early Christianity (e.g. the Ananias and Saphira
episode, the squabbling over the dole for the widows etc.).

[114] Those like Cratippus insisted that *veritas* replace *verisimilitudio*. See North,
"Rhetoric and Historiography," p. 239.

[115] R. Mellor, *Tacitus* (London, 1993), p. 7. People often forget that Tacitus was a very
gifted rhetor and lawyer long before he became a historian.

[116] An elevated subject deserves an elevated or stately style.

[117] R. Morgenthaler, *Lukas und Quintilian: Rhetorik als Erzählkunst* (Zurich: Gotthelf
Verlag, 1993), pp. 393–395. As in his other works Morgenthaler overpresses what
one can learn from statistical analysis but this does not invalidate many of his
observations about Luke's use of rhetoric. The style of writing in Lk. 1.1–4 is clear
but not without rhetorical embellishment. Besides the use of unique words one may
point to the elegant use of hyperbaton in the phrase αὐτόπται καὶ ὑπηρέται, as
well as the reference to have investigated "*everything* carefully."

[118] See now Soards, *The Speeches in Acts* pp. 18ff. Cf. what was said above about
Thucydides offering forensic and deliberative speech material.

22–26.[119] Or again one may note the careful rhetorical argument in Paul's synagogue speech in Acts 13.16b–41.[120] P. E. Satterthwaite has shown that Luke's choice and arrangement of material in Acts shows familiarity with rhetorical conventions in regard to invention, arrangement, and style of a piece if it was to be persuasive.[121]

At point after point Acts can be shown to operate according to conventions similar to those outlined in classical rhetorical treatises. There are some aspects which it is hard to explain other than by concluding that Luke was aware of rhetorical conventions: the preface; the layout of the speeches; the presentation of the legal proceedings in Acts 24–26.[122]

Furthermore, M. Soards has now demonstrated at length that whatever sources Luke may have used for these speeches, he has made them his own in terms of style, vocabulary, syntax, and the like. Thus, it is safe to say that they *at least* reflect Luke's rhetorical skill, since what we have in almost every case is a précis or edited summary of a speech, and not an entire speech.[123] In this regard, however, Luke would not have differed from either Thucydides or Polybius both of whom also wrote up their speech material mainly in their own style and manner.

To conclude, those who study the Acts of the Apostles in its historical context will do well to familiarize themselves with both the conventions of ancient historiography and other

---

[119] See J. Neyrey, "The Forensic Defense Speech and Paul's Trial Speeches in Acts 22–26," in *Luke–Acts: New Perspectives from the SBL Seminar*, ed. C. H. Talbert (1984), pp. 210–224; and B. Winter, "The Importance of the *Captatio Benevolentiae* in the Speeches of Tertullus and Paul in Acts 24.1–21," *JTS* NS 42, 2, (1991), 505–531.

[120] See C. Clifton Black, II, "The Rhetorical Form of the Hellenistic Jewish and Early Christian Sermon: A Response to Lawrence Wills," *HTR* 81 (1988), 1–18, here pp. 8ff.

[121] P. E. Satterthwaite, "Acts against the Background of Classical Rhetoric," in B. W. Winter and A. D. Clarke (eds.), *The Book of Acts in its First Century Setting*, vol. I, (Grand Rapids, 1993), pp. 337–379.

[122] Ibid., p. 378. On rhetoric, the legal proceedings, and Acts 24–26 see B. W. Winter, "Official Proceedings and the Forensic Speeches in Acts 24–26," ibid., pp. 305–336.

[123] On Paul's rhetorical skills see my *Conflict and Community in Corinth* (Grand Rapids, 1994), pp. 1ff. and my forthcoming commentary on Philippians for Trinity Press International.

ancient forms of literature such as biography.[124] It is also
critical to familiarize oneself with the increasing impact of the
conventions of rhetoric on history writing, especially during the
Empire. There is no better place to start this process than by
studying Thucydides and the wealth of literature on his work,
in view of the continuing influence he had on all sorts of writers,
including, in my judgment, Luke.

[124] See Prof. Talbert's chapter below in this volume.

CHAPTER 2

How history should be written[1]

C. K. Barrett

Of those who in the nineteenth century applied the historical method to the study of the New Testament and the early church none were more important than Ferdinand Christian Baur and Joseph Barber Lightfoot. My intention in this chapter is to compare them and the outstanding contributions they made to our knowledge of the period with which they dealt. I do this in the hope of recalling for our profit some of the history of New Testament study and of making the point that New Testament study is, or ought to be, a field for international cooperation rather than international rivalry. At first I hoped that my method, of considering what each of these great men made of a particularly obscure piece of New Testament history, might lead not only to deeper understanding of how historians work but also to a fresh consideration and evaluation of the piece in question; it has proved impossible to go so far within the space available. My underlying concern is, however, with the problem of early Christian history. My title I borrow from the Latin version of a tract by Lucian, Πῶς δεῖ ἱστορίαν συγγράφειν. Lucian will, to my regret, occupy a smaller part of the chapter than I originally intended, but having borrowed the title I cannot omit him altogether.

I am interested in Lucian for two reasons. The first is that he

---

[1] This chapter as originally published (in *New Testament Studies* 28 [1982], 303–320) bore the Latin title "Quomodo Historia Conscribenda Sit," to which occasional allusions are made. It was given at the General Meeting of the SNTS in Rome in 1981. See also "J. B. Lightfoot," *Durham University Journal* 64 (NS 33) (1972), 193–204, and "J. B. Lightfoot as Biblical Commentator," *The Lightfoot Centenary Lectures*, ed. J. D. G. Dunn (Durham, 1992), pp. 53–70.

really did know something about the writing of history. It has been maintained that a historical revolution took place in or about the eighteenth century; that only at that time did critical history come into being. There are some senses in which this proposition is true. It is largely within the present century that archaeology has become something of an exact scientific method. The textual and literary criticism of the documents on which the historian must depend have been developed and brought into the historian's craft. History has been brought out into a wider field and seen as part of a social process; as this has happened a wider range of evidence has been employed, and different kinds of evidence, as well as different pieces of evidence of the same kind, have been compared. Undoubtedly, since 1700 or thereabouts historians have learned more about their job. But it seems to me impossible to read Lucian's little tract – not to mention Thucydides, and a few other ancient authors – and sweep away all pre-Enlightenment history as unscientific and fabulous.

It would be hard to improve upon Lucian's account of the moral qualities required in the historian, though, if we may trust him, not often to be found in those affected by that epidemic of historiography which he compares to the epidemic of Abdera, the symptoms of which were nosebleeding, sweating, and the spouting of iambics (ἰαμβεῖα ἐφθέγγοντο, *Quomodo* 1). Some might catch historiography as a disease, but "the one effect and goal of history is to be useful (τὸ χρήσιμον), and this can come from truth alone (ἐκ τοῦ ἀληθοῦς μόνου)" (*Quomodo* 9). "The one task of the historian is to say exactly what happened (τοῦ δὲ συγγραφέως ἔργον ἕν, ὡς ἐπράχθη εἰπεῖν)" (*Quomodo* 39). "The one property of the historian is to sacrifice to truth alone (μόνη θυτέον ἀληθείᾳ)" (ibid.). The historian must be "fearless, incorruptible, free, a lover of free speech and truth, calling figs figs and a boat a boat" (*Quomodo* 41). This last is as good a piece of advice in regard to style as it is in regard to morals. There is other good stylistic counsel too, which there is no time to relate. Lucian is strong on morals, sound on style; he is, it must be admitted, weakest on historical method, that is, on how the historian actually does his job.

There was no Public Record Office readily available for historical research, and he could hardly be expected to give advice on the use of research tools that did not exist. The historian had to use sources of a more direct and personal kind. Lucian writes in a passage (*Quomodo* 47) which is not without interesting parallels with Lk. 1.1–4: "Facts must not be carelessly put together, but the historian must work with great labor and often at great trouble make inquiry, preferably being himself present and an eyewitness (ἐφορῶντα); failing that, he must rely on those who are incorruptible, and have no bias from passion or prejudice, to add or to diminish anything." Speeches are a somewhat different matter; for the most part they were not recorded, and there was nothing to do but make them up. "When it is necessary to make anyone speak, it is specially important that things should be said which are suitable to the person and to the matter in question. Beyond that let it be said as clearly as possible" (*Quomodo* 58). A bit of rhetorical style will do no harm here.

The parallel with Lk. 1.1–4 suggests the second reason for paying attention to Lucian. He was a writer of approximately Luke's own period, and, though Luke might possibly be found among those many historians of whom Lucian disapproved, there is some likelihood that the two will share some basic principles regarding the historian's craft and duty. There is nothing new in such observations, and I have no time to pursue them. Moreover, they do not guarantee the truth of a single one of Luke's statements. It is possible to be a very well-intentioned historian, and a very bad one; and we have already seen that Lucian was strong on morals, sound on style, but not so good on method. The same may well be true of Luke, with the added fact that Luke had no intention of writing with dispassionate disinterestedness. He had a case to make, though it was the sort of case, I suppose, that would not have been greatly helped by stories that were known to be, or could be shown to be, false. The speeches he very probably composed in the way Lucian described.

In saying these things I am in danger of falling into the sin of generalization and must pause to indicate precisely what I hope to do. I shall consider first *quomodo historia conscripta est*, first by Baur and then by Lightfoot. This I shall describe with reference to what all would agree to be a center of importance and of difficulty in New Testament history, the narrative of Acts 15. A comparison of the two historians and their work may lead to a few observations on *quomodo historia conscribenda sit*, though it will not be possible to continue with an application of these observations to Acts 15.

Baur knew that not Acts but the Pauline corpus constituted the prime source of early Christian history. It is indeed not true that he found no historical value in Acts, though this has been claimed, for example by Horton Harris.[2] On the contrary, Acts remains "eine höchst wichtige Quelle für die Geschichte der apostolischen Zeit," though Baur adds immediately, "aber auch eine Quelle, aus welcher erst durch strenge historische Kritik ein wahrhaft geschichtliches Bild der von ihr geschilderten Personen und Verhältnisse gewonnen werden kann."[3] This is borne out by the chapter headings of Part I ("Das Leben und Wirken des Apostels Paulus") of Baur's *Paulus*, which may possibly come as a surprise to those who have been led to think of Baur as one who consistently denied the trustworthiness of Acts. They run as follows.

Die jerusalemische Gemeinde vor der Bekehrung des Apostels. Ap. Gesch. 3–5
Stephanus, der Vorgänger des Apostels Paulus, Ap. Gesch. 6.7
Die Bekehrung des Apostels Paulus. Ap. Gesch. 9.22.26
Die erste Missionsreise des Apostels. Ap. Gesch. 13.14
Die Verhandlungen zwischen dem Apostel Paulus und den ältern Aposteln zu Jerusalem. Ap. Gesch. 15. Gal.2
Die zweite Missionsreise des Apostels. Ap. Gesch. 16
Der Apostel in Athen, Corinth, Ephesus. Seine Reise nach Jerusalem über Miletus. Ap. Gesch. 17–20
Die Gefangennahme des Apostels in Jerusalem. Ap. Gesch. 21.

It is not surprising that the last chapter ("Der Apostel in Rom, seine Gefangenschaft und sein Märtyrertod") bears no

---

[2] Horton Harris, *The Tübingen School* (1975), p. 259.
[3] F. C. Baur, *Paulus, der Apostel Jesu Christi* (1845), p. 13; 2nd ed., ed. E. Zeller (1866), p. 17.

reference to Acts, but it is worth while to note that in Baur's view the record of the journey to Rome is "das am meisten Authentische, was die Apostelgeschichte über das Leben des Apostels gibt."[4] He adds that he does not deal with it because it contains nothing of any significance for Paul's apostolic work. The references in the chapter headings to relevant passages in Acts do not of course mean that the material is simply taken over. The "strenge historische Kritik" to which I have referred has to be applied.

The root of the matter is that Acts is an apologetic document, written not with a single eye to the truth but in order to make a case. How else can one account for the absence from Acts, which purports to tell the story of the apostolic church, of those polemical features and controversial events which appear either on or just below the surface of the unquestionably genuine and transparently truthful Pauline letters? How else can one understand the careful parallelism between Peter and Paul that Acts presents? The author of Acts is so evidently a partisan of Paul's that this can only have been worked out in the interests of Paul. It is not necessary, at least in the first instance, to accuse Luke of deliberate invention. He has chosen to present only material that is suitable to his apologetic purpose and has left in silence that which is not. Every historian must select, but the kind of selection that produced Acts tells its own story. "An sich schon kann gewiss ein Schriftsteller, welcher so vieles absichtlich verschweigt und schon dadurch die Gegenstände seiner Darstellung in ein anderes Licht stellt, nicht für zu aufrichtig und gewissenhaft gehalten werden, um, sobald es in seinem Interesse lag, sich auch noch in ein schrofferes Verhältnis zur wahren Geschichte zu setzen."[5]

So much in general terms, but continuing my drive to the specific, I turn to Baur's treatment of Acts 15, with its account of a gathering in Jerusalem and of the so-called Decree alleged to have issued from the gathering. The chapter in which Baur deals with Acts 15 consists of forty closely reasoned pages, and

[4] *Paulus*, p. 213; 2nd ed., p. 243. [5] *Paulus*, p. 10; 2nd ed., p. 13.

even a fairly brief résumé would exceed the time allowed for
this chapter. It must suffice to bring out Baur's method. His
chapter is a sustained and brilliant example of what I have
already hinted at. Critical history is possible only when two or
more sources are available for comparison; here we have Galatians 2 to set beside Acts 15, and it is impossible to doubt (says
Baur) that of the two Paul's account must be the authentic one.
It is hardly possible to disagree with this; it is more questionable whether Baur is right in saying that where Luke diverges
from Paul's account it must be because he intended to do so:
"die Apostelgeschichte, deren Darstellung nur als eine
absichtliche Abweichung von der geschichtlichen Wahrheit im
Interesse der besonderen Tendenz, die sie hat, angesehen
werden kann."[6] Error can have other causes, for example pure
ignorance.

The first observation that Baur makes, on the basis of Galatians 2, is that it is the older apostles who are Paul's true
opponents. Why should he take the matter so seriously, why
indeed should he go up to Jerusalem, if he had to contend only
with the παρείσακτοι ψευδάδελφοι? "Der Gang der Verhandlungen selbst zeigt, wie sich die Apostel zu den Grundsätzen
dieser falschen Brüder verhielten. Sie sind ja die Gegner, gegen
welche der Apostel diese Grundsätze bekämpft."[7] It is otherwise in Acts, where the troublemakers are a few Pharisaic
Christians (15.5), and the older apostles, represented by Peter
and James, declare themselves to be on the same side as Paul.
Later we shall have occasion to note Lightfoot's view of the
matter.[8]

It may be said that even the narrative in Galatians represents the Jerusalem apostles as recognizing Paul's apostolate
and the validity of his Gospel. True,

aber diese Anerkennung war eine bloss äusserliche, sie überliessen es
ihm, nach diesen Grundsätzen auch ferner unter den Heiden für die
Sache des Evangeliums zu wirken, für sich selbst aber wollten sie
nicht davon wissen. Das beiderseitige apostolische Gebiet wird daher
streng abgesondert, es gibt ein εὐαγγέλιον τῆς περιτομῆς und ein

---

[6] *Paulus*, p. 105; 2nd ed., p. 120.   [7] *Paulus*, p. 121; 2nd ed., p. 138.
[8] Pp. 45f.

εὐαγγέλιον τῆς ἀκροβυστίας, eine ἀποστολὴ εἰς τὴν περιτομήν, und eine ἀποστολὴ εἰς τὰ ἔθνη, in der einen gilt das mosaische Gesetz, in der andern gilt es nicht, aber beides steht noch unvermittelt neben einander.[9]

This concession was really inconsistent with their principles, but they found themselves forced by circumstances to make it; they were not, however, forced to participate in Paul's mission; they ignored it. Had they agreed with Paul's basic principles they would have been obliged by those principles to join him in his work. In their position we may see the origin of two distinct forms of Jewish Christianity. "Es gab innerhalb des Judenchristentums selbst eine strengere und mildere Ansicht und Partei".[10] The former were logically consistent in seeing that Paul's Gospel meant the end of Judaism, and in consequence they became his declared opponents. The latter were forced out of such logical consistency by their acceptance of the concession. At their head were the original apostles, and they were content to let Paul go his own way. It is this twofold attitude that accounts for Peter's vacillating behavior in Antioch; and it is significant that "auch hievon weiss freilich die Apostelgeschichte nichts," and there can be no doubt that "ihr Stillschweigen über einen so offenkundigen Vorfall ein absichtliches ist."[11]

What resulted from the gathering in Jerusalem? Here we encounter silence on the part not of Luke but of Paul. For of the "Decree" there is no trace anywhere in the epistles. Not only is there silence. After referring to the agreement to two separate apostolates Paul adds (Galatians 2.10) μόνον τῶν πτωχῶν ἵνα μνημονεύωμεν – μόνον: no other requirement was made. It is unthinkable that if the meeting had resulted in such a decision Paul could have omitted it. "Ja, man muss sogar sagen, dass es für den Apostel schlechthin nothwendig war, wenn er einmal auf jene Verhandlungen so speciell zurückgieng, einen solchen Beschluss nicht unerwähnt zu lassen."[12] Time does not permit us to follow Baur's exploration of the way

---

[9] *Paulus*, p. 125; 2nd ed., pp. 142f.   [10] *Paulus*, p. 127; 2nd ed., p. 145.
[11] *Paulus*, p. 129; 2nd ed., p. 147.
[12] *Paulus*, p. 134; 2nd ed., p. 153.

in which Luke introduced from his own time regulations that were not made in Paul's.

This brief sketch should have made clear enough the historical method Baur employs, though no summary could do justice to the sharpness and energy with which he analyzes the alternative sources which purport to provide accounts of the same events. In all this there is no appeal to any theory of history, but only to documentary facts. Confronted with divergent accounts a historian may conceive it to be his task to harmonize them, to fit pieces of the one into the other. There are several points at which Baur refers to attempts that had been made to do this for Acts 15 and Galatians 2; he ruthlessly argues that these attempts fail. The two sources say different things, and it is his method to set these differences in the clearest possible light in order to demonstrate the intentions of each writer, intentions that must be allowed for in the attempt to win historical truth from his story. There for the moment we may leave Baur and move toward Lightfoot.

It has become conventional to describe Lightfoot as the great adversary of Baur, who overthrew his work. "The overall effect of Lightfoot's work was to show that Baur and his followers had built a castle in the sky."[13] "Lightfoot was supremely qualified to be the champion of the Faith on such a field as this" [sc. against Baur].[14] There is an element of truth in this view of the matter, but it has been seriously exaggerated. It must not be supposed that Baur's work was so widely known in England that it called for vigorous opposition. I cannot forbear to recount the story of Earl Stanhope, who, in 1871, asked a fellow of an Oxford college, "Do you consider that the works of the school known as the Tübingen school are extensively read in Oxford?" "No," replied the fellow, Mr. Appleton, "no theology of any school is much read at Oxford."[15] There is more serious evidence than this. There is no explicit

---

[13] W. Gasque, *A History of the Criticism of the Acts of the Apostles*, Beiträge zur Geschichte der Biblischen Exegese 17 (1975), p. 118.

[14] J. A. Robinson in *Lightfoot of Durham*, ed. G. R. Eden and F. C. Macdonald (1932), p. 128.

[15] W. O. Chadwick, *The Victorian Church* (1966–1970), 2.68.

reference to Baur in *Essays and Reviews*, the volume of essays which, published in 1860, caused a furore among English Christians by its readiness to adopt (in a very moderate way) the methods of biblical criticism. There is no allusion in Rowland Williams's essay on "Bunsen's Biblical Researches," and in Jowett's "On the Interpretation of Scripture" one passage might be taken to mean that he was quite unaware of contemporary German work.[16] This inference would be wrong, but perhaps not far wrong. In his commentary on the Pauline epistles he gives a detailed reply, quite free from animosity, to Baur's six arguments against the authenticity of 1 Thessalonians, and refers to Baur in his discussion of the authenticity of 2 Thessalonians.[17] But his knowledge of Baur must have been sketchy and may have been secondhand, for he could discuss[18] the divisions and heresies of the apostolic age without mentioning him and in his essay on "Paul and the Twelve" gives no indication that he knew anything of Baur's views on this subject.

Essays and Reviews was succeeded by *Lux Mundi*.[19] Here there is one puzzling allusion. Gore in his essay on "The Holy Spirit and Inspiration" argues,[20] with particular reference to the Old Testament, that theology should leave the field open for free discussion of the questions raised by biblical criticism. He expects that his plea will be met by the charge to "remember Tübingen." He does not explain this, but the context suggests that many will reply to his argument by claiming that biblical criticism leads to skepticism in theology; Tübingen showed this to be true in relation to New Testament criticism, and it will be the same with the Old Testament. Gore replies that, "if the Christian Church has been enabled to defeat the critical attack, so far as it threatened destruction to the historical basis of the New Testament, it has not been by foreclosing the question with an appeal to dogma, but by facing in fair and

---

[16] *Essays and Reviews* (1860), 377.

[17] *The Epistles of St Paul to the Thessalonians, Galatians and Romans*, 3rd ed., ed. Lewis Campbell (1894), 1.4–17, 70–76.

[18] 1.29–32, 367–381.   [19] *Lux Mundi*, ed. C. Gore (1890).   [20] Ibid., p. 361.

frank discussion the problems raised." There is no ground
here for inferring a profound firsthand knowledge of Baur.

The fact is that English insularity was reinforced by dom-
estic interests. Some Tractarian arguments might have been
given interesting answers on the basis of Baur's *Über den
Ursprung des Episcopats in der christlichen Kirche*,[21] but they were
not answers that the average Evangelical would have cared to
use. Darwin's *Origin of Species*, published in 1859, provided
ample material for debate and thereby deflected attention
from New Testament criticism. Certainly there were exceptions. Niebuhr's *History of Rome* had important echoes in
British study of the history of Israel;[22] as early as 1844 Stanley
was urging that "we ought to study German as well as English
theology."[23] R. L. Nettleship, editing the works of Thomas
Hill Green, mentions[24] the lectures Green gave on the New
Testament. These were "not intended to be original contributions to biblical criticism. He took the material for them
chiefly from German works, especially those of F. C. Baur."
When, however, we turn to the lectures that have been preserved,[25] we find straightforward exegesis and theology, with
no reference to Baur and nothing distinctive of him. Baur's
fate in the English-speaking world is a puzzle. His *Paulus*
appeared in German in 1845; publication of the English translation was not complete till thirty years later, and thus did not
become generally available till after the original force of the
Tübingen school was spent[26] – the second edition of A. Ritschl's *Entstehung der altkatholischen Kirche*, which called for
serious reconsideration of some vital points in Baur's understanding of New Testament history, was published in 1857.[27]
There is an interesting parallel in the fact that Bultmann's

---

[21] Originally in *Tübinger Zeitschrift für Theologie* (1838) part 3, 1–185; now in F. C. Baur,
    Ausgewählte Werke in Einzelausgaben, ed. K. Scholder, vol. 1 (1963), pp. 321–505.
[22] Pointed out to me by J. W. Rogerson and discussed by him in forthcoming essays.
[23] R. E. Prothero, *The Life and Correspondence of Arthur Penrhyn Stanley* (1893), vol. 1,
    p. 325.
[24] *The Works of T. H. Green*, ed. R. L. Nettleship, vol. III, 2nd ed. (1889), p. xci.
[25] Ibid., pp. 186–276.
[26] See Chadwick, *The Victorian Church*, 2.69.
[27] Lightfoot made good use of this work.

Geschichte der synoptischen Tradition awaited English translation till 1963.

These facts go some way toward explaining the otherwise surprising paucity of Lightfoot's references to Baur, which are far less common than the popular picture of Lightfoot would require. Lightfoot would not have fallen under Lake's censure: "Those who speak most evil of the Tübingen school have usually never read their books."[28] He was an omnivorous reader – in English, French, German, Italian, and Spanish[29] – and cannot have overlooked Baur. References are few,[30] and for the most part confined to relatively mild disagreement. The only one that I have noted as displaying any strength of feeling is in Lightfoot's *Clement*: "No man has shown himself more ready to adopt the wildest speculations, if they fell in with his own preconceived theories than Baur, especially in his later days."[31] If there was a sharpening of the polemical element toward the end of Lightfoot's life this may have been due in part to the translation of two of Baur's books and their increased availability to the English clergy, in part to the fact that Lightfoot was now dealing with the Apostolic Fathers, but mainly to the publication of the anonymous work, *Supernatural Religion*.[32] What upset Lightfoot was the groundless attribution of the book to Bishop Thirlwall and the accusation that Westcott had been guilty not only of bad scholarship but of disingenuousness; it was these facts that provoked Lightfoot to write the familiar sequence of review essays. Even in these essays, however, references to Baur are very few and temperate.[33]

---

[28] K. Lake, *The Earlier Epistles of St Paul* (1911), p. 116, n. 3. The text is sometimes – rather misleadingly – quoted without this note.

[29] Eden and Macdonald, *Lightfoot of Durham*, p. 119.

[30] In the dissertation "St Paul and the Three" in the commentary on Galatians (1st ed., 1865) there is a general reference to Baur's *Paulus* (p. 295), and brief references on pp. 327, 333, 341, 347, 353; most of these have to do with patristic rather than New Testament matters. In the dissertation on "The Christian Ministry" in the commentary on Philippians (1st ed., 1868) there are references on pp. 201 and 233 (where it is allowed that, on the point in question, Baur may be partly right).

[31] *The Apostolic Fathers, Part I, S. Clement of Rome*, 2nd ed. 1890), 1.357 f.

[32] 1st ed., 1874. The author was W. R. Cassels.

[33] The essays were collected in the volume *Essays on the Work Entitled Supernatural Religion* (1889). There are references to Baur on pp. 26, 61, 64, 70.

Cassels, the author, in many respects adopted Baur's views, and in attacking Cassels Lightfoot could not but disagree with Baur, but he did not go out of his way to draw attention to the fact.

The difference between Baur and Lightfoot was in truth small.

Dieses Geschichtsbild, das als treibende Kraft der urchristlichen Geschichte die Auseinandersetzung zwischen der im Judentum verbleibenden Urgemeinde, vor allem ihrem radikalen Flügel, und dem gesetzesfreien paulinischen Heidenchristentum ansah, wurde aber nicht nur von einem ausgesprochen kritischen Forscher wie C. Weizsäcker geteilt, sondern am Ende des 19. Jahrhunderts hatten sich diesem modifizierten Baurschen Geschichtsbild auch konservative Forscher wie der Berliner Neutestamentler *B. Weiss* und der durch seine sorgfältigen Kommentare bekannte Cambridger Exeget und spätere anglikanische Bischof J. B. Lightfoot angeschlossen.[34]

This judgment by the leading historian of New Testament studies is now plentifully supported. R. H. Fuller writes,

While it is commonly taken for granted that such scholars as J. B. Lightfoot in England and Theodore [*sic*] Zahn in Germany demolished the Tübingen hypothesis, all that they actually destroyed was the chronology of the Tübingen school. In other words, the dialectical process of Jewish Christianity, Paulinism and the synthesis in early catholicism was accomplished by the end of the first century instead of stretching into the second.[35]

This is perhaps the most important single observation to make about Lightfoot in relation to Baur; it sums up the total effect of his work. Here too, however, before we go on to develop the comparison we must avoid the perils of generalization by some attention to detail. What did Lightfoot make of Acts 15? There are three sources from which this question may be answered. Inevitably they cover much the same ground in much the same way and arrive at much the same conclusions. I shall avoid reduplication as far as possible.

[34] W. G. Kümmel, *Das Neue Testament im 20. Jahrhundert*, Stuttgarter Bibelstudien 50 (1970), p. 73.
[35] R. H. Fuller, *The New Testament in Current Study* (1962), p. 65. I made, independently, a somewhat similar observation in *Durham University Journal* 64 (1972), 203.

The first source is Lightfoot's commentary on Galatians:[36] the notes on the text of Galatians 2.1–10; the note on "The later visit of St Paul to Jerusalem"; and the dissertation on "St Paul and the Three." Believing that Galatians 2 corresponds to Acts 15, Lightfoot is bound to consider the apparent discrepancies between the two narratives. He treats the following points (pp. 125–128):

(1) In Acts it appears that Paul is sent to Jerusalem by the Christians of Antioch in order to settle disputes that had arisen; in Galatians the apostle states that he went up by revelation. But there is no contradiction. The historian records the external impulse; Paul states the inward motive. Lightfoot compares Acts 9.29, 30; 13.2–4; 15.28. The very fact that Paul stresses his response to a divine monition hints, according to Lightfoot, that other influences were at work. The narratives are in fact harmonious.

(2) "St Paul speaks of his communications as made to the Apostles in private: St Luke's narrative describes a general congress of the Church" (p. 125). Lightfoot again stresses the different intentions of the two writers. Paul's concern is to show what he did, or did not, owe to the Twelve; Luke's concern is with the interests of the church at large. Each hints at what the other deals with explicitly. ἀνεθέμην αὐτοῖς, κατ' ἰδίαν δὲ τοῖς δοκοῦσιν implies something beyond the private conference; Acts 15.4, 5, 6 suggest private discussion, and the speeches of Acts 15 are the result of "much wise forethought and patient deliberation" (p. 126).

(3) "Again, it is said, the account of St Luke leaves the impression of perfect and unbroken harmony between St Paul and the Twelve; while St Paul's narrative betrays, or seems to betray, signs of dissatisfaction with their counsels" (p. 126). But the aim of the Council was to produce "Articles of Peace"; hence inevitably there was compromise; Paul was indeed (as he claims) the champion of Gentile liberty, yet he was in the end tactful enough not to push himself forward but to let the Jerusalem Apostles make the main speeches and appear to propose the resolution.

[36] See n. 30; the date is 1865.

(4) Acts quotes, as a result of the gathering, a "Decree," to which Paul makes no reference. This, according to Lightfoot, can be easily explained. (a) The Decree was of limited application and was delivered to those churches to which it was addressed. It was never intended to be universal. (b) Its object was to relieve Gentile Christians of the burden of legal observance. The Galatians sought no such relief; their situation was entirely different. (c) In the circumstances of the attack upon him and his apostolic status in Galatia it was essential that Paul should appeal only to his own apostolic authority.

It is not my intention to discuss these points in detail and to inquire whether Lightfoot's explanations of apparent discrepancies are convincing. What we must note is Lightfoot's presupposition and the way in which he states the problem he sets himself to solve. If two New Testament writers are describing the same event, their accounts cannot be inconsistent; any apparent inconsistency can and must be explained. The difference between this approach and Baur's is immediately apparent; what is not at this point apparent is the "modifizierte Baursche Geschichtsbild." We come nearer to this in the dissertation "St Paul and the Three," where Lightfoot recognizes that the Council did not put an end to hostility. It will be worth while to quote a long passage.[37]

This ample recognition[38] would doubtless carry weight with a large number of Jewish converts: but no sanction of authority could overcome in others the deep repugnance felt to one who, himself a "Hebrew of the Hebrews," had systematically opposed the law of Moses and triumphed in his opposition. Henceforth St Paul's career was one life-long conflict with Judaizing antagonists. Setting aside the Epistles to the Thessalonians, which were written too early to be affected by this struggle, all his letters addressed to churches, with but one exception,[39] refer more or less directly to such opposition . . . everywhere and under all circumstances zeal for the law was its ruling passion. The systematic hatred of St Paul is an important fact, which we are too apt to overlook, but without which the whole history of the Apostolic ages will be misread and misunderstood.

---

[37] *Galations*, p. 311.   [38] Lightfoot refers to Gal. 2.9.
[39] Lightfoot refers to Ephesians, which he takes to be a circular letter.

Toward the end of the dissertation, when he returns to the theme of "theological differences and religious animosities" (p. 374), Lightfoot raises the question by whom the letters of recommendation used by the "extreme Judaizers" (2 Cor. 3.1) were given. "By some half-Judaic, half-Christian brotherhood of the dispersion? By the mother Church of Jerusalem? By any of the primitive disciples? By James the Lord's brother himself?" (p. 373). Evidently Lightfoot is prepared to concede the last as a possibility, though it is one that he does not like.

It is wisest to confess plainly that the facts are too scanty to supply an answer. We may well be content to rest on the broad and direct statements in the Acts and Epistles, which declare the relations between St James and St Paul. A habit of suspicious interpretation, which neglects plain facts and dwells on doubtful allusions, is as unhealthy in theological criticism as in social life, and not more conducive to truth. (p. 373)

The allusion in the final sentence is unmistakable.

The second source of Lightfoot's article on Acts is the second edition of W. Smith's *Dictionary of the Bible*.[40] This constitutes a general introduction to Acts, and in the course of it Lightfoot naturally deals with the questions of authenticity and historicity (which he tends to treat as one question, implying that if the work was written by Luke it will be historically accurate, and vice versa). The brief discussion of Acts 15 arises out of Lightfoot's treatment of objections to authenticity. Here he has in mind the kind of objection made by Baur, though he does not (except in his bibliography) mention Baur's name. The strongest objection is based upon Luke's representation of Peter and Paul, especially his representation of them as being in agreement. Lightfoot gives a general answer by referring to 1 Cor. 1.12f., 23; Gal. 1.18; 2.6f., 14; 1 Clem. 5; Ignatius, *Rom.* 4; Polycarp, *Phil.* 2, 5, 6, etc., which, he claims, confirm the picture to be found in Acts. The most important field of argument, however, is the Council of Acts 15. Here Lightfoot refers to his treatment of the matter in his *Galatians*, and adds that the chapter contains particularly strong indications of its

---

[40] The volume was published in 1893; the article was written long before.

veracity. There is a strong presumption of truthfulness in the
fact that Luke is prepared to show the weaknesses of the church
– the faction and quarrels of 15.1f., and the contention between
Paul and Barnabas (15.36f.). The whole narrative is simple,
straightforward, and natural; the speeches are related to the
epistles attributed to the speakers; Peter and James, Paul and
Barnabas are given the right sort of relation to each other;
Peter is spoken of as Symeon; the Decree is manifestly genuine
– no one could have constructed it at a later period. Only
presuppositions regarding the relations of the apostles to each
other could call the historicity of the narrative in question.
Lightfoot goes on to mention the supposed parallelism between
Peter and Paul. Yes, there are parallel stories, but nothing
suggests that any design was present to the author's mind. 'In
fact parallelisms far more close are common in history" (col.
39a).

It would be hard to deny that at point after point in this
argument we are asked to take Lightfoot's word for what he
says. The simplicity, straightforwardness, and naturalness of
the narrative are simply asserted, and Lightfoot indicates no
criteria by which these qualities may be assessed.

The third source from which Lightfoot's views of Acts 15
may be discovered is his course of lectures on Acts, given while
he was a professor at Cambridge and preserved in his own
manuscript in the Chapter Library at Durham.[41] Here, too,
little is added. There is, in the lecture notes, a long discussion of
the authenticity of the speech attributed in Acts 7 to Stephen,
but no more than a few pages on the Council. It almost seems
that Lightfoot was incapable of seeing serious problems here.
There are, however, a few points which it will be profitable to
discuss.

After dating the Council Lightfoot announces that he will
take his hearers through the text before making any general
observations. From his detailed notes on the text I take three
points. Of these the first is surprising. Commenting on 15.1, καί

---

[41] The date 1877 is written on the manuscript. The lectures contain marginal supplements and were evidently delivered more than once.

τινες κατελθόντες, he argues from verse 24 that these unnamed persons had an "external connexion" with the apostles in Jerusalem, but did not represent them in their demand for circumcision. He adds, however, that the Apostles of Circumcision (meaning presumably Peter, John, and James) "(1) concurred with the principles of these Judaizers," but were "(2) disposed to concession in practice, for the sake of peace." This is a surprising concession on Lightfoot's part, and justifies the description of Lightfoot's position as a modified version of Baur's; indeed, in this respect it is scarely modified.

The second is Lightfoot's comment on the quotation from Amos in Acts 15.16, 17. The difference between the Hebrew and the LXX versions of Amos 9.11f. is not really great. "The Hebrew says that the Tabernacle of David was to hold sway over all the earth; the Greek, that all the nations should seek it, or seek the Lord." The Tabernacle of David is interpreted as the "Church of Christ, the abode of David's Son."

Third is the comment on the Decree in Acts 15.29. Its requirements are negative; they exact no rites, but only abstention from certain practices. The total effect is neither moral nor ceremonial; Gentiles are expected to abstain from those things which, though they may think them trivial, would give great offence to Jews.

Lightfoot sums up very briefly, in two paragraphs. The first is headed "Truthfulness," and has two subdivisions. Of these the first deals with the speeches; they are suitable to the speakers in sentiments and language. The second deals with the letter. It too is couched in suitable language, and it is easy to understand how it came into Luke's hands. By 16.10 he has joined Paul, so that, even if he was not an Antiochene, the "historical connexion" is established. The transition from the first main paragraph to the second is effected in these words. "The genuineness of the document and the truthfulness of the account established, we turn[42] next to the difficulties in connexion with St Paul's Epistles." Again there are two subdiv-

---

[42] The word is illegible; it could be "turn," and this or some synonym is certainly intended.

isions, the first dealing with the differences between Acts 15 and Galatians 2 (the two accounts have different motives and describe the one the private, the other the public conference), the second with the subsequent conduct of the principal agents, Peter and Paul. But the most important thing to note is the astonishing transitional sentence. A great deal of abbreviation and many omissions in lectures intended for undergraduates need no justification, but what can justify the logic – or lack of it – of supposing that the truthfulness of Luke's account can be established before a full confrontation of Acts with the epistles?

This point will serve as well as any as the cue to introduce the comparison of Baur and Lightfoot. Baur's position is clear, Lightfoot's more complex. It is rightly described as a modified Baurian position, yet we see Lightfoot again and again turning back from what seems to be the logical conclusion of his argument and accepting at their face value statements which Baur receives with a good deal of skepticism. Is it enough to say that we are dealing with one man of a skeptical, another of a more orthodox and conservative temperament? Perhaps; but I think it doubtful, and that the difference, being more than a mere difference of opinion, is worthy of further investigation; and only further investigation will eventually teach us for our own advantage *quomodo historia conscribenda sit*.

A hint may be found in the work of the Englishman who, in the first half of the nineteenth century, was probably better acquainted than any other with German thought and litera-ture.[43] Julius Hare discusses the difference between English and German criticism. It is not biblical criticism that he has in mind, but general literary criticism. He illustrates his point from a German essay on the *Amphitryon* of Plautus.

That play, the writer observes, differs from all the other Roman comedies in having a mythological subject, which occasions essential differences in treatment; so that it forms a distinct species: and he proposes to examine the nature of this peculiar form of comedy, according to its external and internal character; not to explain the poetical composition of *the Amphitryon*, considered as an individual

---

[43] Hare left his German library of some 3,000 volumes to Trinity College, Cambridge; A. F. Hort, *Life and Letters of F. J. A. Hort* (1896), vol. I, p. 308.

work of art, but merely to determine the place it is to hold in the history of the Roman drama.[44]

Hare goes on to claim that this is the right way to approach the subject.

For in criticism, as in every other branch of knowledge, *prudens quaestio dimidium scientiae est.* He who has got the clue, may thread the maze. Yet the method of investigation here is totally different from what an English scholar would have pursued. The notion of regarding *the Amphitryon* as a distinct species of ancient comedy, and of considering that species in its relation to the rest of the Roman drama, – the distinction drawn between this historical view of it, and the esthetical analysis of it taken by itself, – these are thoughts which would never have entered the head of an English critic.[45]

Words such as *Formgeschichte* and *Gattung* immediately come into the mind of one who reads this passage 150 years or so after Hare wrote it. But more is involved than this. Another passage from Hare will give us a further clue.

One of the clearest proofs German Philosophy has exhibited of its being on the road toward the truth, has lain in this very fact, that it has been enabled to appreciate the philosophical systems of former ages . . . We see them[46] endeavouring to estimate all prior systems according to their historical position in the progressive development of human thought . . . this historical, genetical method of viewing prior systems of philosophy . . .[47]

This brings us on our way. Baur is often spoken of as a Hegelian in such a way as to suggest that Hegel's only contribution to thought was the formula "Thesis – Antithesis – Synthesis," which is supposed to have provided Baur with the outline of his account of Jewish Christianity, Pauline Christianity, their conflict, and the compromise result of Catholic Christianity. There can be no doubt that this is an incorrect view of the origins of Baur's historical opinions. Rightly or wrongly he found the conflict and the compromise in the historical sources and only subsequently began to interpret what he had found in

[44] *Guesses at Truth by Two Brothers* (J. C. and A. Hare), vol. I, 4th ed. (1851), 274–277.
[45] Ibid., pp. 277f.   [46] The authors have referred to Ritter and Hegel.
[47] *Guesses at Truth*, vol. II (3rd ed., 1855), pp. 249f.

Hegelian terms. These terms, moreover, are not adequately described by the neat threefold formula. Hegel's thought is commonly said to mark the climax of idealism, and as such it sought to place the particular events of history in a universal context and to see history as the expression of an idea. It is this idea that gives meaning to what might otherwise seem to be fortuitous and unconnected. It is mind, infinite mind, that becomes self-conscious and apparent in history; and it is possible to construe infinite mind, as Hegel's successors showed, in theistic, panentheistic, or atheistic terms. Perhaps what matters most as far as we are concerned is the basic conviction that the historian is not achieving his task unless he is able to perceive within history such a developing pattern as is consistent with the expression of mind – of what, in Christian language, might be called revelation.

Baur certainly had much too fine a mind to be dominated by a simple formula, a mold into which the events of history must willy-nilly be forced, and his presuppositions have been wrongly evaluated in other respects too. According to Horton Harris[48] the chief characteristic of Baur and his followers was their objection to the supernatural. "If one had to sum up the aim and object of the Tübingen School in a single statement it would be that the Tübingen School made the first comprehensive and consequent attempt to interpret the New Testament and the history of the early Church from a non-supernatural (indeed anti-supernatural) and non-miraculous standpoint." This will hardly do; P. C. Hodgson is nearer to the truth when he describes Baur the historian as equally opposed to supernatural and rationalist interpretations of history.[49]

Lightfoot, in contrast, was not a philosopher and showed no interest in a theory of history. A. C. Benson says of him, "His own work was a moral rather than an artistic process, and depended more upon patience, clear-headedness, and industry than upon brilliance or suggestiveness."[50] Lightfoot would not

---

[48] *The Tübingen School*, p. 255.

[49] *F. C. Baur on the Writing of Church History*, ed. and trans. P. C. Hodgson (1968), pp. 12–17.

[50] *The Leaves of the Tree* (1911), p. 208.

have demurred. "I brought to the task nothing more than ordinary sense."[51] He reminds one of Lucian's ideal historian. He was a man of inflexible integrity,[52] determined above all to be συνεργὸς τῇ ἀληθείᾳ; he had the moral and stylistic virtue of calling a spade a spade, and he spared no pains in seeking out the most trustworthy sources of information. This was Lightfoot's strength. His feet are always firmly planted on the earth, and he looks at evidence with a plain man's objectivity. His presuppositions are theological, or perhaps one should say religious. He was profoundly convinced of the truth of Christianity, and of his own vocation to defend it; and he could see no other way of defending it than that of maintaining the essential truth, including the historical truth, of the Bible and of the biblical account of Christian origins. "I cannot pretend to be indifferent about the veracity of the records which profess to reveal Him, whom I believe to be not only the very Truth, but the very Life."[53] Jesus as the truth and the life was for Lightfoot inseparable from the historical accuracy of the stories about him and of the apostolic framework in which those stories were set. It may be that we can see here the reason why Lightfoot, always magnificent as an exegete of word, sentence, and paragraph, made his real contribution to history not in the New Testament, where a particular view of the nature of revelation inhibited him, but in the post-apostolic age of Clement, Ignatius, and Polycarp.[54] It is here that he quite simply corrected undoubted mistakes on the part of Baur and put him right. In the earlier period, that of the New Testament itself, he cannot bring himself to admit that his sources err and contradict one another, though facts in the end compel him to admit that the disagreement and conflict, from which Baur began his historical reconstruction, did in fact exist. If the apostles agreed in principle with the Judaizers, they disagreed in principle with Paul. Conflict belongs not

---

[51] *Essays*, p. 180.
[52] I emphasized Lightfoot's integrity in *Durham University Journal* 64 (1972), 195.
[53] *Essays*, pp. viii f.
[54] One should refer also to the great article on Eusebius in W. M. Smith and H. Wace, *Dictionary of Christian Biography*, vol. II (1880), pp. 308–348.

only to the age of the Pseudo-Clementines but to the age of the New Testament.

I said that Lightfoot's presuppositions were theological or religious, but it may be that behind them we should recognize a way of apprehending reality. I do not know that Barth had ever read Lightfoot, but he comes somewhere near the point in the following passage:

We have to describe as a philosophy the systematised commonsense with which at first the rationalists of the 18th century thought that they could read and understand the Bible, and later, corrected by Kant, the school of A. Ritschl, which was supposed to be so averse to every type of speculation and metaphysics . . . There has never yet been an expositor who has allowed only Scripture alone to speak. Even a biblicist like J. T. Beck patently failed to do this . . . It is . . . a grotesque comedy, in which it is better not to take part, that again and again there are those who think that they can point with outstretched finger to all others past and present, accusing them of falling victim to this or that philosophy, while they themselves abide wholly by the facts, relying on their two sound eyes. No one does that, for no one can. It is no more true of anyone that he does not mingle the Gospel with some philosophy than that here and now he is free from all sin except through faith.[55]

Does Lightfoot, who was certainly less of a systematic theologian than Beck, escape? Does his "ordinary sense" represent a kind of empiricism? J. W. Rogerson[56] has spoken of the philosophical climate of British theology in the early nineteenth century as a "Lockean sort of supernaturalism"; revelation, if revelation existed, must come from without and be attested by supernatural accompaniments; hence a great hesitancy to accept any kind of criticism that might seem to cast any doubt on the biblical narrative and the supernatural events included in it. Perhaps it is significant that the idealist philosopher T. H. Green did (according to his biographer and editor) know and use Baur.

Lightfoot characteristically accepts the critical method so

[55] K. Barth, *Church Dogmatics* 1.2 (E.T., 1956), pp. 728f.
[56] In the essays referred to in n. 22 above.

long as the criticism is not skeptical.[57] "In whatever relates to morals and history – in short, to human life in all its developments – where mathematical or scientific demonstration is impossible, and where consequently everything depends on the even balance of the judicial faculties, scepticism must be at least as fatal to the truth as credulity."[58] Over against this, Baur writes, "Eine Kritik, welche nicht auch eine skeptische seyn darf, ist keine Kritik, weil so oft nur der Zweifel zur Wahrheit führen kann, und eine Theologie, welche schlechthin den Grundsatz aufstellt, dass man überhaupt nicht zweifeln und sichten dürfe, thut am besten, die historische Kritik geradezu aus der Reihe der theologischen Wissenschaften zu streichen."[59] It may well be that Baur's use of *skeptisch* is not identical with the common English use of "sceptical." Certainly Käsemann has in mind the passage I have just quoted when he writes in his *Einführung* to the reprint of Baur's works, "Historische Kritik ist die Funktion des lebendigen Glaubens auf seinem Wege aus bewusst gewordener Vergangenheit in die eigene Gegenwart und Zukunft, welche eben diese Vergangenheit in den übergreifenden Zusammenhang der Gesamtgeschichte stellt."[60] Lightfoot and Baur stand over against each other not as believer and unbeliever but as representatives of different philosophical and theological traditions. And as far as facts are concerned, each, the Hegelian idealist and the commonsense empiricist, has his blind spots.

What has all this to tell us as we ask with reference to our own work, 150 years after Baur and 100 after Lightfoot, *quomodo historia conscribenda sit?*

He would be a rash man who claimed to have all the virtues

---

[57] See *Galatians*, p. 373, quoted on p. 47. See the whole context. "Doubtful allusions" is scarcely fair to the position against which Lightfoot is arguing.

[58] *Essays*, p. 26.

[59] *Abgenöthigte Erklärung gegen einen Artikel der evangelischen Kirchenzeitung, herausgegeben von D. E. W. Hengstenberg*, originally in *Tübinger Zeitschrift für Theologie* (1836), part 3, p. 219; now in *Ausgewählte Werke*, vol. 1, p. 307.

[60] *Ausgewählte Werke*, vol. 1, p. XIX. Käsemann goes on to say that *historisch-kritisch* must in the end mean *historisch-spekulativ*. It may be that there is also some difference in usage between *spekulativ* and "speculative."

of Baur, or all the virtues of Lightfoot, rasher still who claimed to combine the virtues of both. I return to Hare's Latin tag: *prudens quaestio dimidium scientiae est.* The practical difference between Baur and Lightfoot may be summed up by saying that Baur's sharp analytical mind, spurred on by a philosophical outlook, excelled in asking questions; Lightfoot's magnificent store of philological knowledge excelled in answering them. Baur, for whom no possibilities were a priori forbidden, asked the right questions, but many of his answers, especially as regards particular persons, documents, and dates, were wrong. When Lightfoot set about questions that were both relevant and suitable to his equipment, such as the authenticity and date of the Ignatian epistles, he could produce answers which after 100 years still hold the field, in books which are still indispensable. Philosophy is a great help in framing questions; it is always dangerous as a guide to the answers. If there is a moral here, it is a very simple one – simple, that is, to state. We must learn with Baur to ask all the questions there are, and to concentrate on the essential ones, using one source to set off the distinctive characteristics of the other; and we must acquire and apply Lightfoot's knowledge of languages and of ancient literature.

This impossible requirement involves another which ought not to be beyond our power to achieve. Lightfoot was to some extent inhibited from asking the right questions by his theological beliefs, by his understanding of authority and especially of the authority of Scripture. This authority, he believed, was bound up with the authenticity of documents and the accuracy of historical statements. He was an absolutely honest man, as well as a very learned one, and he never fudged evidence in order to reach the conclusions that his piety required. But he either failed to put, or blunted the edge of, the sharpest questions, and did not see where his own statement that the apostles in Jerusalem agreed in principle with the Judaizers and his pushing back of the dates of apostolic and post-apostolic documents were leading. What this means is not that Lightfoot was wrong to ascribe authority to Scripture, but that his way of formulating authority was mistaken. On the whole,

German scholars, even conservative ones, do not seem to have shared his inhibitions; Ritschl, for example, whose work Lightfoot found so helpful, seems to have been free from them. How far this was due to the German Reformation, how far to the German Enlightenment, how far to other causes, I am not prepared to estimate. But I see here, in the investigation of underlying philosophical and theological presuppositions, a fruitful field for collaboration, especially as we explore that important area (of which Acts 15, had we time to study it further, would serve as a specimen) in which New Testament theology and New Testament history interpenetrate.

CHAPTER 3

The Acts of the Apostles: monograph or "bios"?

Charles H. Talbert

To be invited to contribute to a volume on Acts and ancient historiography presents a peculiar challenge to one whose published writings argue that Luke–Acts belongs to ancient biography.[1] I assume that my assigned task is to justify my decision to place Acts in the biographical rather than the historiographical tradition and to indicate what difference, if any, I think that makes. That is, in fact, what I shall attempt to do. My chapter will begin with a consideration of certain evidence from Mediterranean antiquity about the genres of history and biography.[2]

In a number of respects ancient history and biography are similar. (1) History is a prose narrative. The dominant type of biography is also prose narration. This sets them apart from epic. (2) Both history and biography are about real people and real events. This sets them apart from romance. (3) Varieties of both share certain aims: apologetics, instruction, entertainment.

Indeed, histories often contain biographical sections (Polybius 9.22; 10.2.2; Dionysius of Halicarnassus 5.48.1; Diodorus Siculus 17; Josephus, *Antiquities* 14–17; Dio Cassius, 45–56; 73 at beginning; 73.11.2–4; Eusebius, *Church History* 6). Biographies often include a narrative of events. The dominant

---

[1] Charles H. Talbert, *Literary Patterns, Theological Themes and the Genre of Luke–Acts*, SBLMS 20 (Missoula, MT: Scholars Press, 1974), chap. 8; *What is a Gospel? The Genre of the Canonical Gospels* (Philadelphia: Fortress, 1977); "Once Again: Gospel Genre," *Semeia* 43 (1988), 53–74; "Biography, Ancient," *Anchor Bible Dictionary*, ed. David Noel Friedman (New York: Doubleday, 1992), vol. I, pp. 745–749.

[2] Except where it is indicated otherwise, all quotations from Greek and Latin authors come from the Loeb Classical Library.

type of biography is prose narrative, which is similar to history except that it is anecdotal and mostly unconcerned about cause and effect. This is in contrast to biographies which are dialogues (for example, Satyrus, *Life of Euripides*; Palladius, *Life of Chrysostom*; Sulpicius Severus, *Life of St. Martin*) and the biographical collections of sayings like Plutarch's "Sayings of Kings and Commanders" (for example, in D, Plutarch says: "their pronouncements and unpremeditated utterance . . . afford an opportunity to observe . . . the working of the mind of each man").

At the point of a historical monograph about a single individual, especially if the story is told in eulogistic terms, the line between history and biography is most blurred. In Cicero's *Letters to his Friends* 5.12 is a request addressed to Lucceius.[3] Cicero desires that his name gain celebrity through Lucceius' works. Lucceius is about finished with the account of the Italian and civil wars he has been writing and is looking forward to writing about subsequent events. Cicero asks him to do one of two things: either to weave his affairs along with those of the rest of the period into a single narrative, or to detach the material relating to Cicero from the continuous history and to treat it eulogistically. "Waive the laws of history for this once." Cicero's preference is for the latter because "in the doubtful and various fortunes of an outstanding individual we often find surprise and suspense, joy and distress, hope and fear." Lucceius has often promised that he will "compose the record of my public career, its policies and events." Now Cicero is impatient because he wants to enjoy a modicum of glory before he dies. It is not a biography that Cicero wants written, but a historical monograph about his public career, and he wants it done in eulogistic terms. In this case, as with Sallust's *Catiline* and *Jugurtha*, the aim is not to set forth the individual's essence but to narrate political events with which the individuals were associated.

In spite of the similarities between history and biography,

---

[3] *Cicero's Letters to His Friends*, trans. D. R. Shackleton Bailey (Atlanta: Scholars Press, 1978), pp. 58–63.

some ancients spoke about a difference between them. On a number of points the difference is noted.

(1) History claims completeness (Cicero, *Orator* 34.120); biography incompleteness (Plutarch, *Alexander* 1.2–3).

(2) History deals with grand events (Herodotus 1.177; Xenophon, *Hellenica* 5.1.4; Polybius 10.21.5–8; Dionysius of Halicarnassus 5.56.1; Statius, *Silvae* 1.2.96–97). Cicero, *Orator* 34.120, speaks about history as "omitting no important event." Biography, however, deals with incidental matters as well as grand events (Plutarch, *Demosthenes* 11.7). Plutarch, *Alexander* 1.2–3, puts it this way:

It is not Histories that I am writing, but Lives; and in the most illustrious deeds there is not always a manifestation of virtue or vice, nay, a slight thing like a phrase or a jest often makes a greater revelation of character than battles where thousands fall.

(3) In history there is an attempt to discern causes (Polybius 3.32; 12.25b1; Cicero, *Orator* 2.15.63). As Dionysius of Halicarnassus put it: "The readers of histories do not derive sufficient profit from learning the bare outcome of events, but . . . everyone demands that the causes of the events be related" (5.56.1). In biography the aim is to reveal character (Plutarch, *Alexander* 1.2–3; *Nicias*; Lucian, *Demonax* 67). Cornelius Nepos, *Pelopidas* 16.1, says: "I do not know exactly how I should describe his character, and I am afraid that if I begin to tell you of his deeds, I will appear not a biographer but a historian."

It is true that sometimes histories included material about an individual's character. Polybius 9.22, for example, says that: "Since the course of affairs has called our attentions to the character of Hannibal, I think I am called upon at present to state my opinion regarding those peculiar traits in it which are the subject of most dispute." When history included a section on an individual's character, it was subsumed under the general explanations of why events happened as they did. Character is one cause among others. In biography, character is the end sought. Events are but one means of the illumination of character. In biography "character is studied in its own right, almost independently of the political framework of historiography in which it had served a functional purpose."[4]

(4) Much history was designed as instruction for political figures as political figures. Dionysius of Halicarnassus 5.56.1 is to the point. "For statesmen I perceive that the knowledge of these things is absolutely necessary, to the end that they may have precedents for their use in the various situations that arise." Much biography aimed to shape the life of the reader as a human being (Plutarch, *Pericles* 21.4; *Cimon* 2.3–5; Tacitus, *Agricola* 46; Lucian, *Demonax* 2). Plutarch, *Aemilius Paulus* 1, says: "I try in one way or another to order my own life and to fashion it in accordance with the virtues of these lives." In *Aratus* 1, he contends that his readers should do the same.

(5) The subject matter of history was states, that is, political and military events. The subject matter of biography was the character of individuals and/or peoples. *Bios* was written of peoples as well as individuals. Dicaearchus in the fourth century BC wrote *Bios Hellados*, a life of Greek culture from the Golden Age to his own time, as well as *bioi* of individuals, like Plato and other philosophers. Varro, in the first century BC, wrote *De Vita Populi Romani*, a social treatment of the Roman people. Although these two *bioi* are not extant, it is possible to discern something about their ethos from a statement by Cornelius Nepos. In his preface, Nepos says:

If these could only understand that what is honorable in one land is often disgraceful in another and that all manners must be judged in the light of national customs, they would not be surprised that in our description of Greek character we carefully consider local practices and conventions.[5]

Whether a *bios* dealt with an individual or a people, the focus was on character: what sort of person he was, what sort of people they were.

There are remarkable similarities between the canonical gospels and ancient biographies of individuals in the form of

---

[4] Charles William Fornara, *The Nature of History in Ancient Greece and Rome* (Berkeley: University of California Press, 1983), p. 187. See also Robert Scholes and Robert Kellog, *The Nature of Narrative* (New York: Oxford University Press, 1966), p. 65.

[5] Cornelius Nepos, *Lives of Famous Men*, trans. Gareth Schmeling (Lawrence, KS: Coronado Press, 1971).

prose narrative. These similarities have been carefully assessed
by the recent work of Richard A. Burridge, *What Are the
Gospels? A Comparison with Graeco-Roman Biography*.[6] Burridge
offers a model of four generic features: (a) opening features
such as title, prologue, and preface; (b) subject; (c) external
features such as size, sequence, and scale; and (d) internal
features such as setting, motifs, style, attitude, and quality of
characterization. He then examines five early and five late
examples of Greco-Roman *bioi* on the basis of this model. The
result is a clear demonstration of a *bios* genre. Next Burridge
uses his model of the *bios* genre to study the four canonical
gospels. His conclusion is that these gospels belong within the
overall genre of ancient biography. It is difficult to see how,
after this careful study, the biographical nature of the canonical gospels can be denied.

There is a problem, however, when Luke and Acts are
taken together as originally one work, because of Acts. To
many scholars Acts seems to be about a community[7] and
looks more like a historical monograph than a biography.
This has led some to take their clue from Acts and, assuming
the unity of Luke–Acts, regard Luke as well as Acts as a
historical monograph,[8] as apologetic history,[9] or as a continuation of biblical history.[10] It has led others to deny the generic
unity of Luke and Acts[11] and to regard Luke as a *bios* and Acts
as either history or romance.[12]

6 SNTSMS 70 (Cambridge: Cambridge University Press, 1992).
7 David L. Balch, "The Genre of Luke–Acts," *Southwestern Journal of Theology* 33
   (1990), 5–19; Gregory E. Stirling, *Historiography and Self-Definition: Josephos, Luke–
   Acts and Apologetic Historiography* (Leiden: Brill, 1992), pp. 19, 320, n. 47.
8 David E. Aune, *The New Testament in its Literary Environment* (Philadelphia: West-
   minster, 1987), chap. 3.
9 Stirling, *Historiography and Self-Definition*, and David L. Balch, "Comments on the
   Genre and Political Theme of Luke–Acts: A Preliminary Comparison of Two
   Hellenistic Historians," *Society of Biblical Literature 1989 Seminar Papers*, ed. David J.
   Lull (Atlanta: Scholars Press, 1989), pp. 343–361.
10 William S. Kurz, SJ, *Reading Luke–Acts: Dynamics of Biblical Narrative* (Louisville:
   Westminster/John Knox, 1993).
11 Mikeal C. Parsons and Richard I. Pervo, *Rethinking the Unity of Luke and Acts*
   (Minneapolis: Fortress, 1993); James M. Dawsey, "The Literary Unity of Luke–
   Acts: Questions of Style – A Task for Literary Critics," *New Testament Studies* 35
   (1989), 48–66. A reading of these pieces is their refutation.
12 Richard Pervo, *Profit with Delight: The Literary Genre of the Acts of the Apostles*

The assumption that Acts, and possibly Luke together with Acts, belongs either to the genre of Greco-Roman history or to so-called biblical history is not as obvious as usually supposed. It is challenged by the judgment of Arnaldo Momigliano, a scholar of repute in the area of ancient history and biography. He says:

> History of salvation was not a Greek type of historiography in pagan days. Nor were the historical books of the Bible of much use as models to the Christians, because they told the story of an existing nation in its obedience or disobedience to God during its periods of organized political life . . . Even for Luke and Acts . . . it is impossible to find a parallel in the extant Greek historians.[13]

Similar challenges focus on the pieces of the argument for Luke–Acts as history. (1) Loveday Alexander's *The Preface to Luke's Gospel: Literary Convention and Social Context in Luke 1:1–4 and Acts 1:1*[14] shows that Luke's prefaces are not closest to those of classical historians. This, she argues, indicates that the author did not desire to present his work to his readers as "history." (2) Charles H. Talbert's "Prophecies of Future Greatness: The Contributions of Greco-Roman Biographies to an Understanding of Luke 1:5–4:15"[15] shows that the opening of the Third Gospel corresponds to the genre of the pre-public careers of great men found in Greco-Roman biographies. This means that an ancient Mediterranean would have heard the opening of the Third Gospel as the beginning of a biography of an individual. (3) Those who appeal to the speeches of Acts as evidence that the document belongs to the historical genre must reckon with two problems. First, "as early as Xenophon

---

(Philadelphia: Fortress, 1987). Stephen P. Schierling and Marla J. Schierling, "The Influence of the Ancient Romances on Acts of the Apostles," *The Classical Bulletin* 54 (1978), 81–88, are more accurate in speaking of novelistic elements in Acts.

[13] "History and Biography," in *The Legacy of Greece: A New Appraisal*, ed. M. I. Finley (Oxford: Clarendon Press, 1981), pp. 178–179.

[14] SNTSMS 78 (Cambridge: Cambridge University Press, 1993).

[15] In *The Divine Helmsman: Studies of God's Control of Human Events, Presented to Lou H. Silberman*, ed. James L. Crenshaw and Samuel Sandmel (New York: KTAV, 1980), pp. 129–142.

(in the *Memorabilia*), biographers attributed to their heroes speeches that they could have made, even if, historically, they did not . . . They are convenient literary vehicles for representing the ideal in the historical figure."[16] Second, even if the speeches of Acts were to be found closer in function to those in history, one must still reckon with the matter of host genres in which elements from other genres reside.[17] For a reader who began reading Luke with all the literary clues pointing to the biographical genre, to encounter speeches in Acts need not demand that Luke's second volume be history any more than its sea journey requires that it be taken as romance. In sum: the contention that Luke–Acts is ancient history is not as obvious or problem-free as has often been assumed.

Burridge's work on the gospels as biographies attempts only in passing to come to terms with the problem of Acts. He offers two options: either (1) Acts, like the Gospel, is linked to *bios* literature as a list or brief narrative of the main subject's followers (as Talbert suggests), or (2) Acts may be a *bios* of the church in the manner of Dicaearchus' biographical work on Greece.[18] The latter option is, to my knowledge, a novel one. The two options may be explored briefly.

The first option, that Luke–Acts reflects the ancient A + B biographical form employed for founders of philosophical schools and their successors, has, for whatever reason,[19] never been adequately understood by the guild. A brief sketch of it is in order. The trajectory of such a biographical type is the place

---

16 Patricia Cox, *Biography in Late Antiquity* (Berkeley: University of California Press, 1983), p. 63.
17 This is a problem sensed by Stirling, *Historiography and Self-Definition*, pp. 15–16. He asks how one can tell when a given work has moved from one genre to another because of the presence of material from another genre.
18 *What are the Gospels?*, p. 246.
19 It may be tied to the reviews offered by David Aune, one a rather overheated, underlighted polemic ("The Problem of the Genre of the Gospels: A Critique of C. H. Talbert's *What is a Gospel?*," in *Gospel Perspectives*, ed. R. T. France and D. Wenham [Sheffield: JSOT, 1981], vol. II, pp. 9–60), and the other a one-page misstatement of the position followed by three specious criticisms (*The New Testament in its Literary Environment*, pp. 78–79). For a full refutation of Aune's criticisms, see Charles H. Talbert, "Reading Chance, Moessner, and Parsons," in *Cadbury, Knox, and Talbert: American Contributions to the Study of Acts*, ed. M. C. Parsons and J. B. Tyson (Atlanta: Scholars Press, 1992), pp. 229–40.

to begin. (1) The earliest evidence that we have for such a biography is in a pre-Christian biography of Aristotle. Here the life of Aristotle is followed by a succession list.[20] Among the Herculaneum papyri, moreover, there may be evidence of other lives of philosophers written in the same way.[21] (2) In Diogenes Laertius certain lives of philosophers reflect this pattern (Socrates, Aristippus, Plato, Zeno, Pythagoras, Epicurus). The B component is sometimes filled out with anecdotes and sayings of the founder's successors, so that B is not a list (as in the case of Socrates, Aristippus, and Plato, for example) but a brief narrative (as in the case of Zeno and Epicurus, for example). (3) In *The Life of Pachomius* we find a Christian appropriation of this type of biography. It is fitting because this biography deals with the life of the founder of cenobetic monasticism and his successors in the community. The early part of the biography deals with the career of Pachomius. In section 117, in language that may be regarded as part of the technical terminology of succession characteristic of the philosophical schools, he appoints Orsisius to succeed him. In the sections that follow we are told what Orsisius did and said (118–129), zealously emulating the life of Pachomius (119). Then Orsisius appoints Theodore (130). Subsequently we are told what Theodore did and said. This biography confirms not only that such a type existed well into our era but also that, when appropriate, there was no obstacle to Christian appropriation of this subgenre of biography. (4) In Hilary of Arles' *Sermon on the Life of St. Honoratus*, we meet an encomium praising Honoratus, the founder of the monastery, that fits into the A + B pattern. In chapter 8, Hilary says he is Honoratus' successor and that his task is to do what the founder had done.

From this charting of the development of the subgenre from pre-Christian times to its later Christian appropriation, certain things are obvious. First, the subgenre had a long life. Second,

---

[20] I. Duering, *Aristotle in the Ancient Biographical Tradition* (Göteborg, Sweden: Göteborgs Universitets Arsskrift, 1957).

[21] W. Scott (ed.), *Fragmenta Herculanensia* (Oxford: Clarendon Press, 1885); A. Traversa (ed.), *Index Stoicorum Herculanensis* (Genoa: Istituto di Filologia Classica, 1952).

it is appropriate where the hero is the founder of a community and whose death demands successors. Third, the material about successors can be given briefly in a list or more fully in a narrative. The narrative tends to expand in length over the lifetime of the subgenre. It is longer in Christian circles than in non-Christian ones. Fourth, in the second component, B, when a list is given, it functions to say that it is part of the character of a philosophical founder to have disciples or successors; when a narrative is given, the emphasis is usually on the successor(s) emulating the founder or otherwise manifesting continuity with him.

Luke–Acts tells the story of the life of Jesus in such a way that he is depicted as the founder of the Christian community who provides for its continuation after his departure. The narrative about the community led by his appointed ones portrays the Twelve and Paul in such a way that they reproduce in their careers the prototypical events of the career of Jesus. The B component is long, longer even than that in the *Life of Pachomius*. It is expanded with historical (for example, speeches?) and novelistic elements (for example, the sea journey) throughout. Nevertheless, Acts remains within the general bounds of an A + B biography in antiquity, both in terms of its pattern and in terms of its function. It deviates no more from the cultural pattern than do Paul's letters from the Greek letter or the Apocalypse of John from the genre of Jewish apocalyptic.

One objection sometimes leveled at this solution is that the technical terminology of succession is missing from Luke–Acts. This is an issue that must be addressed. The principle of succession is found all over the Mediterranean world in antiquity in various contexts: for example philosophical schools, government, magic, medicine. The vocabulary used for the transition to the successors of a major figure is diverse. For philosophical circles, for instance, Diogenes Laertius can use different terminology: for example, regarding Socrates, he speaks of those who succeeded him (τὸν δὲ διαδεχσάμενον αὐτὸν); regarding Aristippus, he talks about those of the Cyrenaic school which sprang from him (διελθόμεν τοὺς ἀπ᾽

αὐτου); regarding Plato, he says simply that his disciples (μαθηταὶ) were . . .

The language shifts slightly when succession is spoken of in military or governmental circles. On the one hand, Diodorus Siculus uses the same terminology used for Socrates' successors by Diogenes Laertius. Diodorus devotes Book 17 to Alexander the Great, from his accession down to his death. In 17.118.4, he writes: "Having reached the death of Alexander as we proposed to do at the beginning of the book, we shall try to narrate the actions of the successors (διαδέχσαμενον πράξεις) in the books which follow." Book 18.1.6 says: "this one, containing the deeds of those who succeeded to his kingdom" (τοῖς δια-δέχσαμενοις τὴν τουτοῦ βασιλείαν). This language reflects the succession from the point of view of the one receiving the kingdom. On the other hand, Josephus uses language that reflects the situation from the perspective of the one giving the kingdom. In *Antiquities* 13.16.1 §407, he says of the Hasmonean king, Alexander, that he "left behind him two sons . . . but committed the kingdom (τὴν βασιλείαν διεθέτο) to Alexandra."

Luke–Acts reflects some of this vocabulary. The most obvious is μαθηταὶ (disciples): Lk. 6.13–16. The most important is the verb διατίθημι. The key passage is Lk. 22.28–30. This is usually thought to be a Q saying (Matt. 19.28). The Matthean version of the saying is clearly eschatological.

In the new world, when the Son of Man shall sit on his glorious throne, you who have followed me will also sit on twelve thrones, judging the twelve tribes of Israel. (RSV, 2nd ed.)

This has predisposed scholars to read the Lucan version in the same way.[22] So

I bequeath (διατίθημι) to you, as my Father bequeathed to me, a kingdom/rule, that you may eat and drink at my table in my kingdom/rule, and sit on thrones judging the twelve tribes of Israel

---

[22] Joseph A. Fitzmyer, *The Gospel according to Luke (X–XXIV)* (Garden City, NY: Doubleday, 1985), pp. 1415, 1419; I. H. Marshall, *The Gospel of Luke: A Commentary on the Greek Text* (Exeter: Paternoster Press, 1978), p. 814.

has been taken to refer to the new world, the messianic banquet, and the role of the apostles in eschatological judgment (1 Cor. 6.2). It should not be read in such a way.

A right reading requires that three expressions be clarified. (1) In Luke–Acts, what is Jesus' rule/kingdom? Acts 2.34–36 indicates that it is his session at God's right hand (cf. Lk. 22.69; 1 Cor. 15.20–28). (2) What does it mean to eat at the king's table? The expression comes from the Hebrew Bible (for example, 1 Sam. 20.29b; 2 Sam. 9.7,9,11 = "ate at the king's table like one of the king's sons"; 2 Sam. 19.28; 1 Kgs. 2.7; 4.27; 18.19). It means to be accorded a place of honor within the king's house such as the king's sons have. (3) What does it mean to judge the tribes of Israel? Again the expression comes from the Hebrew Bible (for example Exod. 2.14, a prince and a judge over us; 18.22, let them judge the people at all times; 2 Sam. 15.4, Absalom said: "Oh that I were judge in the land! Then every man with a suit or cause might come to me, and I would give him justice"; Mic. 7.3, the prince and the judge ask for a bribe). It refers to functionaries in Israel who rendered decisions about what was right. Sometimes such judges were also princes, king's sons.

Taking these three expressions together yields a reading that takes Lk. 22.29–30 as referring to the apostles' role in Jesus' reign from his exaltation to his parousia. It is one of honor. They are as sons of the king in that they eat at his table and function as decision makers among the people. The apostles are not successors as in the later apostolic succession of the Old Catholic Church. They rather rule, as judges did in ancient Israel, within and under the reign of Christ.

This seems to describe the role of the apostles in Acts. Take, for example, the centrality of Jerusalem in the missionary enterprise in Acts (1.4,8; 8.14–15; 11.1–2,22; 15.2). This includes the Jerusalem frame of reference for Paul's entire ministry in Acts (9.27–29; 11.25–26; 13.1–3; 15.2; 16.5; 18.22; 21.17). Jerusalem control of missions in Acts is closely tied to the fact that, for Luke, Jerusalem is the place where the twelve apostles reside (8.1; 9.27; 11.1–2; 15.2,4; 16.4). The twelve apostles in Acts function as appointed people of honor who make key decisions within the early church under the reign of Christ.

The mindset is very much like what Plutarch says about human rulers during the period of the Roman Empire. In his *Precepts for Ruling the State*, 813d–e, he says:

When a man enters on any public office, he must not only keep in mind the considerations of which Pericles reminded himself when he assumed the general's cloak – "Be careful, Pericles; you are ruling free men, you are ruling Greeks, Athenian citizens" – but he must also say to himself: "Although you are ruling you are a subject, and the city you rule is under the control of proconsuls, and of the procurators of Caesar."

The apostles' honor and decision making in Luke–Acts are within the overarching reign of Christ. If the reading offered here of Lk. 22.28–30 is correct, then the Lucan writings do in fact employ at least one of the key technical terms used for succession in antiquity. It is terminology that views the apostles' succession from the point of view of the one who gives it, Christ.

Given what has been said above, would an ancient Mediterranean auditor of Luke and Acts have heard the two volumes, when read together, as analogous to the A + B biographies of founders of communities? Even with the considerable expansion of the B component in Acts, this would have been the closest thing to Luke–Acts in antiquity's literary arsenal. If so, the B component would not have been required to develop the character of Jesus' disciples or to treat their lives in full. The B component served merely to document Jesus' reign and his followers' honor and decision making within the church. That there were often correspondences between the disciples in Acts and the career of Jesus in Luke would serve to reinforce the connection between the two volumes.

If, after such an argument, one remains unconvinced about the biographical character of Acts, then one should give consideration to the suggestion of Burridge that Acts may be a *bios* of a people, the church, analogous to such *bioi* of Dicaearchus and Varro. Acts would be written to describe the character of Jesus' disciples as a distinctive people after the resurrection/

ascension. They would be depicted as the people empowered by the Holy Spirit to give witness to Jesus while they wait for his return. From first (Acts 1.8–11) to last (Acts 28.30–31), this would seem to describe the character of the people called Christians as they are portrayed in the Acts of the Apostles. It may be that some combination of the two biographical hypotheses would work better than either taken alone.

Two related concerns prevent some scholars from taking Luke as biography which aims to speak of Jesus' character. The first assumes that to speak of Jesus' character means that he is understood as a human only and in terms of Greek virtues.[23] The assumption is incorrect. (1) The use of myth in certain biographies guarantees that the hero is understood in more than human terms (for example, Philostratus, *Life of Apollonius*; Pseudo-Callisthenes, *Alexander Romance*). The same is true for the gospels in general and Luke in particular. (2) Character, what sort of person he was, can be described in Jewish apocalyptic categories as well as in terms of the Greek virtues. So, for Luke to depict Jesus as the preacher of the kingdom of God by word and deed and as the one who died rather than sin is for the Evangelist to say who Jesus was. For Luke–Acts to say that Jesus has been raised from the dead to rule at God's right hand is to speak about who he is. That is to speak of what sort of person he was and is, of his character. The second reservation is associated with those who view Luke–Acts as the continuation of biblical history, that is, a continuation of the salvation history that is described in the Old Testament narratives and elsewhere.[24] This is not so much a genre description as a statement of the contents of the Lucan writings. I agree, Luke and Acts tell the continuing story of salvation history. Let us remember, however, that salvation history narrows at the point of Jesus to the story of one individual. At that point, the history of salvation is best told by the literary genre biography.

If one grants the biographical character of Luke and Acts,

23 David P. Moessner, "And Once Again: What Sort of 'Essence'? A Response to Charles Talbert," *Semeia* 43 (1988), 75–84; and "Re-reading Talbert's Luke," in *Cadbury, Knox, and Talbert*, pp. 203–228.
24 Kurz, *Reading Luke–Acts*.

what difference does it make? An answer must be given at two levels: theological and historical. At the theological level, the question is: Is the focus of Luke–Acts theological or is it christological in Luke and ecclesiological in Acts? If Luke–Acts is read as history, it may be the former; if it is read as biography, it is certainly the latter. The issue is whether or not the theological dimensions of the divine plan being worked out in Luke and Acts are the background or the foreground of the narrative.[25] If Luke–Acts or Luke and Acts are biographical, then the divine plan is the backdrop for the christological and ecclesiological focus of the two volumes.

At the historical level, what difference does it make if the Lucan writings are history or biography? Is Acts' historicity more secure with one or the other? To regard Acts as history says nothing about its historical reliability. One has only to read Polybius to see that there were different types of history in antiquity, some reliable and some not.[26] For example, in Polybius 12 there is a contrast between history as Polybius understands it and history as one Timaeus practices it. For Polybius, "if you take away truth from history what remains is but an unprofitable fable" (12.12). Therefore, for him systematic history consists of three parts: (1) the study of memoirs and other documents and a comparison of their contents; (2) a survey of cities, places, rulers, lakes, and in general the peculiar features of land and sea and the distances from one place to another; and (3) a review of political events (12.25e). Timaeus' "pronouncements are full of dreams, prodigies, incredible tales, and to put it shortly, craven superstitions and womanish love of the marvelous" (12.24). His speeches are "untruthfully reported" and "on purpose" (12.25a). Indeed, Polybius thinks that "at the present day . . . what is true and really useful is

---

[25] C. H. Talbert, review of *The Narrative Unity of Luke–Acts*, vol. i, by Robert C. Tannehill, *Biblica* 69 (1988), 135–138.

[26] Martin Hengel, *Acts and the History of Earliest Christianity* (Philadelphia: Fortress, 1979), p. 60, says: "Acts is no less trustworthy than other historians of antiquity." That is certainly true, but which historians: those like Timaeus or those like Polybius? Stirling, *Historiography and Self-Definition*, p. 3, says: "To place Luke–Acts into the framework of ancient historiography does not presuppose a settlement of the issue of veracity."

always treated with neglect, while what is pretentious and showy is praised and coveted as if it were something great and wonderful" (16.20).

Lucian's *How to Write History* echoes the same problems at a later time. For Lucian the historian should be involved in much laborious and painstaking investigation. He should, if possible, be an eyewitness. If not, then he should listen to those who tell the most impartial story (48). Alas, in Lucian's time history is written by those with no knowledge of geography (24). Those who have never set foot outside their city begin with such words as: "Ears are less trustworthy than eyes. I write then what I have seen, not what I have heard" (29). They invent and manufacture whatever "comes to the tip of an unlucky tongue" (32). Clearly in antiquity, to be presented with a writing of the historical genre was no guarantee of historical truthfulness.

Moreover, to say that the Lucan writings are biography does not guarantee anything about their historicity.[27] The sober lives of Suetonius and moralistic *bioi* of Plutarch reflect the more historically reliable variety of biography in antiquity, but alongside them one must reckon with Pseudo-Callisthenes' *Alexander Romance* and Lucian's *Passing of Peregrinus*. The biographical genre, no less than historiography, offers no guarantees about historicity. The matter of the historical value of Acts must be determined on other grounds.

[27] Michael Grant, *Roman Literature* (New York: Cambridge University Press, 1954), p. 120, says: "The border between biography and fiction was never very solid, and Greek 'biographers' had already overstepped it near the outset of the Hellenistic epoch."

CHAPTER 4

The preface to Acts and the historians

Loveday C. A. Alexander

The beginning of a text has a special place in the orientation process which forms an inevitable part of any reader's approach to a new book. In the ancient world, where a book had neither dust-jacket nor publisher's blurb, the opening of a book, whether or not it constituted a formal preface, was particularly important. It was frequently used to identify the subject of the text which followed, sometimes the author or a particular readership. It could also be used, less directly, to identify the genre of the text: in a literary world which operated with a relatively formal code (formal, that is, by twentieth-century standards), the conventions employed at the beginning of the text could alert the reader as to what kind of text to expect.[1]

The commentators on Acts have long been aware of the potential literary significance of its opening words. Cadbury, writing in 1922, stated clearly what was to become a datum of Lucan scholarship: "[Luke's] prefaces and dedications at once suggest classification with the contemporary Hellenistic historians."[2] The influential commentaries of Conzelmann and Haenchen contain classic restatements of this position:

Acts, as the second book of a large historical work, begins in accordance with literary forms with a renewed dedication (to Theophilus) and a backward glance to the first book . . . This opening verse shows

---

[1] D. Earl, "Prologue-form in Ancient Historiography" (ANRW 1.2, ed. H. Temporini (Berlin: de Gruyter, 1972, pp. 842–856)); L. C. A. Alexander, *The Preface to Luke's Gospel*, SNTSMS 79 (Cambridge: Cambridge University Press, 1993) 2,4, 5, *passim*.

[2] *The Beginnings of Christianity*, vol. II, ed. F. J. Foakes Jackson and Kirsopp Lake (London: Macmillan, 1922), p. 15.

that firstly: Christianity is adopting the literary forms. It is therefore on the point of leaving the milieu of ordinary folk and entering the world of literature, the cultural world of antiquity. Thus its aloofness from the "world" in which it grew up, expecting the end of this aeon, is diminishing . . . (Haenchen)

Since the opening includes at least the suggestion of a proem, Luke is making literary claims and introducing his book as a monograph. The dedication is also in accord with literary custom. (Conzelmann)[3]

Comments like these imply what Cadbury had explicitly stated: that the preface of Acts functions as a genre-indicator. The informed reader, beginning at the beginning of the book, is led immediately to place it in the category "history" (Cadbury, Haenchen) or "monograph" (Conzelmann). Whether the rest of the book lives up to these expectations is another matter; in any genre-contract, the reader may well be disappointed to find that the author is unable to fulfill her or his side of the contract.[4] For many scholars, the expectations aroused by the preface of Acts are fully satisfied in the text itself.[5] Others confess almost immediate frustration. Haenchen, oddly, blames the problems on the readers:

The elegant exordium of the third gospel has left many scholars with the impression that Luke would have been capable of writing the

---

[3] E. Haenchen, *The Acts of the Apostles* (Oxford: Blackwell, 1971, trans. from 14th German ed. of 1965), pp. 136–137; H. Conzelmann, *Acts of the Apostles*, Hermeneia commentaries (Philadelphia: Fortress, 1987, trans. from 2nd German ed. of 1972), p. 3. It is clear from the context that Conzelmann has in mind primarily the historical monograph.

[4] See R. A. Burridge, *What are the Gospels?* SNTSMS 70 (Cambridge: Cambridge University Press, 1992), chap. 2, esp. pp. 35–36. For genre as "a system of expectations," cf. p. 35, drawing on E. D. Hirsch, Jr., *Validity in Interpretation* (New Haven, CT: Yale University Press, 1967), pp. 83, 73; for genre as contract, ibid., drawing on H. Dubrow, *Genre*, The Critical Idiom Series 42 (London: Methuen, 1982), p. 31.

[5] The position is classically stated by Sir W. M. Ramsay, *St. Paul the Traveller and the Roman Citizen* (London: Hodder & Stoughton, 1895), pp. 34: "I will venture to add one to the number of the critics, by stating in the following chapters reasons for placing the author of *Acts* among the historians of the first rank." It has been defended many times in this century, notably in the work of F. F. Bruce; for a thorough recent treatment, see C. Hemer, *The Book of Acts in the Setting of Hellenistic History* (Winona Lake, Indiana: Eisenbrauns, 1990).

history of the dawn of Christianity in the style of a Xenophon, if not a Thucydides. However, he lacked at least two requisites for such an undertaking: an adequate historical foundation – and the right readers.[6]

Others would be more inclined to locate the problem with the standards of historiography prevailing in Luke's day:[7] which is to say that although our expectations in reading Acts may be disappointed (if, that is, we expected a dispassionate, objective history of the early church), nevertheless the first-century reader, accustomed to rather different standards of historical writing, would find the outcome of the composition perfectly in line with the expectations set up by the preface. Either way the preface (which is all that concerns us in this chapter) is widely accepted as defining the rules of the particular game Luke is playing.

Our question in this chapter is simply to ask how far this consensus assessment is justified. If the preface acts as a genre-indicator, have its signals been read aright? Have they been read in the way that an informed first-century reader would read them? This is not an invitation to psychologize but an invitation to become readers ourselves: that is, to immerse ourselves in a wide range of contemporary literature in order to facilitate an informed judgment on the range of possible options for reading the preface. The code of etiquette governing genre and other aspects of literary convention should not be seen as setting up *normative* prescriptions for what authors might and might not do: rather, by focusing on what the informed first-century reader could reasonably expect, the literary code encourages us as twentieth-century readers to build up an awareness of what was regarded in

---

[6] Haenchen, *Acts*, p. 103.
[7] E.g. W. L. Knox, *The Acts of the Apostles* (Cambridge: Cambridge University Press, 1948), p. 4; C. K. Barrett, *Luke the Historian in Recent Study* (London: Epworth, 1961), pp. 9–12; E. Plümacher, *Lukas als hellenisticher Schriftsteller* (Göttingen: Vandenhoeck & Ruprecht, 1972); W. C. van Unnik, 'Luke's Second Book and the Rules of Hellenistic Historiography,' pp. 37–60 of *Les Actes des Apôtres: Traditions, rédaction, théologie*, ed. J. Kremer, Bibliotheca Ephemeridum Theologicarum Lovaniensium XLVIII (Louvain: Ed. Duculot, 1979), esp. pp. 42–43.

the ancient world as *normal* or *customary* in a particular genre.[8]

I ONE VOLUME OR TWO?

The recapitulatory nature of the opening sentences immediately raises the question of the relationship between Acts and the "former treatise": more particularly for our purposes, the question how far the preface to the Gospel should also be treated as the preface to Acts. If Acts is "Volume II" of a two-volume composition, does this mean that the preface to "Volume I" (the Gospel) serves equally as a preface to Acts, rather like the preface to a multi-volume series in modern academic publishing? Or is the connection to be interpreted in a rather looser fashion?[9]

There is, of course, no serious dispute that the "former treatise" of Acts I.I is the Gospel of Luke: quite apart from the similarities of style, the identity of the dedicatee suggests that at once, as does the fact that Luke's is the only one of the canonical gospels which fits the description in Acts I. I. But the closeness of the relationship, and its literary consequences, have been variously assessed in recent scholarship. Standard estimates of the literary significance of Luke's prefaces, like those of Cadbury and Haenchen cited above, tend to treat both prefaces together; the assumption is that any genre-indications implied by the Gospel preface may be taken as assumed in the second volume. More recent scholarship, however, has begun to question the widely accepted assumption of the unity of the two-volume work known to scholarship

---

[8] Burridge, *Gospels*, p. 35. The literary "code" might usefully be compared with the dress codes governing certain groups (e.g. schoolchildren) or activities (e.g. sport). Parents of schoolchildren know all too well that the peer group's unwritten conventions about "what is being worn" can be much harder to defy than the school's more prescriptive rules. Similar unwritten codes govern what is (and perhaps even more what is not) worn when playing, e.g., at a golf tournament.

[9] I. H. Marshall, "Acts and the 'Former Treatise'" (pp. 163–182 of *The Book of Acts in its First Century Setting*, vol. I: *The Book of Acts in its Ancient Literary Setting*, ed. B. W. Winter and A. D. Clarke (Grand Rapids: Eerdmans, 1993) provides a helpful discussion of the options.

as "Luke–Acts".[10] This wider debate is of interest to us here only insofar as it concerns the preface.

There are in fact two distinct questions to be borne in mind: to ask "Does the Gospel preface look forward to Acts?" is not the same as asking "Does the preface of Acts look back to the Gospel?" From the starting-point of Lk. 1.1–4, it is a question that concerns the author rather than the reader. These verses contain no explicit indication that a second volume is in prospect: it is only with hindsight, after reaching the beginning of Acts, that the reader is encouraged to explore the connection. From the author's point of view, on the other hand, it is a real question to what extent Luke had Acts in mind when he wrote the preface to the Gospel. When he describes his work in terms of "the tradition handed down to us by the eyewitnesses and ministers of the word" (Lk. 1.2), for example, does this also describe the content of Acts? When he implies that Theophilus has already received "instruction" in the material he is about to read (Lk. 1.4), is this also true of Acts?[11] And what of the genre question? I have argued elsewhere that the conventions employed in the Gospel preface do not accord with the common classification of Luke's work with Greco-Roman historiography: the scope and scale are wrong, dedication is not normally found in historical writings, the customary topics for historical prefaces do not appear, and both the style and the motifs of the Lucan preface are better paralleled elsewhere, in the broad area of Greek literature (too broad to be called a

---

[10] Most recently in M. C. Parsons and R. I. Pervo, *Rethinking the Unity of Luke and Acts* (Fortress: Minneapolis, 1993); see also D. W. Palmer, "Monograph", E. Plümacher, "Monografie" (cited in n. 54).

[11] Alexander, *Preface*, pp. 24, 14f., 206f. In fact it has been argued that some of the statements in Lk. 1.1–4 apply *more* to Acts than to the Gospel (see e.g., Cadbury's argument discussed in Alexander, *Preface* pp. 128–130; Marshall, "Former Treatise," pp. 172–174) – though these readings raise problems of their own given the lack of explicit direction to the second volume in Lk. 1.1–4. Conversely, even if it is accepted that Luke–Acts is a two-volume work, it is natural that the first volume should be more immediately in mind (both to author and to readers) at the point at which the preface appears. Thus few would wish to argue that the "many" of Lk. 1.1 applies also to the Acts narrative; and it is possible to refer Luke's statements on "tradition" primarily to the Gospel without necessarily calling into question the unity of the work.

"genre") which I have called "the scientific tradition."[12] I do not intend to repeat the evidence for these statements here except insofar as they relate to Acts: but we do need to ask how far the genre-indicators implicit in the first preface (whatever they may be) are relevant to the second.

For the reader of Acts, however, the question has a rather different complexion. If at the beginning of the Gospel it is an open question how much the second volume is in view, at the beginning of Acts there is no such comfortable uncertainty. The text explicitly directs the attention of the reader to the earlier volume in its opening words: it presents itself as a continuation of the story begun there, and makes the closing scene of the first volume the opening scene of the second.[13] The reader of Acts thus has little choice about taking account of the existence of the Gospel. What is not clear is exactly what implications this has for our reading.

At the most obvious (and practical) level, it serves as a warning that the narrative on which we are about to embark is not self-contained. Names and allusions will not necessarily be explained: Jesus, Holy Spirit, John, the apostles are introduced without further explanation: passion, resurrection, kingdom are briefly mentioned in the first few verses as if the reader knows exactly what they are. Moreover by using the first person (ἐποιησάμην), the author of Acts points the reader back to one specific gospel, the one that he wrote: he does not here allude (as he does in Lk. 1.1) to other versions of the story which could supply the same essential background information. How far those narrative presuppositions may be extended backwards (for example through allusions to events much earlier in the Gospel narrative) or forwards (will this kind of prior knowledge also be presupposed at later points in

---

[12] Alexander, *Preface*, *passim*: for a definition of the "scientific tradition," see pp. 21f.

[13] Whatever the literary relations between the two versions of the ascension story (on which see the commentaries), this is how the story is presented in the text as we have it. See Plümacher, "Monografie" (cited in n. 54) p. 460: Plümacher argues that the repetition of the ascension story in the first chapter of Acts underlines Luke's concern "to present his two λόγοι as rounded narrative segments relatively independent of each other" ("seine beiden λόγοι als von einander relativ unabhängige, abgerundete und in sich einheitliche Geschehenablaüfe darzustellen").

the Acts narrative?) cannot be determined from the preface alone, and the inquiry would take us too far outside our immediate brief. All that can be stated with certainty is that *as a narrative*, Acts presents itself quite clearly as a "second volume," that is, as a continuation of a story already half-way through. "New readers begin here."

This does not, of course, settle the question of the unity of Luke–Acts by itself: Luke could well have conceived the Gospel as a single-volume work and then have added Acts as an afterthought. All the preface tells us on its own is that the Gospel was already written when Luke wrote the opening verses of Acts, and that he wanted his readers to know that. If, however, the recapitulation with which Acts begins is a recognizable literary convention known from other texts in the Greco-Roman literary world, it is reasonable to ask what light those other texts might shed on the question of unity. Where such a recapitulation occurs, is it normally the case that the second (or subsequent) work is "Volume II" (or III, or IV) in a multi-volume composition? And can the readers also take it for granted that the text they are about to encounter is *the same kind* of text as its predecessor?

Examination of a range of recapitulations in other ancient texts confirms that Greek literature contains numerous examples of multi-volume works linked by a recapitulatory sentence at the beginning of successive volumes: see, for example, the three volumes of the commentary of Apollonius of Citium on the Hippocratic *De Articulis*, or the five volumes of Artemidorus Daldianus' *Oneirocritica*.[14] But it is also true, as I have argued elsewhere, that "the connection between two successive works of a corpus linked by recapitulations is not always as tight as we might expect."[15] The writings of Theophrastus, for example, are linked by recapitulatory sentences describing the contents of previous works, even where the units so linked are not treated (by editors or scribes) as parts of a single composition. Thus the *De Causis Plantarum* presupposes the *Historia Plantarum* (both themselves multi-volume works)

---

[14] Alexander, *Preface*, pp. 143–146.   [15] Ibid., p. 146.

and refers back to it in the opening sentence; similarly *De Ventis* Book 1 states at the outset that part of the topic has been treated "previously" (πρότερον). Here Theophrastus reflects the characteristic Aristotelian concern for logical order and completeness in the arrangement of the whole scientific-philosophical enterprise, but with a relatively new interest in the corpus as a body of written texts.[16] Archimedes exhibits the same interest in the letters which accompanied his mathematical treatises across the Mediterranean.[17]

A similar concern may be seen in later large-scale scholarly enterprises. Philo shows it throughout the corpus (though more in the *Exposition* than in the *Allegory of the Laws*), where many texts begin with a transitional sentence summarizing the contents of the previous book (cf. the openings of *Plant.*, *Ebr.*, *Sobr.*, *Conf. Ling.*, *Quis Rerum*, *Somn.* 1, *Dec.*, *Spec. Leg.* 1, *Virt.*). There is no obvious formal distinction between these "corpus" transitions and those between "Book 1" and "Book 2" of a multi-volume work: compare *De Vita Mosis* 2.1, ἡ μὲν προτέρα σύνταξίς ἐστι περὶ γενέσεως τῆς Μωυσέως καὶ τροφῆς with, *Quis Rerum* 1, Ἐν μὲν τῇ πρὸ ταύτης συντάξει τὰ περὶ μισθῶν ὡς ἐνῆν ἐπ' ἀκριβείας διεξήλθομεν. A similar phenomenon may be observed in Galen, where a one-volume work, or Book 1 of a multi-volume work, may easily begin with a reference to a previous work.[18] Josephus seems to have structured his own *œuvre* with the same large-scale conception of the relation of the parts to the whole, or at least of subsequent compositions to what has gone before: thus the *Antiquities* makes a clear allusion (though not in a formulaic recapitulation sentence) to the *Jewish War*, and the *Apion* (in more formulaic fashion) in turn

---

[16] Cf. *De Signis Tempestatum*, 1.1. Texts in *Theophrasti Opera Omnia*, ed. F. Wimmer (Paris: Didot, 1866, repr. Frankfurt-on-Main: Minerva, 1964).

[17] See *De Sphaera et Cylindro*, Book 1, *De Conoidibus et Sphaeroidibus*, and *De Mechanicis Propositionibus*, all of which refer to a previous work, although none of them is a "second volume."

[18] *De temp.*, Book 1, Kühn 1.509; *De Anatomicis Administrationibus* Book 1, Kühn 11.215; *De Sanitate Tuenda*, Book 1, Kühn VI.1; *De Causis Morborum*, Kühn VII.1; *De Sympt. Diff.*, Kühn VII.42; *De Tremore*, Kühn VII.584; *De Dignosc. Puls.*, Book 1, Kühn VIII.766, where the four books of *De Diff. Puls.* are treated as the first part of a larger project; *De Comp. Med. Sec. Locos*, Book 1, Kühn XII.378.

to the *Antiquities*.[19] Josephus is a particularly valuable instance of this habit in that it is clear that there was a considerable time lapse between the completion of the *War* and the publication of the *Antiquities*.[20]

Comparison with the conventional code governing the use of recapitulations thus establishes clearly that two works linked as Acts is to Luke's Gospel need not necessarily have been conceived from the start as a single work. The comparison cannot, however, of itself establish that they were *not* so conceived: the preface to Acts leaves both possibilities open. The genre question, however, is not so clear. Palmer argues that two works by the same author linked by a recapitulation need not necessarily be of the same genre, and therefore that the genre of Acts may be different from that of the Gospel.[21] Certainly there is good reason for assigning distinct genre-categories to Josephus' three major works: the *War* and the *Antiquities* belong, if not to two different genres, at least to two different subgenres of historical writing, and the *Contra Apionem*, as its name suggests, is structured as an apologetic argument rather than a narrative. However, in these cases the changed subject matter and genre of the new work are indicated clearly in the preface.[22] Acts, by

---

[19] As Darryl Palmer correctly observes, "Monograph" (cited in n. 54), p. 25: cf. *Ant.* 1.4, *Apion* 1.1.

[20] *Ant.* 1.7 speaks of "hesitation and delay" in beginning the *Antiquities*; the date of completion (xx.267) suggests around eighteen years from the publication of the *War* (Thackeray, Loeb Classical Library *Josephus*, vol. iv, p. x). We might also compare Artemidorus Daldianus, *Oneirocritica* (R. A. Pack [ed.], *Artemidorus Daldiarnus. Onirocrition Libri V*, [Leipzig: Teubner, 1963]), where Book 3 in the five-volume sequence is presented as an afterthought: (3, pref.; 4, pref., p. 237). The fourth book seems to have followed after a further interval: it addresses a new dedicatee after the death of the first, and takes up criticisms of the earlier books (4, pref. pp. 237f.).

[21] Palmer, "Monograph" (cited n. 54) p. 25.

[22] "While Polybius and the tradition of political and military historiography served as the primary model for the *War*, it was the antiquarian history represented by Dionysius of Halicarnassus which supplied the model for Josephus' next work": H. Attridge, "Josephus and his Works" (pp. 185–232 of *Jewish Writings of the Second Temple Period*, ed. Michael E. Stone, Compendia Rerum Iudaicarum ad Novum Testamentum sect. ii [Assen and Philadelphia, van Gorcum/Fortress 1984]), p. 217. Cf. Sterling, *Apologetic Historiography* (cited n. 64), pp. 240–245. The genre of the *Antiquities* (as well as its subject) is indicated clearly at 1.5 (τὴν παρ' ἡμῖν ἀρχαιολογίαν). The apologetic mode of the *Contra Apionem* is indicated in the preface equally clearly, though less directly, by a cluster of forensic terms: βλασφημίας, τεκμήριον, λοιδορούντων, ἐλέγξαι, ψευδολογίαν, μάρτυσι, κτλ.

contrast, contains no prospective summary to match the retrospective allusion to the previous volume in verse 1, which seems to make it less likely that a major change of genre is in view. In the case of Philo, the assignment of genre-categories within the corpus is much more problematic. Although it is tempting to regard the "lives" of the patriarchs as belonging to a different genre from the treaties on the pentateuchal Law which follow, the same underlying exegetical structure underlies the whole series. In the *De Vita Mosis*, on the other hand, where there is a more obvious attempt to address a Greek audience with a self-contained text in a distinct genre, the preface makes the change abundantly clear: no previous knowledge of the corpus is assumed, and formal preface-conventions of a type hardly seen elsewhere appear.[23]

As far as the preface is concerned, then, we cannot rule out either option: Acts may be read either as "Volume II" of a unified composition, or as an independent monograph which simply reminds the reader that its narrative is a sequel to the earlier work. In what follows, I have tried to allow equally for both possibilities. I shall not assume that the implications of the Gospel preface also hold good for Acts, but shall treat the preface to Acts on its own merits.

II DEFINING THE PREFACE

Our first task must be to define what we mean by the preface of Acts. Commentators differ markedly in their divisions of the text at this point: the first section is estimated variously from three verses to fourteen. But for our purposes in this chapter there is no real need to define the end of the preface, for the simple reason that in formal terms (that is, in terms of the formal Greek literary conventions which concern us here) the preface to Acts has no ending.

---

[23] On the audience of the *De Vita Mosis*, see esp. E. R. Goodenough, "Philo's Exposition of the Law and his *De Vita Mosis*,' *HTR* 26 (1933), 109–125; E. R. Goodenough, *An Introduction to Philo Judaeus*, 2nd ed. (Oxford: Basil Blackwell, 1962), pp. 33–35; S. Sandmel, *Philo of Alexandria: An Introduction* (Oxford and New York: Oxford University Press, 1979), p. 47.

The point may be illustrated by comparison with the preface to 2 Maccabees (2 Macc. 2.19–32), a passage which clearly follows Hellenistic literary convention and which is distinctly demarcated from the beginning of the narrative with the formula (verse 32), "it would be foolish to lengthen the preface by cutting short the history itself."[24] Even where no such formula is used, syntax and style usually make it clear where the preface ends and the narrative or discourse proper begins: this is the case, for example, with the preface to *ben Sira* and with Luke's own preface to the Third Gospel.[25] The preface to Acts, by contrast, has a curiously open-ended feel to it, not only because of the hanging μέν left without an answering δέ,[26] but also because the authorial first sentence merges uneasily into impersonal narrative, into indirect speech, and then into direct speech, with the transitions marked only by a series of unimpressive conjunctions and relative pronouns. Since the end of the preface is so ill-defined, our primary concern here will be with the beginning, where the use of Greek convention is clear. We shall consider the awkward transition from preface to narrative, and its implications for Luke's use of literary convention, at a later point.[27]

For our immediate purposes, then, the preface of Acts consists of an opening sentence in which the author speaks in the first person singular, addresses an individual (Theophilus) using the vocative, and alludes briefly to the subject matter of his own previous treatise. This brief summary of the previous work then becomes the opening scene of the narrative, which unfolds subsequently without any further return of the second-person address or of the authorial first person singular.[28] The

---

[24] On this preface see Alexander, *Preface*, pp. 148–151.

[25] See Alexander, *Preface*, pp. 151–154 on *ben Sira*; 103–104 on other endings.

[26] See the commentaries and D. W. Palmer, "The Literary Background of Acts 1.1–14," *NTS* 33 (1987), 427–438.

[27] In common with most current scholarship, I shall treat the text as it stands on the assumption that any irregularities are Luke's own, and not the result of redaction or textual corruption.

[28] Wehnert rightly dissociates the "we" of the we-passages from the authorial "I" of the prefaces: J. Wehnert, *Die Wir-Passagen der Apostelgeschichte: Ein lukanisches Stilmittel aus jüdischer Tradition*, Göttinger Theologischer Arbeiten 40 (Göttingen: Vandenhoeck and Ruprecht, 1989), pp. 136–139.

preface thus employs at least three recognizable Greek literary conventions: the authorial first person (as distinct from the impersonal narrator); the dedication to a named second person; and the recapitulation or summary of the contents of the previous book in a series. The manner in which the recapitulation merges directly into the narrative is also a formal feature (if only in a negative sense) for which we may fairly seek parallels, although it is possible that in this case we are dealing with authorial idiosyncrasy rather than with literary convention.

III THE PREFACE TO ACTS AND GREEK HISTORIOGRAPHY

We return now to the question with which we began. Do the conventions used in the preface suggest to the informed reader, in Cadbury's words, an immediate classification with contemporary Hellenistic historiography? Do they arouse literary expectations which, even if they are not fulfilled in the text of Acts, yet exhibit a degree of literary pretension unique in the NT? And how far does the subject matter of Acts and its predecessor, as presented to the reader in the preface of Acts, accord with contemporary expectations as to the proper subject matter for historical writing?

a Authorial first person

The use of the authorial first person in prefaces is common in Greek literature, and can readily be paralleled in historical writing. It appears occasionally in Thucydides (1.3.1,9,1.22.1, 5.26.4–6), and much more freely in Polybius (for example 6.2.1–7, 9.1.1–2.7, 9.1.1a-5) and Diodorus (for example, 1.3.1, 5, 1.4.1–53, 1.42.2, 2.1.2–3, 3.1.3). It should, of course, be observed that the phenomenon is too widespread to be accounted a genre-indicator on its own.[29]

---

[29] See Alexander, *Preface*, pp. 18, 22, 45, 50, 70, 71 on the development of personal prefaces in Greek literature.

It is worth observing, however, that historical writers were notably reluctant to break the mold of impersonal narration inherited from their epic predecessors. The opening words of Herodotus' preface introduce the author in the third person, and the same archaic convention is used by Thucydides (1.1.1, 5.26.1): it remains a recognizable stylistic marker for later historians eager to parade their Thucydidean aspirations.[30] Even where the post-classical convention of the recapitulation is used, the verbs employed may well be impersonal and passive: not "I have written," but "it was demonstrated" (as in the [editorial] internal prefaces in Xenophon's *Anabasis*, or in Diodorus 2.1 and 3.1–2). The same reluctance to use the first person is evident where the author is introduced as a character in his own narrative: Thucydides, and following him Xenophon and Josephus, describe their own actions in the third person, not the first – a point which should be remembered in relation to the so-called "we-passages" of Acts.[31]

b Dedication

The appearance of this literary convention at the beginning of Acts would not encourage the informed reader to think immediately of historiography. The habit of dedicating a treatise to a named individual was not at all common in historical writing:

The apostrophe of the second person, whether in direct address (vocative) or in epistolary form, does not fit with the impersonal narrative style of history, and was generally avoided: in Herkommer's words (my translation), "the dedication of historical works was not customary among the Greeks . . . Further, dedication does not belong by nature to Roman historical writing."[32]

In fact the first extant example of a dedicated historical work is Josephus' *Antiquities*, which was dedicated (as we learn from the end of the *Vita*) to Epaphroditus. Even here, however, the

---

[30] Ibid., pp. 26–27.   [31] Wehnert, *Wir-Passagen*, p. 143.
[32] Alexander, *Preface*, pp. 27–29, with reference to E. Herkommer, "Die Topoi in der Proömien der römischen Geschichtswerke," Diss. Tübingen, 1968, p. 25.

conventional code is not formally breached: the beginning of the *Antiquities* opens in orthodox fashion with a discussion of the author's predecessors in the field and of the magnitude of the subject matter.[33] Epaphroditus appears in the third person, apparently incidentally, at 1.8: the themes introduced here, of the author's reluctant yielding to persuasion and of the learned disposition of the dedicatee, are part of the characteristic courtesy of dedication,[34] but Josephus, sensitive as ever to the stylistic niceties, avoids using the second-person address until the very end of his work (*Vita* 430). Only in the *Contra Apionem* (1.1, 2.1), which is not a historical narrative, do we find dedication given literary expression in a second-person address at the beginning of the text: which seems to suggest that, whatever the underlying social matrix in terms of patronage or place-seeking, the literary code does not encourage the formality of a second-person address in a historical work.[35]

Evidence for earlier, now lost histories which might have borne dedications is difficult to assess unless the opening of the work happens to have survived. Testimonies in later writers that a certain text was written "for" a particular individual do not necessarily imply that a second-person address stood in the preface.[36] However, where possible dedications are attested, it is notable that they tend to cluster on the more "antiquarian" side of Greek historiography (Apollodorus) and with authors who, like Josephus, stand in one way or another outside the mainstream of Greek culture (Berossus, Manetho). The evidence may be summarized as follows:

1. The *Chronica* of Apollodorus. This, according to Pseudo-Scymnus, he "composed for the kings in Pergamum" (τοῖς ἐν Περγάμῳ βασιλεῦσιν ... συνετάξατ'); it was a didactic

---

[33] Alexander, *Preface*, p. 31; Herkommer, "Topoi," pp. 102–112, 164–174.

[34] Alexander, *Preface*, p. 27 and n. 7, pp. 73–75.

[35] The relationship between patronage and dedication is more complex than is often assumed: see ibid., pp. 50–63 (esp. 62), 187–200 (esp. 194). Josephus also records that he presented copies of the *War* to Vespasian, and that Titus arranged for its publication (*Vita* 363): yet neither is addressed in the preface. See Attridge, "Josephus," pp. 192–193.

[36] As is clear from Josephus: see previous note. Cf. J. Ruppert, "Quaestiones ad historiam dedicationis librorum pertinentes," Diss. Leipzig, 1911, pp. 29–30.

summary of world history in iambic verse, a sufficiently odd innovation for Pseudo-Scymnus (who uses the same meter for his geographical summary) to consider it worth a lengthy explanation. That this was a formal dedication at the head of the text is clear:

κεῖνος μὲν οὖν κεφάλαια συναθροίσας χρόνων
εἰς βασιλέως ἀπέθετο φιλαδέλφου χάριν,
ἃ καὶ διὰ πάσης γέγονε τῆς οἰκουμένης,
ἀθάνατον ἀπονέμοντα δόξαν ᾿Αττάλῳ
τῆς πραγματείας ἐπιγραφὴν εἰληφότι.[37]

2. Berossus. Tatian preserves a testimony from Juba of Mauretania, one of the major excerptors of Berossus' work, to the effect that Berossus "drew up the history of the Chaldeans in three books for Antiochus." Neither Josephus nor Eusebius, our major sources for the text of Berossus, mentions the dedication, but there is nothing intrinsically improbable in Juba's testimony. The Antiochus in question was Antiochus I Soter, whose reign can be dated from 293/2 (or 280) to 261/0 BCE. Josephus quotes from Berossus' work (see, for example, *C. Ap.* 1.129–153), and may have been influenced by the literary conventions employed there.[38]

3. Manetho. No authentic dedication survives, but Syncellus preserves the information that Manetho's account of Egyptian history was addressed to Ptolemy II Philadelphus. Unfortunately at least one of the Syncellus texts connects the dedication with the Book of Sōthis, which is a digest of Manetho's work dating probably from the third century CE. The "Letter of Manetho," although it may preserve some authentic information, is "undoubtedly a forgery."[39] Josephus quotes exten-

---

[37] For Apollodorus see F. Jacoby, *Apollodors Chronik: eine Sammlung der Fragmente*, Philogische Untersuchungen 16 (Berlin: Weidmann, 1902). The citations are from Pseudo-Scymnus, *Orbis Descriptio* 16–49 (C. Müller [ed.], *Geographi Graeci Minores* [Paris: Didot, 1855–1861], pp. 196–199).

[38] Berossus: texts and fragments in P. Schnabel, *Berossos und die Babylonisch-Hellenistische Literatur* (Leipzig and Berlin: Teubner, 1923), pp. 5–8. Discussion in Sterling, *Apologetic Historiography*, pp. 104–117.

[39] Waddell, Loeb Classical Library *Manetho*, p. xxviii; text of the letter in Appendix 1, pp. 208–210. On the Sōthis-book, see pp. xxviif. and 234–248; the Syncellus extracts appear on pp. 14, 208. See further Jacoby, *FGH* (Leiden: Brill, 1958),

sively from Manetho (see, for example, *C.Ap.* 1.73–105) without mentioning any dedication.

4. The *Libyan History* of Aristippus. According to Diogenes Laertius 2.83, Aristippus of Cyrene, one of the early Socratics, is credited, among other works, with "three books of *historia* of matters concerning Libya, sent to Dionysius" (τρία μὲν ἱστο-ρίας τῶν κατὰ Λιβύην ἀπεσταλμένα Διονυσίῳ). As so often with Diogenes Laertius, there are conflicting reports on the writings of Aristippus: a second list attributed to Sotion and Panaetius (2.85) makes no mention of the "history." If it is authentic, the dedication would pre-date by several decades the earliest examples known to us in any literary tradition.[40] The *historia* in question clearly belongs to the geographical-ethnographical side of the Ionian tradition: the word could as well be translated "inquiry" as "history."

5. Dionysius of Halicarnassus, *Ant. Rom.* 1.4.3. This refers to some of his predecessors who have "dared to express such views [sc. critical of the origins of Rome] in the writings they have left, taking this method of honouring barbarian kings who detested Roman supremacy – princes to whom they were ever servilely devoted and with whom they were associated as flatterers – by presenting them with 'histories' which were neither just nor true" (βασιλεῦσι βαρβάροις . . . οὔτε δίκαιας οὔτε ἀληθεῖς ἱστορίας χαριζόμενοι: Loeb Classical Library trans.). Here again we are in the area of ethnography and "archaeology," and again the practice of dedication is associated with the monarchies of the Hellenistic age (though Diony-sius describes the recipients of these texts, whoever they were, as "barbarians," i.e. non-Greeks). But again it must be stressed that, as we saw in the case of Josephus, the charge of "writing to please" does not necessarily entail that a formal dedication stood at the head of the text. Dionysius himself is happy to admit (apparently without irony) that his own work is bias-free because he is making a "grateful return" (χαριστηρίους

IIIc609 (Syncellus = T11a, b); Sterling, *Apologetic Historiography* (cited in n. 64), pp. 117–135.

[40] Cf. Alexander, *Preface*, p. 53: perhaps (if genuine) the work should be ascribed to Aristippus' grandson? See further *RE* II.1 s.v. "Aristippos" (8).

ἀμοιβάς) to the city of Rome (1.6.5). Like Josephus, he is able to make a graceful gesture without marking any dedication with a formal address.

6. Phlegon of Tralles (*FGH* 257 *T*3) and Callinicus of Petra (*FGH* 281 *T*1). They date respectively from the second and the third century CE and are thus too late for our purpose of establishing literary custom in the first century.

c Recapitulation

The brief (and by no means exhaustive) survey of recapitulations given above of itself raises the question of literary appropriateness. How far are the practical, academic concerns evidenced by this kind of transitional introduction compatible with the more rhetorical interests of Hellenistic historiography?[41] Theophrastus, Archimedes, Philo, and Galen could not be called by any stretch of the imagination historians: and it would be dangerous to take Josephus, an outsider always conscious of his literary shortcomings,[42] as typical of the whole Greek historiographical tradition.

In fact the construction of a preface in the form of a recapitulatory transition is the exception rather than the rule in Greek historiography. The fifth-century classics, Herodotus and Thucydides, did not divide their works into books, and thus had no need for secondary introductions to separate books. Thucydides does have a secondary preface at 5.26 which reestablishes his authorship of the second section of the *History* (Γέγραφε δὲ καὶ ταῦτα ὁ αὐτὸς Θουκυδίδης Ἀθηναῖος ἑξῆς, ὡς ἕκαστα ἐγένετο), but this is more concerned with bridging the interlude in the war (and counting its extent in years) than with summarizing the contents of the first part of the work. Conformably with his model Thucydides, Xenophon provides no internal prefaces to the *Hellenica*, and the recapitulations in the *Anabasis* are generally accepted as the work of a later redactor. Even when the practicalities of book production made the

---

[41] Well summarized in Sterling, *Apologetic Historiography* (cited in n. 64), pp. 8–9.
[42] See *Ant.* 1.7; *C. Ap.* 1.50.

division of a longer text into volumes a familiar phenomenon, historical writers still preferred to do without recapitulations: in the words of Laqueur's classic 1911 study,[43]

Josephus in the *Jewish War*, Arrian in his *Anabasis*, Tacitus in the *Annals* and the *Histories*, Herodian etc. dispense altogether with any stylistic demarcation of the individual book; we read from one book to the next without finding the slightest indication of the fact that we have got into a new book.

Narrative, it would seem, provides its own principles of internal organization: a clearly structured narrative with a firm chronological sequence can dispense with the external aids to logical ordering used in philosophical or scientific discourse.

The number of surviving recapitulatory prefaces (that is, books which begin with a recapitulation) in historical writing up to the second century CE is remarkably small given the size and scale of Greek historiography. Diodorus Siculus has four or five such prefaces in twenty books: eight further books have a recapitulation at the end of the preface, marking the transition to the narrative, but in these cases the preface itself is structured in a very different way (see further below, "The Preface to Acts and the Historical Monograph").[44] Polybius has one at 2.1 and again at 6.1 (though the back reference is to Book 2, not Book 3). Book 5 has no introduction, and Book 3 begins

---

43   R. Laqueur, "*Ephoros I*: Die Proömien," *Hermes* 46 (1911), 161–206, 166f. (my trans.): "Josephus im Jüdischen Kriege, Arrian in seiner Anabasis, Tacitus in (167) Annalen u. Historien, Herodian usw. verzichten überhaupt auf jede stilistische Herausarbeitung des Einzelbuches; wir lesen von einem Buche zum andern hinüber, ohne auch nur im geringsten die Tatsache angedeutet zu finden, dass wir in ein neues Buch geraten sind."

44   Recapitulatory prefaces: 1.42.1, 2.1.1, 3.1.1, 11.1.1–2. 1.41 is included as marking the transition to the second "volume" of Book 1, though there are doubts as to the authenticity of the bulk of the recapitulation, which is written in the third person (unusually for Diodorus) and sits ill with the first-person prospective sentence at 42.2. Book 17, which is similarly split, has no such demarcation. Recapitulation at the end of the preface: 4.1.5–6, 12.2.2–3, 13.1.2–3, 14.2.3–4, 15.1.6, 18.1.6, 19.1.9–10, 20.2.3. To class all these together, as Sterling does (p. 331, n. 102) is therefore misleading: even here there is still a wide variety of styles, some being much more formulaic than others. What interests us here is the construction of a preface around a recapitulation *and nothing else*: Sacks, indeed, can say that "books ii, iii and xi have only tables of contents," as opposed to the "full prooemium" which appears in Diodorus' other books (K. S. Sacks, *Diodorus Siculus and the First Century* [Princeton: Princeton University Press, 1990], p. 9).

effectively as if it were a new (and large-scale) preface to the whole composition. The prefaces to the remaining books are mostly lost, but the most likely interpretation of his own words in 11.1 is that Polybius chose to preface each Olympiad (that is, every other book) with an integral *proekthesis* or "introductory survey to a book or series of books." These *proektheseis* should be distinguished from the recapitulations of the earlier books.[45] Dionysius of Halicarnassus has only one initial recapitulation in the ten books of the *Roman Antiquities*, at 2.1, and Josephus has four in the twenty books of the *Jewish Antiquities*, at 8.1, 13.1, 14.1, and 16. The last case is puzzling since there is no obvious reason why Josephus should have adopted this convention here and nowhere else: Laqueur suggests the influence of a lost source. But for Polybius, Dionysius, and Diodorus it is possible to see a practical reason for the employment of recapitulations in the early sections of the work, where an extended theoretical or "archaeological" introduction could make it difficult for the reader to find his or her way around.[46] Once the narrative proper begins, this need disappears; and it is noticeable that neither Josephus nor Polybius seems to feel that a summary of the prospective book is necessary in narrative, even where the *anakephalaiosis* formula is used: Josephus *Ant.* 8.1 and 13.1 contain no forward summary, and *Ant.* 14.1 and 15.1, like Polybius 2.1, simply say, "we shall now speak of the events that followed immediately."

The use of a recapitulation at the beginning of a book cannot therefore be described as in any way *customary* or *usual* in Greek historiography, though there are examples to be found. From the perspective of the reader's expectations, it is also relevant to note that such beginnings are far more common elsewhere in Greek literature, notably in the vast and multiform body of texts associated with philosophical and scientific inquiry.[47]

---

[45] F. W. Walbank, *A Historical Commentary on Polybius*, vol. II (Oxford: Clarendon Press, 1967), p. 266; Laqueur, "*Ephoros I*," p. 186.

[46] Laqueur, "*Ephoros I*," pp. 191–192: "Ein prakistsches Bedürfnis hat die ἀνακεφαλαιώσεις hervorgebracht und sie immer dann anwenden lassen, wenn die Verzahnung zum Verständnis der Composition eines Werkes notwendig war."

[47] Alexander, *Preface*, pp. 143–144.

This fits with the reasonable presumption that these summary introductions serve practical rather than rhetorical ends (see n. 46 above): the influence of rhetoric on history writing produced a very different kind of preface, of which I shall say more below. It may also be relevant to note that the highest incidence of these prefaces is in the area of history which overlaps most with the broader *historia* of the Ionians and their successors. It has been argued on other grounds that this area of historiography operated with a conventional code distinct from that which governed contemporary historiography.[48] But for our immediate purposes the important point is that this feature alone is not sufficient to suggest an identification with Greek historiography to the informed reader beginning at Acts 1.1.

d Subject matter

Ancient authors often use the opening words of a preface (or of the text itself) to indicate their subject matter, either generically (as in Josephus *Ant.* 1.1, "Those who attempt to write histories . . ."), or more specifically (as in Josephus *BJ* 1.1, "Since the war of the Jews against the Romans . . .").[49] Where the opening sentence takes the form of a recapitulation describing the subject of the previous volume, we would naturally expect a prospective sentence to introduce the subject of the new book. With Acts the matter is complicated by the fact that we have only the summary of the previous volume: Luke plunges straight into his narrative at 1.3 without giving the

[48] The *locus classicus* for the distinction between political history and "archaeology" or "antiquities" is A. D. Momigliano, "The place of Herodotus in the History of Historiography," pp. 127–142 of Momigliano, *Studies in Historiography* (London: Weidenfeld & Nicolson, 1969); see also "Historiography on Written Tradition and Historiography on Oral Tradition' in the same volume. See also n. 22 above.

[49] See Earl, "Prologue-form." See also Stadter, *Arrian* (cited in n. 62), p. 61: "The subject is presented firmly, though indirectly: Alexander son of Philip. Each sentence [of the preface] discusses Alexander historians, and A.'s name appears five times in these few lines." The habit was not confined to historians: see Alexander, *Preface*, pp. 29, 42–46, 71–73. The fact that in both the cases cited Josephus is actually talking about his predecessors does not affect the fact that these words effectively inform the reader of the genre of the book: *Preface*, pp. 107–108 and n. 7.

reader any prior orientation as to its contents. Whether or not it can be paralleled (see next section), this purely retrospective *anakephalaiosis* does have the effect of limiting the reader's perception of what lies in prospect.

This means that even if Acts is to be read as a self-contained work, rather than a "second volume" (see above), the brief description of the contents of the previous treatise provided in verse 1 is the only summary indication of genre the preface provides; and it is not one which would immediately register to the informed reader, "This is a historical work." The proper subject matter for history in the Greco-Roman tradition was *res gestae*, the actions (*praxeis*) of nations, or cities, or great men.[50] The teachings and doings of an individual (περὶ πάντων . . . ὧν ἤρξατο ὁ Ἰησοῦς ποιεῖν τε καὶ διδάσκειν) are more properly the subject of a biographical work (and a philosophical one at that) than of a history.[51] And even allowing for the possibility of a change of genre between the two books, there is nothing in the succeeding verses to indicate that the second is any more of a history than the first. They provide merely a bewildering succession of unglossed religious terms clustering around the continued activity of the dead teacher described in the previous volume.

This is not to say that the preface does not contain clear pointers as to the subject of the book: simply that they are not the kinds of pointers used to indicate "history" on the Greco-Roman literary spectrum. For the informed reader (and Luke signals clearly in verse 1 that his implied reader is already

---

[50] On the proper subjects for history, see Momigliano, "Herodotus"; O. Geiger, *Cornelius Nepos and Ancient Political Biography*, Historia Einzelschriften 47 (Stuttgart: Steiner Verlag, 1985), pp. 21–29, 46–51, esp. p. 22: "For the Ancients history was political history, its main characters and prime movers kings, statesmen and generals." See also M. Hengel, *Acts and the History of Earliest Christianity* (London: SCM, 1979), pp. 13–14; van Unnik, "Luke's Second Book," pp. 38–39. Most commentators believe that the title ΠΡΑΞΕΙΣ ΑΠΟΣΤΟΛΩΝ was attached to Acts at a later stage of the tradition: see Sterling, *Apologetic Historiography* (cited in n. 64), p. 314.

[51] Classic in this field is A. D. Momigliano, *The Development of Greek Biography* (Cambridge, MA: Harvard University Press, 1971; reissue, 1993). Burridge, *Gospels*, pp. 70–81 gives a good general introduction; on Acts as biography, see L. C. A. Alexander, "Acts and Ancient Intellectual Biography," pp. 31–63 of Winter and Clarke, *Book of Acts*.

acquainted with the Gospel) the opening verses of Acts place the narrative in sequence not only with the Gospel but with the larger narrative which forms its matrix, that is, the narrative of the Jewish scriptures. I shall return to this point in my conclusions.

e Transition

Finally, what of the abrupt transition from recapitulation to narrative? Palmer argues that there are a number of parallels to this apparent irregularity, though the list is not in fact very long.[52] However, I know of no parallel which can match the oddity of Luke's opening sentence: even in the closest parallels, the distinction between authorial comment and narration is matched by a clear syntactical break. This irregularity may be due simply to lack of competence on Luke's part, or to lack of interest in maintaining the formal preface-style with which he begins.[53] But it must be recognized that it is an irregularity, and it must affect our assessment of the relationship between Acts and the Gospel. As I observed above, the Josephan parallels occur within a narrative which has sufficient momentum of itself to allow the author to dispense with a prospective summary. The whole force of such a preface depends on the continuity of the narrative: there is no question that it introduces a self-contained monograph, much less a new genre. Where Josephus does begin a major new work with a reference back to earlier compositions, the transition to the new subject is fully explained (see n. 22 above).

It is becoming increasingly clear that if we are to take

---

[52] Palmer, "Monograph" (cited in n. 54), pp. 22–23 cites Josephus, *Ant.* 8.1, together with the editorial additions to Xenophon, *Anabasis* (date unknown) and Herodian, who dates from the third century CE. Polybius 2.1.1–4, which he also cites, does have a prospective sentence, however brief: "I will now attempt to give a summary view . . . of the events immediately following"; cf. the similar brief prospectus in Josephus *Ant.* 14, 15.1. And in all these cases the narrative transition is rounded off with the appropriate particle (δέ or νῦν) to match the opening sentence. Similarly in Galen, *De Meth. Med.* (Kühn x.594), the one case I have been able to find in scientific literature.

[53] See Alexander, *Preface*, p. 175 on the limitations of Luke's competence and/or interest in the *formalia* of the preface.

seriously the signals emitted by the preface we must either admit that the beginning of Acts does not conform to the conventional etiquette of Greco-Roman historiography or look for a different type of historiography. In this context it is worth giving some attention to the suggestion made by a number of scholars that although the category 'Hellenistic historiography" is too broad to help the reader of Acts, there are useful parallels with more specialized types of historical composition. Two in particular will concern us here: the historical monograph, and the genre of "apologetic historiography."

IV THE PREFACE TO ACTS AND THE HISTORICAL MONOGRAPH

Classification of Acts (or Luke–Acts) as a "historical monograph" goes back to a suggestion of Conzelmann's which has been taken up in a number of more recent studies.[54] The definition of this subgenre is by no means clear (see especially Palmer's discussion of the wide range of options, both in ancient and in modern usage), and its usefulness for the reader of Acts is variously assessed. There are in effect two diametrically opposed approaches. One looks at multi-volume works which use internal prefaces to highlight the individuality of each volume, while the other focuses on smaller-scale works consisting of one or two volumes only. We begin with the former.

Conzelmann's note on Acts 1.1 (*Acts*, p. 4) includes an excursus on "proems" which suggests that it is the very fact that Acts has a preface which marks it out as a "monograph":

---

[54] Ward Gasque, "A Fruitful Field: Recent Study of the Acts of the Apostles", *Interpretation* 42 1988), 129 suggests that while "[v]ery few contemporary scholars would say that Luke is a historian in the tradition of Thucydides or Polybius . . . [t]he consensus of opinion at present seems to be that Luke has written a historical monograph." See especially Hengel, *Earliest Christianity*, pp. 14, 36f.; E. Plümacher, "Die Apostelgeschichte als historische Monografie," pp. 457–466 of *Les Actes des Apôtres* ed. Kremer. Plümacher is followed by D. W. Palmer in "Acts and the Ancient Historical Monograph," pp. 1–29 of *The Book of Acts*, ed. Winter and Clarke, in which see p. 3, n. 9 for further references. Geiger, *Cornelius Nepos*, pp. 47–51 gives a useful summary of the evidence for historical monographs.

Proems originally belonged to the epideictic genre . . . Their pene-
tration into Hellenistic historiography is indicative that such literary
products are thought of as monographs (Diodorus). Thus the presence of the Lucan proem argues against the thesis that Luke's Gospel
and Acts originally formed a single work, separated only for "technical and canonical" reasons.

The reference to Diodorus is elucidated by a footnote bibliography which includes the classic study by Laqueur to which I
alluded earlier (n. 43 above). In this lengthy analysis of the
Diodoran prefaces, Laqueur points out that there are two
distinct types of preface in Diodorus' *Library of History*. The
first, as we have seen, is the "recapitulation" type found in the
first three books. But from Book 4 onwards a completely
different type of preface appears, described by Laqueur as "a
new form . . . unheard of in contemporary literature" (p. 195,
my trans.). Instead of the transitional, purely informative
summaries of the earlier books, we find in these new prefaces
either a methodological discussion about historiography in
general (for example Book 15) or a moralizing introduction
(Laqueur, p. 162) which approaches the theme of the book in
an indirect fashion (for example Book 14). These prefaces recall
the varied opening gambits of epideictic oratory and may be
traced back ultimately to Isocrates. But Diodorus found them,
Laqueur plausibly argues, in the historical work of Ephorus of
Cyme, who was a pupil of Isocrates and who, according to
Diodorus himself, "wrote thirty books attaching a *prooimion* to
each one" (Diodorus 16.76.5: Laqueur, pp. 196–197). Margrit
Kunz challenges Laqueur's assumption that Ephorus was Diodorus' only source for the "epideictic" preface-type,[55] but her
detailed linguistic analysis confirms the distinction drawn by
Laqueur between the rhetorically well-constructed "epideic-
tic" prefaces and the recapitulations. The monotonous

---

[55] Margrit Kunz, "Zur Beurteilung der Prooemien in Diodors historischer Biblio-
thek," Diss. Zurich, 1935, pp. 101–107. Sacks, *Diodorus* (also in "The Lesser
Proemia of Diodorus Siculus." *Hermes* 110 [1981], 434–443) goes further in the
rehabilitation of Diodorus as author rather than compiler, but does not contest the
distinction between the recapitulation and the *prooimion* proper: cf. n. 44 above and
next note.

construction and limited vocabulary of the latter point to Diodorus' own authorship (Kunz, pp. 67–68).[56]

Whether this innovation should be credited to Ephorus or to some other historian, the effect of adding an epideictic preface to every volume of a multi-volume work is that each book becomes a monograph, with its own rhetorically crafted *prooimion*, rather than a purely pragmatic division of a seamless historical narrative. But this is not the kind of preface we have in Acts: as we have seen, it is precisely the unrhetorical, recapitulatory prefaces of Diodorus' earlier books that Acts recalls. By alluding to the "former treatise," in fact, Acts 1.1 actively resists categorization as a monograph (in this sense): whether or not the book was conceived as "Volume II," its opening sentence directs the reader's attention to the relationship of the narrative to a larger whole. Similarly with the examples from Archimedes, Josephus, and Galen noted above, where a recapitulation is used to link separate works: the effect of the recapitulation is to place the current work in a sequence within the author's total *œuvre*. In this sense, then, the preface to Acts would seem rather to militate against classification as a "monograph."

However, the concept of the historical monograph may have a wider relevance to Acts if it is conceived not in the "Ephoran" sense but simply as a historical work of limited scope and/or scale.[57] Even as a two-volume work, Luke–Acts is much shorter than the major works of classical and Hellenistic historiography, and this disparity in scale is a serious obstacle to the identification of Luke–Acts as "history."[58] Hence a number of scholars have realized the importance of investigat-

---

[56] See the prooemium to Book 13 (Künz, pp. 87–88), where Diodorus professes to have no time for a real historical *prooimion*: "If we were composing a history after the manner of the other historians, we should, I suppose, discourse upon certain topics at appropriate length in the introduction (ἐν τῷ προοιμίῳ) and by this means turn our discussion to the events which follow; surely, if we were picking out a brief period of history for our treatise [or: *taking a little time out of our text*], we should have the time to enjoy the fruit such introductions yield" (13.1.1, trans C. H. Oldfather, Loeb Classical Library). What he does have time for (τοῦτο μόνον προειπόντας) (13.1.2) is a recapitulatory sentence summarizing the contents of the previous six books and of the present one (13.1.2–3): which seems to confirm that in Diodorus' eye the recapitulation does not constitute a *prooimion* proper.

[57] Palmer, "Monograph," pp. 4–14; Plümacher, "Monografie," pp. 464f.

[58] See Burridge, *Gospels*, pp. 117–119 on the generic significance of "Size and Length."

ing the evidence for smaller-scale works dealing with a limited chronological period. Most of the evidence for these works is fragmentary, but the studies of Plümacher and Palmer (n. 54 above) focus on Sallust and Cicero as providing good examples of the kind of monograph which was being written (or in Cicero's case talked about) in Rome in the first century BCE. Despite the difficulty of defining a genre for which there is no single ancient term,[59] Palmer concludes (pp. 26–27) that Sallust's works "conform to the theoretical requirements for a short monograph" (namely a single-volume work covering a limited historical period, with the focus on one theme and one person; its literary components include a prologue, narrative, speeches, despatches, and letters). Acts too is a single volume of moderate length, with a limited historical and geographical scope; it focuses on "one leading figure at a time," and contains a prologue, narrative, speeches and letters (Palmer, pp. 28–29).

There are a number of important issues here which are beyond the compass of this chapter: here we can concern ourselves only with the preface. The "prologue" for Palmer is an important formal link between Acts and Sallust (of the Hellenistic Jewish texts which he classes as "monographs," only 2 Maccabees has a comparable prologue: Palmer, p. 27). But the prefaces which Palmer uses elsewhere for comparison with the formal features of the Acts preface are not from monographs but from multi-volume works (Palmer, pp. 22–24) – inevitably, given the foregrounding of the recapitulation in Acts 1.1. Sallust's prefaces have none of the formal features we have identified in the preface to Acts except the use of the authorial first person, which is, of course, far too widespread to act as a genre-indicator on its own. Both books lead into their subject indirectly with a general discussion of historiographical methodology (*Jug.*) or of human ethics (*Cat.*) in a manner strongly reminiscent of the "Ephoran" prefaces used by Diodorus – a fact noted by Quintilian, who ascribes it to the influence of epideictic oratory.[60] Whatever the rights and

[59] Palmer, "Monograph," pp. 4–8.
[60] Quintilian 3.8.9, "quos secutus [Isocrates and Gorgias] videlicet C. Sallustius in bello Iugurthino et Catilinae nihil ad historiam pertinentibus principiis ortus est." See also Laqueur, "*Ephoros I*," p. 202.

wrongs of this attribution,[61] we shall have to look further afield than Sallust to find parallels to the formal features of the Acts preface.

Arrian's *Anabasis of Alexander*, which has been described as "the only perfect surviving example of a Greek historical monograph,"[62] has no dedication and no recapitulations: Arrian favors a direct, workmanlike style, and displays a strong interest in the authenticity of his sources (*Anab.* 1, pref.), but apart from the use of the first person this preface has no formal parallels either with Sallust or with Acts 1.1 (or for that matter with Lk. 1.1–4).[63] A thorough search of the fragmentary remains might throw up some useful parallels (though, as I have observed elsewhere, it is precisely these relatively trivial *formalia* that tend to disappear in the process of epitomizing). But the problem seems to be that historical monographs still belong to the genre of history, and their prefaces display all the variety found in the larger genre: it does not seem possible to isolate a preface-style specifically associated with monographs, and the formal features found in the prefaces of Luke and Acts are no more at home here than they are in Greek historical writing generally.

V THE PREFACE TO ACTS AND "APOLOGETIC HISTORIOGRAPHY"

The subgenre of the historical monograph, then, does not help us to locate the preface within a particular area of Greek historiography. A second, more recent approach may prove more promising. In an important monograph,[64] Gregory

---

[61] Earl, "Prologue-form," pp. 846–849 contests Sallust's debt to epideictic and proposes instead that Sallust had been reading the newly rediscovered Aristotelian corpus: "whether directly influenced by Aristotle's works or not, he began 'Bellum Catilinae' and 'Bellum Iugurthinum' as though they were not works of history but philosophical and ethical treatises" (p. 855).

[62] Geiger, *Cornelius Nepos*, p. 47. On the preface to the *Anabasis*, see P. Stadter, *Arrian of Nicomedia* (Chapel Hill: University of North Carolina Press, 1980), pp. 60–66.

[63] There is a dedication, interestingly (or at least a dedicatory epistle), in Arrian's *Discourses of Epictetus*, and the *Periplus* is structured as a letter to Trajan (Stadter, *Arrian*, pp. 32–41); but neither of these is a historical monograph.

[64] Gregory E. Sterling, *Historiography and Self-definition: Josephos, Luke–Acts and Apologetic Historiography*, Supplements to Novum Testamentum LXIV (Leiden: Brill, 1992).

Sterling has posited a subgenre which he calls "apologetic historiography" as the best location for Luke's work within the Greek historiographical tradition. Prime examples of the genre are Manetho and Berossus, along with the lost Hellenistic Jewish historians and Josephus. Whether this group of writings is sufficiently well defined to merit identification as a genre – and whether "apologetic historiography" is the right name for it – are questions beyond the scope of this chapter.[65] What is significant for our purposes is that all the texts cited by Sterling would fall on the antiquarian-ethnographic side of Greek historiography, i.e. the side where we are most likely to find recapitulations marking the beginnings of books; and that this is also the area of historiography where dedication is best attested, especially among non-Greek writers (see above).

It would be too much to say that the preface of Acts offers positive support of Sterling's thesis: the formal features we have isolated are not sufficient of themselves to identify the genre of Acts as "apologetic historiography." Rather, Sterling's thesis, by focusing on this particular area of Greek historiography, evades the negative problems which we have identified in the preface.[66] If Acts belongs anywhere within the genre of historiography, this (broadly speaking) is the type of historiography which the conventions used in the preface would lead the informed reader to expect.

VI CONCLUSIONS

It seems clear, then, that in simple terms the answer to our initial question is "No": the preface to Acts, taken on its own, does not set up expectations for the informed reader that the text which follows belongs to the genre "Hellenistic Historiography." It should be stressed that this preliminary conclusion

[65] Palmer, "Monograph" pp. 16f. raises the question "whether the apologetic purpose is constitutive of this genre and limited to it."

[66] Sterling accepts the standard view that the prefaces of Luke and Acts (which he treats as a unified work, *Apologetic Historiography*, pp. 331–339) reflect "the primary and secondary prefaces so common in Hellenistic historiography" (p. 339; see also pp. 323–324, 330–346, 348, 367, 369), but does not give much attention to the *formalia* (especially dedication) which in my view act as counter-indicators.

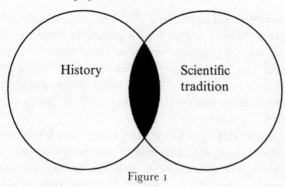

Figure 1

concerns *only* the preface: there may be other good reasons
within the body of the text which would encourage these same
informed readers to revise their expectations, but these do not
concern us in this chapter. All I have tried to do here is to
establish the point, negatively speaking, that the opening conventions used in the Book of Acts are not sufficient to establish
the genre of the work as "history" within the frame of reference
defined by Greek literary convention, whether because they
are not sufficiently genre-specific or because they reflect
literary customs not normally associated with historiography.
Further than "normally" it would be unwise to go: I have not
been concerned here to discuss what is possible for the author,
merely what the literary custom of the first century would lead
the reader to expect.

This conclusion has both negative and positive implications
for the genre of Acts. Negatively, it must be admitted that the
formal features of the Acts preface, though they can be paralleled in Greek historiography, are not in any sense typical of
that literature. On the positive side, these conventions
(especially dedication and recapitulation) are more characteristic of other types of literature: where they occur in historiography, they cluster on the margins of the genre, where it is
furthest from epic or rhetorical pretension and closest to the
scholarly, scientific side of the Ionian *historia*-tradition: in fact,
where historiography intersects with the broader, non-rhetorical tradition of philosophical and technical prose which I have
called "scientific literature" (see n. 47 above).

This may be represented in the form of a simple diagram (see Figure 1). If we are to find a plausible location for Acts within the Greek historiographical tradition it should be where these circles intersect, i.e. on the more scholarly, less rhetorical side of history (archaeology, ethnography), and perhaps especially where the author and/or subject is non-Greek.[67]

One of the advantages of locating Luke's work in this area is that it allows us to place the text in a broader literary framework which is at least consistent with the indications of subject matter provided by the preface. It has long been recognized that the strongly "biblical" language and subject matter of Acts place the book closer overall to biblical historiography than to the Greek tradition.[68] This suggests a possible literary matrix for the text among the lively and creative literary activities of the Greek-speaking Diaspora, which produced a significant number of biographical and historical monographs to set alongside the towering figure of Josephus.[69] None of the prefaces extant within this literature is close enough to that of Acts to suggest an immediate model, but there is sufficiently varied use of prefaces among Hellenistic Jewish writers to provide a literary context for Luke's. A more detailed study of the conventions used in these prefaces might well provide useful insight into the multifarious ways in which Jewish

---

[67] For the purposes of this chapter I have excluded from consideration (what a more extensive study would have to include) other prose narrative genres which overlap with history (and even with ethnography), such as travel writing and the novel. See on this whole area E. Gabba, "True History and False History in Classical Antiquity," *JRS* 71 (1981), 50–62.

[68] See on this E. Plümacher, *Lukas als hellenistischer Schriftsteller* (Göttingen: Vandenhoeck & Ruprecht, 1972); more recently Sterling, *Apologetic Historiography*, pp. 353–363; B. S. Rosner, "Acts and Biblical History," pp. 65–82 of *The Book of Acts*, ed. Winter and Clarke.

[69] The popularity of this subgenre among Hellenistic Jewish writers is clear from the surveys of Hengel (*Earliest Christianity*, p. 37), Geiger (*Cornelius Nepos*, p. 50, n. 49), and Palmer ("Monograph," pp. 18–21). Palmer notes that in fact the *only* single-volume historical monographs to survive before Acts, apart from Sallust's, are Jewish. Note also that these texts, like Acts, tend to fall at the overlap between history and biography (Geiger *Carnelius Nepos*, pp. 50f.; Palmer, "Monograph," pp. 27f.) in a manner which conforms more with a long-established pattern of biblical historiography than with Greek: see on this Momigliano, *Development*, pp. 34–36.

writers of Greek texts plug themselves into the dominant culture.[70]

And what, finally, of the Gospel preface? In this chapter I have deliberately focused on the preface to Acts alone: but it is pertinent in conclusion to bring the Gospel preface back into the picture. Nothing in this study of the preface to Acts has caused me to revise my view of the literary affinities of the Gospel preface. Both in different ways display a strictly limited range of literary conventions, and an equally limited interest in their development and use. In both cases, the literary etiquette displayed by Luke is fully at home in the broad tradition of technical prose, and much less so among the historians, who have a well-recognized repertoire of preface-topics which Luke does not use (and which I have not even touched on in this chapter).[71] There is no need, therefore, to argue for a different genre for the two works on the grounds of their prefaces (there may be other grounds, but they do not concern us here). Whether Luke and Acts are treated as separate works or as a two-volume set, their prefaces belong to the same literary code: and attentiveness to the nuances of this code, I would argue, can actually help us to resolve some long-standing questions about the genre of the two works.

[70] Alexander, *Preface*, chap. 7. It should be stressed that "Hellenistic Jewish literature" is not a genre so much as a literary matrix. Its writers intersect with the dominant Greco-Roman culture as individuals, not as a group, and there are many literary distinctions to be drawn between them. See esp. Sterling, *Apologetic Historiography*, chap. 5; Attridge, "Historiography," chap. 4 of *Jewish Writings of the Second Temple Period*, ed. Stone.

[71] Alexander, *Preface*, chap. 3.

CHAPTER 5

The future of the past: Luke's vision of salvation history and its bearing on his writing of history

Jacob Jervell

I

Luke does not know the term "salvation history." He does not employ the word ἱστορία. But he knows about one particular history, and this history has salvation as its theme.[1] This is the history of Israel. The church, its message and life, is in itself the final part of this history. This is because Luke writes the history of the people of God. Israel is the only nation Luke names "people," λαός.[2] Luke, of course, is aware of the fact that other people have a history, but he does not deal with their history; rather, he only gives slight hints of its existence. This is not because he has chosen to write only the history of Israel and does not want to take other people into account, or because salvation history to him was something isolated within or outside world history.[3] There is, of course, a connection between salvation history and world history. But God has – *sit*

---

[1] Not all scholars identify Luke with the literary genre of historiography: L. Alexander, *The Preface to Luke's Gospel: Literary Convention and Social Context in Luke 1:1–4 and Acts 1:1*, SNTS Mon. Ser. 78 (Cambridge, 1993); R. Pervo, *Profit with Delight: The Literary Genre of the Acts of the Apostles* (Philadelphia, 1987); C. Talbert, *What is a Gospel? The Genre of the Canonical Gospels* (Philadelphia, 1977); cf. E. Trocmé, *Le "Livre des Actes" et l'histoire* (Paris, 1957), pp. 41–50, 113.

[2] See J. Jervell, "Gottes Treue zum untreuen Volk," in *Der Treue Gottes Trauen*, FS Gerhard Schneider (Freiburg, Basle and Vienna, 1991), pp. 15ff.

[3] The widespread opinion that Luke relates the Christ-event to "persons, times, institutions, and epochs of world history" (J. A. Fitzmyer, *The Gospel According to Luke*, vol. 1 [New York, 1981], p. 172) in order to make Jesus a figure of world history and Greek-Roman culture is false. There are some scattered references to world history (Luke 2.1–3; 3.1–2; Acts 11.28; 18.2,12; 25.11; 27.1; see also chapters on the Roman lawsuit against Paul, Acts 21–28). The idea, however, is not to make Jesus and the church a part of world history, but to show the way the Gentiles in the endtimes will be incorporated into the history of the people of God.

venia verbo – neglected the history of other people.[4] Their history is not worth mentioning since it is an "empty" history, as is clearly expressed in Acts 14.16. "The Gentiles were all left alone to go their own way." As an excuse, Luke adds that God has not "left himself without witness," for example rain, fruitful seasons, food and gladness (14.17). But the history of other people is a history of idolatry and ignorance, even if God is the Creator and the universal giver of life who has fixed the epochs of history in general and the limits of the territories of the people (Acts 17.25f., 30). When God once is mentioned directly as Creator, it is in order to demonstrate his power over history (Acts 4.24ff.). And the history of other nations will soon be brought to an end. This is because in the endtimes God is going to incorporate the Gentiles into the history of the people of God, programmatically announced in the Apostolic Council (Acts 15.16–18, cf. 10.34–43). The salvation of the Gentiles, that is, the Gentile people, is a part of the promise to Israel (Lk. 24.47; Acts 2.39; 3.25f.; 13.47; 15.16ff.). And only then do other people become a part of salvation history (Acts 10.36ff.; 15.14ff.). From an eschatological point of view, Luke describes a development that comprises all of history.

There is no salvation in the history of any other people. Only in the history of Israel is salvation to be found. Even if God has been continuously active as savior in the history of Israel (Acts 7.2–52; 13.17–25) and only in that history, the ultimate and final salvation is to be found in the new and last epoch of history, that of the Messiah of Israel, Jesus. Luke has no idea about the Jesus-event and the time of Jesus as "Die Mitte der Zeit,"[5] but Jesus means the inauguration of the last and final epoch of salvation history. Luke presupposes the history of Israel, and he does so *expressis verbis* as he is the only New Testament author who twice gives us detailed representations

---

[4] Luke does not know the phrase "world history," but if anything is world history to him it is the history of the people of God, which is – *sit venia verbo* – the eschatological history.

[5] So the title of the famous book by H. Conzelmann, *Die Mitte der Zeit*, BhTh 17 (Tübingen, 1953) (translated as *The Theology of St. Luke* [New York, 1960]).

of the history of Israel (Acts 7.2–53; 13.17–25).[6] Further, his use of the Scriptures demonstrates that salvation comes from the past, namely from the history of Israel, from the promises and patterns in God's words and acts throughout that particular history.

Unlike other New Testament authors, history means more to Luke than eschatology. Everything in the church comes from the past, and eschatology confirms history. It is not sufficient for Luke simply to presuppose the history of Israel until the coming of the Messiah, but he must tell his readers about the meaning included in his presupposition. But within these pre-suppositions Luke's task is to offer the history of the people of God in the last phase of salvation history, beginning with the coming of the Messiah. For Luke, the history of Israel until Christ belongs to the past, but the rest of the history is to him contemporary history. But the contemporary history is meaningless and no history of salvation if the history of the people of God does not continue without breach in the history of the church.

Luke's idea of history is, in the strictest sense of the word, theo-logically determined. God is the only *causa*, the motor and driving force in history, the only master of history. The cue is βουλή, God's counsel, determination, decree, and will.[7] The word points not only to the will of God, but even to the fact that God himself carries out his will, and fixes the times for its execution (Acts 1.7; 13.37; 17.26; Lk. 21.24, cf. 1.10). God's counsel is irresistible (Acts 4.28; 5.38). Humans are forced to bring about all the things God has foreordained, for example the death of Jesus (Acts 2.23; 3.24f.; 4.28). Luke knows that even humans act in history, but the difference between divine and human acts is announced in the famous words of Gamaliel: "If this counsel of theirs and its execution is of men, it will collapse; but if it is from God, you cannot overthrow it" (Acts 5.38). The will and work of humans have no durability in the course of history, unless they are according to God's will (cf.

---

6 Hebrews 11 is different in that it is a collection of parenetic examples.
7 We find ten of the thirteen occurrences in the New Testament in Luke–Acts.

Acts 3.18; 4.28; 13.27). And not even idolatry and ignorance are possible without God's permission, or as a result of his punishment (Acts 7.42; 14.15f.; 17.30). Another way of pronouncing God as the active and creative force in history is Luke's favorite expression, "from of old" or "long ago" (3.21; 15.7,18,21; cf. Lk. 1.70; Acts 3.24). The origin of everything that happens in the church lies in the past, and salvation means the future of the past. The development of history is predetermined from its very beginning by the will of God.

God acts in history above all through his promises to his people,[8] all the promises being given solely to his chosen people (Acts 2.36,39; 3.24f.; 5.29f.; 13.32f.; 15.15ff.). There are no promises in the history of the Gentiles, and therefore their history has no future. And the promises to the chosen people make their history exclusively salvation history. God not only gives promises, but also fulfills them (Acts 3.18; 13.32f.). The very beginning of the history of Israel started with God's promise to his people (7.1–8). And the history even before Christ shows how God gave and fulfilled his promises. The summaries in Acts 7 and 13 present a history of God's promises and the fulfillment of them by God himself (7.5–8,10,16,17ff., 33f.,35–38; 13.17–25). The time of the church is the time of fulfillments of past promises, but even in the fulfilling of promises new promises are given. Thus, the outpouring of the Spirit is a fulfilled promise, but at the same time the fulfilling points to the consummation with the apocalyptic signs (Acts 1.4; 2.1ff.,17ff.,33). The time after the coming of the Messiah is even a time with fulfillment and promises, partly but not yet completely fulfilled (Lk. 9.31,41; 22.16; 24.26–49; Acts 1.4–11; 3.24, etc).

What has happened and what is going to happen in the church comes from history. If you want to know what is happening today and what is going to happen, you have to look to history.[9] The future is there in the past as promises and

---

[8] God is never seen as God of the nations and the peoples, the world, but only as the God of Israel (Acts 3.23; 5.30; 7.32; 13.17; 22.14; Lk. 1.68; 20.37; etc.).

[9] This is so even in Greek historiography, e.g. in the anthropological orientation of Thucydides, but from another point of view than Luke's.

as patterns in the Scriptures. Every element in the salvation story you find as promise. The coming and appearance of the predecessor of the Messiah, the Baptist, is foretold by the prophets (Lk. 3.4ff.; 7.26ff.). So is the promise of the coming and the appearance of the Messiah, his preaching and acts (Lk. 4.18ff.; Acts 3.22; 7.37). Above all is the very center of the message – Christ's passion and death – in all details given as prophecy (Lk. 18.31ff., 24.25ff.,46ff.; Acts 3.18,24; 4.25ff.; 7.52; 8.32–35; 17.3; 26.22). And what is given as prophecy must be fulfilled because God himself will carry the prophecies through to their fulfillment (Acts 13.32f.). Consider also the resurrection and exaltation long ago referred to as prophecy and promise (Lk. 18.31,33; 24.26,46; Acts 2.25ff.; 3.13ff.,24; 13.33ff.; 17.3; 26.22–23). History even proves that not David but Jesus was raised from the dead and exalted at God's right hand (Acts 2.25–36; 13.33ff.). David died and was buried and his tomb is still there, but he served God only in his own generation. Jesus was raised as the Son of David and King of Israel (Acts 2.30ff.; 13.33ff.). Here is the connection David–Jesus seen both as promise and as pattern. The Scriptures not only have promises of a Messiah but even identify Jesus as that promised Messiah (Acts 17.3; 18.28).

History as such legitimizes through promises and patterns the Christian message. Everything essential is given through history, and nothing essential changes. This is so not only in the Christ-event, in Christ's coming, life, death, and resurrection, but even other parts of the Gospel, the history of the church, the parousia and the kingdom of God, are legitimized through history, that is, the history of Israel given in the Scriptures. The stories of Judas and his death – he was one of the Twelve and he guided those who arrested Jesus (Acts 1.16f.,20) – and the election of a new apostle (Acts 1.20ff.) are reported. We find in Scripture the acts of Pilate, the Romans, and Herod at the death of Jesus (Acts 4.25ff.). Even the forgiveness of sins for the believers in Jesus is legitimized through history (Acts 10.43; Lk. 24.47). The outpouring of the Spirit is given as promise (Acts 1.4; 2.16ff.; Lk. 24.49), and even the prophecies in the church and the miracles are historically legitimized (Acts

2.17ff.). The mission among Jews and Gentiles, starting in Jerusalem, and the missionaries of the church are acceptable only when foreordained by God historically (Lk. 24.26,44; Acts 13.41,47; 15.15ff.; 26.22f.). When parts of Israel will not accept the Gospel, that means that only a part of the people will live in the church. This is no surprise since it is given in the Scriptures (Acts 3.23; 13.41; 26.22; 28.6ff.).

Everything from the past, from history, has been realized except for the very last thing, the parousia. The end of time is still future, but it will come because it is a part of history, that is, Scripture. The church knows only from Scripture that it lives in the endtimes (Acts 2.17; 15.15ff.). The facts do not speak for themselves, but can only be understood from Scripture (Acts 2.15; 15.15). The church has seen the dawn of the kingdom of God. The promises to the fathers God has fulfilled in the church (Acts 13.32f.). The very last time of retribution is still future, but given in detail in Scripture (Lk. 21.22ff.; Acts 3.21). The days of Noah are a pattern for the days of the Son of Man (Lk. 17.22ff.). History even gives the assurance to men about the day of the ultimate judgment: in this case the basis of history is the resurrection of Jesus (Acts 17.31). The outpouring of the Spirit as the prologue to the end of time, points to the apocalyptic events (Acts 2.17–21). And so the promises have two functions: they determine the future before they are fulfilled, and when they are fulfilled, they guarantee the rest of the future, the consummation.

The place of Scripture in Luke's theology is clear. He wants to say that Scripture contains everything – πᾶς is a favorite word for Luke – about the message and life of the church. Scripture is the source for the past history of Israel, for the contemporary history of Israel, namely the church, and even for what is going to happen in the future. Further, it is the key to understanding history. Scripture belongs to the past and Luke is well aware of the fact that Scripture is a historical document. What has happened and is going to happen in the future is all foretold and so determined by God in Scripture. The Scriptures not only are a mirror of history, but also create history. Therefore everything in this past has a future. But

Scripture as a historical document is nonetheless the Word of
God to Luke, and therefore normative both for those who
heard the Word in biblical times and for those who came later.
As the Word of God it transcends time. Therefore nothing is
only history, something of the past, but exists now. And so it is
not appropriate and sufficient to refer to Luke's attitude to
history that we can learn from history or that history might
give us self-knowledge. This particular history does or does not
legitimize what happens. There is no future apart from this
legitimization from Scripture, and the future is known to those
who know history, that is, Scripture. What God has not foreordained long ago will collapse. The historian Luke does
nothing but interpret the Scriptures. This is why his subject is
only the history of salvation.

II

Is Luke a historian? Doubts have been raised on this point, but
they are not justified. Only his intention can give the answer,
and it is out of the way to mix this with the question of whether
or not he was a competent and reliable historian. The way he
acted as historian and wrote history, or the assumption that
contemporary historians could not have considered Luke a
colleague,[10] tell us nothing about Luke's purpose. He wanted
to write history of a special sort, salvation history. He did not
intend to write ecclesiastical history[11] or the history of a religious movement,[12] an oriental sect. As he has salvation history
as his subject, he writes the final chapter in the history of the
people of God, Israel, from Jesus to Paul in Rome. His intention is clear from the very outset (Lk. 1.1–4);[13] he is presenting

---

[10] Pervo, *Profit with Delight*: "Acts violates nearly every single canon advanced by
   Lucian" (p. 7).
[11] The father of ecclesiastical history is Eusebius.
[12] That, according to C. W. van Unnik, "Luke's Second Book and the Rules of
   Hellenistic Historiography," in J. Kremer (ed.), *Les Actes des Apôtres*, BETL XLVIII
   (Gembloux, 1979), "was something unheard of in Antiquity" (p. 39).
[13] I do not regard Luke's Gospel and Acts as once a single book only divided when it
   was accepted into the canon. They represent different genres, each of the two parts

a διήγησις[14] on the basis of his going over the whole course of events from the beginning. Usually we refer to three features when characterizing Acts as a historical book: the preface, the many speeches by principal characters, and the style of the dramatic episodes.[15] These formal features are not adequate to decide upon the genre, however, even if style and form are more than accidents for historiography.[16] In contrast to other historians, Luke has not revealed his name even in the preface.[17] He does not even take the word ἱστορία into his mouth. And throughout the narrative, Luke does not give us information about his own person, or reflections on his work, again unlike other historians. We have to add to the formal criteria others concerning content. The idea in Lk. 1.1–4 is clear. So too are the two summaries, Acts 7.2–52 and 13.17–26,[18] where we find the history of Israel up to and including Jesus, who is himself a part of that history. Luke is aware of the different epochs in the history of Israel including the church (16.16), even if interpreters do not reckon with the same epochs or number of epochs. He reckons with the time of Israel before Christ, the time of the church and the time of consummation. He shows a sustained narrative of events, including references to secular history, and he adopts cause and effect in his

corresponds approximately to the largest size of a standard scroll, and they differ to some extent in the way they deal with some topics. Still the preface to the Gospel bears upon Luke's intention in Acts, as Acts 1.1 refers to Lk. 1.1–4.

[14] The same word is used in Acts 1.1; a technical term even in historiography. Cf. Aristeas 8.322, 2 Macc. 2.32; 6.17; Diodorus Siculus 11. 20.1; Lucian, *De Arte Conscribendae Historiae* 55; Polybius 3.4.1; Dionysius of Halicarnassus, *Ant. Rom.* 1.7.4, *Epistula ad Pompeium* 3; cf. Unnik, "Rules," p. 40; J. Thornton, *Der Zeuge des Zeugen* (Tübingen, 1991), pp. 119f.

[15] On the last, see E. Plümacher, *Lukas als hellenistischer Schriftsteller*, SUNT 9 (Göttingen, 1972), pp. 80–136.

[16] Prefaces and speeches as such are not reserved for the genre historiography.

[17] We cannot rule out the possibility that the name (and title of the book) was there from the beginning; so Thornton, *Der Zeuge des Zeugen*, pp. 143–148.

[18] Such summaries are well known from the Old Testament and contemporary Jewish literature. See the list in A. Weiser, *Die Apostelgeschichte*, vol. 1, OTK 5/1 (Gütersloh, 1981), p. 180. See also Eupolemos, *Euseb. Praep. Ev.* 9.30.1–8. Such summaries occasionally serve as prehistory in the Old Testament, but Luke's summaries differ from the Jewish ones in that they serve parenetic purposes on the whole, whereas for Luke history as such is constitutive – he places Jesus and the church in a historical context.

presentation of history.[19] He even knows that the Word of God, *in casu* the message of the church, is not a timeless but a historical phenomenon, and he can watch the development, the "growth of the Word" (6.7; 12.24; 19.20).

When Luke, in spite of his aspirations as historian, at the same time seems to meet[20] and not to meet[21] the standards of contemporary historiography, this has to do with the special bearing the idea of salvation history has on his writing of history.[22] This is clear from Luke's very choice of subject, which, according to the rules of historiography, should be an essential one, "of a lofty character which will be truly profitable to the reader."[23] Does this apply to Acts? It was unheard of in antiquity to write the history of a religious movement, since history was political history, dealing with significant events.[24] A historian must have at least one qualification: political understanding.[25] A newly formed sect was no suitable subject for a historian. To readers in antiquity, the insignificant happenings told in Acts were not world-historical events, and they would not have understood Luke saying that Jesus was "Lord of all" (Acts 10.36, 42), that is, that the message concerned everyone (Acts 1.8; 13.46,48). But the concept of salvation history turns contemporary historiography upside down; the subject is of the greatest importance, an event of world history, only from this point of view. Salvation history makes it clear that Israel and, being dependent upon Israel, all nations are in the game, something which will be evident in the consummation. And so, as the history of Israel, it even includes political history, but this only as a small part of history, on "the outskirts" of history. It would have been confusing to contemporary readers to find such a subject dealt with by the use of the literary and technical tools of historiography.

[19] See Jervell, "Gottes Ratschluss," *Zum Thema Gott und Geschichte in den Lukasschriften*, in *Gott und Geschichte*, Wiss. Beitr. der Ernst-Moritz-Arndt-Universität (Greifswald, 1988), pp. 47f. For other criteria, see Unnik, "Rules," *passim*.

[20] Pointed out by Unnik, "Rules," *passim*.   [21] Pervo, *Profit with Delight*, pp. 3–8.

[22] Luke is not the inventor of the phenomenon "salvation history," as we find prefigurations and fragments of it in the Pauline letters and in the other gospels.

[23] Dionysius of Halicarnassus, *Ant. Rom.* 1. 1,3; *Epistula ad Pompeium*; cf. Lucian, *De Arte Conscribendae Historiae* 53.

[24] Unnik, "Rules," p. 39.   [25] Lucian, *De Arte Conscribendae Historiae* 34.

Luke's purpose in writing history is clear: history gives his readers the certainty of the matters of which they have been taught, the Gospel (1.4). It is far removed from Herodotus describing the achievements of the past solely in order to prevent them from sinking into oblivion. Luke knows that his readers are well informed and instructed about "the events that have happened among us" (Lk. 1.2; Acts 2.22; 10.37f., etc.). Even if Luke formally and technically works as a tragic-pathetic historian,[26] purpose and content show that he is more of a pragmatic historian[27] in the sense that he writes history to solve problems in his own church(es). Pragmatic historians[28] analyze the mechanisms of political processes in order to understand apparently familiar phenomena better, this in order to give instruction and understanding to politicians. In spite of the relationship Luke has to contemporary Greek historiography, procured by Jewish historiography, his purpose and content aim at something different because he deals in salvation history. History serves as *anamnesis*, recalling what has happened and what happens as binding and normative for the life of his own church.

In the question about the motive forces in the political process, ancient historians were expected to explain the causes and effects of significant events. Their primary task was to offer a plausible description on the basis of reasonable criteria;[29] they sought objective reasons for what had happened. They had to show the coherence in the events. They could even refer to supernatural phenomena, especially portents, but had to qualify their reports by appending "it was told."[30] The super-

---

[26] The role of emotions, sympathy, and experience is as important in understanding history as information gained from facts alone, for tragic-pathetic historians. See H. Strassburger, *Die Wesensbestimmung der Geschichte durch die antike Geschichtsschreibung*, 3rd. ed. (Wiesbaden, 1975), p. 78.

[27] On tragic and pragmatic historiography, see B. Gentili and G. Cerri, *History and Biography in Ancient Thought* (Amsterdam, 1988), pp. 7–33; F. W. Walbank, "History and Tragedy," *Historia* 9 (1960), 233.

[28] Thucydides, Polybius.

[29] H. Hohmeyer, *Lukian: Wie man Geschichte schreiben soll* (Munich, 1965), pp. 218f.

[30] See Dionysius of Halicarnassus 1.48.14; 2.20.3; 2.74.5; Pliny, *Hist. Nat.* 9.18. The criticism of miracles in Josephus (*Ant* 3.25.32; 4.459–464; 8.349; 9.28; 10.261f.) is a concession to Greek historiography. See O. Betz, "Das Problem des Wunders bei

natural and wondrous phenomena had their place mostly in a poetic genre. Historians could touch upon the question of religion and even make long digressions on the subject,[31] but only within the general framework.[32] Even if Herodotus was led by his trust in the divine order of the world, and his etiology has ethico-religious leanings, he gave preeminence to causality.

To Thucydides the historical process is a current of occurrences determined by unchangeable, that is, anthropological, laws.[33] The historian could trace the activity of the capricious goddess Tyche,[34] or the law of chance. Not much scope if any was left for a direct intervening God. This is, of course, different from the Old Testament type of historical writing furthered in Jewish historiography, with the belief in God's intervention, punishment, and help.[35] History instructs in the character and acts of God and appeals for allegiance to him; it is "a form of confessional proclamation."[36]

Luke also explains the causes and effects of the events: the death of Jesus by the hands of Jews and Romans (Acts 2.22,36; 3.13ff.; 4.24ff.; 5.28; 10.39; 13.27ff.) and the progress of the mission of the Church from Jerusalem via Asia Minor, Macedonia, and Achaia to Rome (Acts 1–20, 28). He explains the controversies between the church and the Jewish leaders, and the Roman lawsuit against Paul (Acts 21–28). But because Luke offers salvation history, the main cause in this process is God. And not God seen as divine providence or *deus otiosus*, but

---

Flavius Josephus im Vergleich zum Wunderproblem bei den Rabbinen und im Johannesevangelium," in *Josephus-Studien*, FS O. Michel (Göttingen, 1974), pp. 26f.; G. Delling, "Josephus und das Wunderbare," *NovT* 2 (1958), 281–308.

[31] Above all in Herodotus' second book.

[32] Most interesting is the difference between Luke and Josephus. The latter is more of a historian than Luke as he does not in his historical work give a description of Jewish religion, but only presupposes it as an essential part of "our entire ancient history and political constitution" (*Ant.* 1.5–6).

[33] Such as φιλοτιμία πλεονεζία δεός; see Thucydides 1.22.4.

[34] LAW 1069f.; Thornton, *Der Zeuge des Zeugen*, pp. 157.

[35] Jewish historiography: B. Gärtner, *The Areopagus Speech and Natural Revelation*, ASNU 21 (Uppsala, 1955), pp. 18–26; M. Hengel, *Judentum und Hellenismus*, WUNT 10 (Tübingen, 1969), pp. 161–186; M. E. Stone (ed.), *Jewish Writings of the Second Temple Period*, Compendia Rerum Judaicarum ad Novum Testamentum II (Philadelphia, 1984), pp. 157–184.

[36] R. Maddox, *The Purpose of Luke–Acts*, FRLANT 126 (Göttingen, 1982), p. 16.

as the continuously acting God in all the processes of this history. The real cause of the death of Jesus is God's will (Acts 4.27).[37] In order to show the divine action in history, Luke's report is full of supernatural phenomena in all phases of this history: miracles, healings, wondrous liberations, supernatural punishments, portents, visions, auditions, dreams. Every step taken in the church is in this way guided by God, the God of salvation. This exceeds by far the limits set for historians in antiquity.

In the rules for historiography[38] one of the requirements was that writing history should be "truly profitable to the reader."[39] This even bears upon the idea of the meaning of history. History was called "philosophy derived from examples,"[40] or *magistra vitae*.[41] The advantage of history was the power to influence contemporaries in politics and morals. The readers should gain political and military experience, and be educated for political life.[42] Further, history educates a person's character, and teaches one how to discern between good and evil, etc.[43] In this context we have the idea that the task of the historian is to write contemporary history (at least since Thucydides). Writing history meant literally the history where the historian took an active part in the events, so that history writing *par excellence* meant dealing with contemporary history.[44] Even if Luke does not say *expressis verbis* that he is writing history and history as such is of benefit to his readers, it goes without saying and is implied already in the definition of his aim in the preface to the Gospel (1.4). But Luke's history is useful in a completely different manner from what the historians in antiquity ever considered. "Profitable" is not the word; we should say

---

[37] For further evidence, see pp. 106–108.

[38] There existed a long and rich historiographical tradition, so our dealing with rules refers to what was generally accepted; see Hohmeyer, *Lukian*; G. Avenarius, *Lukians Schrift zur Geschichtsschreibung* (Meisenheim-am-Glan, 1956).

[39] Dionysius of Halicarnassus, *Ant. Rom.* 1. 1.3; cf. Josephus, *Ant.* 1.3; other material in Avenarius, *Lukians Schrift*.

[40] Pseudo-Dionysius, *Ars Rhetorica* 11.2.   [41] Cicero, *De Oratore* 2.9.36.

[42] Polybius 1.1.1.

[43] See Josephus, *Ant.* 1.1–3.

[44] Dionysius of Halicarnassus, *De Thucydide*, 6, ed. H. Usener and L. Rademacher, BSRGT v (Stuttgart, 1965); Gellius, *Noctes Atticae* 5.18.1.

"fateful." Luke's aim as historian has nothing to do with political or even moral benefits as defined by the historians. The reason is again salvation history, and so the benefit of history for Luke is of a strictly religious character. Probably the Greek and Roman historians would not have found that Luke actually met the standards of historiography. Luke writes contemporary history, but he does not confine himself to that. He not only employs the history of Israel as the presupposition of contemporary history,[45] that is, since Jesus, but also gives summaries of that history and refers to it as having a contemporary and highly significant meaning. This again is because his history is salvation history. Therefore, it is history and at the same time far more than ordinary history. This is because Luke intends to write about how God has fulfilled and is fulfilling his promises. Thus he offers holy history, the continuation of the history presented in the Scriptures. As such, Luke obviously has the idea that he is contributing to the Scriptures. Something like that is unheard of in historiography, not only in Greco-Roman but even in Jewish history (as we can see from 2 Macc. 2.24–32; 3 Macc. 1.1ff.; Josephus, *Ant* 1.1–8; *Bell.* 1.1–12).[46]

There were two initial steps to be taken in the historian's work: to collect the material and to give it the shape of ὑπομνήματα, an *aide-mémoire*, before it was written down in a proper form, which in turn demanded some power of expression. In dealing with contemporary history, the first source for the historian was himself. This is the *autopsia*, the author as an eyewitness of the events described,[47] and not only an eyewitness, but one capable of understanding and interpreting what had been seen.[48] It was therefore necessary to have political and military experience and be a well-traveled person. The next source was information collected from trustworthy people who had been present at the events to be reported.[49] The third

---

[45] As Polybius does in his first two books, Polube, *Histoires I-II* (Paris, 1969ff.).
[46] *Bellum Judaicum*, but he wrote *Bellum Judaicum* first.
[47] Polube, *Histoires* 12.27.6; 3.4.13.   [48] Thornton, *Der Zeuge des Zeugen*, pp. 161ff.
[49] Polube, *Histoires* 12.4–6.

was the study of written sources,[50] first of all primary sources,[51] but also secondary ones, the works of other historians.

We do not know exactly how Luke collected his material. We do know that his main source was available to him beforehand, that is, the Scriptures. Even if Luke is writing contemporary history, his main source is not, as for historiography, *autopsia*. The Scriptures are a source in a special way, not only the main source with regard to material, but even Luke's means of control of any other employed source. Therefore his writing of history could be nothing but salvation history, which was given prominence in the Scriptures themselves. And he employed the Scriptures without any critical sifting of them.[52] They were a source not only for the history of Israel before Christ, but even after, as the promises given clearly showed not only that certain things were going to happen, but even how they would occur. If anything in the Jesus story or the history of the church did not tally with Scripture, it had not happened at all. No Greek or Roman historian would have acknowledged Luke as a colleague because in his case there was no question of impartiality when dealing with this source or with the events.

As this main source was a written one, it was not necessary for Luke to have this material in the form of ὑπομνήμα. The rule of ancient historiography, the *autopsia*, is followed as Luke indicates that he personally had taken part in some of the reported events. He announces himself as an eyewitness, coworker, and companion of Paul in using "we" (16.10–17; 20.5–15; 21.1–8; 27.1–28.16).[53] There is a wealth of details in these sections compared to other parts of Acts, even details with no significance for his account.[54] These details are not

---

[50] Ibid., 12.25.1,2.   [51] Letters, contracts, treaties, agreements.

[52] Luke is the fundamentalist among the New Testament authors. See J. Jervell, "Die Mitte der Schrift: Zum lukanischen Verständnis des Alten Testamentes," in *Die Mitte des Neuen Testaments*, FS E. Schweizer (Göttingen, 1983), pp. 79–86.

[53] See Thornton, *Der Zeuge des Zeugen*; J. Wehnert, *Die Wir-Passagen der Apostelgeschichte: Ein lukanisches Stilmittel aus judischer Tradition*, GTA 40 (Göttingen, 1989).

[54] Thornton, *Der Zeuge des Zeugen*, pp. 275ff.; J. Wellhausen, *Noten zur Apostelgeschichte*, NAWG, Phil.-hist. Kl, NF xv/2 (Berlin, 1914), p. 42.

explainable as part of Luke's memory since he wrote Acts 30 years after his voyages with Paul. We can safely assume that Luke took notes when events happened and used his notes years later. On this point he met the standards of historiography, at least formally.

The bulk of Luke's sources were the oral traditions stemming back to the earliest periods of the church. This is another aspect of the old rule of *autopsia*: the first pillar is the author himself; the second pillar is his information from trustworthy people who themselves had been eyewitnesses to the events described. That is exactly what Luke announces in his preface to the Gospel (1.1–2). He writes a historical report on those things "which have been fulfilled [sc. by God] among us,"[55] ἐν ἡμῖν (Luke is obviously included in this "among us"). He himself is a witness, and so are those who handed these things down, the original "eyewitnesses and servants of the Word." They are by definition trustworthy, and therefore it is not necessary for Luke to inquire into their reliability. To be an eyewitness is to be capable not only of giving assurance that the events reported actually took place, but also of testifying to their significance, namely as a part of God's salvation. Everything eyewitnesses have reported must be in accordance with the Scriptures, again with salvation history. And the whole history Luke writes down is based upon *autopsia*.

Luke had written sources, above all the Scriptures,[56] but there are other ones. Some of them Luke obviously meant as primary sources, such as letters (15.23–29; 23.26–30, cf. 9.2; 18.27; 2.25; 22.5; 25.26; 28.21). But Luke knows that many before him had undertaken to give a written account of the history he himself offers (1.1). It is customary in ancient historiography to give a critical evaluation of the other historians, the predecessors, who had dealt with the same history as the

---

[55] The πεπληροφορημένων are the various occurrences in salvation history; things do not just happen, but are being "fulfilled," sc. by God. Πράγματα is the Greek equivalent of the Semitic ῥήματα, דברים.

[56] I am not going to discuss Luke's possible written sources here, only point to the phenomena of written sources.

historian in question.[57] Luke does not place these writers on the same footing as the eyewitnesses "from the beginning" (1.2), even if he considers himself to be one of them (ἔδοξε κἀμοί, 1.3). He therefore avoids any criticism, at least *expressis verbis*. How can he criticize people from the church who have undertaken to write the same history as he himself has done? But the very fact that he himself starts afresh, after he has gone over the whole course of events from the very beginning in detail, and writes a connected narrative, "in order" (Lk. 1.3), shows that he is not satisfied with their work. They have not written down salvation history in full, only in part.

It is well known that Luke has rewritten all his sources, and it is therefore a most complicated task to discern them. And, with the exception of the Scriptures, he has molded his sources into a specific language. This is not literary Greek. Even if Luke had a good command of literary, classical Greek (for example in the preface, 1.1–4), he apparently chose not to present his work in this form. Luke is the stylist within the New Testament with a considerable vocabulary. But he includes only scattered elements of literary Greek, and they do not mark his language. The characteristic feature of his language is that it is permeated by Semitic elements that hold good not only for Luke 1–2 and Acts 1–15, but for his work as a whole. Ninety percent of his vocabulary we find in the Septuagint. The stylistic home is the synagogue. This is especially clear in the speeches, *in casu* the missionary speeches. The many speeches in Acts have always been taken as a proof of Luke's aspiration to write as a historian. Luke followed the rule of Thucydides that the historian should reproduce "what seemed the most probable and appropriate language for each occasion, while preserving as faithfully as possible the general sense of the speech actually delivered."[58] The historian wrote the speeches with his own words, giving them the most appropriate form.[59] This

[57] Josephus, *Bellum* 1.1–2; *Ant.* 1.1–4.

[58] Thucydides 1,22; Tacitus, *Annals* 15.63; see also M. Dibelius, *Aufsätze zur Apostelgeschichte*, FRLANT 60 (Göttingen, 1951), pp. 120–162; Plümacher, *Lukas als hellenistischer Schriftsteller*, pp. 32–79.

[59] Even if he knew a speech from his sources, the speech was reproduced with the historian's own formulations.

does not mean that the historians were allowed to compose the speeches freely, that is, to invent speeches. They had (1) to take the specific situation and the actual speaker into consideration, (2) to refer to speeches actually delivered, (3) to present what was actually said, and (4) to refrain from composing or inventing a speech if the speech in question had been published.[60] The many speeches Luke offers in Acts are written in his own language, as is the rest of his material. Even when he follows the rule laid down by Thucydides, he writes and composes speeches in his own way, differently from the Greek and Roman historians. We see that the missionary speeches of Peter and Paul are worded in the same way (Acts 2.14–30; 3.12–26; 4.8–12; 5.29–32; 10.34–43; 13.16–41,[61] cf. 1.16–22; 4.24–30; 6.2–4; 15.7–11, 14–21). They have not only the same language, but also the same content and way of theological thinking. They proclaim the same things in the same way, and they employ the Scriptures in the same way. We find the Semitisms in the speeches in Acts as a whole, not solely in the first part (1–15): 13.16–41; 15.7–11, 14–21; 20.18–35; 22.6–22; 26.2–23; 28.17–20; 25–28).[62] In all the other speeches in Acts, that is, those given by Christians, we find the same language.[63] In the missionary speeches we find that a sermon for a Jewish audi-

---

[60] See Tacitus, *Annals* 15.63; differently M. Dibelius, *Aufsätze zur Apostelgeschichte*, pp. 122f., 156. That the historians did not always adhere to their principles (e.g. in referring to speeches) goes without saying. Polybius is stricter about the veracity of the speeches than Thucydides. And when historiography entered the union with rhetoric, other ideals were set, that is, from the time of Isocrates. Great importance was attached to an elegant form in the expression of thoughts, but there was great variety.

[61] The exception is the Areopagus speech (Acts 17.22–31), but this is an apologetic, not a missionary, speech.

[62] Even in the Areopagus speech we have Semitisms. See F. J. Foakes-Jackson and K. Lake (eds.), *The Beginnings of Christianity: Part I: The Acts of the Apostles*, v, (London, 1933), p. 419; Plümacher, *Lukas als hellenistischer Schriftsteller*, p. 48, n. 62.

[63] It is a general opinion that the Septuagintalisms are not widespread in Acts 16–28, because the time of the apostles is the decisive and most holy element in the holy time. See Plümacher, *Lukas als hellenistischer Schriftsteller*, p. 69. Was Paul's time, not separated from the time of the apostles, less holy than theirs? And Luke did not imitate something parallel to a Homer or Herodotus, something far back in time, because the apostles were his contemporaries. And the Scriptures were not historical sources to him as we understand such sources, but the Word of God read in the service of the synagogue.

ence is not different from one to a Greek; the missionaries do speak in exactly the same way to Jews and Gentiles, *in casu* God-fearers (Acts 10.34–43; 13.16–52).

In other speeches, for example that of Tertullus (Acts 24.2–8), Luke imitates the style of the rhetor which shows his ability to apply the rules of historiography by making the style of the speech suitable for the occasion. The historians were licensed to be rhetorical and demonstrate stylistic ingenuity, but the speeches should not demonstrate one's own stylistic ingenuity.[64] Nevertheless, the speech of Tertullus is an exception. As a whole, Luke avoids rhetoric, even if there are exceptions. The reason Luke's speeches both linguistically and from a content standpoint were made in a way that antique historians would have disapproved of is again salvation history.[65] The Semitic elements, the Septuagintalisms, are to Luke the language of the Scriptures. And the apostles and missionaries always preach the same message the same way, and the church preaches exactly the same way the Apostles did. The idea is not to imitate a historical epoch of the church, the language of the apostles (this as a parallel to the Greek *mimesis*),[66] but to show that the speeches represent the Word of God as it always has been proclaimed and still will be. There is no Greek rhetoric in the missionary speeches.[67] It is not the style antique historians would have approved.[68]

---

[64] Lucian, *De Arte Conscribendae Historiae* 58; especially Dionysius of Halicarnassus, *De Thucydide* 39–49; Diodorus Siculus 20.1.1–2,22.

[65] It has nothing to do with the phenomenon of *mimesis* in Hellenistic literature. The imitative style Luke obviously knew from Jewish literature. See H. J. Cadbury, *The Making of Luke–Acts* (London, 1968), pp. 122f. Luke represents an analogy to Hellenistic *mimesis*. A. Wifstrand, *Die alte Kirche und die griechische Bildung* (Bern/Munich, 1967), p. 114, n. 3.

[66] *Pace* Plümacher, *Lukas als hellenistischer Schriftsteller*, pp. 38–78.

[67] Cf. *Beginnings of Christianity*, iv, pp. 119f.; H. J. Cadbury, "Acts and Eschatology," in *The Background of the New Testament and its Eschatology*, FS C. H. Dodd (Cambridge, 1954), p. 317; Plümacher, *Lukas als hellenistischer Schriftsteller*, pp. 44f.

[68] The assertion that Luke employs an archaic style, influenced by Hellenistic literature, in order to give, by means of an antiquated coloring, an impression of the holy time of the apostles (so Plümacher, *Lukas als hellenistischer Schriftsteller*, pp. 72–78) is due to a misunderstanding of the well-known Jewishness in Acts, which runs through the whole of Acts, and demonstrates the character of the church from the beginning until Luke's own time and church. See Jervell, "Retrospect and Prospect in Luke–Acts Interpretation," SBL Seminar Papers (Atlanta, 1991), 383–403.

Antique historians did not attach importance to completeness. On the contrary, they had to consider what should be embodied and what omitted in their work.[69] According to Lucian, "much should be omitted."[70] It is a question of the proper selection. The criteria employed were of an aesthetic character, namely what affected the mind of the reader pleasantly. Change and variety were seen as pleasant.[71] The importance of a matter was actually valued according to its effect, not its historical worth.[72] Connected with this is the demand for ἐνάργεια, vividness of the narrative. But this quality should not be stressed at the cost of truth. The criterion is once more the reader: he or she, through the reading, should become a spectator and be engaged in the occurrences told.[73] Much criticism has been raised against Luke by his interpreters because he omits or passes over in a general way all sorts of questions of historical worth, but stresses in detailed accounts certain incidents, and above all among his characters one person, Paul. This has nothing to do with scanty material or lack of information, as he obviously had at his disposal various and rich sources for the whole period with which he deals.[74]

When it comes to vividness, Acts is most impressive: lively stories, great variety, dramatic episodes.[75] Luke is seen as a brilliant and creative author and his "history of primitive Christianity [is] marked by astonishing uniformity and simplicity."[76] And so, Luke is working within the framework of ancient historiography and meets the requirements, at least to some extent, on this point.

---

[69] Dionysius of Halicarnassus, *Epistula* 3.11.

[70] Lucian, *De Arte Conscribendae Historiae* 56.

[71] Dionysius of Halicarnassus, *Epistula* 3.12; Lucian, *De Arte Conscribendae Historiae* 56, cf. Avenarius, *Lukians Schrift*, pp. 127ff.

[72] Avenarius, *Lukians Schrift*, p. 130.

[73] Lucian, *De Arte Conscribendae Historiae* 51; Dionysius of Halicarnassus, *De Lysiade* 7; see also Avenarius, *Lukians Schrift*, pp. 130–140.

[74] J. Jervell, *Luke and the People of God* (Minneapolis, 1972), pp. 19–39; Unnik, "Rules," pp. 54ff.

[75] This vividness is not reserved for antique historiography, of course, but applies as well to the antique novel. And vividness as such is not sufficient for answering the question of Acts' genre.

[76] E. Haenchen, *The Acts of the Apostles* (Oxford, 1971), p. 99.

What about the long-drawn-out description of the trial of Paul, with no progress, no sentence passed, and no outcome of the dramatic appeal to Caesar? I would maintain that antique historians in possession of the same material as Luke would have given us a totally different story, embodying and omitting other parts, if they would have found this story at all worth while to write about. This is because they did not deal with salvation history. Luke gives us the history of primitive Christianity as the history of Paul, with the other apostles, as something like a prolegomenon. He omits a series of possible discussions about the church in Jerusalem, other apostles and evangelists, other missionary areas than the Pauline ones, the organization of the churches, etc. In the lawsuit against Paul, the Romans figure only as extras, whereas the main parts are played by Paul and the Jews. But Luke does not write to inform his readers or to engage them in what is told. They already know the story, and they are engaged. His selection of material, *in casu* dealing with Paul and omitting other important persons, to us opening the doors to subjectivism, has to do with a pillar in salvation history. Luke knows that *extra Israel nulla salus est*, that Israel is the one and only people of God destined for salvation. It is so important to demonstrate the continuity in history, from the Israel of old to Jesus as the Messiah of the people, the twelve apostles, and, above all, to the only missionary to the peoples and founder of 90 percent of the churches, Paul. The Twelve within Israel are no problem, but Paul and his supposed sayings about Christ, the law, and Israel are a headache. A conflict between Paul and the Empire is of scant interest, but the controversies in this context with the Jewish leaders worldwide are essential. The indisputable vividness of Acts is not meant as aesthetic, engaging occurrences, much less as entertainment,[77] but to offer certainty about the salvific effect of the familiar occurrences told and the scenes described (Lk. 1.4).

A proper chronology was important for the method in historiography.[78] It is a fact that Luke has clear deficiencies on this

---

[77] So Pervo, *Profit with Delight*.
[78] The importance of chronology is not diminished by the fact that some antique historians could be careless and even confused on chronology.

point and lacks chronological references. His absolute chronology is problematic as well as his relative one. Again this has to do with salvation history. It is not important to him to relate what happens in the Jesus story and the church to persons and events in world history (for example the history of the Gentiles). Time is to him fulfilled time. Therefore, chronology is important in his surveys of the history of the people of God (Acts 7.1–53; 13.16–23). Chronology is important in connection with the events of the life of Jesus and his predecessors, and the church (Luke 1.5,24f.,26,59; 2.1,21,42; 3.1f.,23; 4.2; 24.21; Acts 1.3; 2.1). What is important is not when things happened, but if what actually happened has its roots in the past, was "from of old" (3.21; 15.7,18,21).

Important to antique historiography is the character of the historian, which could be revealed in his work. The great aim of the historian is the truth, and so he should be impartial and independent, trustworthy, incorruptible, unfettered by power holders, unsubservient, and plain-speaking.[79] He should therefore offer as objective a narrative as possible. This was an ideal of a historian, and various prefaces, where the historian mentions and characterizes his predecessors, show that only some met the requirements.[80] Did Luke? Only some of them, such as to be plain-speaking,[81] unsubservient, incorruptible, and unrestrained by power holders. The others, independence and impartiality, touch a sore point. This is certainly not because Luke is an eyewitness himself to part of the history he tells, but should be seen from his own premises again: his subject is salvation history. He is in no way a neutral observer, and he starts with the presupposition that the history he offers is the

---

[79] Lucian, *De Arte Conscribendae Historiae* 41; Avenarius, *Lukians Schrift*, pp. 40–46.

[80] Cf. Josephus, *Ant.* 1.1–4; *Bell* 1.1–16; *C. Ap.* 1.24ff.; Dionysius of Halicarnassus, *Epistula ad Pompeium* 4.2. It is interesting to see how Josephus regards himself as a competent historian, *in casu* of the war of the Jews against Rome, as he: (1) had taken part in the action and not collected information from hearsay; (2) in the beginning of the war had fought himself, but in the sequel was an onlooker. Josephus admits that he cannot conceal his private sentiments, but he asks the indulgence of his reader "for a compassion which falls outside a historian's province" (literally, "contrary to the law of history") (*Bell.* 1.11).

[81] παρρησία is one of the key words in Acts: 2.29; 4.13,29,31; 9.27f.; 13.46; 14.3; 18.20,26; 19.8; 26.26.

truth; and he aims at giving his readers security and assurance of the instruction of the church, that this history is the history of salvation. When he employs the Scriptures, not as historical documents, but as documents of the Word of God, there is neither independence nor impartiality.

III

Luke could not write history along the lines of his contemporaries, not even the Jewish ones.[82] Still, he wanted to write history, but of a special sort. Others in the church before him had given prefigurations and parts of salvation history. Luke wanted to give it in full. He transcends what other Christians had done, and he is to our knowledge the first in the church to employ the tools of historiography.[83] Why? Did he know the idea among contemporary historians that the one who knows the past even knows the future? Surely his intention was not to set Christianity within the realms of world history, that is, to have Christianity accepted as a part of world history. He did not conceive of Christianity as an integral part of the world. Both his idea about Israel as the only people of God with its exclusive place in history and his eschatology built upon the same idea speak against such an understanding. Neither did he want to create *Welt-Literatur*. His language with all the Semitisms opposes this idea. His readers are not from the pagan world, not highly educated people, but Christians with a Jewish background of thought. His synchronisms as well as his neglecting chronology point in another direction than a wish to have the church considered as a part of world history.

Luke was obviously an educated man, perhaps even trained in rhetoric and history. He did not write the history of a religious movement or sect, but the final part of the history of the people of God of Israel. He knew from the Scriptures that the people of God had gone through a special and unique history. Further, Scripture was no novel, no philosophical

---

[82] They did not know any messianic fulfillment, and so salvation was primarily something of the future.
[83] These tools are well known to Jewish historians, e.g. Josephus.

treatise with timeless ideas, or a codex of laws. He knew about the importance of "the beginnings" and "from of old." So he chose historiography even if he was aware that he transcended its limits by far.

PART II

Historical and theological difficulties in Acts

CHAPTER 6

Acts 6.1–8.4: division or diversity?

Craig C. Hill

> Now in these days when the disciples were increasing in
> number, the Hellenists murmured against the Hebrews
> because their widows were neglected in the daily
> distribution.   Acts 6.1 (RSV)

The predominant interpretation of Acts 6.1–8.4 holds that the
"Hellenists" and "Hebrews" were separate, ideologically
defined parties within the early Jerusalem church.[1] The
Hellenists, being universalistic in outlook and liberal in temperament, came after a short time to realize – in a way that the
narrow, conservative Hebrew believers could not – the full
implications of the Gospel of Jesus Christ. This new understanding was voiced most clearly and powerfully by the
Hellenist leader Stephen, who was put to death for his criticism
of the Jewish Law and Temple. The persecution that arose
following his martyrdom affected only his fellow Hellenists; the
Hebrews, who had no share in those views of the Hellenists that
were offensive to Judaism, were not touched. Thus the infant
church's underlying division came to full expression: henceforth, Hellenist and Hebrew factions, represented by the Christian communities of Antioch and Jerusalem and the figures of
Paul and James, would go their own ways, the liberal
Hellenists into a Christian universalism, and the conservative
Hebrews into a retrenched Jewish legalism.

---

[1] In this chapter I summarize (with kind permission of Augsburg-Fortress Press) some
of the key arguments made in the first three chapters of my book *Hebrews and
Hellenists: Reappraising Division within the Early Church* (Minneapolis, 1992). Please
refer to that work for more detailed analysis and bibliography.

This interpretation was first advanced a century and a half
ago by the great Tübingen scholar Ferdinand Christian Baur.
Unlike most other components of his historical reconstruction,
Baur's description of relationship between the Christian
Hellenists and Hebrews has seldom been challenged. Indeed,
in our century the essential elements of this reconstruction have
assumed the status of critical orthodoxy. This acceptance may
be illustrated by reference to the annotations in two popular
contemporary Bibles. In *The New Oxford Annotated Bible* we are
told that the Hellenists were "Greek-speaking Jews or Jews
who have adopted Greek customs." The Hebrews, by contrast,
"probably spoke Aramaic and were more conservative."
Furthermore, it is said that "Stephen saw more clearly than
others that Jesus' teaching *would change the customs*," and that "it
was wrong for *Solomon* to build *a house*."[2] The *NIV Study Bible*
has this to say about Acts 6.1:

> At this stage of its development, the church was entirely Jewish in its
> composition. However, there were two groups of Jews within the
> fellowship: (1) *Grecian Jews.* Hellenists – those born in lands other
> than Palestine who spoke the Greek language and were more Grecian
> in their attitudes and outlook. (2) *Hebraic Jews.* Those who spoke the
> Aramaic and/or Hebrew language(s) of Palestine and preserved
> Jewish culture and customs.[3]

In contemporary New Testament introductions, theologies,
and histories, in studies of Paul, and in Acts commentaries
alike, we find the same basic idea repeated: the earliest church
was divided into two groups, Hellenists and Hebrews, who, as
such, thought differently theologically.[4] Doubts concerning
this view arise in response to recent insights into the complex
relationship between Hellenism and Judaism in the ancient
world. Scholars now realize that first-century Judaism was
more Hellenized than had previously been supposed. The
picture that emerges is of a pluralistic and eclectic religion – a

---

[2] *The New Oxford Annotated Bible with the Apocrypha. New Revised Standard Version* (New
York, 1991), pp. 168, 169, 171.
[3] *The NIV Study Bible: New International Version with Study Notes and References, Concordan-
ces and Maps*, ed. K. Barker (Grand Rapids, 1987), p. 1620.
[4] Numerous additional examples are included in *Hebrews and Hellenists*, pp. 9–15.

signally different phenomenon from that reflected in earlier schematisms of Diaspora and Palestinian "Judaisms." In other words, scholarship has moved from division to diversity as its model for conceptualizing the distinctions within first-century Judaism. In light of this, it must be asked whether the popular depiction of the Hellenists and Hebrews of Acts 6.1 is founded upon anything but stereotype.[5] Why should our acceptance of the cultural complexity of first-century Judaism stop at the door of Jewish *Christianity*? Surely the historically credible picture here, as in the case of Judaism itself, is the complex one. We should expect to find Jewish Christians of various opinions irrespective of their particular nationalities. We ought not to be surprised, for example, to learn of "liberal" Hebrews and "conservative" Hellenists.

Disputations concerning the theoretical foundation underlying the traditional understanding of the Hellenists and Hebrews can take us only so far. Ultimately, the legitimacy of any interpretation must be tested within the framework of a study of the texts upon which it is based. For the purpose of this chapter, we shall confine ourselves to an examination of two key passages, Acts 8.1 and Acts 6.8–7.60, on the basis of which it is averred: (1) that the Christian Hellenists were selectively persecuted because of their distinctly radical theology, and (2) that this theology was first propagated by their leader, Stephen, who openly opposed both Temple and Torah. In these few pages I hope to show that the text of Acts is incapable of bearing this heavy load of interpretation.

ACTS 8.1: THE PERSECUTION OF THE HELLENISTS

According to Acts 8.1, after the death of Stephen "a great persecution arose against the church in Jerusalem; and all were scattered throughout the region of Judea and Samaria, except the apostles." Commented Baur, "This may justly surprise us";

---

[5] Or prejudice. Much effort has been expended over the years in the attempt to rescue Paul (and Pauline Christianity) from Judaism. The bifurcation of the Jerusalem church is part and parcel of this program.

after all, what persecution is directed at followers but not
leaders?

However, it cannot be doubted that they [the apostles] remained
behind in Jerusalem . . . But if they remained we cannot believe that
they were the only ones who did so, but rather that the persecution
first directed against the Hellenist Stephen was in fact carried on
against the Hellenistic part of the Church.[6]

This selective persecution of the Hellenists produced results of
enormous consequence for the early church:

The two elements composing it, the Hellenistic and Hebraistic . . .
now became outwardly separated from each other. At that time the
Church at Jerusalem was purely Hebraistic; as such it adhered closely
to its strictly Judaizing character, and a strenuous opposition to the
liberal Hellenistic Christianity was consequently developed.[7]

For their part, the Hellenists, having been driven from
Jerusalem, progressed naturally to "a universal system in
which Jew and Gentile stood equal side by side."[8] In equal and
opposite reaction, the church of Jerusalem, now wholly rigid
(i.e. Jewish),[9] came to oppose the rapidly developing Gentile
mission of the Hellenists.[10] This antagonism is evidenced most
clearly in the confrontation between Paul and his Jerusalem-
sponsored Judaizing opponents.

Hence, we see that the opposition between Jewish Petrine
and universalist Pauline perspectives, which dominated Baur's
conception of the early church, was traced by him to its
original manifestation in the tension between the Hebrews and
Hellenists of Acts. Accordingly, Stephen, the exemplary Hellenist, was termed by Baur "the most direct forerunner of the
Apostle Paul."[11]

The significance for subsequent scholarship of Baur's interpretation of Acts 8.1 can hardly be overstated. Time and time
again scholars have appealed to the selective persecution of the
Hellenists as the controlling datum in their interpretation of

---

[6] F. C. Baur, *Paul, the Apostle of Jesus Christ*, trans. A. P. and A. Menzies (London and
   Edinburgh, 1873 [vol. I], 1875 [vol. II]) vol. I, p. 39, my italics.
[7] Ibid., vol. I, p. 40.   [8] Ibid., vol. I, pp. 60–61.
[9] Compare Baur's description of the Jews, ibid., vol. I, p. 51.
[10] Ibid., vol. I, p. 40.   [11] Ibid., vol. I, p. 62.

the rest of Acts 6.1–8.4. Ernst Haenchen, for one, explicitly espouses this method in his interpretation of Acts 6.1–7:

> But the tangle may not be so easily unravelled. One must begin at the other end, and this means looking beyond the passage under discussion. We are told in 8.1 that the whole primitive community, apart from the Apostles, was persecuted and dispersed . . . This inference [namely that the Hellenists were selectively persecuted], once admitted, sets off a chain reaction.[12]

It may be objected both that this inference ought *not* to be admitted, and that it is *not* in any case sufficient to its suggested consequences. The selective persecution of the Hellenists is unlikely history and, by the most optimistic reckoning, indeterminate evidence. Faith in the traditional perspective must leap gaps both in exegesis and in logic.

A variety of reconstructions of the events recorded in Acts 8.1 and following is possible. Although these are not all equally plausible, we shall consider each of them in turn in order to demonstrate that none supports the popular view of the Hellenists and Hebrews. The alternatives are as follows:

(1) Was there a "great persecution" as Luke records?
    YES   NO
(2) Who was persecuted?   (8.1 a Lucan construct)
    Only the Hellenists   The entire church
(3) By whom?
    Hellenists Authorities   Authorities

We begin by assuming an answer of "Yes" to question (1). Acts 8.1b is, therefore, taken to be historically accurate; some type of large-scale persecution of the church did occur at this time. But – question (2) – who, specifically, was persecuted? The most common option would be to conclude that opposition was aroused only against the Hellenists. If so, question (3) must be pressed – who were their persecutors? One alternative is to imagine that the Hellenists were opposed by fellow Hellenists (that is, Greek-speaking Jews). Those who regard

---

[12] E. Haenchen, *The Acts of the Apostles: A Commentary*, trans. B. Noble and G. Shinn (Philadelphia, 1971), p. 266.

the trial scene in 6.12–7.1 as artificial are most likely to take
this approach. According to this view, the non-Christian
Hellenists attacked those disturbing their community, acting
spontaneously (as in the mob actions of Acts 6.8–12 and
7.54–60) or acting perhaps in recognition of their responsibility
to discipline their own.[13]

However reasonable this view may seem, it must be noted
that such an "intra-Hellenist conflict"[14] would not have constituted a διωγμὸς μέγας ("great persecution") in Lucan terms.
As Luke has it, the persecution is directed from the top: the
high priest himself sits in judgment of Stephen (7.1) and
authorizes Paul's persecution of the church (9.1–2). Indeed,
the further one pushes the theory of a general yet selective
persecution by Hellenists, the more complicated and unbeliev-
able the result becomes. One is left to imagine a state of affairs
ín which Hellenist synagogue officials or Hellenist mobs could
continue (that is, beyond the death of Stephen) to do as they
pleased across Jerusalem, and in which the high priests and
elders themselves took no interest in the resultant commotion,
though it was reputed to concern both Temple and Law, and,
further, in which no appeal to higher authority was ever made,
either by Hellenist or by Hebrew Christians (the Hebrews, for
their part, being ready to sacrifice the Hellenists to keep the
peace).[15] Surely, if one feels compelled to move in this direct-

---

[13] Says M. Hengel, "ethnic synagogue associations in Jerusalem certainly had the
possibility of exercising discipline within the community . . . It seems to me that the
martyrdom of Stephen was connected with a synagogue assembly of this kind. No
wonder that the Roman authorities did not intervene" (*Between Jesus and Paul:
Studies in the Earliest History of Christianity*, trans. J. Bowden [London, 1983], p. 20).
Compare the synagogue punishment of Paul in 2 Cor. 11.24 and the warning in
Mark 13.9. See also E. P. Sanders, *Paul, the Law and the Jewish People* (Philadelphia,
1983), pp. 190–192 ("Conflict with his Own People").

[14] As J. D. G. Dunn terms it (*Unity and Diversity in the New Testament: An Inquiry into the
Character of Earliest Christianity* [London, 1977], p. 274).

[15] Cf. Dunn's speculation "that the Hebrew Christians had virtually *abandoned*
Stephen, so antagonized were they by his views on the temple . . . Perhaps they
believed that Stephen had brought his fate upon his own head." Subsequently, "the
Hellenist Christians who shared Stephen's views would have few friends to shelter
them; whereas local Hebrew Christians still loyal to temple and law would be
relatively secure"(*Unity and Diversity*, pp. 273, 274). Division (and even animosity)
of such an extent between the groups seems to me to be quite incredible, particularly as it is not supported by any tradition or by the facts as we know them

ion, it is more reasonable simply to accept the facts as Luke presents them: that opposition begun within the Greek-speaking community of Jerusalem was subsequently taken up by the Jewish authorities.

The simple fact is that unless the antagonists of Acts 8.1–3 were in a position to attempt a general persecution of the church, their failure to do so proves nothing. Therefore, if the Hellenists were selectively persecuted, and if their persecutors were fellow Greek-speaking Jews, then we are left to admit that the persecution itself tells us nothing about the relationship between the Hellenist and Hebrew Christians.

Let us (together with most commentators) say then that Luke's account is accurate, that opposition begun within the Greek-speaking community was subsequently taken up by the Jewish authorities. Moreover, let us assume that only the Hellenists were affected by this persecution.[16] On the one hand, this view manages to avoid the difficulties mentioned in connection with the previous proposal. On the other hand, it leads us straight into a further dilemma: The argument from persecution is in fact one of the most vital pieces of evidence for the Hellenists' solidarity with – and not their distinctiveness from – the Hebrews, for the Hebrews are, if anything, the more persecuted by these same Jewish leaders. In 4.1–22, John and Peter are arrested by "the priests, the captain of the temple, and the Sadducees," taken before "rulers, elders and scribes . . . and Annas the high priest, Caiaphas, John, and Alexander, and all who were of the high-priestly family," and threatened. In 5.17–41, the "apostles" are arrested by "the high priest . . . and all who were with him (that is, the sect of the Sadducees)" and, after having been miraculously freed, are sought and then summoned to appear "before the council [Sanhedrin]," where they are beaten. In 12.1–11, we are told that Herod "laid violent hands upon some who belonged to the

concerning the subsequent relationship between the churches of Antioch and Jerusalem.

[16] That is, in reference to the chart above, (1) there was a "great persecution," (2) it affected only the Hellenists, and (3) it was authorized or promoted by the Jewish authorities.

church." He killed James with the sword and then, "after he saw that it pleased the Jews," had Peter arrested as well. Again, Peter is miraculously delivered "from the hands of Herod and from all that the Jewish people were expecting" (verse 11) and, it seems likely, forced to flee Jerusalem (verse 17). If these do not suffice, we have the example of James the brother of Jesus, by all accounts the leader of the Hebrews, put to death at the instigation of the high priest Ananus the Younger (brother-in-law of Caiaphas, the high priest who, according to Acts 7.1, sat in judgment of Stephen).[17] We also have the testimony of Paul in 1 Thess. 2.14–16 concerning the persecution of the churches "in Judea."[18] Finally, passages in the Synoptic Gospels appear to presuppose a state of persecution (for example Matt. 10.23, locating this specifically in Israel). Therefore, if persecution may be taken to mean something in the case of the Hellenists, then recurrent persecution of the Hebrews by these same Jewish leaders means something equally significant.

So the difficulty is unavoidable: Either the Hellenists were opposed by the same persons who opposed the Hebrews, or the opposition they met was from fellow Hellenists and therefore was something less than the "great persecution" of Acts 8.1. In either case, the most basic of the arguments marshaled in support of the theological distinctiveness of the Hellenists is disallowed.

Up to this point we have assumed that the phrase "except the apostles" precludes the possibility that the Hebrews were persecuted along with the Hellenists. Just to exhaust all possibilities, let us assume for the moment that there was a large-scale persecution, and that it was not limited to the Hellenists (after all, Luke does say that it was against "the church" and that "all," except the apostles, were scattered). As we have seen, it is simpler to assume that such a persecution would have been carried out by the Jewish authorities and not by the anti-Christian Hellenists. Such a detail is hardly worth discuss-

---

[17] See *Hellenists and Hebrews*, pp. 190–191.

[18] The authenticity of 1 Thess. 2.14–16 is discussed in *Hellenists and Hebrews*, pp. 36–37, n. 69.

ing, however, if we realize that any general persecution of the church that did not distinguish between Hellenist and Hebrew would only serve to underscore our conclusion: The Hellenists and Hebrews were not distinctive ideological groups.

What is the most reasonable appraisal of Acts 8.1? I would suggest that Luke is, as it were, setting up his pieces for the next game. It is in his design both to get the Gospel out – "in all Judea and Samaria and to the end of the earth" (1.8) – and to keep the apostles (not the Hebrews) in, centered on Jerusalem, where they belong. It is no coincidence that if we were left with Acts as our only source, we would know nothing of the wider travels of Cephas, "the other apostles and the brothers of the Lord" (1 Cor. 9.5). It is in Luke's design that the Twelve (recall Acts 1.15–26) keep their authoritative feet planted firmly in the holy city. This is required for the sake of the Lucan apology: Now as before, Jerusalem is the epicenter of God's saving activity. That it is also the church's center is thus not a matter of indifference.[19]

On reflection, it is difficult to believe that scholars would ever have interpreted a verse like Acts 8.1 with such minute literalism, except for the fact that an entire superstructure is built upon it. This is not to suggest that Luke's account is fabricated. It is possible that it reflects what was a genuine heightening of tensions between the primitive church and Judaism, tensions which may have broken out in violence, particularly within the Greek-speaking Jewish community. Those who were not resident in Jerusalem (i.e. predominantly Hellenist pilgrims) might well have thought it best to leave the city at this time, as Luke records in Acts 8.4–5 and 11.19–20. Luke would have known in any case that Paul was at one time a persecutor of Christians. His introduction within the context

---

[19] Johannes Weiss saw Acts 8.1b as "only a redactional expedient to explain how it came about that the church continued peacefully on its way in spite of everything. The same thing occurs here as in so many later descriptions in which the author can never say too much in picturing the horrors of persecution; one can hardly understand how any one could ever have been left alive" (*Earliest Christianity: A History of the Period A.D. 30–150* [2 vols., New York, 1959], vol. 1, p. 170). While I accept the second half of this statement, I think that there is more significance to the verse than Weiss describes.

of the first general persecution of the church is therefore
entirely understandable. It could even be argued that Luke
located the persecution itself, along with Paul, in Jerusalem.
Obviously, in such a case there would be no point in considering the (imaginary) persecution of the Hellenists. But this is
only speculation, as any proposal must be that goes beyond the
confines of the modest account of Acts 8.1–4.

Thus, all interpretive roads lead finally to the same destination: There is nothing in the account of the persecution of
Acts 8 that would cause us to believe that the church of
Jerusalem was divided into ideological camps corresponding to
the labels "Hellenists" and "Hebrews." If the persecution was
selective, and the Hellenist Christians were persecuted by their
fellow Hellenists, we are able to infer nothing concerning their
relationship with the Hebrews. If, on the other hand, the
Hellenists were persecuted by the chief priests, we know only
that they were opposed by those persons who on other occasions also opposed the Hebrews. If the persecution *was not*
selective, then it would serve to unite, rather than to distinguish between, the Hellenists and the Hebrews. If, however,
there was no "great persecution" such as Luke describes, then
the matter is laid to rest entirely.

ACTS 6.8–7.60: STEPHEN'S CRITICISM OF LAW AND TEMPLE

At the center of the Hellenist debate stands the figure of
St. Stephen. His importance to the author of Acts is manifest:
The speech credited to him is the longest in a book of speeches;
his death precipitates the outward movement of the Gospel
from Jerusalem (a leitmotiv of Acts); and he is ennobled as the
church's first martyr, one whose death is patterned after the
passion of Jesus himself.[20]

Stephen is no less important to modern expositors wishing to
uncover the theology of Luke's Hellenists. Martin Hengel sides

---

[20] On the relationship between the two martyrdom stories, see *Hellenists and Hebrews*,
pp. 58–61.

with the majority when he calls Stephen the spokesman of the Hellenist community.[21] It is commonly assumed that Stephen not only spoke for the Hellenist party, but was in fact the progenitor of their distinctive theology. For this reason, we encounter the Hellenists of Acts appearing under the name "the Stephen circle" in much of the relevant literature.

For the purposes of this chapter, I wish to make only the most important point about the Stephen materials of Acts 6 and 7: There is nothing in these chapters that supports the widely held view that Stephen was a radical critic of either the Temple or the Law. That Stephen could have made inflammatory utterances, such as the repetition of Jesus' warning concerning the destruction of the Temple, is not denied. The question is not, Did Stephen advocate beliefs offensive to Jewish authorities, but, Did Stephen advocate beliefs offensive to Hebrew (but not Hellenist) Christians? Let us not forget that from an early date the Hebrews also aroused opposition. James, the brother of John, was himself executed (Acts 12.2), but it is seldom if ever imagined that James shared Stephen's supposedly extremist views. Did Stephen's death require different and greater causes than that of James?

Temple and Law criticism are thought by many to be evidenced in the accusations of chapter 6 and/or the speech of chapter 7. Let us consider each of these passages in turn.

THE ACCUSATIONS

According to Luke, the charges against Stephen (which, admittedly, concerned the Law and the Temple) were set forth by *false* witnesses. Almost universally, commentators have assumed the opposite: that the supposedly false witnesses were in fact telling the truth. This interpretive reversal is accomplished by means of an intriguing sleight of hand. It is said that Luke knows and wants to report the reason for Stephen's death, and yet the witnesses he employs to do so must be "false" since they are witnessing against Stephen, who is

---

[21] Hengel, *Between Jesus and Paul*, p. 19.

"true." Wilfred Knox calls this "a genuine literary curiosity": "any witness who gives evidence against a martyr must be a 'false' witness since he is against the truth."[22] Or, as Martin Scharlmann has written, the charges were indeed false, "but not in the sense of being contrary to fact"![23] But it would have been obvious to Luke and to his readers, living after AD 70, that the charges were precisely contrary to fact. The temple had in truth been destroyed – but not by Jesus. Heikki Räisänen is one of the few commentators to have recognized this: "The reader of Luke's Gospel will also know that Jesus, according to that book, never said that he will destroy the temple, but only that it will be destroyed."[24] It also needs to be said that it is fully in keeping with Luke's purposes in Acts that he both introduce and refute the charge of "blasphemy" against Moses. S. G. Wilson, in his thoughtful monograph *Luke and the Law*, concludes that in Luke's perspective, "there is no conflict in living according to the law, indeed doing so zealously, and being a Christian."[25] In fact, Luke "viewed living according to the law as a natural and appropriate way of life for Jews and Jewish-Christians."[26] Moreover, Luke goes to considerable lengths to demonstrate the piety of the Jewish Christians in general, and of the apostle Paul in particular. There is no doubt that, to Luke, the witnesses are patently false.

It can be argued that there might still be some truth to the accusations. After all, the false charges against Paul in Acts 21.21, 28 are clearly exaggerations of charges that could genuinely have been leveled against him. This is true, but in Paul's case we have the means for verifying the considerable extent to which the accusations have been falsified by "exaggeration." In Stephen's case no such verification is possible; we

---

[22] W. Knox, *The Acts of the Apostles* (Cambridge, 1948), p. 25.

[23] M. H. Scharlmann, *Stephen: A Singular Saint*, Analecta Biblica 34 (Rome, 1968), p. 102.

[24] H. Räisänen, *The Torah and Christ: Essays in German and English on the Problem of the Law in Early Christianity* (Helsinki, 1986), pp. 164–165 (cf. Lk. 13.34–35; 20.9–19; 21.6). See also G. H. Stanton, "Stephen in Lukan Perspective," in *Studia Biblica 1978. III. Papers on Paul and Other New Testament Authors*, ed. E. A. Livingstone (Sheffield, 1980), pp. 345–360, here pp. 348–349.

[25] S. G. Wilson, *Luke and the Law* (Cambridge, 1983), p. 102.

[26] Ibid., pp. 114–115.

are left only to speculate about what historical kernel may lie hidden within the supposedly overstated charges of the false witnesses. A healthy dose of skepticism about such speculation is entirely in order. In studies of this sort one usually finds whatever kernel one is looking for.

It is also necessary to consider the possibility that it was the question of Paul's faithfulness to the Law that was actually at issue in Acts, and that Luke reads the Pauline defense – that is, the one that he knows and the one that most concerns him – back into the story of Stephen. This would, of course, explain the striking but otherwise coincidental parallelism between the charges against Paul in Acts 21.28 and those against Stephen in 6.13. Whether or not this is the case, it is clear that Luke is arguing a point with respect to the Law; it is the Jews who have disobeyed, not the Christians (7.53). Given Luke's apologetic (or, I might say, polemical) agenda, it would be very hazardous to stake out our claim to the Stephen of history on the basis of this one, stereotyped accusation.[27]

Many scholars who look to Acts 6.11–14 for evidence of Stephen's radicalism claim that certain literary peculiarities betray the text's non-Lucan (and therefore traditional) origin. For example, Earl Richard, one of the most cautious interpreters of Acts 6.1–8.3, writes that "[a] careful examination of the style of v. 11 has convincingly shown that the verse owes a considerable debt to tradition."[28] This assertion is based in part on the presence in verse 11 of the adjective βλάσφημος, used elsewhere in the New Testament in this grammatical construction only in 2 Pet. 2.11, where it is not accompanied by the preposition εἰς.[29] It is difficult to see how this wording necessitates a source. While it is true that Luke does not use the adjectival form of βλασφημέω elsewhere, the noun βλασφημία *is* used in Lk. 5.21, and the verb itself appears seven times in

---

[27] See Acts 18.13 and 21.24, 28, as well as Paul's defense against the same charge, *by this time already understood* by the reader, in 25.8.

[28] E. Richard, *Acts 6.1–8.4: The Author's Method of Composition* (Missoula, 1978), p. 288.

[29] Richard considers this point especially significant: "the combination of the elements found in 6.11 is unique, particularly the adjective βλάσφεμος followed by εἰς" (ibid., p. 288).

Luke–Acts, once in connection with εἰς ("blaspheming against the Holy Spirit," Lk. 12.10; see also Mark 3.29). The term modified by βλάσφημα–ῥήματα ("words") – is a "good Lucan" word,[30] while "blasphemy" itself might almost be called a "good" Lucan theme. Just as it is the Jews who disobey the Law,[31] it is the Jews who are guilty of blasphemy.[32] In Acts 26.11, Paul even describes his persecution of the church as an attempt to compel Christian Jews to blaspheme! So we are brought again to a by-now familiar consideration, namely the Lucan apologetic vis-à-vis Judaism: Stephen is falsely charged with the crime of which the Jews themselves are culpable. Other, similar claims concerning the supposedly non-Lucan character of Acts 6.11–14 (and 7.1–60, for that matter) are equally questionable.[33]

THE SPEECH

Many scholars turn to Acts 7 for evidence of Stephen's Law- and Temple-criticism. Are the "true" accusations of the "false" witnesses substantiated by the speech? Martin Dibelius addressed this question perceptively when commenting on the alleged Temple-criticism of the speech: "the speech is extremely reticent and seems to be very loosely connected with the charge – indeed, we ourselves shall probably be reading into it any significance that we may find."[34] This observation should be extended to both of the charges against Stephen. It is very doubtful that the speech would ever have been inter- preted as Law-critical if it were not for the charge in 6.13 that "this man never stops saying things . . . against the law." If anything, the speech is emphatically "pro-law." This is most evident in the treatment of Moses, the one who received the "living oracles" (7.38) at Mt. Sinai. Johannes Munck rightly remarked that Acts 7 "gives us the highest appreciation of

30 Räisänen, *The Torah*, p. 263.   31 Acts 7.53.
32 Lk. 22.65; 23.39; Acts 13.45; 18.6; 26.11.
33 These are dealt with in detail in *Hellenists and Hebrews*, pp. 58–67 and pp. 82–89.
34 M. Dibelius, *Studies in the Acts of the Apostles*, ed. H. Greeven, trans. M. Linz and P. Schubert (London, 1956), p. 168.

Moses that we meet in the New Testament."[35] It is likely that Moses and the Law have been elevated for the dramatic purpose of heightening the guilt of the Jews. The Law itself was received εἰς διαταγὰς ἀγγέλων ("as ordained by angels").[36] The fault lay with the Jews, who failed to keep it. It is not the Law that is the subject of Luke's attention; it is the Jews. Luke needs the Law in much the same way that Paul needs it in Rom. 2.17–24; it is the bar at which the Jews may be arraigned.

Scholars who consider the Hellenists to be a bridge to Paul on the question of Law-criticism are in a fascinating dilemma. They want to emphasize the law-critical side of Stephen, but there is no evidence. A somewhat better case can be made for criticism of the Temple – at least here there is some ambiguity as to Stephen's position – but an attack on the Temple seems something of an irrelevance. While questions about the Law did concern the early Aramaic- and Greek-speaking churches (such as Jerusalem and Antioch), there are no data to suggest that the Temple was also a point of controversy. In fact, the one type of Temple "criticism" that can adequately be defended on the basis of the speech is not unique and fails to attack the institution of the Temple itself.[37] Further, the persecution of Stephen and the Hellenists over the Temple might not distinguish them from but rather unite them with Jesus and the Hebrews, both of whom may have suffered for similar reasons.[38] Consequently, it must be shown that Stephen's criticism of the Temple was of such a fundamental nature that it

[35] J. Munck, *The Acts of the Apostles* (Garden City, 1967), p. 221, n. 1.

[36] Verse 53; see also verses 30, 35, and 38. Unlike Paul's disparaging reference to angelic agency in Gal. 3.19, Luke mentions the angels at Sinai in order to emphasize the sanctity and importance of the Law (compare angelic agency in Lk. 1.11–20, 26–38; 2.9–15, 21; and Acts 5.19–20; 8.26; 10.3–7, 22; 11.13; 12.7–11, 23; 23.9; 27.23–24). The mediation of angels in the giving of the Law is also referred to in Heb. 2.2.

[37] That is, the idea that the destruction of the temple came as a result of Jewish unbelief. See Matt. 21.33–41, 42–44, and parallels. Such a view does not, however, constitute *criticism* of the Temple.

[38] On the temple and the death of Jesus, see E. P. Sanders, *Jesus and Judaism* (Philadelphia, 1985), pp. 296–306. While it is not known why, for example, James the brother of Jesus was killed, it is once again the high priest who was responsible for his death (Josephus, *Antiquities* 20.197–203).

brought into question the validity of the Law itself. It is for this reason, I believe, that Stephen's negative statements concerning the Temple are portrayed as being so strong.[39] This is a necessity if he is to be made a critic of Torah.

There are two principal places in the speech where scholars claim to find radical criticism of the Temple. The most significant of these is in verses 46–48a:

[David] found favor with God and asked that he might find
a dwelling place for the house of Jacob.
But it was Solomon who built a house for him.
Yet the Most High does not dwell in things made with human hands.

The primary debate concerns the supposed contrast between "finding a dwelling place" and "building a house." If such a contrast exists, it is usually interpreted to mean that the simple, approved intentions of David were thwarted in the actual disposition of his son, Solomon. So, for example, Haenchen remarks that, "The speaker understands σκήνωμα ["dwelling place"] in the sense that the pious David wanted to 'find' God only a tented dwelling, i. e. the tabernacle [σκηνή, "tent"], not build him a solid house."[40]

This seems highly doubtful. Verse 46b draws directly upon Psalm 132, ἕως οὗ εὕρω τόπον τῷ κυρίῳ, σκήνωμα τῷ θεῷ 'Ιακωβ ("until I find a place for the Lord, a dwelling place for the God of Jacob" verse 5), a song of ascents celebrating the establishment of the Davidic line and the Jerusalem cult. (Luke's choice of the verb αἰτέω ["ask"] in Acts 7.46 almost certainly

---

[39] For example, Julius Wellhausen wrote that "Stephen . . . rejects it [the Temple] a priori; he puts it in opposition to the legitimate cultic place of the tabernacle, and on the same level with the golden calf and shrine of Moloch" ("Kritische Analyse der Apostelgeschichte," in *Abhandlungen der königlichen Gesellschaft der Wissenschaften zu Göttingen, philologisch-historische Klasse*, NS 15.2 [1914], 1–56, here p. 13). Similarly, Robert Maddox stated that according to Acts 7, "the building of the Temple was an act of rebellion" (*The Purpose of Luke–Acts* [Göttingen, 1982], p. 53). C. K. Barrett put the matter this way: "David . . . found favour with God and planned to make him a σκήνωμα, a word that is used occasionally for the tabernacle. At this point the decisive rot set in. Solomon built God a house, οἶκος. This was contrary to God's will" ("Old Testament History according to Stephen and Paul," in *Studien zum Text und zur Ethik des Neuen Testaments: Festschrift zum 80 Geburtstag von Heinrich Greeven*, ed. W. Schrage (Berlin and New York, 1986), pp. 57–69, here p. 67).

[40] Haenchen, *Acts*, p. 285. The same interpretation is found in Baur, *Paul*, vol. i, pp. 47–52.

indicates that he himself was thinking of 2 Sam. 7.1–2 – in which David expresses to the prophet Nathan his desire to build a temple – as the background to Ps. 132.2–5.)[41] This is, of course, quite enough to account for the peculiar phrase εὑρεῖν σκήνωμα ("to find a dwelling place"). Similarly, the vocabulary of verse 47 (οἰκοδομεῖν οἶκον ["to build a house"]) is to be found in a number of related verses in the LXX (2 Sam. 7.13; 1 Kgs. 5.3 [alluding to David's wish]; 6.2; and 8.16–17), where it also refers to the building of the Temple.

It is worth noting that the categories "tent" and "house" are not used consistently by the author. Specifically, we are told of a bad σκηνή in Acts 7.43 ("the tent of Moloch") and, if the reading is correct, of an apparently good οἶκος in verse 46. If the author genuinely had intended to create a contrast between the terms, he could certainly have done a better job of it.

Thus it seems most reasonable to take verses 46–47 at face value and not be diverted by them. It is true that the author wishes to make a point about the Temple – amongst other things – but it is overly subtle to detect the sort of contrast that so many have found in these verses.

A fact almost universally ignored in discussions of this passage is that verse 48, which summarizes verses 46 and 47 (and almost certainly the author's own point of view), omits the words οἶκος ("house") and σκήνωμα ("dwelling place") entirely. Thus, the verse makes a simple point that has nothing to do with an opposition between temples and tents: God does not reside in things made by human hands. It is a point that any Jew might make in a polemic against paganism and about which no Jew would probably be able to disagree (see 1 Kgs. 8.27). At most, it represents the perspective of one who would resist any tendency to localize worship exclusively in the Temple. The assertion of verse 48 takes on additional significance, however, when it is made in the context of a Gentile church or mission, and that after the destruction of the Temple in AD 70. This is a theme to which we shall return shortly.

---

[41] Marcel Simon contended that behind this text lies, not David's desire to build a house (as in 1 Kgs. 5.3), but *only* David's earlier wish to move the ark to Jerusalem. This interpretation is disputed in *Hellenists and Hebrews*, pp. 72–73.

The real problem with verses 46–50 is their relationship to Stephen's accusations against the Jews in verses 51–53. These are so vehement in tone that it seems necessary to find justification for them in preceding verses. Thus scholars are led to overestimate the force of the polemic in verses 48–50 and to assume that a repudiation of the Temple is at the heart of the Stephen speech. Says Haenchen, "The swift passage to the string of charges in verses 51–3 which goad the audience into fury can only be explained if the preceding verses form a radical denunciation of the Temple worship."[42] In point of fact the allegations of verses 51–53 have nothing to do with the temple. In these verses, "the author appears to have as his goal to list as many accusations as possible against the Judaism of NT times."[43] The Jews are "stiff-necked" and "uncircumcised in heart" "and ears." They "are forever opposing the Holy Spirit," having killed the prophets, and are now becoming the "betrayers" and "murderers" of the righteous one. For the crowning accusation he returns, not to the Temple or even to the death of Jesus, but to that which has occupied the greatest part of his attention, the rejection of Moses and the Law: "You are the ones that received the law as ordained by angels, and yet you have not kept it" (verse 53).

It is worth considering this last statement more carefully. It is my understanding that the dominant (although by no means the only) question being addressed in the Acts of the Apostles is, Who are the people of God? Accordingly, it is not the institutions of Judaism, which are by definition good, but the unbelieving Jews themselves that are assailed. This is as true in the Stephen speech as it is in the rest of Acts.[44] Jewish dis-

---

[42] Haenchen, *Acts*, p. 286. Given Haenchen's views concerning the composition of the speech, it is curious that he makes an argument based on the probable response of a fictitious audience.

[43] Richard, *Author's Method*, p. 138.

[44] See, for example, J. T. Sanders, *The Jews in Luke–Acts* (London, 1987), and his "The Jewish People in Luke–Acts," in *SBL 1986 Seminar Papers*, ed. K. H. Richards (Atlanta, 1986), pp. 110–129, and his "The Salvation of the Jews in Luke–Acts," in *SBL 1982 Seminar Papers*, ed. K. H. Richards (Chicago, 1982), pp. 467–483; L. Gaston, "Anti-Judaism and the Passion Narrative in Luke and Acts," in *Anti-Judaism in Early Christianity*, vol. 1, *Paul and the Gospels*, ed. P. Richardson and D. Granskou (Waterloo, 1986), pp. 127–153; S. G. Wilson, "The Jews and the

obedience, although to some extent a theme of the entire speech, is centered upon the rejection of Moses and his teaching. The point is twofold: (1) it shows by their earlier example that the Jews are likely to be wrong in their present rejection of Jesus, and (2) it demonstrates the tragic consequences to which rejection of this "Second Moses" must lead. This is the true heart of the Stephen speech.

It is important to recognize that although Jewish institutions are not attacked directly, their value is necessarily depreciated. The Christian church was not, after all, a back-to-Moses movement. The author is not contending that the Jews need simply become better (i.e. more law-abiding) Jews. He is not asking, in other words, that they accept their heritage, but that they accept the thing to which he believes their heritage should lead. To Luke, Judaism is inherently good but also inherently not good enough.

This insight goes a long way toward explaining the strangely contradictory attitude of Acts toward the Jews, and it certainly helps us to understand the inclusion of verses 48–50 within the Stephen speech. Luke's perspective encourages a spiritualizing tendency that is also to be found in verse 51 ("uncircumcised in heart and ears") and perhaps in the story of Abraham as well ("he [God] did not give him [Abraham] any of it as a heritage, not even a foot's length," verse 5 [Deut. 2.5]; compare Heb. 11.39–40). In a sense this allows him the luxury of denying what he must at the same time necessarily affirm. Christians accept the Law and the Temple – rightly understood.

Even if the tendency to minimize the significance of the Temple is understandable, we have not yet answered the question as to why the theme is brought into the speech. A number of plausible answers could be offered, but I believe that one in particular makes more sense of the presence of the Temple, and indeed of its dramatic location within the speech, than any other. The key may be found in the attitude expressed in Lk. 13.34–35a:

Death of Jesus in Acts," in *Anti-Judaism*, pp. 155–164; D. L. Tiede, "Glory to Thy People Israel!: Luke–Acts and the Jews," *SBL 1986 Seminar Papers*, pp. 142–151; and R. C. Tannehill, "Rejection by Jews and Turning to Gentiles: The Pattern of Paul's Mission in Acts," in *SBL 1986 Seminar Papers*, pp. 130–141.

Jerusalem, Jerusalem, the city that kills the prophets and stones those
who are sent to it! How often have I desired to gather your children
together as a hen gathers her brood under her wings, and you were
not willing! See, your house is left to you!

It is highly likely that the sentiment expressed in these verses
lies beneath the treatment of the Temple in the Stephen
speech. Indeed, a number of key words reappear in Acts 6–7:
Ἰεροσαλήμ, ἀποκτείνω, οἱ προφῆται, λιθοβολέω, οὐκ ἠθελήσαι,
ὁ οἶκος ("Jerusalem," "kill prophets," "stone," "you would
not," "house"). Viewed in this light, the Temple takes on
enormous symbolic significance. The destruction of the
Temple is Luke's contemporary parallel to the incident in the
wilderness, in which "God handed [the Jews] over" for their
rejection of Moses (verse 42). The reference to Babylon in verse
43 (cf. "Damascus" in the original text of Amos 5.27) thus sets
in parallel the destruction of the Jerusalem Temple and the
scattering of the Jewish people under Babylon and under Rome.
If Luke was writing in the years after AD 70, the relationship
between these events could hardly have been missed by his
readers. The Stephen speech is very much at the center of the
program of Acts, and the inclusion of the Temple is one critical
element in its presentation.[45] Verses 46–50 do not fit logically
within the speech if they are related only to the occasion of
Stephen's martyrdom, but their logic is inescapable if one looks
beyond to the underlying movement of the Book of Acts.

Heikki Räisänen has written that "Stephen's speech does not
contain the vehement criticism of the temple and its sacrifices
sometimes ascribed to it . . . The temple section does not really

---

[45] It may even be that Luke has shifted the saying of Mark 14.58 to its present context
in Acts for this reason. One of the themes of Luke–Acts is the gradual hardening of
the Jews (F. F. Bruce, *Commentary on the Book of Acts: The English Text with Introduction, Exposition and Notes* [London, 1954], p. 92). The stoning of Stephen is in this
sense even more significant than the crucifixion of Jesus. Hitherto, the real possibility of present (not future, eschatological) Jewish national repentance seems to
have been held forth (see Acts 3.17–19). As a consequence of the death of Stephen,
however, the tide has turned, and the offer of the Gospel is increasingly focused
upon the Gentiles, who will listen (28.28). Thus Stephen's death may presage the
destruction of the Temple even more than did the death of Jesus, whom the Jews
and their rulers crucified "in ignorance" (3.17). An echo of this may perhaps be
found in the contrast between the green wood and dry wood of Lk. 23.31.

lead anywhere."[46] We may now appreciate the perceptiveness
of the first of these assertions while choosing to disagree with the
second. Stephen does not vehemently criticize the Temple, it is
true, but the vehemence his remarks incite does portend the
rejection of the Temple and of the Jewish nation. The Temple
section does indeed lead somewhere.

The kind of Temple-criticism most often (and erroneously)
attributed to the speech ("God was happy with a tent but never
wanted a house") does not present so fundamental a challenge
to the Law as that discerned by some in the account of Israel's
idolatry in the wilderness in 7.39f. The impetus for this interpretation comes from the citation of Amos 5.25–27 in verse 42:
God was not the object of their sacrifices. Indeed, God never
wished to be. Thus the cult and the "adulterated Law" that
enshrined it were merely an Israelite extension of the Golden
Calf of Egypt.[47] Stephen "draws a distinction between the
divinely ordered "lively oracles," i.e. the authentic Law of
Moses, and [all] the ordinances concerning sacrifices and
temple, which were invented by the Jews."[48] For this reason the
people of Israel were finally removed by God "beyond
Babylon" (verse 43).[49]

The obvious difficulty with this interpretation is the fact that
it is not sustained in the verses that follow. In verse 44 the
polemic suddenly disappears. The tabernacle was a "tent of
witness" whose construction was directed by God. It was
brought by the people into the land that God gave to them.
David himself is said to have found favor with God. There
simply is no reasonable way to argue that the people were
unrelenting idolaters given up by God after the incident with
the Golden Calf.

---

[46] Räisänen, *The Torah*, p. 274.

[47] M. Simon, *St. Stephen and the Hellenists* (London, 1958), p. 46. See also Knox, *St. Paul and the Church of Jerusalem* (Cambridge, 1925), p. 44; and B. B. Bacon, "Stephen's Speech: Its Argument and Doctrinal Relationship," in *Biblical and Semitic Studies: Critical and Historical Essays by the Members of Semitic and Biblical Faculty of Yale University* (New York, 1901), pp. 211–276, here pp. 264, 269–276.

[48] Simon, *Stephen*, p. 48.

[49] "The substitution of Babylon for Damascus seems – and most commentators agree – best explained as a post-exilic correction" (Richard, *Author's Method*, p. 126; see also n. 233).

Many who do not go to these lengths still believe that there is an essential link between the wilderness story and the building of the Temple. This correspondence is based on the account of the idolatrous Israelites, who rejoiced "in the work of their hands" (verse 41). The Temple is characterized in verse 48 as χειροποιήτοις ("handmade"). Hence it is concluded that "the superstitious attachment of the Jews to their temple is made to appear as a continuation of their idolatry in the desert."[50]

Again, the claim of Temple-criticism is dubious. For one thing, it ignores the fact that the tabernacle was also hand-made. It may be objected that the construction of the tabernacle was, however, directed by God (verse 44).[51] This is true, but it is also true that David, whose idea it was to construct the Temple, is treated favorably and is not chastised for his wish. The treatment of Solomon is neutral or else an amazingly subdued criticism (cf. verses 51–53, where the author could scarcely be accused of subtlety). And verses 48–50, as we have seen, minimize the role of the Temple (countering the notion that God dwells only [or perhaps is uniquely present] in a handmade structure) without attacking it directly. The same point is repeated (including the use of χειροποίητος)[52] in Paul's speech on the Areopagus in Acts 17.24.[53] Räisänen's observation is right on target: "This makes it probable that verses 48–50 represent *Luke's own* point of view."[54]

The solution to the difficulties of verses 39–43 should by now be clear. The severity of these verses is directly attributable to the severity of the judgment awaiting the Jews (from the perspective of Stephen's – and realized by Luke's – day). If Israel's rejection of Moses led to God's rejection of Israel

---

[50] J. Dupont, *The Salvation of the Gentiles: Essays on the Acts of the Apostles* (Toronto, 1979), p. 134.

[51] C. H. H. Scobie, "The Origins and Development of Samaritan Christianity," *NTS* 19 (1972–1973), 390–414.

[52] The form of the Temple accusation in 6.14 most closely resembles that of Mark's Gospel (14.58). Mark's term χειροποίητος is not, however, taken up in Acts 6. Instead it appears in the answer to the charge, here in chapter 7 (verse 48).

[53] This theme is, of course, already present in the story of the dedication of the Temple in 1 Kgs. 8.

[54] Räisänen, *The Torah*, p. 274.

(verse 42), what other consequence might the reader expect of present Jewish rejection of the "prophet like Moses?"[55] The corollary works only if the first judgment can be made to parallel and thus to justify the second. Thus the finality of God's judgment in verses 42–43, while making a logical non-sense of verse 44f., makes its own admirable sense. To regard these verses as the tokens of some obscure theology of the two laws encompassing a rejection of the sacrificial system is to miss the point entirely.

A final observation: All of the evidence we possess strongly suggests that early churches arrived at Law- (not to mention Temple-) criticism only gradually, and then in response to concrete circumstances, especially as occasioned by the Gentile mission (for example as in Acts 11.19–20; Gal. 2.1–14; and Acts 15). Law-criticism did not come "packaged whole" from the earliest days in Jerusalem.[56]

In summary, then, there is no evidence that would lead us to believe that Stephen was a radical critic of either the Law or the Temple. It is entirely possible that the historical Stephen was put to death because of something he said about the Law or the Temple, and that this memory lies behind the composition of Acts 6 and 7. But there is nothing here that would substantiate the claim that Stephen died because of a peculiarly harsh attack on the Law and the Temple. In the latter case, let us not forget that Jesus himself was probably put to death at least in part because of statements he made concerning the Temple, and it is the Temple authorities who almost certainly are implicated in the deaths of James the brother of John (Acts 12.1–3) and of James the brother of Jesus, the leader of the so-called Hebrews.

[55] D. Moessner has argued that Luke's presentation of Stephen is itself modeled in Deuteronomic fashion after "the pattern of a prophet like Moses" ("Paul and the Pattern of the Prophet like Moses in Acts," in *SBL 1983 Seminar Papers*, ed. K. H. Richards (Chico, 1983), pp. 203–212, here pp. 203–209). Cf. B. Dehandschutter, who sees in Luke's portrayal of Stephen the archetypal presentation of a prophet's destiny of suffering ("La Persécution des chrétiens dans les Actes des Apôtres," in *Les Actes des Apôtres. Traditions, rédaction, théologie, BETL* 48 [1979], pp. 541–546, here p. 544, n. 10).

[56] See *Hellenists and Hebrews*, pp. 138–142.

CONCLUSION

The first Jerusalem Christians were positioned at the intersec-
tion of two histories: that of Jesus of Nazareth and that of the
church universal. One's perception of these early believers
profoundly influences one's understanding of the development
of subsequent Christian history and theology. For example,
scholars of a previous generation who delineated stages of
christological development like "Palestinian Jewish," "Hellenistic Jewish," and "Hellenistic Gentile" presupposed that the
Hebrew Christians of Jerusalem would have thought only in
certain predictable ways. Those today who are aware of the
complexity of first-century Palestinian Judaism must allow for
the possibility that first-century Palestinian Jewish *Christians*
also thought in diverse and even surprising ways.

The secondary literature on the New Testament abounds in
deprecating references to the "extreme conservatism" and
"narrow legalism" of the (Hebrew) Jerusalem church. The
"liberal," "universalist" Hellenists, in contrast, have enjoyed
an almost heroic status. But the evidence of the New Testament
does not justify this two-toned portrait of Jewish Christianity.
Indeed, it suggests an opposite picture: a colorful and dynamic
church in which there was as much disagreement within as
between individual congregations. For example, in the
accounts of both the Jerusalem Conference and the Antioch
Incident (Acts 15 and Gal. 2.1–14), we see debate within and
compromise between the churches of Jerusalem and Antioch,
the putative centers of Hebrew and Hellenist ideology.[57]
Nevertheless, assumptions about the bad (Jerusalem, James,
etc.) and good (Antioch, Paul, etc.) factions within Jewish
Christianity continue to affect (even, at times, to govern) the
interpretation of books as varied as Acts, Galatians, Romans,
Matthew, and James.[58]

Generalizations are of only limited usefulness, but there is
nothing *wrong* with generalizing; it is our common means of
managing complexity. Not all generalizations, however, are

[57] Ibid., pp. 103–147 on Galatians 2 and Acts 15.   [58] Ibid., chaps. 4 and 5.

equally valid; to the extent that they distort more than they clarify, darken more than they illumine, generalizations may be judged a hindrance to understanding and an impediment to scholarship. The penchant of academics to think in terms of groups, parties, and schools has been, in the case of the early church, uncommonly unfortunate in its results. Jewish Christianity was too large and too varied an entity to fit neatly into Hellenist and Hebrew ideological pigeonholes.[59] It appears that Christian theology did not develop along such straightforward or readily accessible lines. Instead, its development was a phenomenon as complex as the world within which it arose.

[59] On the complexity of Jewish Christianity see ibid., pp. 193–197.

CHAPTER 7

James and the Gentiles (Acts 15.13–21)

Richard Bauckham

INTRODUCTION

The speech of James in Acts 15.13–21 plays a key role in Luke's account of the Council of Jerusalem (and therefore in his whole account of the origins of the Gentile mission). Peter's speech, which opens the proceedings, reminds his hearers of the conversion of the first Gentile converts, when the evident charismatic phenomena (15.8; cf. 10.44–47; 11.15–17) constituted a clear declaration by God himself that Gentiles were acceptable to him as Gentiles (15.9; cf. 11.12). Thus Peter's argument is from miraculous events making God's will clear.[1] Barnabas and Paul follow up this argument in the same vein, alleging "the signs and wonders that God had done through them among the Gentiles" (15.12) as evidence that their Gentile mission is the valid continuation of what began in the house of Cornelius. But Luke does not represent this line of argument as the finally decisive one. After all, the matter under discussion is one of *halakhah* (15.5), which could only be decided from Scripture.[2] It is therefore left to James to provide the clinching argument: that according to Scripture itself the Gentiles who, it predicts, will join the eschatological people of God will do so as Gentiles. On this basis James proposes the terms of the Apostolic Decree (15.19–20; cf. 15.28–29; 21.25) as a definitive decision on the issue of what the Torah itself requires of Gentile

---

[1] See P. E. Esler, "Glossolalia and the Admission of Gentiles into the Early Christian Community," *BTB* 22 (1992), 136–142.

[2] Cf. B.T. B. Mez. 59b, and A. I. Baumgarten, "Miracles and Halakah in Rabbinic Judaism," *JQR* 73 (1982), 238–253.

Christians.[3] The key role which James' speech here plays in determining the Jerusalem church's stance with regard to the Gentile mission makes it worth asking, amid the complex of other difficult historical problems which surround Luke's narrative in Acts 15.1–35,[4] whether the argument of the speech has any historical credibility as an argument deriving from the Jerusalem church itself.

Study of the speeches in Acts has unfortunately paid little attention to this speech of James. The observation that not only is the scriptural quotation in 15.16–18 dependent on the LXX of Amos 9.11–12, but also its value for James' argument seems to depend on precisely the LXX text where it differs from the MT of Amos 9.12, has often been considered sufficient to rule out any possibility that the argument of the speech goes back to the historical James or to the Jerusalem church. Either the whole speech, with its scriptural quotation, is simply a Lucan composition,[5] or else Luke is dependent, as some think he is in the other speeches in the first half of Acts, on Hellenistic Christian exegetical tradition,[6] which supplied him with the quotation as a prooftext for the Gentile mission.

What has been lacking is a thorough study of the speech in the light of first-century Jewish exegetical methods.[7] In the

---

[3] J. Jervell, *Acts and the People of God: A New Look at Luke–Acts* (Minneapolis, 1972), pp. 188–193, gives a good account of the way Luke's narrative makes James' speech, rather than Peter's, decisive, but his explanation for Luke's portrayal of the role of James (that James had more authority than Paul for Luke's readers) is unconvincing.

[4] For a discussion of the attitude of the Jerusalem church to the Gentile mission, which sets the argument of the present chapter in a wider context, see R. Bauckham, "James and the Jerusalem Church," in R. Bauckham (ed.), *The Book of Acts in its Palestinian Setting* (Grand Rapids, 1995).

[5] E.g. E. Richard, "The Divine Purpose: The Jews and the Gentile Mission (Acts 15)," in P. J. Achtemeier (ed.), *Society of Biblical Literature 1980 Seminar Papers* (Chico, 1980), pp. 267–282.

[6] E.g. G. Lüdemann, *Early Christianity according to the Traditions in Acts*, trans. J. Bowden (London, 1989), pp. 169–170; J. Dupont, *The Salvation of the Gentiles: Studies in the Acts of the Apostles*, trans. J. R. Keating (New York, 1979), pp. 139–140; cf. F. Bovon, *Luke the Theologian: Thirty-three Years of Research (1950–1983)*, trans. K. McKinney (Allison Park, 1987), pp. 98, 101, 107.

[7] For some account of Jewish exegetical methods in other speeches in Acts, see E. E. Ellis, "Midrashic Features in the Speeches of Acts," in *Prophecy and Hermeneutic in Early Christianity*, WUNT 18 (Tübingen, 1978), pp. 198–208.

context of what we now know of these, especially from the study of the Qumran pesharim, the peculiar text-form of the conflated quotation in Acts 15.16–18 requires to be studied and understood as a product of skilled exegetical work. Such a study, pursued in this chapter, will show that the quotation is more precisely adapted to the issue under discussion at the Council in Acts 15 than has usually been recognized and also that it is more closely connected than has previously been noticed with the terms of the Apostolic Decree, to which, in James' speech, it leads. These conclusions will put the historical question in a new perspective, in which it can be seen to be probable that Luke has accurately, if rather summarily, preserved the exegetical basis on which the Jerusalem church, under James' leadership, was able to endorse Paul's Gentile mission, with the important proviso embodied in the Apostolic Decree.

THE QUOTATION IN ACTS 15.16–18

Acts 15.16–18	*Amos 9.11–12 LXX*	*Amos 9.11–12 MT*
Μετὰ ταῦτα ἀναστρέψω	'Εν τῇ ἡμέρᾳ ἐκείνῃ	בַּיּוֹם הַהוּא
καὶ ἀνοικοδομήσω	ἀναστήσω	
τὴν σκηνὴν Δαυειδ τὴν	τὴν σκηνὴν Δαυιδ τὴν	אָקִים אֶת־סֻכַּת דָּוִיד
πεπτωκυῖαν,	πεπτωκυῖαν,	הַנֹּפֶלֶת
	καὶ ἀνοικοδομήσω	
	τὰ πεπτωκότα αὐτῆς,	וְגָדַרְתִּי אֶת־פִּרְצֵיהֶן
καὶ τὰ κατεστραμμένα	καὶ τὰ κατεσκαμμένα	
αὐτῆς ἀνοικοδομήσω	αὐτης ἀναστήσω	וַהֲרִסֹתָיו אָקִים
καὶ ἀνορθώσω αὐτήν,	καὶ ἀνοικοδομήσω αὐτὴν	וּבְנִיתִיהָ
	καθὼς αἱ ἡμέραις τοῦ	כִּימֵי עוֹלָם:
	αἰῶος,	
(17) ὅπως ἂν ἐκζητήσωσιν	(12) ὅπως ἐκζητήσωσιν	12 לְמַעַן יִירְשׁוּ
οἱ κατάλοιποι τῶν	οἱ κατάλοιποι τῶν	
ἀνθρώπων τὸν κύριον,	ἀνθρώπων	אֶת־שְׁאֵרִית אֱדוֹם
καὶ πάντα τὰ ἔθνη	καὶ πάντα τὰ ἔθνη	וְכָל־הַגּוֹיִם
ἐφ' οὓς ἐπικέκληται	ἐφ' οὓς ἐπικέκληται	אֲשֶׁר־נִקְרָא שְׁמִי עֲלֵיהֶם
τὸ ὄνομά μου ἐπ' αὐτούς,	τὸ ὄνομά μου ἐπ' αὐτούς	נְאֻם־יְהוָה
λέγει κύριος	λέγει κύριος ὁ θεός	עֹשֶׂה וֹּאת
ποιῶν ταῦτα	ὁ ποιῶν ταῦτα.	
(18) γνωστὰ ἀπ' αἰῶνος.		

James' quotation is far from simply a quotation of the LXX

text of Amos 9.11–12 "with small variations."[8] It is a conflated quotation, with its text-form both selected and adapted to suit the interpretation, in the manner now familiar to us not only from the New Testament[9] but also from the Qumran pesharim. The opening words (μετὰ ταῦτα ἀναστρέψω) and the closing words (γνωστὰ ἀπ᾽ αἰῶνος), which do not come from Amos 9.11–12, frame the main text with allusions to other texts which have been interpreted in close relationship to it (Hos. 3.5; Jer. 12.15; Isa. 45.21). We shall return to these after studying the text of Amos 9.11–12. Here there is obvious dependence on the LXX, but also significant and evidently deliberate divergences.

In the description of the restoration of the "tent" of David, Acts 15.16 omits two whole clauses of the LXX (καὶ ἀνοικοδομήσω τὰ πεπτωκότα αὐτῆς and καθὼς αἱ ἡμέραις τοῦ αἰῶνος). It also replaces the two occurrences of ἀναστήσω in the LXX (rendering אקים) with ἀνοικοδομήσω and the one remaining occurrence of ἀνοικοδομήσω in the LXX (rendering ובניתיה) with ἀνορθώσω.[10] These substitutions are acceptable translations of the Hebrew verbs, though ἀναστήσω is a more literal translation of אקים than ἀνοικοδομήσω. But it should be noticed that they would not have been made had the exegete who produced this form of the text not wished it to be quite clear that the reference is to the restoration of a *building*. There is no possibility that, as has sometimes been suggested,[11] he understood Amos 9.11 as a prophecy of the resurrection of Christ, since the LXX's repeated ἀναστήσω, for which he substitutes ἀνοικοδομήσω, would have been admirably suited to such an interpretation. Nor would an interpretation of the text as referring to the restoration of the Davidic family to the throne (in the messianic rule of Jesus) easily account for our exegete's insistence that it is a building that is to be built.

[8] K. Lake and H. J. Cadbury, in F. J. Foakes Jackson and K. Lake (eds.), *The Beginnings of Christianity: Part I: The Acts of the Apostles*, vol. IV (London, 1933), p. 176.

[9] For Paul's quotations, see now C. D. Stanley, *Paul and the Language of Scripture* (SNTSMS 69; Cambridge, 1992).

[10] Variation between κατεστραμμένα and κατεσκαμμένα occurs in the manuscripts of both Acts 15:16 and Amos 9:11 LXX, so that it is virtually impossible to know whether the original text of Acts here differed from the LXX.

[11] E.g. E. Haenchen, *The Acts of the Apostles: A Commentary* (Oxford, 1971), p. 448.

Most likely the exegete understood the σκηνή Δαυειδ to be
the *Temple* of the messianic age. This would be a quite natural
understanding of the text of the LXX, which regularly uses
σκηνή to render both אהל and משכן with reference to the
tabernacle, and in Tobit 13.11 uses σκηνή of the Temple that
will be built again in Jerusalem in the eschatological age. If, as
we shall see is likely, our exegete consulted the Hebrew text, he
could also have found reason for understanding סכת דויד to be
the eschatological Temple. Most other occurrences of סכת in
the Hebrew Bible would give no help in the interpretation of
the phrase, but שׂך, which is a variant of the same word, occurs
in Lam. 2.6 with clear reference to the Temple, while the
obscure בסך in Ps. 42.5 was evidently understood by the LXX
translator as a reference to the Temple (LXX Ps. 41.5: ἐν τόπῳ
σκηνῆς). Moreover, a reader of Amos might well connect the
סכת דויד in 9.11 with סכות מלככם in 5.26, as the author of
CD 7.14–16 did. Though the LXX translator took the latter
phrase (or at least סכות מלך) in connection with the idolatry
to which the rest of 5.26 refers and translated it τὴν σκηνὴν τοῦ
Μολόχ, it could also be taken in connection with 5.25 as a
reference to the tabernacle.

It is noteworthy that the σκηνή of Amos 9.11/Acts 15.16 is
both associated with David *and* to be built by God. Jewish
writers of this period were accustomed to contrast the present
Temple, made by human hands, and the eschatological
Temple, which God himself will build.[12] Thus 4QFlor. 1.1–13,
which is a pesher of 2 Sam. 7.10–14, takes the "house" which
YHWH will build (2 Sam. 7.11b) to be the eschatological
Temple to which Exod. 15.17 ("the sanctuary of YHWH
which your hands have established") also refers, and pointedly
omits 2 Sam. 7.13a, which predicts that David's seed, the
Messiah, will "build a house for my name."[13] Such an inter-

---

[12] A similar contrast is between the earthly Temple, built by human hands, and God's
Temple in heaven, not built by hands: SibOr 4.8–11; Heb. 9.11, 24; ApPet 16.9; cf.
2 Enoch 22.2; Acts 7.48; 17.24.

[13] 4QFlor. 1.12 quotes part of Amos 9.11 ("And I will raise up the booth of David
which is fallen") in connection with 1 Sam. 7.12–14, but takes "the booth of
David" to mean "the branch [סוכה, found in later Hebrew for biblical שׁוכה,
'branch'] of David," identified with the צמח דויד (1.11), i.e. the Messiah of David.

pretation of Exod. 15.17 as referring to the eschatological Temple which God will build with his own hands is also found in the Mekhilta of R. Ishmael.[14] (For the expectation that God himself will build the eschatological Temple, see also 11QT 29.9–10; 1 Enoch 90.29; Jub. 1:15–17.) Although 4QFlor. evidently thinks it incompatible with the idea that the Messiah will build the Temple, such a view was not always taken. Sibylline Oracle 5.414–434 ascribes the building of the eschatological Temple both to the Messiah (422–423)[15] and to God (423–433). The Messiah presumably acts as God's agent. Even more relevantly for our purposes, Jesus' alleged prophecy of the destruction and rebuilding of the Temple is quoted in Mark 14.58 in the form: "I will destroy this Temple that is made with hands, and in three days I will build another not made with hands" (cf. Matt. 26.61; John 2.19). Here the term ἀχειροποίητος alludes to the Jewish tradition of interpretation of Exod. 15.17.[16] The eschatological Temple will be built miraculously, by divine action, but the building is at the same time associated with the Messiah, in accordance with 2 Sam. 7.13; Zech. 6.12–13. Thus the exegete whose work is embodied in Acts 15.16–18 may have understood the phrase σκηνή Δαυειδ to mean that God himself will build the eschatological Temple miraculously through the agency of the Davidic Messiah, though he may simply have taken it to refer to the Temple of the messianic age, which God will build when "David" rules God's people (cf. Ezek. 37.24–28).

We are now in a position to understand the omission of the two phrases καὶ ἀνοικοδομήσω τὰ πεπτωκότα αὐτῆς and καθὼς αἱ ἡμέραις τοῦ αἰῶνος from the LXX text of Amos 9.11

But it is therefore notable that 4QFlor. does not quote the rest of Amos 9.11 where reference to a building is unavoidable.

[14] Quoted in D. Juel, *Messiah and Temple: The Trial of Jesus in the Gospel of Mark*, SBLDS 31 (Missoula, 1977), p. 151.

[15] The figure described in lines 414–415 is the figure of Daniel 7.13 interpreted as the messianic ruler: see A. Chester, "The Sibyl and the Temple," in W. Horbury (ed.), *Templum Amicitiae*, FS E. Bammel, JSNTSS 48 (Sheffield, 1991), pp. 49–50. For the expectation that the Messiah will rebuild the Temple, see also Tg. Zech. 6.12; Isa. 53.5.

[16] Juel, *Messiah*, pp. 147–154, rejects this possibility because in Mark 14.58 it is the Messiah, not God, who builds the Temple "not made with hands."

in Acts 15.16.[17] The first could have been regarded as merely repetitive of the previous clause. But if our exegete was working with the Hebrew of Amos as well as the Greek, he had a stronger reason to omit these words. The Hebrew וגדרתי את־פרציהן ("and I will repair the breaches [in the walls]") suggests more obviously the walls of a city than those of a temple. The phrase καθὼς αἱ ἡμεραις του αἰῶνος will have been omitted because it conflicts with the common belief that the eschatological Temple will be vastly superior to the Temple of the present age (1 Enoch 90.29; SibOr 5.422–425; 2 Bar. 32.4; 4 Ezra 10.55).

The text of Amos 9.12 in Acts 15.17 is much closer to the LXX than that of the previous verse. Moreover, whereas in Amos 9.11 the LXX is a faithful translation of the MT, in 9.12 the LXX diverges notably from the MT. The words ἐκζητήσω-σιν οἱ κατάλοιποι τῶν ἀνθρώπων must presuppose a Hebrew text which had ידרשו ("they will seek")[18] for MT's יירשו ("they will possess") and אדם ("humanity") for MT's אדום ("Edom") (and presumably also lacked the accusative particle את). When Lake and Cadbury remark that the LXX here is "apparently based on a misreading of the original Hebrew," and conclude that, "It is incredible that a Jewish Christian could thus have used the LXX in defiance of the Hebrew,"[19] they entirely misunderstand the way in which Jewish exegesis of this period treated the biblical text, as the Dead Sea Scrolls in particular have now made clear to us. A Jewish Christian familiar both with the Hebrew and the LXX of this verse would not regard the latter as a misreading of the Hebrew. He may have known a Hebrew text like that translated by the LXX, but, even if not, would have recognized that the LXX represents, not a misreading, but either a variant text or a

---

[17] For omissions from the text as an exegetical device in the Qumran pesharim, see G. J. Brooke, *Exegesis at Qumran: 4QFlorilegium in its Jewish Context*, JSOTSS 29 (Sheffield, 1985), pp. 91–92.

[18] In LXX ἐκζητεῖν most often translates דרש.

[19] In Foakes Jackson and Lake, *Beginnings*, vol. IV, p. 176; cf. C. K. Barrett in D. A. Carson and H. G. M. Williamson (eds.), *It Is Written: Scripture Citing Scripture*, B. Lindars FS (Cambridge, 1988), p. 244: "James appears to quote the LXX where it differs from the Hebrew. Is it conceivable that he would do this?"

deliberate alternative reading of the text. Jewish exegetes were accustomed to choosing among variants the reading which suited their interpretation, or to exploiting more than one. But in a case such as ours, it is scarcely possible to distinguish a variant text which has arisen accidentally in the transmission of the text from one which results from the exegetical practice of deliberately reading the text differently by means of small changes (known as 'al tiqrē' in later rabbinic terminology).[20] The "misreading" of the Hebrew text presupposed by the LXX of Amos 9.12 is quite comparable with many examples of deliberate "alternative readings" ('al tiqrē') in the Qumran pesharim.[21] Thus there is not the slightest difficulty in supposing that a Jewish Christian exegete, familiar with the Hebrew text of the Bible but writing in Greek, should have welcomed the exegetical potential of the LXX text of Amos 9.12 as a legitimate way of reading the Hebrew text of that verse.

In addition to following the LXX text of the first clause of Amos 9.12, Acts 15.17 adds an interpretive gloss: τὸν κύριον.[22] The verb ἐκζητήσωσιν clearly requires an object, lacking in the

---

[20] For a striking example of 'al tiqrē' in LXX, see D. I. Brewer, *Techniques and Assumptions in Jewish Exegesis before 70 CE*, TSAJ 30 (Tübingen, 1992), p. 178. For 'al tiqrē' in the Targumim, see Brooke, *Exegesis*, pp. 29–36; for 'al tiqrē' in the Qumran literature, see Brooke, *Exegesis*, pp. 281, 284, 288–289, 306, 327; A. Chester in Carson and Williamson (eds.), *It Is Written*, pp. 143–144; G. J. Brooke, "The Biblical Texts in the Qumran Commentaries: Scribal Errors or Exegetical Variants?," in C. A. Evans and W. F. Stinespring (eds.), *Early Jewish and Christian Exegesis: Studies in Memory of William Hugh Brownlee* (Atlanta, 1987), pp. 95–97; Brewer, *Techniques*, pp. 197–198. Brooke, "The Biblical Texts," pp. 85–100, argues in detail that, whereas some variant readings in the Qumran pesharim represent already existing textual variants, many were deliberately created for exegetical reasons. (The rabbinic use of 'al tiqrē' does not alter the text as such, but amends it temporarily for exegetical purposes: Brewer, *Techniques*, p. 173.)

[21] See especially those for 1QpHab listed in A. Finkel, "The Pesher of Dreams and Scriptures," *RQ* 4 (1963–1964), 367–368; Brooke, *Exegesis*, pp. 288–289; Brooke, "The Biblical Texts," pp. 95–97.

[22] LXX MS A also has τὸν κύριον after ἀνθρώπον. It is not impossible that this text of the LXX underlies Acts 15.17, but more likely that it results from assimilation to Acts 15.17. For the tendency of the A-text to assimilate to the NT, see E. Richard, *Acts 6: 1–8:4: The Author's Method of Composition*, SBLDS 41 (Missoula,1978), p. 154; and on this text, cf. B. Lindars, *New Testament Apologetic* (London, 1961), p. 35,n. 3. But for the view that Luke attests the currency of the A-text in the first century, see Bovon, *Luke*, p. 99.

LXX, and τὸν κύριον is quite frequently in the LXX the object of ἐκζητεῖν (rendering דרש את־יהוה). But in the present context of words attributed to the Lord (λέγει Κύριος) and surrounded by verbs in the first person and the phrase ὄνομά μου, a gloss intended purely to assist the sense should have been με, not τὸν κύριον.[23] The explanation of the latter may well be that it is an example of the practice of expanding a text by allusion to another text with which it shares common words (gezērâ šāwâ) or themes.[24] In this case, the allusion is to Zech. 8.22 LXX: "And many peoples and many [MT: strong] nations (ἔθνη) shall come to seek the face of the Lord Almighty (ἐκζητῆσαι τὸ πρόσωπον Κυρίου παντοκράτορος, translating לבקש את־יהוה צבאות) in Jerusalem." The link between Amos 9.12 and Zech. 8.22 depends on the use of ἐκζητεῖν in the Greek texts of each (rendering respectively דרש and בקש), but our exegete may have been aware that ἐκζητῆσαι τὸν Κύριον would be a more literal translation of the Hebrew of Zech. 8.22. The phrase τὸ πρόσωπον Κυρίου in Zech. 8.22 LXX is itself an interpretation which makes it clear that it is the presence of YHWH in the Temple that the nations will seek (cf. Ps. 26[27]: 4,8). Zech. 8.22 is strongly linked thematically with Amos 9.11–12 as understood by our exegete: It predicts that, following the laying of the foundation for the rebuilding of the Temple (8.9) and YHWH's return (cf. Acts 15.16a) to dwell in Zion (8.3), the Gentiles will be drawn to seek the presence of YHWH in his Temple.

We are now in a position to consider the beginning of Acts 15.16, which substitutes Μετὰ ταῦτα ἀναστρέψω καί for the opening words of Amos 9.11 LXX: ἐν τῇ ἡμέρᾳ ἐκείνῃ.[25] At first

---

[23] Eusebius, *Dem. Evang.* 2.3 quotes the LXX text with the addition of με.

[24] Brewer, *Techniques*, pp. 180–181.

[25] These opening words of Amos 9.11 (MT ביום ההוא) must have been missing from the Hebrew text from which part of the verse is quoted in 4QFlor. 1.12 and CD 7.16: [CD הנופלת] הנופלת [CD דוד] דויד סוכח את והקימותי. Both of these quotations begin with והקימותי in place of MT אקים. Since this agrees with the placing of καί before ἀ9οικοδομήσω in Acts 15.16, J. de Waard, *A Comparative Study of the Old Testament Text in the Dead Sea Scrolls and in the New Testament*, STDJ 4 (Leiden, 1965), pp. 24–26, followed by Brooke, *Exegesis*, pp. 210–211, postulates a text tradition common to Acts, 4QFlor., and CD. But in Acts 15.16 the καί is

sight the change is puzzling, since Μετὰ ταῦτα presupposes preceding events which are not explained. By contrast, in Acts 2.17 the words μετὰ ταῦτα in Joel 2.28 LXX are replaced by ἐν ταῖς ἐσχάταις ἡμέραις. We may be justified in wondering whether the quotation of Amos 9.11–12 in Acts 15.16 has been extracted from a larger context, but in any case the opening words of Acts 15.16 must be intended to make it clear that the building of the eschatological Temple will take place after a situation in which God has turned away from Israel in judgment. However, the words are not improvised. They allude to other biblical prophecies of the building of the eschatological Temple and the conversion of the nations to the God of Israel.

The words μετὰ ταῦτα probably come from Hos. 3.5.[26] In the LXX Hos. 3.4–5a reads:

For the children of Israel shall dwell many days without king or ruler or sacrifice or altar or priesthood or Urim. And *after these things* the children of Israel shall *return*[27] and *shall seek the Lord* their God (μετὰ ταῦτα ἐπιστρέψουσιν οἱ υἱοὶ 'Ισραηλ καὶ ἐπιζητήσουσιν κύριον τὸν θεὸν αὐτῶν) and *David* their king.

The links with Acts 15.16–17 are both verbal (italicized words above) and thematic. Both passages associate the restoration of the Temple and seeking the Lord in it with the restoration of Davidic rule.

For the source of the Lord's promise to return (ἀναστρέψω) in Acts 15.16a, we must turn to two other passages. An allusion to Zech. 8.3 LXX ("I will return to Zion [ἐπιστρέψω ἐπὶ Σιων] and I will dwell in the midst of Jerusalem") is possible, in view of the probable allusion to Zech. 8.22 which we have detected in Acts 15.17. But a more probable source is Jer. 12.15. Following a passage which refers to God's abandonment of the

required by the preceding ἀναστρέψω, which, I shall argue below, derives from Jer 12.15. The association of Jer. 12.15 with Amos 9.11–12 depends on the interpretation of both as referring to the inclusion of the Gentile nations in the eschatological people of God. Such an interpretation would certainly not have been followed at Qumran. So, although והקימותי shows that in the text of Amos 9.11 used at Qumran some other words stood in place of MT's ביום ההוא, it is unlikely that they corresponded to Μετὰ ταῦτα ἀναστρέψων (Acts 15.16).

[26] Ezek. 20.39 LXX is less probable.   [27] Cf. Acts 15.19.

Temple (Jer. 12.7) and judgment of his people, Jer. 12.14–17 refers to Israel's pagan neighbors. In the LXX, verses 15–16 read:

And it shall be that, *after* I have cast them out, *I will return* (ἐπιστρέψω) and have mercy on them, and will cause them to dwell, each in his inheritance and each in his land. And it shall be that, if they will indeed learn the way of my people, to swear by my name, "The Lord lives," as they taught my people to swear by Baal, then also they *shall be built* (οἰκοδομηθήσονται) [*v.l.*: it shall be built: οἰκοδομηθήσεται] in the midst of my people.

Here the reference to building could easily have been understood as a reference to the eschatological Temple, especially if, as we shall argue, the Jewish Christian exegete who created the text in Acts 15.16–18 understood the eschatological Temple, not as a literal building, but as the eschatological people of God, composed of both Jews and Gentiles. In that case, Jer. 12.16 would be understood similarly: The Gentile nations are to be "built in the midst of my people," i.e. form part of the eschatological Temple.

In both Zech. 8.3 and Jer. 12.14, the LXX has ἐπιστρέψω (in both cases translating forms of שוב), whereas Acts 15.16 has ἀναστρέψω.[28] This may be due to a desire to relate this verb to the following verbs (ἀνοικοδομήσω, ἀνορθώσω), but it might indicate that at this point our exegete was not dependent on the LXX.[29]

Turning now to the end of the quotation (Acts 15.18), we note that the words ποιῶν ταῦτα, which occur in the LXX of Amos 5.12, are given a different sense by the addition of γνωστὰ ἀπ' αἰῶνος.[30] The resulting clause (ποιῶν ταῦτα γνωστὰ ἀπ' αἰῶνος, "making these things known from eternity") conflates Amos 5.12 with Isa. 45.21, where the Hebrew

---

[28] But the D-text of Acts has ἐπιστρέψω.

[29] Both ἐπιστρέφειν and ἀναστρέφειν are good translations of שוב, which both are used to translate in the LXX.

[30] The longer readings at Acts 15.16 probably result from the assumption that a sentence must end with ταῦτα, where the text of Amos 9.12 LXX ends, and so expand γνωστὰ ἀπ' αἰῶνος into a sentence. The defence of the longer reading by G. D. Kilpatrick, "Some Quotations in Acts," in J. Kremer (ed.), *Les Actes des Apôtres*, BETL 48 (Louvain, 1979), pp. 84–85, is not convincing.

מי השמיע זאת מקדם ("Who made this to be heard from ancient times?") is translated in the LXX: τίς ἀκουστὰ ἐποίησεν ταῦτα ἀπ' ἀρχῆς. There seems no reason for a deliberate change of ἀκουστὰ ἀπ' ἀπχῆς to γνωστὰ ἀπ' αἰῶνος (Acts 15.18), and so it seems likely that our exegete was using not the LXX but the Hebrew of Isa. 45.21.

The reason for the allusion to this verse is that, once again, its context (Isa. 45.20–23) predicts that the nations (verse 20: "the survivors of the nations," LXX: οἱ σῳζόμενοι ἀπὸ τῶν ἐθνῶν; verse 22: "all the ends of the earth") will draw near to God (verses 20, 21 נגש; verse 21 ἐγγίζειν), turn to God and be saved (verse 22). From the allusion to Isa. 45.23 in Phil. 2.10 (cf. Rom. 14.11; Justin, *Apol.* 1.52) we know that this was one of the many passages of Deutero-Isaiah which were important to early Christian exegetes.

Thus we can see that all variations of the text of Acts 15.16–18 from that of Amos 9.11–12 LXX belong to a consistent interpretation of the text with the help of related texts which refer to the building of the eschatological Temple (Hos. 3.4–5; Jer. 12.15–16) and the conversion of the nations (Jer. 12.15–16; Zech. 8.22; Isa. 45.20–23) in the messianic age. The modified and conflated text expresses the close connection between these two themes: In the messianic age, when Davidic rule is restored to Israel, God will build the eschatological Temple, as the place of his presence on earth, *so that* (ὅπως) all the Gentile nations may seek his presence there, as he has purposed and predicted throughout history. The conflation of several prophetic texts explains the introductory formula in Acts 15.15: "with this the words of the prophets agree, as it is written."

Two questions about the way this conflated quotation was understood by the exegete who created it remain. First, what is the Temple of the messianic age which God builds? In a Jewish Christian context in which Amos 9.11–12 is understood to predict the inclusion of Gentiles in the eschatological people of God, it is clear that the eschatological Temple must be understood as the Christian community. This interpretation of the eschatological Temple as the people of God, otherwise known

only at Qumran,[31] was very widespread in early Christianity
(1 Cor. 3.16–17; 2 Cor. 6.16; Eph. 2.20–22; Heb. 13.15–16; 1
Pet. 2.5; 4.17; Rev. 3.12; 11.1–2;[32] Did. 10.2; Barn. 4.11; 6.15;
16.1–10; Hermas, *Vis.* 3; *Sim.* 9; Ignatius, *Eph.* 9.1).[33] This in
itself suggests its early origin. But Paul's description of James,
Peter, and John as "those who are regarded as pillars" (Gal.
2.9) enables us to be sure that the early Jerusalem church
understood itself in this way, since it most probably means that
they were regarded as pillars in the eschatological Temple (cf.
Rev. 3.12).[34] Moreover, the letter of Jude, which in my view
provides good evidence of the kind of scriptural exegesis, comparable with that of the Qumran pesharim, which was pursued
in James' circle[35] and of which therefore Acts 15.16–18 could

[31] For the Temple as community at Qumran, see B. Gärtner, *The Temple and the Community in the Qumran Scrolls and the New Testament* (Cambridge, 1965), pp. 16–46; Juel, *Messiah*, pp. 159–168; H. Lichtenberger, "Atonement and Sacrifice in the Qumran Community," in W. S. Green (ed.), *Approaches to Ancient Judaism*, vol. II, Brown Judaic Studies 9 (Chico, 1980), pp. 159–171; Brooke, *Exegesis*, pp. 178–193.

[32] For the Temple image here, see R. Bauckham, *The Climax of Prophecy: Studies on the Book of Revelation* (Edinburgh, 1993), pp. 266–273.

[33] Other instances of the frequently used metaphor of "building" the Christian community are probably also evidence of the widespread currency of the image of the church as the eschatological Temple: see Matt. 16.18; Acts 9.31; 15.16; 20.32; Rom. 14.19; 15.2,20; 1 Cor. 8.1; 10.23; 14.3–5, 12, 17, 26; 2 Cor. 10.8; 12.19; 13.10; Gal. 2.18; Eph. 4.12, 16; Col. 2.7; 1 Thess. 5.11; Jude 20; Polycarp, *Phil.* 3.2; 12.2; OdesSol 22.12.

[34] C. K. Barrett, "Paul and the 'Pillar' Apostles," in J. N. Sevenster and W. C. van Unnik (eds.), *Studia Paulina*, FS J. de Zwaan (Haarlem, 1953), pp. 1–19. For an alternative interpretation, see R. Aus, "Three Pillars and Three Patriarchs: A Proposal Concerning Gal. 2.9," *ZNW* 70 (1979), 252–261 (comparing the Jewish tradition that Abraham, Isaac, and Jacob were the three pillars on whom the world was supported). But the idea of pillars in the eschatological Temple was current (1 Enoch 90.28–29; JosAsen 17.6; Hermas, *Vis.* 3.8.2) and coheres best with other early Christian imagery. On Rev. 3.12, see also R. H. Wilkinson, "The Στῦλος of Revelation 3:12 and Ancient Coronation Rites," *JBL* 107 (1988), 498–501.

Since the account of the eschatological Temple in 1 Enoch 90.28–29 emphasizes its pillars, this text may be the source of the image of the pillars in early Jewish Christianity. In that case, it is notable that 1 Enoch 90.33 portrays all the Gentile nations "gathered together in that house." Since the letter of Jude reveals how important 1 Enoch was in the messianic exegesis of circles close to James (see R. Bauckham, *Jude and the Relatives of Jesus in the Early Church* [Edinburgh, 1990], especially chap. 4), it is possible that 1 Enoch 90.28–36 was an important text in convincing James and his circle that Gentiles should be included in the church, in addition to Amos 9.11–12. If so, it would not be surprising that Acts omitted reference to this non-canonical text. (Cf. the use of 1 Enoch 91.13 in Barn. 16.6–10.)

[35] See Bauckham, *Jude and the Relatives*, especially chap. 4.

preserve another example, also uses the image of the church as Temple (verse 20).[36]

Acts 15.16–18 is not the only text which associates the inclusion of the Gentiles in the eschatological people of God with an interpretation of the eschatological Temple as the eschatological people of God. Eph. 2.11–22 and 1 Pet. 2.4–10 do the same, and although the association is not explicit in Paul it is surely implied, especially in 2 Cor. 6.16–18. It must have been a critically important association of ideas. The Temple was at the heart of Israel. It was where God's people had access to God's presence, whereas Gentiles, allowed only into the outer court of the Second Temple, were banned, on pain of death, from the sacred precincts themselves. A people of God defined by and centered on this Temple as the place of God's dwelling with them could not include Gentiles unless they became Jews. But numerous prophecies portrayed the Temple of the messianic age as a place where the Gentiles would come into God's presence (Ps. 96.7–8; Isa. 2.2–3; 25.6; 56.6–7; 66.23; Jer. 3.17; Mic. 4.1–2; Zech. 14.16; 1 Enoch 90.33).[37] If these were understood to refer to the Gentiles *as Gentiles*, rather than to Gentiles as proselytes,[38] then the early church's self-understanding as itself the eschatological Temple, the place of God's presence, could accommodate the inclusion of Gentiles in the church, without their becoming Jews by circumcision and full observance of the Mosaic Law. It is therefore entirely plausible that Amos 9.11–12, interpreted as a prophecy that God would build the eschatological Temple (the Christian community) so that Gentiles might seek his presence there, should have played a decisive role in the Jerusalem church's debate and decision about the status of Gentile Christians.

---

[36] For the temple image here, see R. Bauckham, *Jude, 2 Peter*, WBC 20 (Waco, 1983), pp. 112–113.

[37] On this theme in OT prophetic literature, see D. L. Christensen, "Nations," in D. N. Freedman (ed.), *The Anchor Bible Dictionary*, vol. IV (New York, 1992), pp. 1044–1047.

[38] T. L. Donaldson, "Proselytes or 'Righteous Gentiles'? The Status of Gentiles in Eschatological Pilgrimage Patterns of Thought," *JSP* 7 (1990), 3–27, argues that the predominant Jewish eschatological expectation was that in the endtimes the Gentiles would be converted to the God of Israel *as Gentiles*, rather than by having

However, the issue which divided the Jerusalem church at the time of the Council of Acts 15 was evidently not whether Gentiles could join the messianically renewed Israel, but whether they could do so without becoming Jews. Few of the prophecies of the Gentiles coming to worship in the eschatological Temple could have been used to decide that issue. To understand how Amos 9.11–12 could be so used we must turn to the second remaining issue of interpretation, which concerns the phrase: πάντα τὰ ἔθνη ἐφ' οὓς ἐπικέκληται τὸ ὄνομά μου ἐπ' αὐτούς ("all the nations over whom my name has been invoked"). Discussion of the quotation in Acts 15.16–18 has rarely appreciated the significance of this phrase.

The expression ἐφ' οὓς ἐπικέκληται τὸ ὄνομά μου επ' αὐτούς is a literal rendering of the Hebrew idiom אֲשֶׁר־נִקְרָא שְׁמִי עֲלֵיהֶם (Amos 9.12). In its relatively frequent use in the OT the idiom expresses ownership, and is used especially of YHWH's ownership of the ark, the Temple, the city of Jerusalem, and the people of Israel. Israel is the people "over whom the name of YHWH has been invoked" (Deut. 28.10; 2 Chron. 7.14; Jer. 14.9; Dan. 9.19; cf Isa. 43.7), whereas the Gentiles are "those over whom your name has not been invoked" (Isa. 63.19).[39] As an expression of God's election of Israel as his own people, the phrase is equivalent to the covenant term סְגֻלָּה which denotes Israel as God's "special possession" (Exod. 19.5; Deut. 7.6; 14.2; 26.18; Ps. 135.4; Mal. 3.17). In post-biblical Jewish literature it seems to have become more common than the latter as an expression of Israel's covenant status (Sir. 36.17; 2 Macc. 8.15; Bar. 2.15; PsSol 9.9; LAB 28.4; 49.7; 4 Ezra 4.15; 10.22; cf. 2 Bar. 21.21).[40] Its use in Amos 9.12 with reference to "all the nations" is very striking, even in the MT, where its original meaning no doubt referred to the

---

to become proselytes. But it is not at all clear that the evidence he examines really supports this conclusion.

[39] In all these texts the LXX renders the Hebrew idiom literally, as in Amos 9.12.

[40] In view of the connection with the eschatological Temple in the interpretation of Amos 9.11–12 in Acts 15.16–18, it is remarkable how often reference to Israel as the people "over whom the name of YHWH has been invoked" is connected explicitly (2 Chron. 7.14; Isa. 63.19 [cf. 18]; Dan 9.19 [cf. 17]; Sir. 36.17 [cf. 18–19]; 4 Ezra 10.22) or implicitly (Jer. 14.9) with the Temple.

subjection of Israel's neighbors to Davidic rule. Even the MT could easily have been understood by a Jewish Christian as predicting the extension of Israel's covenant status and privileges to the Gentile nations. The LXX merely makes this implication clearer.

The significance of Amos 9.12, especially in the LXX, is very close to Zech. 2.11 (Heb. 2.15): "Many nations shall join themselves [LXX: καταφεύξονται, "flee for refuge"] to YHWH on that day, and shall be my [LXX: his] people." But whereas this verse might more readily be understood to mean that the Gentiles will join the people of God as proselytes, Amos 9.12 says that the nations *qua* Gentile nations belong to YHWH. It is not implied that they become Jews, but that precisely as "all the nations" they are included in the covenant relationship. It is doubtful whether any other OT text could have been used to make this point so clearly. By not paying sufficient attention to these words of the text, commentators have consistently missed the very precise relevance of Amos 9.12 to the debate at the Council of Jerusalem.[41]

The decisiveness of Amos 9.12 for the issue under discussion in Acts 15 may have been even greater if the OT expression ἐπικαλεῖται τὸ ὄνομα κυρίου ἐπί τινα was already in use with reference to Christian baptism. In Jas. 2.7, the rich oppressors of Christians are said to "blaspheme the excellent name that was invoked over you" (τὸ καλὸν ὄνομα τὸ ἐπικληθὲν ἐφ' ὑμᾶς). Apart from Acts 15.17, this is the only occurrence of the expression in the NT. Since the letter of James is probably addressed to Jewish Christians (1.1), it is unlikely that the expression here is derived from Amos 9.12, and there is no other OT occurrence of the expression that is likely to be a specific source. Rather, this is an instance of the application of OT terminology for Israel as God's covenant people to the Christian community as the renewed Israel of the messianic era (cf. 1.1). Most likely the invoking of the name over Christians was understood as a reference to baptism in the name of Jesus, as it

---

[41] Cf., e.g., Lüdemann, *Early Christianity*, p. 168: "[The quotation] does not wholly fit the context of the question whether Gentile Christians are to observe the law of Moses."

certainly is later in Hermas, *Sim.* 8.6.4 (which refers back to
Sim. 8.1.1, where the expression is different, but probably, like
Sim. 9.14.3, echoes Isa. 43.7), the only occurrence of the
expression in early Christian literature outside the NT.[42] In
that case we may compare the use of the expression ἐπικαλεῖν
τὸ ὄνομα κυρίου, whose Christian usage derived especially
from Joel 2.32 (Heb. 3.5; Acts 2.21; Rom. 10.13) and was used
with reference to baptism (Acts 22.16; cf. 2.21; Rom. 10.13) as
well as more generally (Acts 9.14, 21; 1 Cor. 1.2). This is a
quite different expression from the one we are considering and
should certainly not be confused with it,[43] but in both cases an
OT phrase referring to the name of YHWH is interpreted as a
reference to the name of the Lord Jesus invoked in Christian
baptism.

If Jas. 2.7 is evidence that, in the early Jerusalem church, the
phrase ἐπικαλεῖται τὸ ὄνομα κυρίου ἐπί τινα was already used
for Christian baptism into the eschatologically renewed people
of God, independently of Amos 9.12 and the question of the
admission of Gentiles to the church, then the argument would
be all the more cogent that its use in Amos 9.12 indicates the
incorporation of the Gentiles into the eschatological people of
God with no requirements for admission other than baptism in
the name of the Lord Jesus.

THE INTRODUCTION IN ACTS 15.14B

There is no doubt that the final clause of verse 14 (λαβεῖν ἐξ
ἐθνῶν λαὸν τῷ ὀνόματι αὐτοῦ) is intended to connect Peter's

---

[42] By "early Christian literature," I mean the literature covered by W. Bauer, W. F.
Arndt, and F. W. Gingrich, *A Greek–English Lexicon of the New Testament and Other
Early Christian Literature*, 2nd ed., ed. F. W. Danker (Chicago, 1979); a list is on
p. xxix. See also 1 Clem. 64.1 (πάσῃ ψυχῇ ἐπικεκλημένη τὸ μεγαλοπρεπὲς καὶ ἅγιον
ὄνομα αὐτου), where the perfect passive ἐπικεκλημένη, the resemblance to Isa. 45.7,
and the immediately preceding phrase εἰς λαὸν περιούσιον (cf. Exod. 19.5 etc.) all
suggest that the words are an echo of Isa. 45.7 and mean: "to every soul that has
been called by his glorious and holy name," rather than: "to every soul that has
called upon his glorious and holy name." In that case, as in Hermas, *Sim.* 8.1.1;
9.14.3, a simpler Greek expression is being used as equivalent to the one we are considering (see also, for the description of the name in 1 Clem. 64.1, 2 Macc. 8.15).

[43] As it is, e.g., by M. Wilcox, *The Semitisms of Acts* (Oxford, 1965), p. 77; Richard, *Acts
6:1–8:4*, p. 276.

account of the conversion of the first Gentile Christians with the quotation that follows and in doing so to provide an anticipatory paraphrase of the main point of the quotation. From this point of view it confirms our conclusion that the key words of the quotation are πάντα τὰ ἔθνη ἐφ᾽ οὓς ἐπικέκληται τὸ ὄνομά μου ἐπ᾽ αὐτούς. However, it is also possible that, as frequently in the Qumran pesharim, these words of interpretation of the quotation themselves echo other passages of Scripture. Most plausible is an allusion to those passages of the Torah (Exod. 19.5; 23.22 [LXX]; Deut. 7.6; 14.2; 26.18–19) which refer to Israel as God's special possession (סגלה, λαὸς περιούσιος), whom he chose from among the nations to be a people for himself (for example Deut. 14.2 LXX: ἐξελέξατο . . . γενέσθαι σε λαὸν αὐτῷ περιούσιον ἀπὸ πάντων τῶν ἐθνῶν).[44] This is more probable in that Rev. 5.9–10 uses the language of Exod. 19.5–6 to refer, not to Israel as one people selected from all the peoples, but to the church as composed of members drawn from all the nations.[45] If Acts 15.14b alludes to these pentateuchal statements about the covenant people, then it substitutes λαὸν τῷ ὀνόματι αὐτοῦ for λαὸν αὐτῷ περιούσιον,[46] as an equivalent phrase which points forward to the key phrase from Amos which appears in the quotation in 15.17. This is probably sufficient explanation of the introduction of a reference to God's name in 15.14b.[47] But it is possible that λαὸν τῷ ὀνόματι αὐτοῦ already contains an allusion to the idea of the

---

[44] For this allusion, see J. Dupont, "ΛΑΟΣ 'ΕΞ 'ΕΘΝΩΝ (Acts xv. 14)," *NTS* 3 (1956–1957), 47–50, and the subsequent discussion by P. Winter, "Acta 15,14," *EvTh* 17 (1957), 400–405; N. A. Dahl, "A People for his Name," *NTS* 4 (1957–1958), 319–327; J. Dupont, "Un peuple d'entre les nations (Actes 15,14)," *NTS* 31 (1985), 321–335.

[45] Bauckham, *Climax*, p. 327.

[46] This phrase (in various Greek translations) is used of the Christian church, including Gentiles, in Eph. 1.14; Titus 2.14; 1 Pet. 2.9.

[47] Dahl, "A People," pp. 320–327, explains λαὸν τῷ ὀνόματι αὐτοῦ by reference to the Targums, in which "a people for my/his/YHWH's name" translates "a people for me/him/YHWH" (e.g. Frg. Tg. Exod. 6.7; 19.5; 26.18–19; Tg. Ps.-Jon. Lev. 26.12). But this is an instance of the frequent use of "the name of the Lord" as a substitute for "the Lord" in the Targums, whereas in Acts 15.14 λαὸν τῷ ὀνόματι αὐτοῦ is a substitute not just for λαὸν αὐτῷ but for λαὸν αὐτῷ περιούσιον (לו לעם סגלה). See also Richard, "The Divine Purpose," pp. 279–280, n. 33; Dupont, "Un peuple," p. 322.

eschatological Temple as the eschatological people of God, which, as we have seen, is presupposed in the use of Amos 9.11 in Acts 15.16. While the phrase λαὸν τῷ ὀνόματι αὐτοῦ never appears in the OT, the phrase οἶκος τῷ ὀνόματι αὐτοῦ is frequent, with reference to the Temple, and in particular occurs in 2 Sam. 7.13, which, messianically interpreted, could be understood as a reference to the eschatological Temple (the σκηνὴν Δαυειδ of Amos 9.11).

THE RELATIONSHIP TO THE APOSTOLIC DECREE

According to Acts 15.19–20, the scriptural quotation in verses 16–18 is the basis on which James proposes that the Gentile Christians should not be required to keep the Law of Moses as a whole, but should observe just four prohibitions.[48] These are the terms of the Apostolic Decree (15.28–29). What is not apparent in the text of Acts is the reason for imposing the four prohibitions. While the quotation in 15.16–18 provides the scriptural basis for not imposing the Law as a whole on Gentile Christians, it does not obviously provide a basis for the specific provisions of the Apostolic Decree. On the other hand, it has been widely recognized that the terms of the Apostolic Decree are based on Leviticus 17–18[49] and therefore have an exegetical basis which is not explained in Acts. This recognition will provide us with a starting-point for uncovering the connection, underlying the text of Acts, between Acts 15.16–18 and the terms of the Decree.

In Leviticus 17–18 MT there are five occurrences of the full phrase "the alien who sojourns in your/their midst" (Lev. 17.10, 12, 13; 18.26: הגר הגר בתוכם/בתוככם; Lev. 17.8: הגר אשר־יגור בתוכם; the LXX adds a sixth in Lev. 17.3). Two of these (17.10, 12) repeat the same prohibition. The four

---

[48] The D-text here is widely, and rightly, regarded as a secondary revision.

[49] Haenchen, *Acts*, p. 469; J. T. Townsend, "The Date of Luke–Acts," in C. H. Talbert (ed.), *Luke–Acts: New Perspectives from the Society of Biblical Literature Seminar* (New York, 1984), p. 50; P. F. Esler, *Community and Gospel in Luke–Acts*, SNTSMS 57 (Cambridge, 1987), p. 99; J. T. Sanders, *The Jews in Luke–Acts* (London, 1987), p. 115.

things that are thus prohibited to "the alien who sojourns in your midst" correspond to the four prohibitions of the Apostolic Decree in the same order (Acts 15.29):[50] (1) "Things sacrificed to idols" (εἰδωλοθύτων) are prohibited in Lev. 17.8–9, since these verses concern not only burnt offerings but also sacrifices whose meat could be eaten by the worshipers, and since it is assumed (cf. verse 7) that sacrifices not brought to the tabernacle are not offered to YHWH but to idols.[51] (2) "Blood" is prohibited in Lev. 17.10,12. (3) "Things strangled" (πνικτῶν) are prohibited in Lev. 17.13. The difficulty with this term in the Apostolic Decree has arisen simply because Lev. 17.13 is a positive prescription: that animals killed for eating must be slaughtered in such a way that their blood drains out. Abstention from πνικτά is the negative corollary, for an animal killed in such a way that the blood remains in it is "choked."[52] It is significant that πνικτῶν in the Apostolic Decree refers to Lev. 17.13, not, as sometimes alleged, to Lev. 17.15,[53] which refers to the "alien" (גר) but does not use the full phrase: "the alien who sojourns in your midst." (4) "Sexual immorality" (πορνείας) refers to Lev. 18.26, where all the forms of sexual relations specified in Lev. 18.6–23 (relations within the prohibited degrees, intercourse with a menstruating woman, adultery, homosexual intercourse, bestiality) are prohibited to the

---

[50] The order is different in Acts 15.20.

[51] The objection of S. G. Wilson, *Luke and the Law*, SNTSMS 50 (Cambridge, 1983), p. 87, that "the specific issue of eating εἰδωλόθυτα, while not unrelated to Leviticus 17, scarcely catches the flavour of the passage" misses the point that the Apostolic Decree, like all Jewish interpretation of the Torah, is concerned not to read the Law like a modern historical critic but to apply it to contemporary circumstances.

[52] Philo, *Spec. Leg.* 4.122: meat from which the blood has not been drained is meat killed by "strangling and choking" (ἄγχοντες καὶ ἀποπνίγοντες); and cf. JosAs 8.5; 21.14; m. Hull. 1.2. Wilson, *Luke*, pp. 88–92, finds quite unnecessary difficulty with πνικτῶν in relation to Lev. 17, because he entirely misses the relevance of Lev. 17.13. In fact, having cited Haenchen, who correctly derives the two prohibitions against blood and things strangled from Lev. 17:10–14, Wilson then quotes, as the terms used in Lev. 17.13–14, the terms which are actually used in Lev. 17.15 (*Luke*, p. 88). See also Sanders, *The Jews*, p. 115, for criticism of Wilson; and E. P. Sanders, *Judaism: Practice and Belief 63 BCE–66 CE* (London, 1992), pp. 216, 520, n. 11.

[53] This is confirmed by Clem. Hom. 7.8; 8.19, which (in an expansion of the prohibitions of the Apostolic Decree) add to "things strangled" the two categories of meat prohibited in Lev. 17.15.

"alien who sojourns in your midst." The general term πορνεία covers all these.[54]

Thus the four prohibitions in the Apostolic Decree constitute a precise reference to the laws in Leviticus 17–18 which are said to be binding on "the alien who sojourns in your midst." But it remains to be seen why these laws should have been selected as uniquely binding on Gentile Christians. The prohibitions in the Apostolic Decree should not be related to the later rabbinic concept of the seven Noahic commandments which are binding on all descendants of Noah (including the gēr tôšāv, the resident alien), since although these overlap with the prohibitions in the Apostolic Decree, they are not based specifically on Leviticus 17–18.[55] There is, in fact, no known Jewish parallel to the selection of precisely these four commandments from the Law of Moses as those which are binding on Gentiles or a category of Gentiles.[56] Moreover, there are other Mosaic laws, most notably the Sabbath commandment (Exod. 20.10; Deut. 5.14), which are specifically said to apply to resident aliens,[57] so that even were the equation of Gentile Christians with resident aliens explicable, it would still be necessary to explain the selection of the four laws in Leviticus 17–18.[58] Finally, the pragmatic desire to facilitate table fellowship between Jewish and Gentile Christians cannot itself

---

[54] It is often supposed that the connection with Lev. 18.26 requires πορνεία in the Apostolic Decree to mean marriage within the prohibited degrees (e.g. R. P. Martin, *New Testament Foundations*, vol. II [Exeter, 1987], p. 113; J. A. Fitzmyer, *To Advance the Gospel* [New York, 1981], p. 88), but this is not the case. Lev. 18.26 refers to all the "abominations" of 18.6–23, which (with the exception of verse 21) are all sexual, but by no means all forms of incest. Thus πορνεία in the Apostolic Decree can be allowed its ordinary general meaning, rather than the implausible specialized meaning of relations within the prohibited degrees (cf. G. Zuntz, *Opuscula Selecta* [Manchester, 1972], p. 228; the evidence discussed by Fitzmyer, *To Advance*, pp. 95–97 does not really show that πορνεία without further explanation could be understood to mean marriage within the prohibited degrees).

[55] For the contrast, see Townsend, "The Date," p. 50.

[56] T. Callan, "The Background of the Apostolic Decree (Acts 15.20, 29; 21.25)," *CBQ* 55 (1993), 284–297, who would like to see some such background for the Decree, shows by his review of the relevant Jewish sources that no parallel exists in the evidence.

[57] See the list ibid., p. 286.

[58] Wilson, *Luke*, p. 86, makes this a reason for denying the dependence of the Apostolic Decree on Leviticus 17–18.

explain the selection of precisely these four laws.[59] The reason
for the selection must be sought in specifically Jewish Christian
exegesis of Scripture.

Because the connection between the scriptural quotation in
Acts 15.16–18 and the Apostolic Decree has usually been
thought to be either very general or completely artificial, the
exegetical basis of the Apostolic Decree has been overlooked.
Amos 9.12 establishes that Gentiles may belong to the eschatological people of God precisely as Gentiles, without becoming
Jews. While this exempts them from the Law of Moses as a
whole, it does not necessarily mean that none of the specifically
Mosaic laws applies to them. Guidance as to which Mosaic
laws apply to Gentile Christians is to be found in two other
prophecies about the conversion of the Gentiles. One of the
prophecies about the Gentiles who join the eschatological
people of God which has contributed to the conflated quotation in Acts 15.16–18 says that they are to be "in the midst of
my people" (Jer. 12.16: LXX ἐν μέσῳ τοῦ λαοῦ μου, rendering
בְּתוֹךְ אַמִּי). Similar phraseology occurs in another prophecy
which is not one of those conflated in Acts 15.16–18 but is so
closely related to them as to be an obvious resource for any
Jewish Christian exegete pursuing this theme: Zech. 2.11
(Heb. 2.15). This verse follows YHWH's promise to Zion to
"come and dwell in your midst" (2.10/14), a reference to the
eschatological Temple comparable with Amos 9.11 (Acts
15.16). Zech. 2.11 then parallels Amos 9.12 (Acts 15.17).
There are differences between the LXX and MT of Zech.
2.11a/15a:

MT: Many nations shall join themselves (וְנִלְווּ) to YHWH in that
day, and shall be my people; and I will dwell in your midst (וְשָׁכַנְתִּי
בְתוֹכֵךְ).
LXX: Many nations shall flee for refuge (καταφεύξονται)[60] to the
Lord in that day, and shall be his people, and they shall dwell in your
midst (κατασκηνώσουσιν ἐν μέσῳ σου).

---

[59] Wilson, *Luke*, pp. 74–75; Sanders, *The Jews*, p. 120.
[60] καταφεύγειν translates the niphal of לוה also in LXX Jer. 27.5 (= Heb. 50.5); cf.
also LXX Isa. 54.15; and JosAsen 15.7 (alluding to Zech. 2.11/15).

The LXX presupposes a text which had (or deliberately reads the text as) וְשָׁבְנוּ instead of וְשָׁבְנְתִּי.[61] This form of the text provides a clue to the legal status of the converted Gentiles. As those who dwell "in the midst" (בְּתוֹךְ) of Israel, these Gentiles are specifically mentioned in the Torah.

The point is not that Jer. 12.16 and Zech. 2.11/15 give these Gentiles the status of the resident aliens to whom the Torah refers by means of a variety of expressions. It is rather that, using the principle of gezērâ šāwâ,[62] these Gentiles are those to whom the Torah refers in a *verbally corresponding way*. As we have noticed, the laws in Leviticus 17–18 on which the Apostolic Decree is based all apply to "the alien who sojourns *in your/their midst*" (בְּתוֹכְכֶם/בְּתוֹכָם). The use of בְּתוֹךְ, as in Jer. 12.16 and Zech. 2.11/15, is the principle of selection, and so other laws, such as the Sabbath commandment (Exod. 20.10; Deut. 5.14) or the laws of Lev. 24.16–22, which are said to be binding on resident aliens but do not describe them with a phrase including בְּתוֹךְ, are not considered relevant to Gentile Christians.[63] Besides the laws in Leviticus 17–18, the only laws in the Torah which the alien resident "in the midst" (בְּתוֹךְ) of Israel is obliged to obey are Lev. 16.29; Num. 15.14–16, 29; 19.10, but all these refer specifically to the Temple cult. We can well imagine that Jewish Christian exegetes who understood the eschatological Temple to which Gentile Christians are admitted to be the Christian community would not apply these laws literally to Gentile converts. Thus exegesis of Jer. 12.16 and Zech. 2.11/15 can explain, as no other attempted explanation of the Apostolic Decree can, why the Apostolic Decree contains precisely the four prohibitions it does contain.

It should be noted that this exegesis, with its precise use of

---

[61] For similar textual variants involving a change of person, probably the result of deliberate exegetical alteration of the text, in the Qumran pesharim, see Brooke, "The Biblical Texts," pp. 8–9.

[62] This is the use of gezērâ šāwâ which Brewer, *Techniques*, p. 18, distinguishes as Gezerah Shavah II. In this case, as often in the rabbis, it is used to clarify a legal issue.

[63] As we have already noticed, even within Leviticus 17–18, the law of Lev. 17.15 is not echoed in the Apostolic Decree, since it applies to the "sojourner" (בְּגֵר), not to "the alien who sojourns *in your midst*."

gezērâ šāwâ, depends on the Hebrew text of both Zechariah and
the Torah. There is no verbal correspondence in the LXX
between the texts of Jer. 12.16 and Zech. 2.11/15, on the one
hand, and those of Lev. 17.8, 10,12, 13; 18.26, on the other; nor
does the LXX distinguish verbally between the resident alien
of those verses and the resident alien in the Sabbath commandment (Exod. 20.10; Deut. 5.14). But in any case, it could not be
the LXX text that provided the basis for the Apostolic Decree.
The LXX calls the resident alien in those chapters, as elsewhere in the Torah, "the proselyte (προσήλυτος) who sojourns
among you." But the point of the Apostolic Decree is precisely
that Gentile Christians are not required to become proselytes,
who would be obliged to keep the whole Law.[64] Only by
disregarding the LXX's interpretation could the laws of Leviticus 17–18 be understood to apply to Gentile Christians not
otherwise obliged to keep the Law.

Our conclusion that the prohibitions in the Apostolic Decree
are based not simply on Leviticus 17–18, but on the exegetical
link between Jer. 12.16; Zech. 2.11/15 and Leviticus 17–18, is
of considerable significance. Not only does it explain the
Decree itself more satisfactorily than other explanations. It also
shows that a logical sequence of thought connects the use of the
conflated quotation in Acts 15.16–18 with the terms of the
Apostolic Decree. Acts 15.16–18 establishes that Gentiles do
not have to become Jews in order to belong to the eschatological people of God, and so authorizes James' decision
announced in Acts 15.19. The proviso in Acts 15.20 is not an
arbitrary qualification of this decision, but itself follows, with
exegetical logic, from Acts 15.16–18. If Gentile Christians are
the Gentiles to whom the prophecies conflated in Acts
15.16–18 refer, then they are also the Gentiles of Jer. 12.16;
Zech. 2.11/15, and therefore the part of the Law of Moses
which applies to them is Leviticus 17–18. Just as the conversion
of the Gentiles has been made known by God in prophecy from
long ago (Acts 15.17b-18 = Isa. 45.21), so the laws which apply

[64] Wilson, *Luke*, p. 86, sees this as a reason why the Apostolic Decree cannot be based
on Leviticus 17–18. That it could be based on the Hebrew text of these chapters
seems not to occur to him.

to them are not novel inventions, but have been read out in the synagogues in every city from ancient times (Acts 15.21).[65] Only as a summary from which the exegetical argument has been omitted does the sequence of thought in Acts 15.19–21 make sense, but as such a summary – and given the presuppositions of ancient Jewish exegesis – it makes excellent sense.

THE SOURCE OF JAMES' SPEECH

The preceding discussion has established:

(1) The scriptural quotation in Acts 15.16–18 embodies skilled exegetical work, adapting the text, conflating passages which are verbally and thematically related, and probably referring to the Hebrew Bible as well as using the LXX.

(2) The quotation is precisely designed to be relevant to the debate at the Jerusalem Council, in that it shows that Gentile Christians do not have to become Jews in order to join the eschatological people of God and to have access to God in the Temple of the messianic age. Its unmistakable reference to Jesus the Davidic Messiah (Acts 15.16 = Amos 9.11) makes its relevance to the Christian community undeniable, while its use of terminology designating the covenant people of God with reference to the Gentile nations precisely as Gentiles makes it uniquely decisive for the issue in debate.

(3) Between the quotation in Acts 15.16–18 and James' decision announced in 15.19–20, i.e. the terms of the Apostolic Decree, there is a very close connection, which strongly suggests that they belong originally together, although the connection is by means of exegetical argument not explicit in the text of Acts.

(4) This exegetical argument, which alone accounts satisfactorily for the terms of the Apostolic Decree, presupposes the Hebrew text of the Old Testament, not the LXX.

---

[65] The phrase ἐκ γενεῶν ἀρχαίων (Acts 15.21) may well be an allusion to Isa. 41.4 (LXX: ἀπὸ γενεῶν ἀρχῆς), whose context (Isa. 41.1–5) has obvious affinities with Isa. 45.20–25, to which Acts 15.18 alludes. It also forms, at the end of James' speech, an *inclusio* with ἀφ' ἡμερῶν ἀρχαίων at the beginning of Peter's speech (15.7). For an argument which finds an allusion to Deutero-Isaianic prophecy in Acts 15.7, see Zuntz, *Opuscula*, pp. 229–233.

(5) Once the exegetical basis of the Apostolic Decree is recognized, it can be seen to represent a resolution of the problem of Gentile Christians and the Law which reflects and meets precisely the concerns of Jewish Christians who wish to uphold the authority of the Law of Moses. Prophecies of the conversion of the Gentiles to God in the messianic age show that, while these Gentiles are not obliged to become Jews and to observe the Law as a whole, the Law itself envisages them and legislates for them. To require of Gentile Christians obedience only to the four commandments which the Law itself imposes on them is not to set aside the authority of the Law but to uphold it:[66] "The law of Moses continues to be valid for Jews as Jews and for Gentiles as Gentiles."[67]

These conclusions do not necessarily warrant the further conclusion that Luke's account of James' speech is an accurate historical report. The speech could be an example of Luke's skill in composing speeches specifically appropriate to the speaker and the occasion, and the skilled exegetical work both behind the text and explicit in the text could be Luke's own.[68] Moreover, there are two reasons for thinking that James' speech as it stands is a Lucan composition:

(1) The whole account of the speeches at the Council (Acts 15.7–21) is a carefully composed unit. The two speeches of Peter and James present two complementary forms of argument: from experience of God's action and from Scripture.

---

[66] It is often argued that the provisions of the Apostolic Decree were intended to make possible table fellowship between Christian Jews and Christian Gentiles (e.g. Esler, *Community*, pp. 98–99; N. Taylor, *Paul, Antioch and Jerusalem*, JSNTSS 66 [Sheffield, 1992], pp. 140–142). There are serious problems with this view as usually presented (Sanders, *The Jews*, p. 120). In the light of Gal. 2.12, it is likely that the Decree was expected to solve the problem of table fellowship. However, it did so not by means of an *ad hoc* and rather arbitrary compromise, but by insisting that Gentile Christians keep those laws which the Torah obliges them to keep. These are conditions for table fellowship, not between Jews and Gentiles in general, but between Jews and Gentiles in the new situation of the eschatological people of God which includes both.

[67] Richard, "The Divine Purpose," p. 273.

[68] The scriptural quotations and exegesis in the speeches of Acts are often attributed to Luke's sources: e.g. Bovon, *Luke*, p. 101: "We are sure that Luke depended on Hellenistic Jewish exegetical traditions" (cf. pp. 97–98). But Richard, *Acts 6:1–8:4*, pp. 248–267, holds Luke entirely responsible for Stephen's speech, with its elaborate exegesis.

They frame the report of Barnabas and Paul (15.12). They are linked by James' opening reference to Peter's (15.14a) and by the *inclusio* between the beginning of Peter's speech (15.7: ἀφ' ἡμερῶν ἀρχαίων) and the end of James' speech (15.21: ἐκ γενεῶν ἀρχαίων).

(2) Acts 15.19–20 is a paraphrase of the words of the Decree itself (15.28–29). That the latter are more original and the former Luke's paraphrase is strongly suggested by the fact that the order of the four prohibitions in 15.29 corresponds exactly to the order of Leviticus 17–18, whereas in 15.20 it does not.[69]

However, if James' speech is Luke's composition, it by no means follows that he did not use a source in composing it. The freedom of ancient historians in composing speeches did not mean that they did not attempt to represent as well as possible, using whatever sources were available to them, the substance of what would have been said on a given occasion.[70] Luke may not have had precisely a report of what James said at the Council among his sources, but in composing the speech he could have used good evidence of the arguments deployed by the Jerusalem church in propounding the Apostolic Decree. The following points, not all of equal weight, add up to a good case for supposing that James' speech is not Luke's free invention:

(1) The opening words of the quotation (Acts 15.16: μετὰ ταῦτα) are not from Amos 9.11 but result from a deliberate conflation with Hos. 3.5, which supplies only these two words of the quotation. If the conflated quotation was composed by Luke for its context in Acts 15.13–21, it is very difficult to understand why it should have been deliberately made to begin in this way[71] (contrast Acts 2.17, where the opening

---

[69] For a different argument to the effect that 15.29 preserves the oldest form of the Decree, see A. J. M. Wedderburn, "The 'Apostolic Decree': Tradition and Redaction," *NovT* 35 (1993), 372–378.

[70] C. J. Hemer, *The Book of Acts in the Setting of Hellenistic History*, WUNT 49 (Tübingen, 1989), pp. 75–79, 421.

[71] Richard, who thinks Luke composed the quotation, can only say that μετὰ ταῦτα is "a favourite expression of this author" ("The Divine Purpose," p. 280, n. 36). It occurs 9 times in Luke–Acts (Luke 5.27; 10.1; 12.4; 17.8; 18.4; Acts 7.7 [echoing Gen. 15.14]; 13.20; 15.16; 18.1) (cf. 7 times in John, once in Hebrews, once in

words μετὰ ταῦτα in the text of Joel 2.28 LXX are replaced by ἐν ταῖς ἐσχάταις ἡμέραις). It is therefore more probable that Luke derived the quotation from a context in which it followed reference to God's turning away from Israel in judgment.[72]

(2) Neither the connection between the quotation in Acts 15.16–18 and the four prohibitions in the Apostolic Decree nor the derivation of the latter from Leviticus 17–18 is apparent in James' speech as it stands. The latter point is actually obscured by the order of the four prohibitions in 15.20, as compared with the order in 15.29. It seems clear that Luke himself was not interested in the exegetical basis for the prohibitions in the Apostolic Decree.[73] Indeed, he may have regarded them as a temporary compromise, no longer observed in all the churches he knew at the time of writing, and so would not have wished to highlight their scriptural basis. In any case, he seems to have abbreviated a source in which the quotation in Acts 15.16–18 and the terms of the Apostolic Decree were connected by exegetical argument.

(3) The terms of the Apostolic Decree are widely regarded, for good reasons,[74] as not Luke's invention. But if, as I have argued, the terms of the Apostolic Decree were formulated on the basis of an exegetical argument connected with the quotation in Acts 15.16–18, then Luke must have drawn this quotation, along with the terms of the Apostolic Decree, from a source.

(4) The idea of the Christian community as the eschatological Temple, which I have argued is important to the use of

---

1 Peter, 9 times in Revelation, 105 times in LXX). But in all other occurrences in Luke–Acts it occurs, as one would expect, within a sequence of actions.

72 Perhaps Amos 5.25–26, which can easily be connected with Amos 9.11–12 by *gezērâ šāwâ*, preceded it. Note that Luke's quotation of these verses in Acts 7.42–43 is introduced by ἔστρεψέ δὲ ὁ θεός, cf. 15.16: μετὰ ταῦτα ἀναστρέψω. There are close links between the whole of Acts 7.42–50 and Acts 15.16–19 (see Richard, "Divine Purpose," p. 272), which may indicate that Luke used the same source in both cases. The relationship between these two passages of Acts deserves fuller discussion, which space unfortunately precludes here.

73 See S. G. Wilson, "Law and Judaism in Acts," in P. J. Achtemeier (ed.), *Society of Biblical Literature 1980 Seminar Papers* (Chico, 1980), p. 259.

74 Haenchen, *Acts*, p. 470; Townsend, "The Date," pp. 49–50, 55–56; Esler, *Community*, p. 98; G. Lüdemann, *Paul: Apostle to the Gentiles: Studies in Chronology*, trans. F. Stanley Jones (London, 1984), pp. 72–74.

Amos 9.11–12 in Acts 15.16–17, is never explicit in Luke's writings, even if it is sometimes implicit.[75]

Finally, in addition to the reasons already given at the beginning of this section for finding Acts 15.16–18 and its connection with the Apostolic Decree highly appropriate to the situation described in Acts 15, there are further respects in which the source I am postulating for James' speech coheres well with what we know of the Jerusalem church under the leadership of James and his circle:

(1) The kind of skilled exegesis, resembling that of the Qumran pesharim, which is evident in 15.16–18 and which can be inferred as the basis for the prohibitions in the Apostolic Decree, is characteristic of early Palestinian Jewish Christianity, including the circle of the Lord's brothers.[76]

(2) From Gal. 2.9 we know that the interpretation of the eschatological Temple as the Christian community was important in the Jerusalem church under James' leadership (see above).

(3) If the letter of James derives, as I believe it does, from the early Jerusalem church, then it is evidence that the Old Testament covenant expression designating Israel as those "over whom the name of the Lord has been invoked" was used of the Christian community as the eschatologically renewed Israel (Jas. 2.7). This would give special point to the selection of a text applying this expression to the Gentiles (Acts 15.17) (see above).

In attempting more closely to define Luke's source, we must note first that it was written in Greek. The significance of the use of the LXX in Acts 15.16–18 has been very frequently misunderstood[77] and needs careful statement. The argument of James' speech *presupposes* exegetical work on the *Hebrew* text of the Bible (especially as the basis for the four prohibitions), but also *quotes* a conflated quotation which must have been com-

---

[75] J. B. Chance, *Jerusalem, the Temple, and the New Age in Luke–Acts* (Macon, 1988), pp. 35–45.

[76] Bauckham, *Jude and the Relatives*, chap. 4.

[77] Dupont, *The Salvation of the Gentiles*, p. 139, is typical of many who think that this reflects "the 'Hellenistic' stage of the apostolic preaching rather than its primitive Aramaic stage."

posed in *Greek*, making use of the LXX. As we have seen, there is not the slightest difficulty in attributing the latter to a Jewish Christian exegete who read both the Hebrew Bible and the LXX. He could have composed this conflated quotation in Hebrew, but in fact he composed it in Greek. There is also no difficulty at all in supposing that the Jerusalem church under James' leadership composed religious literature in Greek.[78] The church itself must still have included "Hellenists" (i.e. Jews who spoke only Greek)[79] as well as "Hebrews" (i.e. Jews who spoke both Aramaic and Greek) (Acts 6.1), and must have been in constant contact with Greek-speaking Jews from the Diaspora visiting Jerusalem. If Luke correctly represents James as addressing an assembly of the whole Jerusalem church (Acts 15.12,22), which would include non-Aramaic-speakers, then it is certainly not impossible that James spoke in Greek. But Luke's source was less likely a report of James' speech than a document written for those Christians in the Diaspora, Jewish and Gentile, for whom the Apostolic Decree was primarily intended. Such a document would have to be written in Greek.

I have already observed that the order of the four prohibitions in 15.29 (followed also in 21.25) is more original than that in 15.20. It follows that 15.28–29a is closer to Luke's source, while 15.19–20 is Luke's paraphrase of the same source. Luke has certainly rewritten the letter from the Jerusalem church leaders to the churches of Antioch, Syria, and Cilicia (15.23–29).[80] It is possible that an original, longer form of this letter was Luke's source and that his knowledge of the Jerusalem Council derived primarily from it. He used material from it to compose James' speech (15.13–21), omitted altogether the exegetical basis for the four prohibitions, and rewrote the letter itself, reproducing the terms of the Decree

---

78 For examples of Jewish Greek literature composed in Palestine, see M. Hengel, *The Pre-Christian Paul*, trans. J. Bowden (London, 1991), pp. 60–61. For the use of Greek for religious purposes by Palestinian Jewish Christians whose mother tongue was Aramaic, see Bauckham, *Jude and the Relatives*, pp. 283–284.

79 E.g. Mnason of Cyprus (Acts 21.16).

80 For the linguistic evidence for this, see A. Harnack, *Luke the Physician*, trans. J.R. Wilkinson (London, 1907), 218–223. But there is no reason to doubt that 15.28–29a is close to the source.

(15.28–29a) but omitting the exegetical argument. Alternatively, perhaps Luke knew some other document circulated by the Jerusalem church after the Council, perhaps composed by Judas Barsabbas and Silas (15.22,27,32), which he used to compose both James' speech and the letter. We cannot be sure, but the probability that the substance of James' speech derives from a source close to James himself is high.

CHAPTER 8

Kerygmatic summaries in the speeches of Acts

Richard Bauckham

INTRODUCTION

In 1919 Martin Dibelius drew attention to a basic pattern common to the evangelistic sermons in Acts 2.14–36; 3.12–26; 10.34–43; 13.16–41, i.e. those sermons preached by Peter and Paul to audiences either of Jews or of Gentiles who already worshiped the God of Israel. The scheme common to these speeches consists of three elements: (1) the kerygma, i.e. a very short narrative of what God has done in the history of Jesus; (2) scriptural proofs demonstrating that these events fulfilled prophecy; (3) an exhortation to repentance and faith. Although Dibelius assumed that these speeches were Lucan compositions, he thought the lack of variation in Luke's composition of them shows that he must have been constrained by a preaching pattern of some antiquity.[1]

Dibelius rather exaggerated the lack of variation in these speeches. The three elements by no means always occur in straightforward simple sequence. Often they are interwoven to some degree. Moreover, not only do the introductions to the sermons vary according to the occasion,[2] but so do the three elements themselves. In Peter's sermon to Cornelius, for example, the theme of fulfillment of prophecy occurs (10.43a), but it is not developed by quotations of Scripture as instances

[1] M. Dibelius, *From Tradition to Gospel*, ET from 1933 German ed. by B. L. Woolf (London, 1934), pp. 16–17; see also "The Speeches in Acts and Ancient Historiography," in M. Dibelius, *Studies in the Acts of the Apostles*, ET M. Ling (London, 1956), pp. 165–166, where he is more inclined to stress that the preaching pattern was that of Luke's own day.
[2] As Dibelius points out in *Tradition*, pp. 16–17.

185

of such fulfillment, as happens in the other sermons. Presumably Luke thought that this would be less appropriate in a
sermon to a Gentile Godfearer. The two sermons in Jerusalem
(2.14–36; 3.12–36) lack the detail about the ministry of Jesus
prior to his death which can be found in the other two sermons
(see 10.37–38;13.23–25). The reason is that the two earlier
sermons are addressed to an audience assumed to be familiar
with the outward facts about Jesus' public life and ministry,
while the two later sermons are addressed to people who know
little, if anything, about Jesus.[3] This is an interesting relationship between the content of the speeches and their context in
the narrative, because it means that presumably in this respect
the sermons in 10.34–43 and 13.16–41 are closer to Luke's
conception of early Christian preachers' typical manner of
proclaiming the Gospel to an audience of Jews or Godfearers.
The fuller narrative kerygma would be the norm, which
exceptional circumstances have caused to be abbreviated in
the sermons in Jerusalem.[4] But finally, we should note that
despite the formal correspondence in the three-part scheme,
there is rather little repetition of precise content from one
speech to another. Even when a similar point is being made,
such as the connection of John the Baptist with the beginning
of Jesus' ministry (10.37–38; 13.24–35) or the guilt of the Jews
who were responsible for Jesus' death (2.23; 3.13–15;
13.27–29), the different speeches allude to different aspects of
the Gospel story in order to make the same point. Such variations are not contextual, but are for the sake of the interest
and edification of Luke's readers. In this way Luke follows a

---

[3] G. Lüdemann, *Early Christianity according to the Traditions in Acts*, ET J. Bowden
(London, 1989), p. 128. Lüdemann oddly combines this correct recognition that the
speech to Cornelius suits the audience portrayed in the narrative with the mistaken
assertion, all too common in writing about the speeches in Acts, that "those
addressed [in verse 37] are the readers of Luke and Acts." Speeches in ancient
historiography were not means for the author directly to address his readers, but
were supposed to be appropriate to the speaker and his audience in the narrative
context: See C. Gempf, "Public Speaking and Published Accounts," in B. W. Winter
and A. D. Clarke (eds.), *The Book of Acts in its Ancient Literary Setting* (Grand Rapids,
1993), pp. 259–303, esp. pp. 279–280.

[4] Cf. G. N. Stanton, *Jesus of Nazareth in New Testament Preaching*, SNTSMS 27 (Cambridge, 1974), chap. 1.

common pattern, while avoiding the tediousness of substantial repetition.

Observing such variations between the speeches does not detract from the validity of Dibelius' basic argument: that the scheme common to the speeches must represent a pattern of preaching with which Luke was familiar. Of course, as Dibelius observed, "what Acts offers as the content of a speech which was really delivered, is proved by its brevity to be rather the skeleton than the substance of a speech."[5] This applies especially to the first element of the threefold pattern, the kerygma, which is the element in which Dibelius was especially interested and which is also the subject of this chapter. Luke must have intended these brief narratives to *represent* a much more substantial element in a real sermon. Dibelius supposed that in actual preaching specific stories about Jesus, such as we have in the Gospel traditions, would be told in order to illustrate and to support the kerygma.[6] Indeed, this was his real interest in discussing the speeches in Acts at this point in his work. They provide an indication that the church's preaching of Jesus Christ was the *Sitz im Leben* for the individual oral Gospel traditions which were later collected in the Gospels. For this reason, Dibelius did not inquire very much further into the kerygma as it appears in the speeches of Acts. He did, however, compare the brief narrative outlines that Luke provides with the formula (or fragment of a formula)[7] that Paul records in 1 Cor. 15.3–5 as a formula Paul himself had received and which he had handed on to the Corinthian church. Unlike the summaries in Acts, which, although they contain old, traditional material,[8] do not reproduce a fixed formula in exact words, Paul, in Dibelius' view, reproduces a fixed formula exactly. It shows that the kind of summary of the kerygma to be found in the speeches of Acts goes back to a much earlier date than the writing of Acts, although, because Dibelius regarded the Pauline formula as a product of "Hellenistic circles,"[9] he

---

[5] Dibelius, *Tradition*, p. 25.   [6] Ibid., pp. 25–26.

[7] According to Dibelius, ibid., p. 19: "We cannot infer how the formula ended, nor how it began, nor indeed what it said about the life of Jesus."

[8] Ibid., pp. 17–18.   [9] Ibid., p. 20.

thought Paul received it in Damascus or Antioch, not in Jerusalem.

It is in discussing the formula in 1 Corinthians 15 that Dibelius explains what he conceived to be the function of such traditional outlines of the kerygma:

Even these Hellenistic churches [i.e. Damascus and Antioch] apparently handed to their new converts or to the missionaries whom they sent out a short outline or summary of the Christian message, a formula which reminded the young Christian of his faith and which gave a teacher of this faith guidance for his instruction.[10]

Only here does Dibelius come within sight of a plausible theory as to the origin of the form of kerygmatic summary which appears in the speeches in Acts. Such brief summaries would not presumably have been reproduced as such in preaching, but could function as an outline on which a preacher could expand by drawing on the Gospel traditions. More generally, the function of the summaries themselves would have been not unlike the creeds and "the rule of faith" (which were in some sense derived from them) in the later second- and third-century church. They functioned in any context where a succinct summary of the kerygma was needed. Luke has incorporated this form in the sermons in Acts because it is an appropriate *substitute*, in a brief literary representation of a sermon, for the much fuller narration which a real sermon would include.

C. H. Dodd's view of these speeches in Acts[11] was in some important respects similar to Dibelius'. He analyzed the scheme common to the speeches in six points (not all of which are actually present in all four speeches),[12] but in effect recognized the same three elements Dibelius identified. (His analysis recognizes that Dibelius' second element is not always distinct from the first.) Neither Dibelius nor Dodd thought that the speeches in Acts were likely to be reports of what the apostles

---

[10] Ibid., p. 19.

[11] C. H. Dodd, *The Apostolic Preaching and its Developments*, 2nd ed. (London, 1944), chap. 1.

[12] Ibid., pp. 21–24. Dodd based his analysis on Acts 4.10–12; 5.30–32, as well as Acts 2.14–36; 3.12–26; 10.34–43; 13.16–41.

actually said on the occasions narrated by Luke, though Dodd considered that this might be true of some speeches in Acts.[13] But whereas Dibelius, though confident that Luke used older material in these four speeches, was vague as to the degree of Lucan composition, Dodd stressed the evidence for Luke's use of sources. Of Peter's speeches he thought that "We may with some confidence take these speeches to represent, not indeed what Peter said upon this or that occasion, but the *kerygma* of the Church at Jerusalem at an early period."[14] Of Paul's speech at Pisidian Antioch he thought it credible that it "may represent in a general way one form of Paul's preaching, that form, perhaps, which he adopted in synagogues when he had the opportunity of speaking there."[15]

Dodd was more interested than Dibelius in the content of the kerygma in these speeches in Acts, and supported his case for its early character by comparing it with a reconstruction of the kerygma presupposed in Paul's letters. But his major concern, like Dibelius', was to relate the kerygma to the Gospel traditions. Dodd's original contribution was to argue that Mark compiled his Gospel around an outline of the story of Jesus, which was an expanded version of the kind of kerygmatic summary that appears in the speeches of Acts. In this way he was able to argue not only that Mark took the individual pericopae of his Gospel from oral tradition, but also that the framework within which he placed them was traditional.[16]

Since Dibelius and Dodd much discussion has focused on the issue of whether Luke used sources for these speeches or freely composed them himself.[17] This way of posing the question may

---

[13] Dodd, *Apostolic Preaching*, pp. 18–19.   [14] Ibid., p. 21.   [15] Ibid., p. 30.
[16] Besides *Apostolic Preaching*, see also "The Framework of the Gospel Narrative," *ET* 43 (1931–1932), 396–400; reprinted in C. H. Dodd, *New Testament Studies* (Manchester, 1953), pp. 1–11. The thesis was criticized by D. E. Nineham, "The Order of Events in St. Mark's Gospel – an Examination of Dr. Dodd's Hypothesis," in D. E. Nineham (ed.), *Studies in the Gospels*, R. H. Lightfoot FS (Oxford, 1955), pp. 223–239. According to R. Guelich, "The Gospel Genre," in P. Stuhlmacher (ed.), *Das Evangelium und Die Evangelien*, WUNT 28 (Tübingen, 1983), p. 204, the "greatest vulnerability of Dodd's argument" lies in the existence of a basic outline of the kerygma that helped structure Mark's Gospel.
[17] For example, on Acts 10.34–43, see U. Wilckens, *Die Missionsreden der Apostelgeschichte* (Neukirchen, 1961) pp. 63–70; F. Bovon, "Tradition et rédaction en Actes 10,1–11,18," *TZ* 26 (1970), pp. 22–45; Stanton, *Jesus of Nazareth*, chap. 3;

not be entirely helpful. If we accept the validity of Dibelius'
fundamental observation that the *scheme* Luke follows in these
speeches must be an old traditional one, then Luke's debt to
tradition cannot be evaluated purely by the language he uses.
Our interest in this chapter is especially in the first element of
the three Dibelius identified – the kerygma – though we shall
argue that this was very closely connected with the second –
the proof from prophecy. I shall argue that in his summaries of
the history of Jesus in these speeches Luke follows a form – I
shall call it the kerygmatic summary – which was very traditional but also very flexible and variable. It was a form which
had gathered a stock of specific items which could be selected
for use in any particular case. It was a theme on which new
variations were constantly being improvised. Luke neither
composed his kerygmatic summaries *ex nihilo* nor reproduced a
source. The form he used provided him with traditional materials which he could vary and supplement in accordance with
his narrative contexts and literary purposes. As a particularly
skilled writer, Luke probably adapted the form rather more
extensively than other writers whose use of kerygmatic summaries we shall study. But the difference is one of degree. The form
was hospitable to variation and innovation.

To establish this thesis we need comparative material. Discussions of the kerygmatic summaries in Acts have previously
discussed parallels only in the Pauline epistles (especially 1
Cor. 15.1–7).[18] This was primarily because the concern, in the
work of both Dibelius and Dodd, was to find evidence that
something like the kerygmatic summaries in Acts goes back to
an early stage of Christian history. However, if our concern is
to demonstrate that the kerygmatic summary was a traditional
form which Luke used, it is also relevant to consider Christian
literature contemporary with or later than Acts. If the form

K. Haacker, "Dibelius und Cornelius: Ein Beispiel formgeschichtlicher Überliefer-
ungskritik," *BZ* 24 (1980), 234–251; Guelich, "Gospel Genre," pp. 209–211;
A. Weiser, "Tradition und lukanische Komposition in Apg 10,36–43," in *A cause de
l'évangile*, J. Dupont FS, LD 123 (Paris, 1985), pp. 757–767; Lüdemann, *Early
Christianity*, pp. 127–128.

[18] Dodd, *Apostolic Preaching*, chap. 1, identified a variety of Pauline passages as
fragments of the primitive kerygma and thereby reconstructed a Pauline kerygmatic outline.

exists, independently of Acts, in such literature, then this may not only be evidence that Luke used such a form, but may also prove informative as to the character of the form and the extent to which Luke's use of it follows tradition.

KERYGMATIC SUMMARIES IN THE ASCENSION OF ISAIAH

The Ascension of Isaiah is one of the most neglected of early Christian works,[19] and its allusions to Gospel traditions have been even more neglected than other aspects of the work.[20] It should probably be dated at the beginning of the second century,[21] though it could be somewhat earlier and cannot be later than the middle of the second century.[22] Against older

[19] The most important recent work has come out of the team of Italian researchers (M. Pesce, E. Norelli, A. Acerbi, C. Leonardi, A. Kossova Giambelluca, P. C. Bori, and others) who have been preparing the new edition of the Ascension of Isaiah for the Corpus Christianorum Series Apocryphorum. A. Acerbi, working in connection with but relatively independent of the group, has produced two books: *Serra Lignea: studi sulla fortuna della Ascensione di Isaia* (Rome, 1984); *L'Ascensione di Isaia: cristologia e profetismo in Siria nei primi decenni del II secolo*, Studia Patristica Mediolanensia 17 (Milan, 1988). M. Pesce (ed.), *Isaia, il Diletto e la Chiesa: Visione ed esegesi profetica cristiano-primitiva nell'Ascensione Isaia*, Testi e Ricerci di Scienze Religiose 20 (Brescia, 1983) contains the papers given at a conference including members of the group and others. See also E. Norelli, "Interprétations nouvelles de l'Ascension d'Isaïe," *Revue des Etudes Augustiniennes* 37 (1991), 11–22. These Italian scholars have revolutionized the study of the Ascension of Isaiah, and the full results of their work in the CCSA edition will be, not only the first fully adequate editions of the texts, but also an authoritative account of the background and nature of the Ascension of Isaiah. However, enough of their work has already been published for it to be scandalous that treatments of the Ascension of Isaiah in recent major reference works (M. Knibb, "Martyrdom and Ascension of Isaiah," in J. H. Charlesworth [ed.], *The Old Testament Pseudepigrapha*, vol. II [London, 1985], pp. 143–155; C. Detlef G. Müller in W. Schneemelcher (ed.), *New Testament Apocrypha*, vol. II, ET R. McL. Wilson [Cambridge, 1992], pp. 603–605; J. L. Trafton in *Anchor Bible Dictionary*, vol. III [New York, 1992], pp. 507–509) take no account of their work.

[20] See E. Norelli, "La resurrezione di Gesù nell' Ascensione di Isaia," *Cristanesimo nella Storia* 1 (1980), 315–366; J. D. Crossan, *The Cross that Spoke* (San Francisco, 1988), who makes some reference to the striking parallels between the Ascension of Isaiah and the Gospel of Peter, especially in the resurrection narrative, but ignores the highly relevant work of Norelli; J. Verheyden, "L'Ascension d'Isaïe et l'Evangile de Matthieu: Examen de AI 3,13–18," in J.-M. Sevrin (ed.), *The New Testament in Early Christianity*, BETL 86 (Louvain, 1989), pp. 247–274.

[21] In favor of an early second-century date are Acerbi, *L'Ascensione di Isaia*, pp. 281–282; R. G. Hall, "The *Ascension of Isaiah*: Contemporary Situation, Date and Place in Early Christianity," *JBL* 109 (1990), 289–306; Norelli, "Interprétations nouvelles," p. 15.

[22] For its use by the Acts of Peter, see Acerbi, *Serra Lignea*, pp. 16–22.

theories which thought of it as a compilation of several sources, Jewish and Christian,[23] recent work has tended to stress its uniformly Christian character[24] and its unity, though Acerbi divides the work into two Christian sources,[25] while Norelli holds that it was written in two stages.[26] My own view is that the work is easily explicable as the unified work of a single author, but in any case the three passages which concern us (3.13–20; 9.12–18;10.17–11.33)[27] are unquestionably closely related, and are generally acknowledged to come, if not from a single author, at least from the same circle.

In AscIsa 7.2–11.35 the prophet Isaiah recounts, in a first-person account to King Hezekiah, a visionary ascent through the heavens to the seventh heaven. The climax of this experience was a vision of the descent of the Beloved (the pre-existent Christ) through the heavens into the world, his earthly life as Jesus, his descent to the place of the dead, his resurrection, and ascension back to the seventh heaven. This vision of the descent and ascent of the Beloved is narrated in 10.17–11.33. A shorter and different account of it is also given in 3.13–4.18, where the vision extends beyond the Beloved's ascension to his parousia and the events of the end of history. These two accounts of the vision are probably intended to be complementary, focusing on different aspects of the Beloved's career and his defeat of evil. Both include, within a wider mythological-christological framework, a summary of the events of the history of Jesus, introduced in the case of the account in 10.17–11.33 by an extended account of the conception and birth of Jesus

---

[23] This view is still taken by Knibb, "Martyrdom and Ascension of Isaiah."

[24] This is the view of M. Pesce, "Presupposti per l'utilizzazione storica dell'*Ascensione di Isaia*: formazione e tradizione del testo; genere letterario; cosmologia angelica," in Pesce, *Isaia, il Diletto*, pp. 13–76; Hall, "*Ascension of Isaiah*"; Acerbi, *L'Ascensione di Isaia*; Norelli,"Interprétations nouvelles."

[25] Acerbi, *L'Ascensione di Isaia*, especially chaps. 7–8.

[26] Norelli, "Interprétations nouvelles," pp. 21–22.

[27] The passage 11.2–22 occurs only in the Ethiopic version, but certainly belongs to the original text: see R. H. Charles, *The Ascension of Isaiah* (London, 1900), pp. xxii–xxiv; A. Vaillant, "Un apocryphe pseudo-bogomile: la Vision d'Isaïe," *Revue des Etudes Slaves* 42 (1963), 111–112.

(11.2–16). In addition to these two summaries of the history of Jesus, there is another in 9.12–18, where the descent and ascent of the Beloved are predicted by the angel who has conducted Isaiah through the seven heavens. The purpose of this account is the more limited one of explaining how the righteous dead will ascend to heaven with Christ at his ascension and will then receive their thrones and crowns in heaven, but it too includes a very brief summary of the earthly history of Jesus. It is clear that all three accounts constitute kerygmatic summaries which bear comparison with those in Acts. The relevant parts of the three passages are as follows:

3.13–18[28]	9.13–18[29]	11.17–22[30]
13 the going forth of the Beloved from the seventh heaven, and his transformation, and his descent, and the likeness into which he must be transformed in the likeness of a human being,	13 The Lord will indeed descend into the world in the last days, he who is to be called Christ after he has descended and become like you in form, and they will think that he is flesh and a man.	[10.17–31: extended account of Isaiah's vision of the Lord's descent through the heavens; 11.2–16: extended account of his birth from Mary]
		17 And I saw that in Nazareth he sucked the breast like an infant, as was customary, that he might not be recognized. 18 And when he had grown up he performed great signs and miracles in the land of Israel and in Jerusalem.
and the persecution with which he will be persecuted, and the punishments with which the children of Israel must punish him, and the discipling of the Twelve,		

[28] This passage is extant in a single Greek manuscript. My translation is from the Greek text in Charles, *Ascension of Isaiah*.

[29] The translation of the Ethiopic version is by Knibb, "Martyrdom and Ascension of Isaiah," p. 170.

[30] The translation of the Ethiopic version is by Knibb, ibid., p. 175.

and how he must [before the Sabbath be crucified on a tree and][31] be crucified together with criminals,

and that he will be buried in a tomb,
14 and the Twelve who are with him will be offended by him, and the guarding of the guards of the grave,
15 and the descent of the angel of the church in heaven, whom he will summon in the last days,[33]
16 and that the angel of the Holy Spirit and Michael the chief of the holy angels will on the third day open his grave,
17 and the Beloved will come out sitting on their shoulders,

14 And the god of that world will stretch out his hand against the Son, and they will lay their hands upon him and hang him upon a tree, not knowing who he is . . .

16 And when he has plundered the angel of death he will rise on the third day

and will remain in that world for 545 days.

19 And after this the adversary envied him and roused the children of Israel, who did not know who he was, against him. And they handed him to the king,[32] and crucified him, and he descended to the angel who is in Sheol.
20 In Jerusalem, indeed, I saw how they crucified him on a tree,

21 and likewise how after the third day he rose

and remained [. . .] days[34] . . .
23 And I saw when he

---

[31] The Greek lacks the bracketed words, which are found in the Ethiopic. Their omission in the Greek is explicable by haplography.

[32] The word which normally means "king" is here translated "ruler" by Knibb, because he assumes that the reference is to Pontius Pilate. It is more likely that the Ascension of Isaiah, like the Gospel of Peter and some other extra-canonical traditions, gives Herod, rather than Pilate, the key role in the crucifixion.

[33] The Greek text of 3.15 is defective, but can be restored by means of the Ethiopic: see especially Norelli, "La resurrezione," pp. 320–324.

[34] Knibb supplies "(many)," but no doubt the figure 545 (as in 9.16) has been lost in the Ethiopic version. It may have been deliberately suppressed (as also in the Latin and Slavonic versions of 9.16) because of the conflict with Acts 1.3.

and how he will send
out his [twelve]³⁵
disciples,

17 And then many of
the righteous will
ascend with him . . .

sent out the twelve
disciples

and ascended.

18 and they will
instruct all nations
and all tongues in the
resurrection of the
Beloved, and those
who believe in his
cross and in his
ascension to the
seventh heaven,
whence also he came,
will be saved . . .

These three passages share the same mythological-christological framework. The Beloved is conceived as a divine
heavenly being, who descends unrecognized into the world.
His identity is concealed by the transformations he undergoes.
As he descends into each of the heavens below the seventh he
adopts the form of the angels who belong to that heaven (this is
the meaning of "his transformation" in 3.13; it is described in
detail in 10.17–31). Arriving on earth he adopts human form
(3.13; 9.13), being born miraculously from Mary (11.2–14).³⁶
His heavenly origin is thereby concealed (11.14) – not only
from human beings (9.13), but, even more importantly, from
the powers of evil who dominate this world (11.16). He
behaves like a normal human infant so that he might not be
recognized (11.17). The christology here has a strongly docetic
tendency, because the concern is with the deliberately concealed presence of a heavenly being in this world. His humanity is his disguise. Despite his miracles (11.18), neither the
supernatural nor the human agents of his death know his true
heavenly identity (9.14; 11.19). This enables the final stage of

³⁵ This word is supplied from the Ethiopic.
³⁶ The account stresses the way in which, not only is the conception virginal, but the
birth itself is miraculous (11.7–14).

his descent (cf. 9.15) – to the region below the earth, the place of the dead, where he delivers the righteous dead from the angel of death (9.16; 11.33). His resurrection is the first stage of his ascent back to the seventh heaven, but the ascent differs from the descent both in the fact that he is no longer incognito, but is now seen in his own divine glory and recognized (11.23–32), and also in that the righteous dead now ascend with him (9.17). But just as his descent from the seventh heaven to Sheol is interrupted by a period in this world, in which he instructs the Twelve (3.13), so also his ascent from Sheol to the seventh heaven is interrupted by a period in this world (9.16; 11.21), in which he sends out the Twelve (3.17; 11.23).

Within this mythological framework, which structures all three passages, each focuses on a different aspect of it. The sole concern of the shortest passage (9.13–18) is that the Beloved descends to deliver the righteous dead from Sheol and ascends to take them back with him to the seventh heaven. The two other passages both give much more attention to the earthly career of the Beloved, but complement each other in that one gives extensive attention to the way in which the Beloved enters this world in the course of his descent from the seventh heaven (11.2–16), while the other focuses especially on the way in which he enters this world in the course of his ascent from Sheol (3.14–17). These – the birth from Mary and the resurrection and exit from the tomb – are parallel, as both miraculous events of the Beloved's entry into this world, but are distinguished as, in one case, the hidden beginning of the Beloved's earthly career, unrecognized, in human form, and, in the other case, the beginning of his triumphant ascent, recognized by the supernatural powers, in his own glory. It is appropriate that the account in chapter 3 should focus on the latter, because it is this account which goes on to describe the proclamation of his resurrection and ascension in the world, by his disciples, and the fortunes of the church until the parousia. The respective emphases of chapters 3 and 11 therefore explain why in chapter 11 the brief narrative form of the kerygmatic summary is introduced by a full narrative of the birth of Jesus from Mary, which is more like a Gospel narrative than a kerygmatic summary, while in chapter 3, the summary form becomes unusually full in verses 14–17, which describe the circumstances and manner of the risen Christ's exit from the tomb. The respective interests of the two accounts also explain why the hiddenness of the Beloved in his life on earth from birth to death, which is not explicit in chapter 3, is the main concern of chapter 11's account of this period (11.11–19), while in chapter 3, there is a special emphasis on the role of the Twelve (3.13,14,17–18; cf. 3.21; 4.3), as well as a reference to the descent of the angel of the church (3.15).[37]

Thus both the mythological-christological framework common to the three passages and also the particular emphases and concerns of each have to quite a large extent determined the selection of material about the earthly history of Jesus (from birth to resurrection appearances) which appears in these accounts. If we focus on what does not belong purely to the mythological framework, but derives from traditions about the history of Jesus, material which is common to more than one account is small, though significant:

3.13–18	9.13–18	11.17–22
crucified on a tree	upon a tree	crucified on a tree
on the third day	rise on the third day	after the third day he rose
	remain for 545 days	remained [. . .] days
send out his twelve disciples		sent out the twelve disciples

It is noteworthy that the language of these repeated elements is characteristic not of the Gospel traditions as we have them in written Gospels, but of kerygmatic summaries. Reference to the cross as "a tree" is never made in the Gospels, but occurs in kerygmatic summaries in Acts (5.30; 10.39; 13.29; cf. 1 Pet. 2.24), reflecting the application of Old Testament *testimonia* to the cross (Gal. 3.13; Barn. 5.13; 8.1, 5; 12.1,7; Justin, *Dial.*

---

[37] On the angel, see Norelli, "La resurrezione," pp. 332–340; and cf. Acerbi, *L'Ascensione di Isaia*, p. 212.

86.6; TBenj 9.3; SibOr 5.257; 6.26).[38] Ascension of Isaiah 9.14,
which uses the expression "hang him upon a tree," preserves a
fuller allusion to Deut. 21.22–23, as do two of the kerygmatic
summaries in Acts (5.30;10.39). A statement that Jesus rose[39]
(from death) is never made, as such, in Gospel narratives,[40]
where its place is taken by the empty tomb and resurrection
appearance narratives, but is characteristic of kerygmatic summaries and other credal-type references to the resurrection.[41]
Similarly the phrases "on the third day" (AscIsa 3.16; 9.16)
and "after the third day" (11.21) are not used in Gospel
narratives of the empty tomb or the resurrection appearances,
but are characteristic of kerygmatic summaries (Acts 10.40; 1
Cor. 15.4; Aristides, *Apol.* 2 [Syriac])[42] and of similar summaries of what Old Testament Scripture prophesied of Jesus,
including the passion predictions in the Gospels (Matt. 16.21;
17.23; 20.19; 27.63; Mark 8.31; 9.31; 10.34; Lk. 9.22;18.33;
24.7,46; also Justin, *Dial.* 51.2). Behind this usage lies, once
again, an Old Testament prophecy (Hos. 6.2).[43] The state-

---

[38] See M. Wilcox, "'Upon the Tree' – Deut 21.22–23 in the New Testament," *JBL* 96
(1977), 85–99.

[39] It is noteworthy that the Ascension of Isaiah uses this traditional language, despite
its own understanding of the resurrection as ascent from Sheol into this world.

[40] It is found in the passion predictions, which resemble kerygmatic summaries, in the
message of the angel(s) at the tomb (Matt. 28.6; Mark 16.6; Lk. 24.5; GPet 56), and
in other references to what Scripture prophesied must happen (Mark 9.9–10; Lk.
24.7,46; John 20.9); cf. GHeb 7. Such references illustrate not how the resurrection
was narrated in the Gospel traditions, but how it was referred to in such contexts as
credal formulae and kerygmatic summaries.

[41] Where Jesus is the subject, most commonly the passive of ἐγείρω is used (e.g. 1 Cor.
15.4; Ignatius, *Trall.* 9.2; cf. Justin, *1 Apol.* 31.7), but for the intransitive use of
ἀνίστημι, which was most likely used in the Greek original of AscIsa 9.16;11.21, see
Mark 8.31; 9.31;10.34;16.9; Lk. 18.33; 24.7,46; John 20.9; Acts 17.3; 1 Thess. 4.14;
Justin, *Dial.* 51.2. Of these, Justin, *Dial.* 51.2 is in a kerygmatic summary, Mark
16.9 is in a passage resembling a kerygmatic summary (see below), and 1 Thess.
4.14 is in a credal formula. The other references are all to what must happen
according to prophecy, and most use with ἀνίστημι the phrase "after three days" or
"on the third day" (Mark 8.31; 9.31;10.34; Lk. 18.33; 24.7,46; cf. also Hippolytus,
C. Noet. 1.7 and other later credal formulae), as in AscIsa 9.16; 11.21. This suggests
that the use of ἀνίστημι in such contexts derives from Hos. 6.2 (LXX: ἐν τῇ ἡμέρᾳ τῇ
τρίτῃ ἀναστησόμεθα), *contra* B. Lindars, *New Testament Apologetic* (London, 1961),
pp. 65–66.

[42] Continuous with these are the many later occurrences in credal formulae: e.g.
Tertullian, *De Praescr.* 13; *De Virg. Vel.* 1; Hippolytus, *C. Noet.* 1.7.

[43] Lindars, *Apologetic*, pp. 60–66.

ment (AscIsa 9.16; 11.21) that he remained 545 days (after the resurrection), while following an extra-canonical tradition about the length of the period of the resurrection appearances (cf. ApJas 2.19–20; 8.3; Irenaeus, *Adv. Haer.* 1.3.2; 1.30.14),[44] parallels the statements in the kerygmatic summary in Acts 13.31 ("for many days he appeared . . .") and in Acts 1.3, which is more like a kerygmatic summary than a Gospel narrative. Finally, reference to the commissioning of the apostles is found in other kerygmatic summaries, though not in the same language (Acts 10.42; Justin, *1 Apol.* 31.7; Aristides, *Apol.* 2 [Syriac]; cf. Lk. 24.47; Justin, *1 Apol.* 50.12; 4 Bar. 9.20).

In addition to this material shared by more than one of the three passages in the Ascension of Isaiah, the material peculiar to each of the two major passages (3.13–18 and 11.17–22) also includes language characteristic of kerygmatic summaries rather than Gospel narratives. Two phrases in 3.13 are notable: "the persecution with which he will be persecuted, and the punishments with which the children of Israel must punish him" (ὁ διηγμὸς ὃν διωχθήσεται, καὶ ἁι κολάσεις αἷς δεῖ τοὺς υἱοὺς τοῦ Ἰσραὴλ αὐτὸν κολάσαι). The verb διώκειν is used in the Gospels, with Jesus as the object, only in John (5.16; 15.20), but it occurs in a kerygmatic summary in Ignatius, *Trall.* 9.1.[45] While κολάζειν is never used of Jesus in early Christian literature,[46] κόλασις is so used just once, in a fragment of the Kerygma Petrou, in a similar context in a kerygmatic summary (KerPet 4[a], ap. Clement of Alexandria, *Str.* 6.15.128: τὰς λοιπὰς κολάσεις πάσας ὅσας ἐποίησαν αὐτῷ οἱ

---

44 Though Gnostics took up this tradition, as they did various Jewish Christian traditions, there is no reason to regard it as Gnostic in origin: *contra* W. Bauer, *Das Leben Jesu im Zeitalter der neutestamentlichen Apokryphen* (Tübingen, 1909) p. 266; A. K. Helmbold, "Gnostic Elements in the 'Ascension of Isaiah,'" *NTS* 18 (1971–1972), 223, who makes this part of his very slender evidence for regarding the Ascension of Isaiah as Gnostic. Though it contains some themes which Gnostics also took up, the Ascension of Isaiah cannot usefully be classified as Gnostic.

45 διωγμός is never used of Jesus in early Christian literature (i.e. the literature covered by W. Bauer, W. F. Arndt, and F. W. Gingrich, *A Greek–English Lexicon of the New Testament and Other Early Christian Literature*, 2nd ed., ed. F. W. Danker [Chicago, 1979]; a list is on p. xxix).

46 For the definition of this term, see the preceding note.

Ἰουδαῖοι).[47] Furthermore, both κόλασις and κολάζειν are quite frequently used of Jesus by Celsus (ap. Origen, *C. Cels.*),[48] where, as in the Ascension of Isaiah and the Kerygma Petrou, it is the Jews who inflict the punishments on Jesus (*C. Cels.* 2.4; 4.22). Celsus is ostensibly quoting Christian use of this terminology, and sometimes his words sound like an echo of a kerygmatic summary (*C. Cels.* 2.55, 59).

AscIsa 11.18 refers to Jesus' miracles as "signs and wonders" (the Greek must have been σημεῖα καὶ τέρατα, as in 3.20), a phrase which is never used of them in the Gospels (except with a derogatory overtone in John 4.48),[49] but is used in kerygmatic summaries in Acts 2.22 (δυνάμεσι καὶ τέρασι καὶ σημείοις, though it should be noted that this phrase picks up τέρατα and ·σημεῖα from verse 19, and combines them with the usual synoptic term for Jesus' miracles)[50] and Testament of Adam 3.1 (see also Barn. 4.14; 5.8).[51] The phrase "in the land of Israel and in Jerusalem" (AscIsa 11.18), a summary statement of the places of Jesus' ministry not found in the Gospels, has equivalents in kerygmatic summaries in Acts 10.39 ("in the country of the Jews and in Jerusalem") and in the Acts of Paul (Hamburg Papyrus, p. 8: "Jerusalem and . . . all Judea"). Finally, the statement that the Jews "handed him [over] to the king" (AscIsa 11.19) reflects a use of παραδιδόναι which is found quite frequently in the Gospel passion narratives (Matt. 27.2,18, 26; Mark 15.1,15; Lk. 20.20; 23.35; John 18.30,35; 19.16; GPet 5; cf. 1 Cor. 11.23),[52] but is also especially characteristic of the passion predictions (Matt. 17.22; 20.19; 26.2; Mark 9.31;10.33; Lk. 9.44; 18.32) and kerygmatic summaries (Acts 2.23; 3.13; cf. Rom. 4.25). This is because, like other

---

[47] This is fragment 4(a) in the numeration used in Schneemelcher, *New Testament Apocrypha*, vol. II, p. 40. For the text, see E. von Dobschutz, *Das Kerygma Petri kritisch untersucht*, TU 11/1 (Leipzig, 1893), where this fragment is numbered 9.

[48] E.g. κόλασις: *C. Cels.* 2.47, 55,59; κολάζειν: 2.4; 4.22; 8.41–42.

[49] The phrase, common in the LXX, is used of miracles of the apostles and other Christian leaders in Acts 2.43; 4.30; 5.12; 6.8; 14.3;15.12; Rom. 15.19; Heb. 2.4; AscIsa 3.20.

[50] See Stanton, *Jesus of Nazareth*, pp. 81–82.

[51] For other kinds of references to Jesus' miracles in kerygmatic summaries, see Acts 10.38; Justin, *1Apol.* 31.7; Acts of Thomas 47; Acts of Paul, Hamburg papyrus, p. 8.

[52] Of course the Gospels also use it of Judas' betrayal of Jesus.

terminology we have found to be characteristic of the kerygmatic summaries, it alludes to Old Testament prophecy (Isa. 53.6, 12 LXX).[53]

Finally, we should notice the use of δεῖ (AscIsa 3.13 twice), which is used in the same way – to indicate the divinely ordained sufferings of Christ, set out in prophecy – both in the Gospel passion predictions (Matt. 16.21; 26.54; Mark 8.31; Lk. 9.22; 17.25; 22.37; 24.7, 46; John 3.14) and in kerygmatic summaries (KerPet 4[a], ap. Clement of Alexandria, *Str.* 6.15.128; see also Acts 17.3; Justin, *Dial.* 51.2; and equivalent expressions in Acts 2.23; 3.13).

Other elements in AscIsa 3.13–18 and 11.17–22, while their forms of expression are not distinctive of kerygmatic summaries rather than of the Gospel traditions, can be paralleled in kerygmatic summaries elsewhere. "The discipling of the twelve" (AscIsa 3.13) is paralleled in Acts of Paul (Hamburg Papyrus, p. 8: "he chose from the tribes twelve men whom he had with him in understanding and faith"); that he "must be crucified together with criminals" (AscIsa 3.13) is paralleled in Epistle of the Apostles 9 ("was crucified between two thieves"); that he "will be buried in a tomb" is paralleled in Acts 13.29; 1 Cor. 15:4; Epistle of the Apostles 9; and the reference to Nazareth (AscIsa. 11.15–17) is paralleled in Acts of Paul (Hamburg Papyrus, p. 8: "brought up in Nazareth").

Not all this evidence is of equal weight, but it is quite sufficient to show that the author of these passages of the Ascension of Isaiah did not compose his summaries of the history of Jesus directly from written Gospels or from the oral Gospel traditions, but followed a traditional pattern of kerygmatic summary which narrated the history of Jesus in a series of brief statements. He knew traditional forms of expression which were regularly used in such summaries. He probably knew, not a single set of items which always occurred in such summaries, but a stock of traditional items from which the contents of such summaries were selected. Therefore he felt free

---

[53] See Lindars, *Apologetic*, pp. 80–81; A. E. Harvey, *Jesus and the Constraints of History* (London, 1982), pp. 23–25.

to vary the contents of each of his summaries in accordance with the requirements of the context. We should not suppose that the traditional form of kerygmatic summary he knew used the mythological descent–ascent scheme as a framework. Although the scheme itself is not unparalleled,[54] it is nowhere else combined with summaries of the history of Jesus in the way that we find in these passages of the Ascension of Isaiah. Kerygmatic summaries elsewhere relate the earthly, observable events of the history of Jesus, from, at the earliest, his birth, to, at the latest, his ascension, although sometimes a statement of his exaltation to God's right hand in heaven and/or reference to his coming parousia are added (Acts 2.33; 3.21; 10.42; KerPet4[a]; Justin, *1Apol.* 31.7; Irenaeus, *Adv. Haer.* 1.10.1).[55] It was the author of the Ascension of Isaiah who incorporated kerygmatic summaries into *his* highly developed mythological-christological framework. As we have seen, it is this framework which has partly determined his selection of items from the tradition of kerygmatic summaries.

We should also notice that the requirements of adapting the kerygmatic summaries to their context in the Ascension of Isaiah, where 9.13–18 is in the form of a prediction by an angel and 11.17–22 is an account of what Isaiah saw in his vision, mean that the precise literary form of the kerygmatic summaries the author knew is unlikely to have been conserved in his text. However, the two grammatical forms used in 3.13–18 can,

---

[54] For elements of it, see John 3.13;6.62; 1 Cor. 2.8; Eph. 4.9–10; 1 Tim. 3.16; Heb. 4.14; ApJas;Ignatius,*Eph.* 19.1; OdesSol. 7.4,6; 19.5; 22.1;42. 11; TBenj 9.3; SibOr 8.292–293;Irenaeus, *Dem.* 84; EpApost 13–14 (this last probably dependent on AscIsa). See further J. Daniélou, *The Theology of Jewish Christianity*, trans. J. A. Baker (London, 1964), pp. 206–213, 233–263; C. H. Talbert, *What is a Gospel?* (Minneapolis, 1977), chap. 3; U. Bianchi, "L'*Ascensione di Isaia*: tematiche soteriologiche di *descensus/ascensus*," in Pesce, *Isaia, Il Diletto*, pp. 155–178; Acerbi, *L'Ascensione di Isaia*, pp. 173–194. Some of the striking resemblances between the Ascension of Isaiah and the Apocryphon of James were already pointed out by W. C. van Unnik, "The Origin of the Recently Discovered 'Apocryphon Jacobi,'" *VC* 10 (1956), 155.

[55] Kerygmatic summaries, in our sense of the term, must be distinguished from such passages as Phil. 2.6–11 and 1 Tim. 3.16, which describe the career of Christ in mythological terms, involving preexistence, cosmic powers, and so on, making only the most minimal reference, if any, to events in the earthly history of Jesus. If we imagined material like that in the kerygmatic summaries in Acts incorporated within the christological hymn of Phil. 2.6–11, we should have something more formally corresponding to the passages we have studied in the Ascension of Isaiah.

as a matter of fact, be paralleled in kerygmatic summaries elsewhere. The series of nouns (3.13,14b-15a; cf. 1.5) is the form used in Kerygma Petrou 4(a) and Irenaeus, *Adv. Haer.* 1.10.1 (see below), while the series of ὡς and ὅτι clauses in 3.13–17 resembles Acts 10:38 (ὡς) and 1 Cor. 15:3–5 (ὅτι), though these usages are contextual and should not be assumed to derive from the traditional forms Luke and Paul knew.

I have emphasized the independence of the elements of the kerygmatic summaries from the Gospel traditions, because it is essential to recognize that the kerygmatic summary was a traditional form in its own right, which existed alongside the Gospel traditions. But it was a flexible form. It was open to anyone who used it to supplement its traditional contents with material summarized directly from the Gospel traditions. It seems fairly clear that this is what the author of the Ascension of Isaiah has done in 3.14b–17a, where he has summarized a resurrection tradition similar to those in Matt. 27.62–66; 28.2–4,11–15 and Gospel of Peter 28–49.[56] (In 11.2–15, however, he has broken out of the form of kerygmatic summary altogether, and told this part of the history of Jesus in full narrative form.)[57] Thus we should regard the kerygmatic summary as *relatively* independent of the Gospel traditions. It is only to be expected that those who used it, being familiar also with the Gospel traditions, should have adapted and supplemented it from their knowledge of the Gospel traditions.

Finally, it seems likely that the author of the Ascension of Isaiah knew the traditional kerygmatic summary as a traditional way of summarizing the history of Jesus as *fulfillment of the Old Testament prophecies*. We have noticed that a number of the forms of expression distinctive of the tradition (to hang him on a tree, he rose on the third day, they handed him over)

---

[56] Whether the Ascension of Isaiah is dependent on Matthew (so Verheyden, "L'Ascension d'Isaïe et l'Evangile de Matthieu") or on oral tradition which was here related to Matthew's special material (so Norelli, "La resurrezione," pp. 324–331; Acerbi, *L'Ascensione di Isaia*, p. 212) is not important for our present purposes.

[57] Cf. EpApost 9–10, where what begins as a kerygmatic summary turns into a full narrative of the women's discovery of the empty tomb and the appearance of the Lord to them.

allude to prophecy, while the use of δεῖ indicates the prophesied necessity of the sufferings of Christ. Moreover, other specific items included in the summaries may well have been selected precisely because they are fulfillments of prophecy (for example 3.13: "crucified together with criminals," cf. Isa. 53.12; 3.14: "the twelve who were with him will be offended by him," cf. Isa. 53.6; Zech. 13.7). As we shall see later, several other kerygmatic summaries are explicitly presented as the content of what the prophets had predicted about Jesus. In fact, this is also the case in the Ascension of Isaiah, for 3.13–18 and 11.17–22 are parts of the two accounts of Isaiah's prophetic vision of the Beloved. This vision, as recounted in the Ascension of Isaiah, is no more than a more explicit version of what is also contained in the prophecies of the canonical Book of Isaiah (AscIsa. 4.19–21) and in the other prophetic Scriptures (4.21–22).[58] So it may well be that the Ascension of Isaiah's use of kerygmatic summaries to depict the history of Jesus as Isaiah foresaw it in prophetic vision was a use for which the traditional use of kerygmatic summaries had already prepared.

KERYGMATIC SUMMARIES IN IGNATIUS OF ANTIOCH

Like the Ascension of Isaiah and probably at around the same time, Ignatius of Antioch also provides us with three examples of kerygmatic summaries, which have both resemblances to each other and differences from each other:

Trall. 9.1–2	*Smyrn.* 1–1.2	*Eph.* 18.2
τοῦ ἐκ γένους Δαυείδ,	ἀληθῶς ὄντα ἐκ γένους	ἐκυοφορήθη ὑπὸ Μαρίας
τοὐ ἐκ Μαρίας,	Δαυείδ κατὰ σάρκα,	κατ᾽ οἰκονομίαν, ἐκ
	υἱὸν θεοῦ κατὰ θέλημα	σπέρματος μὲν Δαυείδ
	καὶ δύναμιν,	πνεύματος δὲ ἁγίου·
ὃς ἀληθῶς ἐγεννήθη,	γεγεννημένον ἀληθῶς	ὃς ἐγεννήθη
	ἐκ παρθένου,	
	βεβαπτισμένον ὑπὸ	καὶ ἐβαπτίσθη
	Ἰωάννου ἵνα πληρωθῇ	
	πᾶσα δικαιοσύνη ὑπ᾽	

---

[58] For the way in which the whole account of the Beloved in the Ascension of Isaiah depends on exegesis of Isaiah and other canonical prophecies, see Acerbi, *L'Ascensione di Isaia*, pp. 32–42, 50–82.

ἔφαγέν τε καὶ ἔπιεν,
ἀληθῶς ἐδιώχθη ἐπὶ
Ποντίου Πιλάτου,
ἀληθῶς ἐσταυρώθη
καὶ ἀπέθανεν,
βλεπόντων [τῶν]
ἐπουρανίων καὶ ἐπι-
γείων καὶ ὑποχθονίων·
ὅς καὶ ἀληθῶς ἠγέρθη
ἀπὸ νεκρῶν, ἐγείραντος
αὐτὸν τοῦ πατρὸς αὐτοῦ,
κατὰ τὸ ὁμοίωμα ὅς
καὶ ἡμᾶς τοὺς
πιστεύοντας αὐτῷ
οὕτως ἐγερεῖ ὁ πατὴρ
αὐτοῦ ἐν Χριστῷ Ἰησοῦ
. . .

αὐτοῦ,
ἀληθῶς ἐπὶ Ποντίου
Πιλάτου καὶ Ἡρώδου
τετράρχου
καθηλωμένον ὑπὲρ
ἡμῶν ἐν σαρκί· ἀφ᾽ οὗ
καρποῦ ἡμεῖς ἀπὸ τοῦ
θεομακαρίστου αὐτοῦ
πάθους·

ἵνα ἄρῃ σύσσημον εἰς
τοὺς αἰῶνας διὰ τῆς
ἀναστάσεως εἰς τοὺς
ἁγίους καὶ πιστοὺς
αὐτοῦ . . .

ἵνα τῷ πάθει τὸ ὕδωρ
καθαρίσῃ.

---

who was of the family
of David, and who
was of Mary,

being truly of the
family of David
according to the
flesh, Son of God
according to the will
and power of God,

was conceived by
Mary according to the
plan of God, both
from the seed will of
David and of the Holy
Spirit; he was born
and was baptized

who truly was born,

truly born of a virgin,
baptized by John in
order that all
righteousness might
be fulfilled by him,

both ate and drank,
truly was persecuted
under Pontius Pilate,
truly was crucified
and died, while those
in heaven and on
earth and under the
earth observed, who
also truly was raised
from the dead, when
his Father raised him,

truly nailed in the
flesh for us under
Pontius Pilate and
Herod the tetrarch
(from its fruit are we,
from his divinely
blessed suffering)

who in the same way will also raise us in Christ Jesus, who believe in him . . .	in order that he might raise an ensign for ever through the resurrection for his saints and faithful people . . .	in order that by his suffering he might cleanse the water.

Since it has been widely recognized that in these three passages Ignatius is echoing traditional formulations,[59] the point need not be proved here. What has been less clearly recognized is that Ignatius is using a traditional form which had both structure and flexibility. If we list elements which occur in two or more of the three passages above, and add some references to other places in his letters where Ignatius seems to be echoing, more briefly, the same traditional expressions, the following basic pattern emerges:[60]

from David's family	(T, S; *Eph.* 20.2)
or seed	(E; *Rom.* 7.3)
from God/Holy Spirit	(S, E)
Mary	(T, E; *Eph.* 7.2; 20.2)[61]
born	(T, E, S)[62]
baptized	(S, E)
crucified	(T, S; cf. E)
under Pontius Pilate	(T, S; *Magn.* 11.1)[63]
raised	(T, S)

All these elements must have had a firm place in the traditional form of kerygmatic summary Ignatius knew, but some could be omitted and others added. There seems to have been

[59] See, e.g., H. Paulsen, *Studien zur Theologie des Ignatius von Antiochien*, Forschungen zur Kirchen und Dogmengeschichte 29 (Göttingen, 1978), pp. 46–54; W. R. Schoedel, *Ignatius of Antioch*, Hermeneia (Philadelphia, 1985), pp. 8–9, 84–85,152–155, 220–224.

[60] T,S,E refer to the three passages of Ignatius printed above.

[61] For reference to Mary by name in kerygmatic summaries, cf. EpApost 3; Acts of Paul (Hamburg Papyrus, p. 8); Tertullian, *De Praescr.* 13; *De Virg. Vel.* 1.

[62] For reference to the birth of Jesus in kerygmatic summaries, cf. Justin, *1 Apol.* 31.7 (from a virgin); Acts of Paul (Hamburg Papyrus, p. 8); Irenaeus, *Adv. Haer.* 1.10.1 (from a virgin); etc.

[63] For reference to Pontius Pilate in kerygmatic summaries, cf. Acts 3.13; Justin, *1 Apol.* 13.3; 61.10; EpApost 9; Irenaeus, *Adv. Haer.* 3.4.2; Tertullian, *De Virg. Vel.* 1.

a variety of ways of combining reference to David, Mary, and God in such a way as to indicate Jesus' dual origin, human and divine, but some such indication seems to have been a standard beginning of the summary. It is a distinctive feature of the form of kerygmatic summary to which Ignatius testifies.[64] (The absence of reference to divine origin in T may be due to Ignatius' anti-docetic concern, which made the assertion of the human origin of prime importance.) Also distinctive of the three passages in Ignatius is the way in which a soteriological implication, different in each case, is drawn out at the end of the summary (in S and E it replaces the end of the summary). Whether this feature is due to Ignatius himself or traditional is difficult to tell.

In all three cases Ignatius' purpose in including the summary is to combat docetic christology by referring to traditional christological statements which made the true humanity and truly human experience of Jesus clear. The repetition of ἀληθῶς (four times in T, three times in S) clearly serves this purpose, and so it is likely that the use of the word is not traditional but Ignatius' distinctive variation on the traditional form. Also serving Ignatius' anti-docetic purpose are the particular way of referring to the crucifixion in S (καθηλωμένον ἐν σαρκί)[65] and the assertion that he "both ate and drank" in T. Ignatius could have selected these, as appropriate to his purpose, from the stock of traditional items, but they are probably more likely to be his original improvisations. The latter occurs in no other example of a kerygmatic summary, and it is hard to imagine it being included except as an anti-docetic statement.[66] However, it is possible that Ignatius has transferred it from a post-resurrection position, where its significance was as evidence of the reality of the resurrection.

---

[64] There would appear to be some relationship to Rom. 1.3–4, especially in *Smyrn.* 1.1, where it cannot be ruled out that Ignatius' own knowledge of the Pauline text has influenced his formulation. Rom. 1.3–4 is a christological formula, not a kerygmatic summary, but it is possible that Paul derived it from a kerygmatic summary, or that it later influenced kerygmatic summaries.

[65] Cf. Tertullian, *De Praescr.* 13: "was nailed to the cross."

[66] It cannot plausibly be related to Matt. 11.19.

That the apostles ate and drank with the risen Christ is stated in the kerygmatic summary in Acts 10.41 (cf. also Justin, *Dial.* 51.2).[67]

The abundance of proper names (David, Mary, John, Pontius Pilate, Herod the tetrarch) in these three passages may also serve Ignatius' anti-docetic purpose, since they highlight not only Jesus' genuinely human origins but also the concrete historicity of the events of his life and death. But if so, this is a feature which Ignatius has emphasized and augmented, rather than creating, since at least the names David, Mary, and Pontius Pilate seem to have been traditional.[68]

However, if many elements of these summaries have been selected or added by Ignatius to serve his anti-docetic purpose,[69] this is not true of all elements. In particular, the reference to the baptism of Jesus (S, E) is difficult to see as polemical[70] and must have been frequent in the tradition. Presumably it was included as marking the beginning of Jesus' public ministry, as it does in the Gospel traditions also. References to John's ministry perform a similar function in the kerygmatic summaries in Acts 10.37; 13.24–25. But in *Smyrn.* 1.1, the reference to Jesus' baptism continues with an explanation for it ("in order that all righteousness might be fulfilled by him") which is closely related to Matt. 3.15. The traditional kerygmatic summary has been expanded by recourse to this Gospel tradition, whether in the form of the written Gospel of Matthew (as most scholars hold, since Matt. 3.15 is usually regarded as redactional) or in the form of the oral tradition on which Matthew drew.[71] Since Ignatius seems to have no con-

---

[67] Cf. also *Const. Apost.* 6.30, though this is dependent on Acts.

[68] With the reference to Pontius Pilate and Herod the tetrarch, compare EpApost 9: "crucified in the days of Pontius Pilate and of the prince Archelaus" (Ethiopic) (where Herod Archelaus and Herod Antipas are confused; for similar confusion, cf. Gospel of the Ebionites, ap. Epiphanius, *Haer.* 30.13.6; Justin, *Dial.* 103.3).

[69] See further Schoedel, *Ignatius*, pp. 153–155.

[70] Ibid., p. 84, gives further reason for seeing the references to the baptism as traditional.

[71] For the issue, see R. Bauckham, "The Study of Gospel Traditions Outside the Canonical Gospels: Problems and Prospects," in D. Wenham (ed.), *Gospel Perspectives 5: The Jesus Tradition Outside the Gospels* (Sheffield, 1984), pp. 394–395. H. Koester, *Synoptische Überlieferung bei den apostolischen Vätern*, TU 65 (Berlin, 1957),

textual reason for making this expansion himself, it seems most likely that it was already traditional. It is a good illustration of a point already made with reference to the kerygmatic summaries in the Ascension of Isaiah: that although the form was relatively independent of the Gospel traditions, it was by no means wholly independent. The content of kerygmatic summaries could be augmented from the Gospel traditions.

Study of Ignatius' kerygmatic summaries therefore confirms the conclusions drawn from the study of those in the Ascension of Isaiah, except that in Ignatius' case there seems to be no relationship to the fulfillment of prophecy. As for the grammatical form of the summaries, we should notice the use of the relative pronoun (ὅς: twice in T, once in E) and participial expressions (S). The former usage is also found in the kerygmatic summaries in Acts (3.13,15; 10.38,39; 13.31), the latter in Justin (*1 Apol.* 31.7).

OTHER KERYGMATIC SUMMARIES

Of other kerygmatic summaries in extra-canonical Christian literature to which reference has already been made for comparison, three are of special interest because they attest the strong connection of kerygmatic summaries with the proof from prophecy. The earliest is fragment 4(a) of the Kerygma Petrou (ap. Clement of Alexandria, *Str.* 6.15.128):

But we [the apostles] opened the books of the prophets which we had, which partly in parables, partly in enigmas,[72] partly in clear and express words, name Christ Jesus, and we found his coming (παρουσίαν), his death, his cross and all the rest of the punishments (κολάσεις) which the Jews inflicted on him, and his resurrection

---

pp. 58–61, holds that the traditional form Ignatius followed was dependent on Matt. 3.15, and regards this as the only point at which Ignatius is even indirectly dependent on Matthew. He is followed, cautiously, by Schoedel, *Ignatius*, p. 222. J. Smit Sibinga, "Ignatius and Matthew," *NovT* 8 (1966), 282, argues that Ignatius is here dependent, not on Matt. 3.15 itself, but on Matthew's source. For the general methodological issue of determining whether Ignatius' many parallels to Matthew are due to his dependence on Matthew's Gospel or to his knowledge of the oral traditions on which Matthew drew in his *Sondergut*, see Bauckham, "The Study of Gospel Traditions," pp. 386–398.

[72] Cf. AscIsa 4.20–22; EpApost 3.

(ἔγερσιν) and his assumption (ἀνάληψιν) into heaven before the judgment[73] of Jerusalem, how there were written all these things which he had to suffer (ἃ ἔδει αὐτὸν παθεῖν) and which would happen after him.[74]

The context (after the resurrection, though apparently not in the presence of the risen Christ) bears comparison with that of Lk. 24.44–47, confirming the impression that Lk. 24.46–47 is related to the tradition of kerygmatic summaries.

The other texts are from Justin and Irenaeus:

In these books of the prophets, then, we found foretold Jesus our Christ as coming (παραγινόμενον), born of a virgin, and growing to manhood, and healing every disease and sickness (θεραπεύοντα πᾶσαν νόσον καὶ πᾶσαν μαλακίαν),[75] and raising the dead, and being envied (φθονούμενον), and not being recognized (ἀγνοούμενον),[76] and being crucified, and dying, and being raised again, and ascending into heaven, and being called the Son of God, and certain people being sent by him into every nation to proclaim these things, and that the people from the nations rather [than the Jews] would believe in him. (Justin, 1 Apol. 31.7)[77]

the Holy Spirit, who through the prophets proclaimed the dispensations (οἰκονομίας) and the coming (ἔλευσιν) and the birth from the virgin and the suffering and the resurrection (ἔγερσιν) from the dead and the corporeal assumption (ἀνάληψιν) into heaven of the beloved Christ Jesus our Lord, and his coming (παρουσίαν) from heaven in the glory of the Father. (Irenaeus, Adv. Haer. 1.10.1)[78]

---

[73] Correction of κτισθῆναι to κριθῆναι (so von Dobschütz).

[74] My translation from the text in E. von Dobschütz, Das Kerygma Petri kritisch untersucht, TU 111 (Leipzig, 1893), where this fragment is numbered 9. For a discussion of the passage, see pp. 58–64.

[75] This phrase is exactly the one used in Matt. 4.23; 9.35, and peculiar to Matthew among the Gospels. Is Justin's text a reminiscence of Matthew's, or did Matthew borrow the summarizing phrase from a kerygmatic summary known to him? Justin's kerygmatic summary here displays no other verbal reminiscence of the Gospels. Dodd's thesis, which attempted to relate kerygmatic summaries to the summarizing passages in Mark, may bear re-examination.

[76] The use of this verb is a striking parallel to its use in a kerygmatic summary in Acts 13.27.

[77] My translation from the text in E. J. Goodspeed, Die ältesten Apologeten (Göttingen, 1914), pp. 46–47.

[78] My translation from the text in A. Rousseau and L. Doutreleau (eds.), Irenée de Lyon. Contre les Hérésies. Livre I, vol. II, SC 264 (Paris, 1979), pp. 155–157.

These three passages correspond closely in the basic sequence: coming – birth – suffering/death – resurrection – assumption to heaven. Irenaeus has little more than the basic sequence; the Kerygma Petrou expands it a little, Justin a lot. All three use this kerygmatic summary to summarize what the prophets foretold.

That these passages stand in a tradition that goes back to a very early time can be confirmed by the fact that the one unquestionably very early kerygmatic summary we have (1 Cor. 15.3–7) is also explicitly concerned with the fulfillment of Old Testament prophecy in the history of Jesus. The repeated κατὰ τὰς γραφάς (15.3–4), in connection with Christ's death for our sins (cf. Isa. 53.4–12) and his resurrection on the third day (cf. Hos. 6.2), serves no contextual purpose of Paul's and must be traditional. Thus the close connection between the kerygmatic summary and the proof from prophecy runs from the sources of Paul's tradition through the Ascension of Isaiah, the Kerygma Petrou and Justin, to Irenaeus. It is not surprising that the same connection is found in the speeches in Acts.[79]

Two further observations on the kerygmatic summary in 1 Cor. 15.3–7 may be made. In the first place, the assumption that the form Paul had received and handed on to his churches began with the death of Christ (15.3) is unjustified.[80] Paul cites that part of the summary which is relevant to his purpose: a discussion of resurrection. There is no reason why Paul should not have known a form in which it was usual to summarize the ministry of Jesus as well as his death and resurrection. Secondly, there is no reason to suppose that Paul refers to a completely fixed form. The list of five resurrection appearances no doubt existed in the tradition he knew (and perhaps other appearances were known in this tradition too), but they need not all have been cited every time the form was used. Sometimes a more summary statement that there were resurrection

[79] This also accounts for the parallels we have noticed between kerygmatic summaries and the passion predictions in the Gospels.

[80] Cf. Dibelius, *Tradition*, p. 19: "We cannot infer how the formula ended, nor how it began, nor indeed what it said about the life of Jesus."

appearances might have been used (as in Acts 13.31). Paul's own purpose in using the tradition in this context accounts for his focusing on these traditional items and his listing them at length. Moreover, as has often been pointed out, at least part of verse 6 must be Paul's own contribution, while he has, of course, added verse 8. But such original variations on the tradition were normal in the context of the flexible form we have been studying. Attempts to determine the precise para-meters of the tradition Paul inherited, though they have been many,[81] are not appropriate to the nature of the form in question.

However, 1 Cor. 15.3–7 is interesting evidence that one form the latter part of a kerygmatic summary took was a list of various resurrection appearances. It may be that this explains the origin of the Longer Ending of Mark. C. H. Dodd pointed out how the sequence πρῶτον . . . μετὰ δὲ ταῦτα . . . ὕστερον (Mark 16.9, 12, 14) resembles the sequence in 1 Cor. 15.5–8: εἶτα . . . ἔπειτα . . . εἶτα . . . ἔσχατον δὲ πάντων.[82] The Longer Ending of Mark could have had as its basis the latter part of a kerygmatic summary,[83] summarizing the resurrection appear-ances, the commissioning of the apostles (cf. Acts 10.42; AscIsa 3:17; 11.23), the ascension (cf. AscIsa 11.23; KerPet. 4[a]; Justin, 1 Apol. 31.7) and exaltation to the right hand of God (cf. Acts 2.33; 5.31; 1 Pet. 3.22), and the worldwide proclamation of the Gospel (cf. AscIsa 3:18–20; Justin, 1 Apol. 31.7). The summary has been expanded (rather in the manner of AscIsa 3:14–17), not with full narratives at each point, but with material from the Gospel traditions, on a scale which is some-where between the series of brief statements found in a keryg-matic summary and a sequence of full Gospel pericopae. A formally rather similar passage, which probably had a similar origin, but in this case in the early part of a kerygmatic

[81] For a survey of views, see N. Taylor, *Paul, Antioch and Jerusalem*, SNTSMS 66 (Sheffield, 1992), pp. 176–178.

[82] C. H. Dodd, "The Appearances of the Risen Christ: An Essay in Form-Criticism of the Gospels," in D. E. Nineham (ed.), *Studies in the Gospels*, R. H. Lightfoot FS (Oxford, 1955), p. 29.

[83] Reference to a list of resurrection appearances in kerygmatic summary form might also explain John 21.14.

summary, is Epistle of the Apostles 3–5.[84] Perhaps in these passages we have some indication of the way in which a kerygmatic summary would be used as an outline in preaching.[85]

THE KERYGMATIC SUMMARIES IN ACTS

We now have the comparative material for establishing that the kerygmatic summaries in the speeches of Acts belong to the same, broad, and diverse tradition of kerygmatic summaries of which a variety of other early Christian writings preserve evidence. In the first place, we may notice that the four major kerygmatic summaries (Acts 2.22–24, 32–33; 3.13–15; 10.36–42; 13.23–31) exhibit both correspondences and variation between them, to a degree which is not unlike the similarities and differences between the three kerygmatic summaries in the Ascension of Isaiah. The form was inherently flexible, and Luke has taken full advantage of its flexibility in order to suit his narrative contexts and in order to spare his readers the tedium of repetition.

Secondly, we have seen that the kerygmatic summary was often used as a summary of the history of Jesus as predicted by the prophets. This is in fact the case with all the major examples which we have studied, except for those in Ignatius. The close connection between the kerygmatic summaries and the proof from prophecy in Acts is therefore entirely characteristic of the tradition of kerygmatic summaries. It appears not

---

[84] This may explain the mixture of miracle reports and short miracle narratives to which J. Hills, *Tradition and Composition in the Epistula Apostolorum*, HDR 24 (Minneapolis, 1990), chap. 2, draws attention. We are not dealing here with the miracle list as an independent form, since chapters 4–5 of the Epistle of the Apostles continue the narrative begun in chapter 3, and since the narrative is continued, after interruption, in chapter 9. The miracle list as an independent form in early Christian literature (of which Hills gives many examples on pp. 40–44) may well have grown out of the kerygmatic summary.

[85] Note also EpApost 9–11, where the kerygmatic summary, resumed from chapter 5, becomes, by the end of chapter 9, full narrative. A similar instance is the (unfortunately fragmentary) sermon of Paul in Acts of Paul (Hamburg Papyrus, p. 8 and Heidelberg Papyrus, pp. 79–80), where what begins as kerygmatic summary turns into a full report of a dialogue between Jesus and his disciples about his miracles.

only in general statements that the events fulfill prophecy (Acts 3.18, 24; 10.43; 13.27–29; cf. 17.2–3) and specific citations of texts which are explained as fulfilled in the events (Acts 2.25–36; 3.22–26;13.32–37), but also in allusions to Scripture in the way the kerygmatic summaries themselves report the events of the history of Jesus. We have already noticed several instances of such allusions which Acts shares with other examples of kerygmatic summaries: reference to the cross as "the tree" and crucifixion as "hanging on a tree" (Acts 5.30; 10.39; 13.29; cf. AscIsa. 3.13; 9.14; 11.20); resurrection "on the third day" (Acts 10.40; cf. 1 Cor. 15.4; AscIsa 3.16; 9.16; 11.21); and the use of παραδιδόναι (Acts 2.23; 3.13; cf. AscIsa 11.19). Other instances of this phenomenon in Acts are in Acts 10.36 (allusions to Ps. 107.20; Isa. 52.7); 10.38 (Isa. 61.1; cf. Acts 4.27); 10.38 (Ps. 107.20); 13.24 (Mal. 3.1?); 13.26 (Ps. 107.20?).[86] In general, not only is the close integration of kerygmatic summaries and the proof from prophecy in the sermons of Acts true to the tradition of such summaries. It may well also reflect an actual practice of using such summaries, together with collections of *testimonia*, as outlines for sermons which demonstrated the fulfillment of the prophecies in the history of Jesus.

Thirdly, the kerygmatic summaries in Acts frequently use terminology which is not characteristic of the Gospel tradition, but occurs in other kerygmatic summaries. Some of the allusions to prophecy just noticed are in this category: "the tree," "hanging on a tree," "on the third day." Other instances already noticed are "wonders and signs" (2.22; cf. AscIsa 11.18; TAdam 3.1); "in the country of the Jews and in Jerusalem" (10.39; cf. AscIsa 11.18; Acts of Paul [Hamburg Papyrus, p. 8]); "from this man's [David's] seed" (13.23: σπέρματος, as in Ignatius, *Eph.* 18.2; *Rom.* 7.3); "did not recognize him" (13.27: ἀγνοήσαντες;[87] cf. Justin, *1 Apol.* 31.7:

---

[86] These allusions are discussed in Stanton, *Jesus of Nazareth*, pp. 72–76, 83. But for some criticism of Stanton's case, see D. L. Bock, *Proclamation from Prophecy and Pattern: Lucan Old Testament Christology*, JSNTSS 12 (Sheffield, 1987), pp. 231–234.

[87] This is the only instance of the verb with Jesus as the object in early Christian literature.

ἀγνοούμενον).[88] It would not be difficult to list many other expressions which, while not paralleled in other known examples of kerygmatic summaries, are not used in the Gospel traditions and may well have been traditional in the tradition of kerygmatic summaries known to Luke. The tradition of the kerygmatic summaries was terminologically relatively independent of the Gospel tradition, and Luke's use of the tradition reflects this independence.

Fourthly, we have seen that the flexibility of the kerygmatic summary allows it to be augmented from the Gospel traditions. There is therefore no inconsistency in supposing that, while Luke draws much of his material in the summaries from tradition, he also sometimes expands and improvises, drawing on the Gospel traditions in his own Gospel. This may well be the case, for example, with the specific details about the events leading to Jesus' death in Acts 3.13b–14; 13.28. Although a reference to John's ministry of baptism may well have been a traditional feature of kerygmatic summaries (cf. Jesus' baptism in Ignatius, *Smyrn.* 1.1; *Eph.* 18.2), the full account in Acts 13.24–25, including John's testimony to Jesus, is very likely Luke's expansion, drawing rather freely on the traditions in his own Gospel (Lk. 3.3, 15–16). It resembles, in this respect, the incorporation of material from Matt. 3.15 (or its source) in the kerygmatic summary in Ignatius, *Smyrn.* 1.1, or the rather full summary of a resurrection tradition in AscIsa 3.14b–17a. The tradition of the kerygmatic summaries was, I have argued, relatively independent of the Gospel traditions, but we have noticed a number of instances in which the Gospel traditions are drawn on to expand a kerygmatic summary. There is nothing untypical about the instances of this in Acts.

Fifthly, it is worth noticing that the kerygmatic summaries in Acts begin no earlier than the ministry of John the Baptist (10.37; 13.24). They do not refer to the birth of Jesus, still less his coming into the world, though 13.23 refers to his descent from David. Nearly all other kerygmatic summaries we have

---

[88] In AscIsa 9.14–15; 11.14,16, 17,19; SibOr 8.292–293 (cf. 1 Cor. 2.8), the theme is rather different: the deliberate concealing of Christ's divine nature and heavenly origin so that he may not be recognized.

noticed refer to Christ's birth (AscIsa 11.2–16; Ignatius, *Trall.* 9.1; *Smyrn.* 1.1; *Eph.* 18.2; EpApost. 3; Justin, *1 Apol.* 31.7; Acts of Paul [Hamburg Papyrus, p. 8]; Irenaeus, *Adv. Haer.* 1.10.1) and/or his "coming" (KerPet 4[a]; Justin, *1 Apol.* 31.7; Irenaeus, *Adv. Haer.* 1.10.1) or otherwise to his incarnation (AscIsa 3.13; 9.13). It seems likely that kerygmatic summaries beginning with the birth of Jesus go back to Luke's time. If so, he has chosen not to follow these in the speeches of Acts, even though his own Gospel takes the story of Jesus back to his conception. Luke's kerygmatic summaries are not, as such, summaries of his own Gospel. They are attempts to represent what the apostles preached. Luke knew that the apostolic proclamation of the Gospel told the story of Jesus' public ministry, beginning with reference to John the Baptist.

In conclusion, it is likely that the examples of kerygmatic summaries which we have studied are merely the literary tip of a vast oral iceberg. The kerygmatic summary was essentially an oral form. During the first century of its use, it must have taken many diverse forms. Most of the literary examples we have are adaptations of the form for some literary purpose which was not the primary function of the oral form. Paul only recorded part of the tradition he had delivered to the Corinthian church when he founded it because he wished to base an argument about resurrection on it. Similarly Ignatius only reproduced kerygmatic summaries for the sake of anti-docetic argument, a polemical use which was secondary to their primary, positive purpose of summarizing the kerygma. We are probably closest to one of the main functions of the oral form in those texts which use the kerygmatic summary to summarize what, they claim, the prophets had predicted about Jesus. The sermons in Acts are among those texts, but in addition they may bear some relationship to one real *Sitz im Leben* of the oral summaries. The sermons in Acts are not, of course, really sermons: They are literary representations of sermons. Luke wishes to give his readers an impression of the kind of thing that would have been said in the narrative contexts in which the sermons occur, but he cannot reproduce a full-length sermon. If Christian preachers in fact used the kerygmatic summaries as outlines, which they would fill out from their knowledge of the Gospel traditions and to which they would attach appropriate scriptural *testimonia* with exposition of how these prophecies had been fulfilled, then these kerygmatic summaries were the most appropriate form for Luke's use. No doubt Luke's use of the form was relatively free, but this freedom itself was appropriate to a highly flexible form, whose use always involved selection and improvisation.

CHAPTER 9

The "script" of the Scriptures in Acts: suffering as God's "plan" (βουλή) for the world for the "release of sins"[1]

David P. Moessner

The ironic if not sobering conclusion of much of critical scholarship on Luke–Acts is that the suffering or death of Christ in itself plays no constitutive role in effecting the salvation that is proclaimed in Luke's second volume. "There is no trace of any Passion mysticism, nor is any direct soteriological significance drawn from Jesus' suffering or death. There is no suggestion of a connection with the forgiveness of sins."[2] Conzelmann's judgment has by and large remained in force some forty-plus years with only slight modifications. The divine necessity of the Christ to suffer is attributed to the comprehensive "will of God," and Luke's use of traditional formulae in the Last Supper longer reading, 22.19b–20, and in Acts 20.28 reflects his own willingness to admit some association, however muted, of Jesus' death with the cultus of sacrifice. Kümmel's survey and modification of Conzelmann's position is representative of much contemporary sentiment: "While Luke by no means entirely removes the redemptive

---

[1] Special gratitude is due the Pew Charitable Trusts for a year-long grant (1993/4) which enabled me to accomplish the research and writing for this chapter and to the German Academic Exchange (DAAD), which made it possible for me to carry out much of the research at the University of Tübingen.
[2] H. Conzelmann, *The Theology of St. Luke* (New York, 1960), p. 201; cf. U. Wilckens, *Die Missionsreden der Apostelgeschichte*, 3rd ed., WMANT 5 (Neukirchen-Vluyn, 1974), p. 216; E. Haenchen, *The Acts of the Apostles* (Oxford, 1971), pp. 91–92; for surveys, F. Bovon, *Luc le théologien: Vingt-cinq ans de recherches (1950–1975)*, 2nd ed. (Geneva, 1988), pp. 175–181; J. A. Fitzmyer, *The Gospel According to Luke*, (Garden City, NY, 1981), vol. I, pp. 22–23, 219–227; J. A. Fitzmyer, *Luke the Theologian: Aspects of his Teaching* (New York, 1989), pp. 203–233; W. G. Kümmel, "Current Theological Accusations Against Luke," *ANQ* 16 (1975), 134, 138.

significance of the death of Jesus he does not stress it."[3] This evaluation would seem particularly striking in light of Luke's two quotations from the Servant of Isaiah passages. But neither in Jesus' own quotation from Isa. 53.12 at the Last Supper nor in the reading from Isa. 53.7–8 of the Ethiopian finance minister in Acts 8.32–33 do the citations continue or include lines from the immediate contexts in which a vicarious atoning death is explicitly predicated of the Servant. According to the "ruling" viewpoint, it would seem almost as if Luke is going out of his way to avoid soteriological linkage to this Servant figure. I. H. Marshall sums up this popular appraisal for both Luke and Acts: "In the Servant . . . we see the supreme case of a person who goes to suffering by the will of God and is subsequently vindicated by God . . . there is no evidence that he [Luke] himself has positively evaluated the Servant concept in terms of redemptive suffering."[4] Indeed for many it is this "Servant pattern" which points to the real saving events in Lucan *Heilsgeschichte*, namely the resurrection, ascension or exaltation of Christ. Whether the death of Jesus be accorded token soteriological significance or none at all, the sentiment prevails that Luke lacks a deeper or profounder understanding of the cross of the more pristine Pauline or Marcan variety. As Käsemann put it, "the Cross of Jesus is no longer a scandal but only a misunderstanding on the part of the Jews which the intervention of God palpably and manifestly corrects."[5]

But does Luke make sense of all that climaxes at the "place of the skull" essentially by a powerful *deus ex machina* at Easter? Is

---

[3] Kümmel, "Accusations," p. 138; similarly, but with more emphasis on the cross, Fitzmyer, *Luke the Theologian*, p. 212 (on Lk. 23.43): "The real question about the Lucan story is whether God is portrayed in it bringing to realization his salvific plan *despite* the suffering and death of Jesus or *through* that suffering and death. In my opinion, it is the latter."

[4] I. H. Marshall, *Luke: Historian and Theologian* (Grand Rapids, 1970), p. 172.

[5] E. Käsemann, *Essays on New Testament Themes*, SBT 41 (London, 1964), p. 92. There are several notable exceptions to this "reading": e.g., J. Neyrey, *The Passion According to Luke: A Redactional Study of Luke's Soteriology* (New York, 1985), esp. pp. 184–192; R. J. Karris, "Luke 23.47 and the Lucan View of Jesus' Death," *JBL* 105 (1986), 65–74; R. J. Karris, *Luke: Artist and Theologian. Luke's Passion Account as Literature* (New York, 1985); J. M. Ford, "Reconciliation and Forgiveness in Luke's Gospel," in *Political Issues in Luke–Acts*, ed. R. J. Cassidy and P. J. Scharper (Maryknoll, NY, 1983), pp. 80–98.

a more provocative, scandalous *theologia crucis* diluted or even replaced by Luke with a *theologia gloriae* with the result that through the mighty resurrection and enthronement of Christ the great release of sins is finally triggered and the "word of this salvation" now triumphs from Jerusalem to Samaria, and on to the ends of the earth? As this popular notion of Luke's "atonement theology" goes, it is surely ironic that the one Gospel writer who stresses the scriptural mandate for the rejection or death of Israel's Messiah at Israel's own hands would see this fulfillment as largely "filler" for a more important moment in the plot of God's saving action. And can we be satisfied with the treatment of narrative summary statements that are patently "loaded" exegetical moments for the construal of the whole but whose interpretation remains largely traditio-historical analyses of its concepts apart from its primary context in the narrative of Luke–Acts?[6] For instance, what are we to make of Jesus' own ponderous portrayal of his entire public ministry at table before his death at the "Skull?": "For I tell you that this which stands written must (δεῖ) come to its completion in me: 'And he was reckoned with the lawless' [LXX Isa. 53.12d]. For indeed that which is written concerning me (περὶ ἐμοῦ) is now reaching its intended goal (τέλος ἔχει)" (Lk. 22.37). But what kind of "goal" is this if it is only a "presupposition" or backdrop for the "real" saving event, or what kind of God would "require" the merciless death of an innocent Jew by sadly "mistaken" Jews only to reveal that this rejection is in any case fundamentally superfluous to any consequences, except to the negative consequence that awaits Israel for its "ignorant" mistake?[7] Do we have in this interpre-

---

[6] E.g. Conzelmann, *Theology of Saint Luke*, pp. 80–83.

[7] E.g. E. Haenchen, *The Acts of the Apostles*, 14th ed. (Oxford, 1971), p. 128: "Three times over . . . it is explained that the Jewish people (λαός 28.26) has forfeited its salvation. For Luke the Jews are 'written off'"; Conzelmann, *Theology of Saint Luke*, p. 145 (on Acts 13.46): "There is . . . a reference to the cutting off of the Jews from redemptive history . . . We can say that the Jews are now called to make good their claim to be 'Israel'. If they fail to do this, then they become 'the Jews'"; J. Jervell, *Luke and the People of God* (Minneapolis, 1984), p. 68 (on an "Israel alongside" Israel as the church): "The reason is that this Israel includes the Jews who were excluded from the people of God on account of their rejection of the gospel and who have no right to the name 'Israel'"; J. T. Sanders, *The Jews in Luke–Acts* (Philadelphia,

tation perhaps more to do with a sadly mistaken, negative valuation of Israel and of God's will (βουλή) for the Jewish people's participation in Jesus' suffering than with a reading of Luke's distinctive portrait?

The thesis to be defended here is that Luke presents the proclamation of the risen Christ, his resurrection or exaltation, and especially his rejection/crucifixion as the three critical components of the fulfillment of God's saving "plan" for the world which has been announced in advance in Israel's Scriptures. Jesus' death along with his raising up to become the "proclaimed proclaimer" in fact follows a closely knit "plot" as depicted and "predicted" in various suffering righteous figures of the Scriptures, foremost of whom are Moses and David. More specifically, this "script" is: (1) summarized in a variety of ways and expressions such as "the divine necessity" (δεῖ)[8] of a suffering "Christ" in (all) the Scriptures (Moses and the prophets); or "the plan of God" (ἡ βουλή τοῦ Θεοῦ) (for the whole of human history);[9] or "the fulfillment of (all) the Scriptures";[10] (2) perceived by Luke as comprehending the whole of Israel's history, especially as it is fulfilled eschatologically in the continued rejection and suffering of its messianic "way." In particular, Luke uses the phrase, "the plan/counsel/will of God" similarly to the way Hellenistic historians speak of a divine principle of order or fate (for example τύχη, εἰμαρμ-ενη, γνώμη, ἀνάγκη) through which they ascertain a larger "rationale" or movement in history and order their material accordingly;[11] (3) utilized by Luke as a principle of unity and

1987), p. 83: "The true role of the Jewish people is prefigured in the Nazareth episode, where Jesus' audience turns with one accord against him."

[8] Acts 1.16 (21–22); 9.16; 14.22; 17.3; 19.21; 23.11 (27.24); cf. Lk. 9.22; 13.33; 17.25; 22.37; 24.7,26,44–46.

[9] Acts 2.23; 4.28; 5.38 (ironically); 13.36; 20.27; cf. Lk. 7.30.

[10] Acts 1.16; 3.18; 13.27, 29; cf. Lk. 2.21–22, 39, 43; 4.21; 18.31; 21.22; 22.37; 24.44.

[11] For "providence"/"fortune"/(divine) "will" (πρόνοια/τύχη/γνώμη and other terms) as an ordering principle, see, e.g., Polybius (*Hist.* 1.4.1–2); Dionysius of Halicarnassus (*Rom. Ant.* 1.4.2); Arrian (*Anab.* 5.1.2); Diodorus (*Bib. Hist.* 1.1.3); cf. Josephus (*Ant.* 1.14, 46); Philo (*De prov.* [*passim*]; *De sobr.* 63); etc. For "fate"/"chance"/"necessity" (εἰμαρμένη/πεπρωμένη/ἀνάγκη and similar terms), see, e.g., Diodorus (*Bib. Hist.* 15.63.2; 3.15.7; 19.2; 10.21.3 etc.); Josephus (*Ant.* 16.397–398; *War* 2.162–164); Dionysius (*Rom. Ant.* 3.5.2; 11.1; 5.8.6; 9.8.1; 10.45.4); Lucian of Samosata, *Zeus Catechized*. For excerpts and/or discussions, see, e.g., A. J. Toynbee,

harmonization for the widely divergent traditions of the growing "messianic" movement. Typical of Hellenistic historians Luke uses the speeches of his main characters to comment on the meaning of the events as they have been unfolding as well as to "complicate" and drive the larger plot of the messianic history.[12] All five instances of "the will of God," for example in the Book of Acts, occur in set speeches or utterances of leading characters at pivotal moments in the thickening plot. By such a maneuver Luke has characters as different as a Peter or a Paul or even a Gamaliel subsume all of the differing reactions and viewpoints to an overarching understanding of what is taking place in the story of Israel. What has happened according to these characters is nothing less than the unfolding script of Israel's *raison d'être* in bringing new life for the whole world as it culminates in the death and enthronement of Israel's anointed.

The scope of this chapter does not allow a tracing of this script in the overall plot of Luke–Acts or an analysis of several of the related themes such as the "divine necessity" in God's fore-ordination, fore-knowledge of history, etc.[13] We shall con-

---

Greek Historical Thought (New York, 1952), esp. pp. 126–149; A. Momigliano, "The Origins of Universal History," in *The Poet and the Historian: Essays in Literary and Historical Biblical Criticism*, ed. R. E. Friedman, HSS 26 (Chico, 1983), pp. 133–154; W. den Boer, "Graeco-Roman Historiography in its Relation to Biblical and Modern Thinking," in *History and Theory* 7 (1968), 60–75; A. Schlatter, *Wie Sprach Josephus von Gott?*, Beitrage zur Forderung christlicher Theologie 14 (Gutersloh, 1910); H. W. Attridge, *The Interpretation of Biblical History in the "Antiquitates Judaicae" of Flavius Josephus*, HDR 7 (Missoula, 1976) (*passim*); J. T. Squires, *The Plan of God in Luke–Acts*, SNTSMS 76 (Cambridge, 1993), pp. 15–77, 155–185.

[12] See, e.g., E. Plümacher, *Lukas als hellenistischer Schriftsteller*, SUNT 9 (Göttingen, 1972), pp. 32–79; E. Plümacher, "Die Missionsreden der Apostelgeschichte und Dionys von Halikarnass," *NTS* 39 (1993), 161–177, esp. 164–171; W. C. van Unnik, "Luke's Second Book and the Rules of Hellenistic Historiography," in *Les Actes des Apôtres*, ed. J. Kremer, BETL 48 (Gembloux, 1979), pp. 37–60; K. S. Sacks, "Rhetorical Approaches to Greek History Writing in the Hellenistic Period," in *Society of Biblical Literature 1984 Seminar Papers*, ed. K. Richards (Chico, CA, 1984), pp. 123–133.

[13] See, e.g., C. H. Cosgrove, "The Divine *Dei* in Luke–Acts," *NovT* 26 (1984), 168–190. For the role of the cross in the *plot* of the Gospel of Luke, see D. P. Moessner, "'The Christ Must Suffer,' the Church Must Suffer: Rethinking the Theology of the Cross in Luke–Acts," *Society of Biblical Literature 1990 Seminar Papers*, ed. D. J. Lull (Atlanta, 1990), pp. 165–183; D. P. Moessner,"Good News for the Wilderness Generation: The Death of the Prophet Like Moses," *Good News in*

centrate rather on several speeches or shorter dialogues in which God's "plan" is elaborated in some detail. It will be seen that although Luke does not articulate the effects of Jesus' death in the atonement terminology of a Mark or Paul,[14] the phrase "release/forgiveness of sins" (ἄφεσις τῶν ἁμαρτιῶν) is Luke's characteristic formulation of the saving, atoning action of God,[15] and that this conception is peculiarly linked to the suffering or death of Christ.

1 ACTS 1.15–26

Peter tells the gathered 120 that Scripture "had to be fulfilled" (δεῖ πληρωθῆναι) with respect to Judas as a "guide to those who arrested Jesus" (1.16b) and to fill this "office" with another who will become with the eleven a "witness to his resurrection" (1.21–22). In Ps. [LXX] 68(69).26, cited in Acts 1.20, the one(s) whose "dwelling"/"cottage"/"cabin" is to become desolate are those in the psalm who have persecuted and tormented a righteous servant (παῖς, 68.17) who has suffered reproach for God's cause (68.5–12). Moreover, the "desolation of their habitation" is to take place since they have wounded the one whom God has *smitten* (πατάσσω, 68.25–26; cf. Lk. 22.49,50). Peter, in other words, appears to be looking back and describing the "things that have happened" (Lk. 24.18) in terms of a plot found in Scripture. Judas is identified in the "script" as a persecutor of a (God's) righteous, suffering servant (cf. the offering of "vinegar" [ὄξος] as part of the *suffering*, Ps. 68.21 and Lk. 23.36).

This identification is confirmed by the citation of Ps. 108(109).8, which immediately "enriches" Psalm 68 in Acts 1.20c. His "office" or "position of overseer" (ἡ ἐπισκοπή) refers to *one* who in particular (108.6–19) out of a larger group

---

History: Studies in Honor of Bo Reicke, ed. E. L. Miller, Homage Series (Atlanta, 1993), pp. 1–34.

[14] Luke, for example, does not express Jesus' death as a *lutron* ("ransom"/"manumission sum"), Mark 10.45; but cf. Acts 7.35.

[15] For the OT (LXX) background of this phrase, see Fitzmyer, *Luke*, vol. 1, pp. 223–224.

of adversaries (108.2–5, 20, 25, 28–31) has "falsely accused" (108.4, 20) a suffering, righteous servant (δοῦλος, 108.3b, 28–29) and is even thinking to put to death this one who has become pricked/pained in the heart but who continues to *pray for his accusers* (108.4b–5; Lk. 23.34!). Judas' "office" of leading the accusers against Jesus, God's "righteous one" (Lk. 23.47), was dictated in Scripture by a divine necessity (ἔδει, Acts 1.16) and must (δεῖ, 1.21) be filled by one who has witnessed this whole drama "from the time the Lord Jesus went in and out among us, beginning from the *baptism of John* [cf. Lk. 7.29–30, where his baptism is called τὴν βουλὴν τοῦ Θεοῦ] until the day he was taken up from us" (1.22a). But this means, then, that the phrase, "witness to his resurrection" refers to one who has participated in the whole plan of events of Jesus as *spoken "in advance" in Scripture*. What is more, the apparent contradiction of juxtaposing two psalm quotations in which the first (Ps. 68) admonishes no replacement but rather "desolation" for the legacy of the persecutor, Judas, whereas the second (Ps. 108) exhorts a continuance of the role of such "overseeing," is now resolved. Peter is declaring that Scripture had pre-"spoken" through David (1.16) that within their own ranks as the closest followers and "overseers" of Jesus' activity a "leader" of the false accusers *must* emerge and that this opposition *must* be so critical to Scripture's pre-scription that the original "number allotted to this ministry" (1.17) *must* be continued in order to keep this God-ordained "witness" to Jesus' death in force. In other words, Jesus' rejection even, or rather especially, from among his own followers is so central to the divine necessity that the "ministry" of this "witness" in the Acts of the Apostles *must* be re-consolidated into the very notion of apostleship. Jesus' commission of the (eleven) "apostles whom he had chosen" (1.2; cf. Lk. 6.13) to be his "witnesses in Jerusalem and in all Judea" (Acts 1.8; cf. Lk. 24.46–48) is now being explicitly defined as "receiving a *place* in the apostleship of this ministry from which Judas turned aside to go to his own *place*" (i.e. to the "field of blood," 1.19) (1.25). Witnessing to Judas' "place" as well as to their own in this larger script of the Scriptures becomes a benchmark for the very notion of "apostle" and serves as a pre-view to the continuing script which is to unfold in Luke's second volume (Acts 1.8). *To sum up*, it appears that the main plot of the developing events in both the Gospel of Luke and its sequel in Acts is already outlined in the Scriptures. To see whether this is in fact the case, we must continue to investigate this notion of a "script" within the Scriptures.

2 ACTS 2.14-40

In the center of his speech at Pentecost (2.14-36), Peter summarizes the career of Jesus from Nazareth, attested/appointed by God through powers, wonders, and signs, killed/executed by Israel ("you") by the agency of law-less folk, and raised up by God from the pangs/cords of death (2.22-25). What is emphasized in this sketch is the resurrection of Jesus to fulfill David's prophecy, Ps. 15(16).8-11, of God's "Holy One" who would not "see decomposition/corruption" (Acts 2.25-35). What is identified most closely, however, with the "predetermined plan and foreknowledge of God" (ὡρισμένη βουλῇ καὶ προγνώσει τοῦ Θεοῦ) is the "delivering up/over" of Jesus by the people to execution/crucifixion by "affixing him," which forms the framework for Peter's discussion of Jesus' resurrection and enthronement (2.23-24, 36b). Jesus' death is thus highlighted again when the people respond to Peter's second charge, verse 36b, that "you crucified Jesus." "Pricked/pained to the heart" (Ps. 108.16!), they are told to repent/change their perspective on what has happened and what they did, and become baptized in the name of Jesus Messiah for the release/forgiveness of sins and gift of the Holy Spirit (2.38). As in the Gospel (for example Lk. 24.44-49) repentance is an integral component of eschatological release, but now it is directed particularly toward the rejection or killing of Jesus in the necessary plan of God.

What role, then, does the resurrection/exaltation play in this plan? The phrase, "pangs of death" (ὠδῖνας τοῦ θανάτου, verse 24) from which the resurrection has "loosed" Jesus occurs *only* in Ps. 17(18).4 (2 Kgdm. 22.6)[16] and Ps. 114(116).3, in which David or an anonymous giver of thanks is presented as a righteous sufferer who is saved by the Lord. In Psalm 17 David is an anointed (χριστός) servant (παῖς, 17.1, 50) who identifies with the lowly (ταπεινός, verse 27), is "raised up"/"exalted" (ὑψόω, verse 48) over unrighteous enemies who hate him (verses 17, 40), and will thus be saved by God from the "pangs of death" (verse 4)[17] "because God has pleasure/delights in him" (verse 19) and in "his offspring forever" (verse 50). In Psalm 114 one who is "lowly" or "childlike" (νήπιος, verse 6) has been "humiliated" (ταπεινόω, verse 6), but is saved from the "pangs of death" (verse 3) by the Lord, who "will take pleasure in him in the land of the living" (verse 9). Psalm 15(16) depicts David as one who, in solidarity with all the persecuted "saints" (οἱ ἅγιοι . . . τας συναγώγας αὐτῶν ἐξ αἵματων, verse 4), sees the "Lord" "always before him," and is therefore confident that the Lord will not abandon his soul/life in Hades nor let the Lord's "holy one" (ὁ ὅσιος, verse 10) "see" the "corruption"/"decomposition" of the grave (verse 10).

The emphasis on the resurrection of Jesus now becomes clear. Jesus is the righteous sufferer, God's holy one, who has been saved/vindicated by God before the very people who rejected and killed him. Peter is thus expounding the role of the resurrection in this preset plan of salvation (see σῴζω, 2.21, 40), especially as it relates to their delivering Jesus to death and their accompanying need of repentance. It is manifest from Psalm 15 that David could not be speaking of himself as the Lord's "holy one" since he himself died and saw corruption (Acts 2.25–29). Moreover, in another psalm (109 [110]; Acts 2.34–35) the Lord addresses another (David's) "Lord" who has been raised/exalted to the right hand and given power over

---

[16] 2 Sam. 22, the Song or Praise of David, serves to sum up David's significance in a fashion similar to Peter's summary of Jesus' career utilizing a key phrase from 2 Sam. 22. All citations from the OT will be from the LXX unless otherwise indicated.

[17] Cf. I. H. Marshall, *The Acts of the Apostles* (Grand Rapids, 1980), pp. 75–76, quoting F. Field: "a remarkable mixed metaphor, in which death is regarded as being in labour and unable to hold back its child, the Messiah."

all his enemies in the midst of the *splendor of the saints* (109.1–3). David, then, a "prophet" (Acts 2.30; cf. 1.16), not only prefigures the Christ in being delivered from his unrighteous enemies, i.e. from death, as he dwells in hope; but also fore-sees the fate of the Christ, one of his "offspring" (2.30b–31), that the Christ would also be delivered from his unrighteous accusers but by being spared the decomposition of the grave and being exalted as Lord to God's own "throne" (verse 30b). Thus Peter is able to come full circle back to the Joel text (2.17–21) and his explanation of how it is that the Holy Spirit is being poured out by Jesus, this one whom "you crucified." In declaring that "God has established this Jesus as both Lord and Christ" (2.36), Peter sums up the whole "predetermined will (βουλή) and foreknowledge of God" (2.23) that is enacted through the careers of the suffering righteous David and his offspring Jesus. All the events that led both to the rejection/death and to the resurrection/enthronement of Jesus constitute Jesus' status as Lord and Christ. But it is the raising up of Jesus in fufilling David's fore-seeing of one like himself that is being singled out by Peter as that event in God's plan which identifies Jesus most confidently as the predicted suffering-exalted one. Therefore the people of Israel must repent/change their whole understanding and orientation to these events and be joined to this eschatological *release of sins* (ἄφεσις τῶν ἁμαρτιῶν, 2.38–39). *To sum up*, the end result of the whole "predetermined plan and foreknowledge of God" is the release of sins which comes through Jesus the Lord and Christ who fulfills the script of the suffering, righteous exalted one of the (David's) Psalms.

3 ACTS 3.12–26

Whereas in Peter's first speech both the rejection/death and resurrection/exaltation of Jesus are placed squarely in the center of God's saving plan with emphasis on the scriptural significance of the resurrection in that plan, all emphasis in this second speech is on the scriptural import of the denial/death of Jesus. Peter opens (3.12–13) by linking the name of "the God of Abraham, Isaac, Jacob" as revealed to Moses at his call or sending to Israel (Exod. 3.6,15–16) to God's servant (παῖς) Jesus, whom the people ("you") delivered over and denied and God glorified; he closes with the affirmation that these same people are the children/offspring of Moses and all the prophets and the heirs of the covenant to Abraham of blessing to all the nations (3.22–25). For this reason God had sent to them first this servant (παῖς) Jesus to "turn each of them from their evil" (3.26).

That by παῖς Peter is referring to the atoning effect of the Servant of Isaiah as well as to the pattern of the righteous servant *in general* is certain: (1) several of the distinctive terms of Isaiah's Servant passages cluster about the παῖς here – δοξάζω,[18] παραδίδωμι,[19] δίκαιος,[20] μάρτυς,[21] διαθήκη,[22] διατίθεμαι,[23] πονηρός;[24] (2) it is the Servant who (in the Gospel) goes first to Israel with the mission of restoration from sin but in so doing also becomes Yahweh's means of salvation to the nations (for example Lk. 4.18–27; Acts 3.25–26; cf. esp. Isa. 49.1–6); (3) as in the Gospel, where ignorance of God's means of release of sin is linked to Jesus' suffering/death, so again "not knowing" is linked to God's necessity that his "Christ" must suffer (for example Lk. 22.19–38; Acts 3.17–18; cf. esp. Isa. 53.4–6); (4) as also in the Gospel, all of the Scriptures point to a fulfillment in a suffering anointed one (Lk. 24.26–27, 44–49; Acts 3.18, 22–24; cf. Isa. 42.1–4; 43.10; 49.4; 50.6–7; 53.1–12); (5) as in the Gospel, a "change of mind"/"repentance" (μετάνοια or "turning" (ἐπιστρέφω) is an integral part of the saving release/"expunging" of sin through suffering/death (Lk. 24.25–26, 44–49; Acts 3.19; cf. esp. Isa. 44.21–22; 49.6 [45.22; 46.8; 55.7; see also the section on 4.23–31 below]); (6) furthermore, as the suffering Χριστός Jesus is preeminently the "prophet like Moses," spoken of by Moses, as the voice from heaven in the Gospel had already echoed in the midst of Jesus' discussion of his "exodus"/"death" with Moses and Elijah (Lk. 9.28–36; Acts 3.18,22–24; cf. Isa. 40.3–5; 48.20–49.2,8–12; 52.6–15 [41.17–20; 42.14–17; 43.1–3,14–21]); (7) finally, as

[18] Isa. 49.3,5; 52.13 (44.23).   [19] Isa. 53.6,12 (twice).   [20] Isa. 53.11.
[21] Isa. 43.9,10,12 (44.8).
[22] Isa. 42.6; 49.6,8.   [23] Isa. 61.8.   [24] Isa. 53.9.

in the Gospel, the rejection, suffering, and death of the Christ have led to "glory" in "heaven" (Lk. 24.26; Acts 3.13, 21; cf. Isa. 43.7; 52.1,13–14). We have then again as in Peter's first speech the blueprint of the plan or necessity of God's salvation which encompasses both the death and the resurrection of the Christ for the forgiveness/release of sins. Here it is the rejection, suffering, and death that are being singled out in this plan. *In sum*, the rejection of Jesus the righteous Servant forms the focal point of the plot which God fulfilled and had already declared through the mouth of all the prophets (Acts 3.18).

4 ACTS 4.23–31; 5.27–42

Like Acts 2.23, 4.28 speaks of God's/the Lord's predetermined/ ordained "plan" (βουλή) and fuses it directly to the Lord's "anointed" "Servant" Jesus *in his rejection*. Already in Psalm 2 David, the Lord's *anointed* παῖς (2.2; Acts 4.25), had spoken about the violent rejection of Jesus, the Lord's *anointed* παῖς (Acts 4.26–27), and David's words continue to describe the harsh treatment of Peter and John, the Lord's *servants* (δουλοί, 4.29), at the hands of Israel's leaders (οἱ ἄρχοντες, 4.25–28). This fluctuation between an individual servant (παῖς) and a larger group of the servant (δοῦλος) who are sent to restore Israel *through suffering* is found already in the second Servant song, LXX (δοῦλος as "Israel," 49.3, 5, sent to gather Israel and yet in features also characteristic of an individual called, named, formed from the womb, hidden, protected as one among many, 49.1, 2, παῖς, verse 6).

The early Jerusalem community prays that the Lord will continue to use Peter and John despite the threats (ἀπειλή) of the leaders by continuing the bold preaching and powerful signs and wonders through the name of the Lord's holy Servant Jesus (4.29–30). Not unlike the prayer of the δοῦλος of Ps. 108.4 for his persecutors, the prayer of the messianist community of δουλοί is thus for the continuing *mediation* of eschato- logical life through suffering on behalf of the whole λαός of Israel. It is curious that our narrator places this prayer of the "filled" or "anointed" servant community (4.31) between two persecutions of the apostles-witnesses (4.1–22; 5.17–26) and their calls for the rest of Israel to change their mind (μετάνοια, 3.19, 5.31) and turn (ἐπιστρέφω, 3.19; cf. 4.12) to the plan of God in Jesus their Anointed One (cf. Isa. 49.6, ἐπιστρέφω, and the Servant's mission to "turn" the scattered Israel "back" to the Lord and the message of "changing their mind" and "turning" throughout Deutero-Isaiah: 46.8, μετανοεῖν and ἐπιστρέφω [the Servant to Israel]; 44.22 [to the Servant as all Israel], 45.22 [to nations], 55.7 [to Israel]).

In Acts 5.30–31 Peter and the apostles repeat God's basic scheme which effects release from sin: "God . . . has raised Jesus upon whom you laid violent hands by hanging him upon a tree. This one, the leader of life and Savior,[25] God exalted at his right hand, granting repentance and release of sin to Israel." Gamaliel's response, contrary to the rest of the Sanhedrin and Council (5.21b), is to compare the movements of Theudas and Judas the Galilean (who shared hopes not unlike those expectations of liberation/redemption of the pious in the Gospel, for example Lk. 1.51–53, 69–75; cf. the "Egyptian," Acts 21.38) with that of Jesus (5.31–37). Gamaliel cautions that the latter could, ironically, be of the "plan" (βουλή) of God (5.38).[26] Peter and the apostles, "released" by Gamaliel's point of view, count themselves honored to be the *suffering mediators* of the "name" of this plan (5.41).

5 ACTS 8.26–40

"On the way" *from* Jerusalem the Ethiopian finance minister, upon reading Isa. 53.7–8 (LXX), poses the question the Emmaus disciples should have asked when a stranger likewise came up to join their journey (Lk. 24.13–35). Like Jesus, Philip *begins* (ἄρχομαι) with this Scripture of a suffering anointed one in declaring the present "good news about Jesus" (8.35), which

---

[25] Syntax as in Acts 7.35b; 2.23, 32, 36b; cf. Vulgate (1843 ed.): "Hunc principem et salvatorem Deum exaltavit"; (1979 edition): "Hunc Deus principem et salvatorem exaltavit."

[26] Ironically as Paul, who is the opposer of Jesus and yet "student" of Gamaliel (Acts 22.3), will be (see below).

leads directly to the chamberlain being baptized (8.36,38). What is featured in the citation is the Servant who endures injustice, persecution, and death without protest for the sake of his mission. Philip himself is one who was forced to flee Jerusalem because of the persecution initiated against Stephen's witness (8.1–2). Stephen, in solidarity with Jesus "the Righteous One," the prophet like Moses (7.37, 52; cf. Isa. 53.11b), the Son of Humankind in glory (7.55–56), had exemplified one who like Jesus did not strike back but even prayed for the forgiveness of those who were persecuting him (7.60; cf. Lk. 23.34; Ps. 108.4).

Our narrator, then, demonstrates again how the mediation of the release of sin effected through the suffering-death and resurrection-exaltation of Jesus Messiah continues on to Israel and beyond through the "script" of the Servant unfolding through his servants. Through Stephen's rejection by Israel and suffering mediation, Philip takes the Servant Gospel to non-Jewish Samaritans in fulfilling the mission of Isa. 49.6 to "re-establish the tribes of Jacob and to turn back the diaspora of Israel." The chamberlain is probably to be identified as a God-worshiping eunuch and therefore "marginal" (i.e. not unlike the "tax collectors and sinners" in the Gospel), prevented by the law from entering into the Temple and therefore from becoming a full worshiping member of Israel (for example Deut. 23.1). If so, his full inclusion now represents the fulfillment of Isa. 56.3–5, similar to Samaria representing the strangers (ἀλλογενεῖς) whose inclusion fulfills the "gathering of the dispersed of Israel" as "servants" in 56.6–8 (ὁ ἀλλογενὴς . . . δουλοί, 56.3, 6; cf. Lk. 17.18)![27] In any case, Acts 1.8 (Isa. 49.6b) is being realized as the eunuch's baptism anticipates the baptisms of Saul and Cornelius and the mission to the nations in Acts 9–10.

In sum, the Ethiopian eunuch and the Samaritan "foreigners" are being scripted by the narrator into the broader and more ancient script of the Servant(s') mission in Isaiah of

---

[27] Acts 15.3 indicates clearly that Samaritan conversion is not regarded as the Gentile mission.

reestablishing the twelve tribes of Israel. It is noteworthy, moreover, that Philip, like Jesus on the Emmaus road, *begins* his explanation of the events of the Christ with a particular (servant) passage with the implication that many more passages or sections of the Scriptures divulge the same recurring "script" (see esp. Lk. 24.27, 44).

6 ACTS 9.1–18

The narrator first introduces Saul/Paul precisely when Stephen is suffering from the "threats" (ἀπειλή) of the Sanhedrin (7.58; cf. 4.29; 9.1). Later the narrator will have Paul present a summary of his entire calling to Israel when Paul himself is nearly killed by the people of Israel (21.22–40) and invokes the "blood of Stephen your [Jesus'] witness," whose "murder" Paul had once been "actively approving" (22.1–16, 17–22). This link is hardly fortuitous, for in Paul we see one of the most dramatic examples of a radical "turning" or shift in point of view.[28] All three accounts of his call underscore the fact that his persecution of those who call upon the name of Messiah Jesus (9.14, 21–22) was actually a persecution of Jesus himself (9.4–5; 22.7–8; 26.14–15: Σαοὺλ, Σαούλ, τί με διώκεις;). This solidarity in suffering between Jesus and the community makes explicit what was all but stated in the section on 4.23–31 above, where suffering for the sake of the name is linked to the name which is present to grant repentance and release of sin as well as healing.

As in Acts 4.23–31, the Servant mission of Isaiah, especially 49.1–6(7), is peculiarly programmatic. This plot of the "divine must" for God's saving act is substantiated in the details of Paul's call: (1) Paul, like Jesus the chosen/elect Son, is a "chosen instrument"/"agent" (σκεῦος ἐκλογῆς, 9.15) of the Lord's (Jesus') purposes. "Chosen/elect vessel" calls to mind such passages as Jer. 18.3–6 and Isa. 54.17–18, in which a

---

[28] As imaged, e.g. in the ironic use of "to bind" (δέω): Paul, who is zealous to *bind* all those who call on the name of the Lord Jesus (Acts 9.2, 14, 21; 22.5) becomes preeminently the one *bound* by his fellow Jews (24.27; cf. 28.20), even as he is *bound* "in the Spirit" (20.22) to be *bound* in Jerusalem (21.11, 13, 33; 22.29).

prophet, a smaller group of Israel, or Israel as a whole is chosen by God to be an agent of restoration through God's remolding/ saving activity (see also Acts 22.14; 26.16; Galatians 1.15; Rom. 1.1). (2) Paul is to "bear my name" before the "nations, kings, and the people of Israel." These three categories match the three audiences of the Servant's (individual and corporate) call in Isa. 49.5–7 and 52.15–53.6[29] and recall Philip's "audience" on the road to Gaza. The "name of the Lord/Jesus" is the presence of Jesus the Christ himself for "salvation" (Acts 2.21; 4.12), the "release of sins" (2.38), "healing" or "signs and wonders" (3.6,16; 4.10,30), and the authoritative presence by which one is empowered to speak or act (4.7, 17, 18; 5.28, 40) and to *suffer* (5.41; cf. 4.30) for those tasks. (3) Paul's "bearing" of the name is inseparably tied to this suffering for the sake of that "presence." It is a "divine must" (δεῖ, 9.16) that suffering be the means or agency through which the name of Christ is effective.

To sum up, Paul is called to open his eyes and to "see the light" from heaven's point of view, so that the light of salvation may shine *through suffering* upon Israel and the nations thus to fulfill Simeon's prophecy for the Servant-Christ (Lk. 2.29–35). It is no "wonder," then, that Paul in Damascus begins to preach "immediately that this Jesus is the *Son of God*" (9.20; cf. Lk. 3.22; 9.35), "confounding the Jews" in the synagogues that "*Jesus is the Christ*" (9.22; cf. Lk. 4.16–27, where Jesus as the anointed [χριστός] prophet/servant of Isa. 61 argues from the Scriptures in the synagogue). Like Jesus he receives the prophets' "reward" at the edge of town (9.23–25; cf. Lk. 4.28–30).

7 ACTS 13.13–52

From Acts 13 our narrator orders all his material to present Paul's calling within the "Lord's" larger "plan" (βουλή, 13.36) and places a speech near the beginning of Paul's activity

---

[29] On Isa. 49.1–6(7) as a "prophetic call," see K. Baltzer, *Die Biographie der Propheten* (Neukirchen-Vluyn, 1975), pp. 171–177.

in the Diaspora (Antioch of Pisidia) which, like Acts 2 and Luke 4, becomes emblematic of all that follows. In rehearsing God's dealings with "this people Israel" (verses 17–25) Paul is concerned to point everything to David's significance in bringing from his offspring (σπέρμα) a "Savior" to Israel (verse 23b). We shall see that both Jesus' death and his raising up are integrally woven together as the climax of Scripture but now with a new wrinkle in its "script."

Paul's presentation of the events that have culminated in the "Savior Jesus" (verses 26–41) would appear to reach a climax in verse 29: "When they [i.e. the residents of Jerusalem and their rulers, verse 27] fulfilled (τελέω) all the things written in the Scriptures concerning him [i.e. the Savior Jesus, verse 23b], they took him down from the tree and laid him in a tomb." Yet Paul continues immediately with "and/but God raised [ἐγείρω, cf. verse 37] him from the dead" (verse 30) and describes Jesus' appearances "over many days" to "his witnesses to the people" who "had come up with him from Galilee to Jerusalem" (verse 31). This announcement of Jesus' resurrection, however, does not even conclude at this mention of Galilean witnesses but extends to Paul's (and Barnabas') own sending to Pisidian Antioch (verse 32). Paul declares that his "preaching the Good News" (εὐαγγελίζομαι) is nothing less than a fulfillment of God's own "fulfilling" (ἐκπληρόω) of his "promise (ἐπαγγελία) to the ancestors" which God has made evident by "raising (ἀνίστημι) Jesus" from the dead (verse 33a). Paul then crowns his argument (verses 26–32 – "just as it is indeed written," verse 33b) by quoting God's pronouncement in Psalm 2 to David ("You are my Son, today I have begotten you") and immediately clarifies its import by adding two other Scripture citations (Isa. 55.3 and Ps. 15.10 in Acts 13.34–35).

But what does Psalm 2 have to do with Jesus' death or resurrection, or what does David's enthronement have to do with Paul's (and Barnabas') preaching in the Diaspora? And just as pointedly, what is the "promise" that God "has fulfilled"? Is it Jesus' resurrection *per se*, his death and resurrection, the preaching of Good News, or some combination of these? To elucidate any connections that Paul through the narrator may have in mind we must go back to Paul's earlier mention of David in his rehearsal of Israel's history (verses 22–23). There, after Saul's "removal," David is "raised up" (ἐγείρω) by God to become "king," of whom God "bears witness" (μαρτυρέω) by declaring (verse 22b), "I have found in David, son of Jesse, a man after my own heart" (cf. Lk. 3.22). David enjoys such favor since "he will do everything in accordance with my [God's] will" (θέλημα, verse 22b). God's words appear to derive from several scriptural passages such as Ps. 88.21 ("I have found David my servant (δοῦλος), I have anointed him with holy oil") or 1 Kgdms. 13.14 ("a man after his [the Lord's] own heart," referring to Saul's removal as king and to his replacement by David) or Isa. 44.28, "he shall do all my will," referring to Cyrus, "my [the Lord God's] anointed" (45.1), who will restore God's reign over Israel, God's "servant," in Jerusalem (45.4). Paul jumps immediately to the "Savior Jesus" by linking God's *will* in David "through this one's seed (σπέρμα) according to promise" (κατ᾽ ἐπαγγελίαν, verse 23). This promise must refer forward not only to verse 33 and Paul's "proclaiming Good News" but also back as well to a passage such as 2 Sam. 7.12–16, which speaks of the time after David "sleeps" (κοιμάω [see Acts 13.36]) when the Lord will "raise up" (ἀνίστημι) his "seed" (σπέρμα) to reign forever as "my son" (cf. Ps. 88.4, 19–29, 33–37, 49–51). Any reader of Luke and Acts should recall that this notion of God's eschatological reign in a Davidic ruler had already been sounded at the beginning for Jesus by Gabriel's annunciation (Lk. 1.32–33) and was interpreted by the law-abiding righteous of Israel as the fulfillment of liberation through a mighty Davidic deliverer (Lk. 1.47–55, 67–75; 2.38). But, in Paul's reasoning, what does David's kingship have to do with his descendant's death and resurrection?

As we should suspect from the role that Scripture plays in the passages treated above, our answer comes in the way Paul relates the significance of the three Scripture citations (13.33b–35) to the content of the "Good News" he proclaims (13.26b):

(1) Our first clue comes from the way he concludes his survey of Israel's history with John's "advance preaching (προκηρύσσω) of a baptism of repentance/change of mind" (Acts 13.24). John already preaches something constitutive of the "Good News" that Paul himself presents as "the word/ message of this salvation" (ὁ λόγος τῆς σωτηρίας ταύτης) which "has been sent to us" (verse 26). It would appear that John's emphasis on a "change of mind/orientation" (μετά-νοια), concerning what the "Savior" (verse 23) would be like, is what marks John's message as "advance Gospel preaching," since Paul adds that John had to make it clear to all the λαός of Israel that he himself was *not* the one who was coming (verse 25)! Curiously the narrator has Paul allude to Lk. 3.15–17, where the λαός are wondering whether John might be "the Christ." All of this transpires within the narrator's frame of John's call as a prophet fulfilling the "voice in the wilderness" "just as it is written in the book of the sayings/message(s) (λόγοι) of Isaiah the prophet" (Lk. 3.1–6,18). John is the voice of the prophet who "prepares the way of the Lord" and heralds the coming "saving act of God" which "all flesh shall see" (Lk. 3.4b-6, citing Isa. 40.3–5). John's limited "course" (δρόμος) consisted then of challenging the people of Israel at the cross-roads of their eschatological fulfillment to change their menta-lity or whole perspective on "God's saving act" (Acts 13.25; cf. Lk. 16.16).

(2) This interpretation of John's "preaching of good news" (εὐαγγελίζομαι, Lk. 3.18) is borne out by the progression of Paul's argument. For Paul follows John's approach with a similar challenge to his own audience to change their whole understanding of what took place in Jerusalem with "Savior Jesus." By again summoning the "voices of the prophets that are read every sabbath" (13.37) as the focus of their "word (λόγος) of exhortation" from "the law and the prophets" that were just read in the Sabbath worship that day (13.14b–15), Paul was indicating that the synagogue audience may be in the same situation as "the residents of Jerusalem and their rulers" (verse 27) and "Pilate" (verse 28), who "did not know this one [τοῦτον, verse 27, i. e. "Savior Jesus," verse 23b] or the voices

of the prophets." These three groups – paralleling the groups "assembled against the Lord and his anointed" in Acts 4.25–27 – unwittingly, ironically "fulfilled" (πληρόω) these same voices of the prophets by condemning Jesus to death. As in Acts 3 and the Gospel, we find the paradox of a larger divine scheme of salvation, indeed, "the message of this salvation" (13.26), being fulfilled *by means of* the execution of Jesus through a people "not knowing" the basic "plot" of the Scriptures. Whereas in Acts 3 "God" is said "to fulfill (τελέω) the Scriptures by having Jesus executed, here the human agents "carry out/fulfill all the things written concerning him" (13.29). But unlike Peter with his *Jerusalem* audience, who follows the charge of their "ignorance" of the Scriptures with a call to repentance, Paul follows this indictment with God's *continuing* action through resurrection (cf. Lk. 18.31; 24.25–27, 44–46).

(3) What role, then, does the resurrection play in God's overall will/ salvation, and what is the promise (verses 23, 32), that is fulfilled? Again as in Peter's speech at Pentecost (Acts 2), Scripture citations, primarily from the Psalms, fuse the first two parts of fulfillment into one united whole. But now Paul's citations provide concrete examples of the people's "not knowing" the voices of the prophets, including a "new" strain that emerges as well. Paul's quoting of Ps. 2.7 in 13.33 ostensibly produces evidence of the fulfillment of the promise through resurrection. "You are my Son, today I have begotten you" speaks of resurrection, whereas in the psalm itself this line describes the "ordinance of the Lord" when the Lord established the speaker (David) as *king upon Zion* and promised to give the nations (ἔθνη) to the king as "your inheritance" (κληρονομία), "even the ends of the earth as your possession" (Ps. 2.7–8). And as Paul qualifies this quotation with a citation of Isa. 55.3 it becomes manifest that God's action alone of raising up Jesus is not all or even the primary result that is being hailed. Rather, Isa. 55.3 shows that Jesus' raising up was to be an ultimate reality in which there would be no return to corruption: I will give "you the firm/trustworthy holy things of David." Within Isaiah 55 this phrase is embedded in a promise of the Lord to Israel (exiles) of an everlasting covenant

(διαθήκη) in which David, as "witness (μαρτύριον), ruler, and commander of the nations" (ἔθνη), had prefigured the eternal fulfillment when these "nations shall flee for refuge to you [Israel] for the sake of the Lord your God" (55.3b-5). Moreover, this coming "witness" and "rule" over the Gentiles is the result of the Lord's having "glorified" Israel (55.5b). Consequently, Isa. 55.1–5 refers to the same promise given to the suffering exiles in the Servant passages, that through the Servant's suffering witness as a "covenant (διαθήκη) resulting in light to the nations" (42.6; 49.6,8), Israel will convey to all nations the true worship of the Lord which will redound to their own glory.[30] Paul clinches this dimension of the argument with another psalm citation (verse 35 – "therefore") by asserting that the resurrection of Jesus to incorruptibility was already explicitly promised by God to David: "You will not let your Holy One see decomposition/corruption (Ps. 15[16].10). The thrust of the scriptural citations is thus now clear: the *promise* to David of a universal, eschatological reign has indeed been fulfilled in Jesus' enthronement by resurrection from the dead/corruption.

(4) The thread that weaves these three passages together into a coherent scriptural argument can now be delineated in light of the "plan/will of God" (13.36) that is most fully exposited in Luke–Acts here by Paul as he intricately interweaves the script of David and the suffering righteous of the Psalms with the suffering Servant and servants of Isaiah (the prophets). As we have just seen, the first two passages within their larger and immediate contexts speak of David's role or legacy for Israel in "inheriting" the Gentiles (Ps. 2.8b, as the χριστός, Isa. 55.4–5, through his eschatological reign). In Psalm 15 David is in grave danger from enemies; Paul ties this predicament to the suffering/persecution of all the saints in the land in whom the Lord takes pleasure (θέλημα, 15.3; cf. Acts 13.22b), and glimpses the time of his deliverance as not being

---

[30] On Isa. 55.4–5, see O. Eissfeldt, "The Promises of Grace to David in Isaiah 55: 1–5," in *Israel's Prophetic Heritage*, ed. B. W. Anderson and W. Harrelson (New York, 1962), p. 206: "there can be no doubt that Israel is here given the same promise which is found elsewhere in Isa. 40–55, particularly in the 'Servant Songs.'"

abandoned to the place of death (Hades). This preview of the "Lord always before me," where "delights are at his right hand forever as the ways/paths that bring life" (Ps. 15.8, 11), are David's *inheritance through the Lord's deliverance*. But clearly David did not see his inheritance at the right hand of God, for he died and his body decomposed (Acts 13.36). Thus it is also clear that David did not live to see an eternal covenant of rule over the Gentiles (Isaiah 55) "according to promise" (Acts 13.23, 32), nor as the Lord's χριστός did he "inherit all the ends of the earth" (Ps. 2.8). Rather it is the Lord's Holy One (ὁ ὅσιος) Jesus who by virtue of being raised up (ἀνίστημι) from the realm of the dead has inherited these firm/trustworthy holy things (τὰ ὅσια). What is more, this one who was condemned and hung on a tree by the "people," "rulers," and a "king of the earth" (Ps. 2.1–2) *was delivered by* resurrection from death/ Hades to become the king in whom the promise of kingship, "you are my Son, today I have begotten you," becomes fulfilled. This then becomes the reason why Paul can say of David that he, precisely as a suffering righteous anointed servant, by anticipation "served the plan of God (ἡ τοῦ Θεοῦ βουλή) with respect to his own generation, died (κοιμάω) and saw corruption" (13.33–37).

(5) But Paul's climax does not come even with the accomplished fact of enthronement in the promise to David. He concludes ("therefore," verse 38), rather, that the fulfilled promise of eschatological rule by a descendant of David has led to the *release/forgiveness of sins* (ἄφεσις ἁμαρτιῶν). The great plan of God is consummated in the presence of the enthroned crucified one who is offering eschatological release of sin through the proclamation of Paul and Barnabas: "Let it be known to you, men, brothers and sisters, that *through this one* (διὰ τούτου) release of sin *is being proclaimed* (καταγγέλλεται) to you" (verse 38). The "Savior Jesus," "Son," and "Holy One" is "bearing witness, ruling and commanding the nations" through the "preaching of good news," "the word of this salvation." It is significant that this release is *not* tied directly to the act or process of Jesus being raised up any more than it is linked to his rejection and death. Both fulfillments, rather, are

critical to the script or "plan of God." What is tied directly to
the *proclaiming* of the release of sins is the warning injunction
not to miss the clear message of that "which has been *spoken* in
the prophets" (verse 40). Paul, in other words, continues the
emphasis of John the Baptist, of Jesus, and Peter, in calling for
a "turning around" of their mishearing of the script of the
Scriptures: "Look, you scoffers, wonder and then be extin-
guished, because I am accomplishing a work/objective in your
days, a work which you will never believe, even when someone
should declare it in detail to you" (13.41 citing Hab. 1.5).
Now, according to Paul, "this one" is himself present to
"rectify" all that they have misheard or "been unable" to do
"by means of/in the law of Moses" if they will just come to
"believe" in the plan of God (13.38b–41).

Our outline above of the "plan of God" is confirmed a
"week later" when "the Jews" "filled with zeal/jealousy"
begin to "speak against the things being said by Paul and revile
him" (verse 45). Paul thus becomes a "sign spoken against"
(Lk. 2.34), and by no accident interprets what is occurring in
their rejection by again quoting Scripture – Isa. 49.6b: Now
the "Lord" (κύριος) who "has commanded us" refers to the
Lord Jesus and the "you" (σέ) is Paul and cohorts who are the
(corporate) Servant fulfilling the mission of mediating the light
of the "word of salvation" to the nations, even to the end of the
earth (Lk. 2.32; Acts 1.8b). It was a divine *necessity* (ἀναγκαῖον,
verse 46; cf. verse 26) that the "word of God" be spoken *first* to
Israel (cf. 3.26: πρῶτον . . . τὸν παῖδα . . . ἀπέστειλεν . . .
πονηριῶν). Since they reject it *en bloc*, Paul and companions
"turn toward the nations." We have once again the Servant
"script" that is constitutive of the plot of Luke–Acts. Jesus, the
anointed, rejected-enthroned Servant-Son, is present proclaiming light through his servants, who mediate this presence
as salvation (σε εἰς φῶς . . . τοῦ εἶναι σε εἰς σωτηρίαν) of
unending life[31] to Israel and the nations. The firm/trustworthy
holy things promised to David are coming true. Our narrator

---

[31] For the image of light as an expression of "life," see K. F. Euler, *Die Verkündigung
vom leidenden Gottesknecht: Aus Jes 53 in der griechischen Bibel*, BWAT 14 (Stuttgart and
Berlin, 1934), pp. 122–125.

hardly need add that the nations (τὰ ἔθνη) "glorified this Word of the Lord" "when they heard" Paul (verse 48; cf. Lk. 7.29; see also Isa. 42.10,12; 45.24–26; cf. 43.4,7,23; 44.23; 46.13; 49.3, 5; 52.1; 55.5) but that "the Jews" "stirred up persecution against Paul and Barnabas and drove them out of their district" (cf. Lk. 4.16–30; Acts 9.23–25). But "the disciples were being filled with joy and the Holy Spirit" (13.50–52). *In sum*, with Paul's mission the expanded Servant script of the Scriptures is itself expanding into the Diaspora: While more and more of Israel reject their Servant-Messiah, more and more of "the nations" "believe" and join those of Israel who do embrace "the message of this salvation."[32]

8 ACTS 15.1–21

Certain Pharisees from among the believers in Jerusalem claim that "the door of faith opened" to the Gentiles (14.27b) includes the divine necessity (δεῖ) of circumcision, with its obedience to the Law of Moses (15.5). James provides the clinching rebuttal in his fusion of three citations from the LXX. All three envision the time of Israel's eschatological restoration after its judgment/destruction of 587 BCE. Jer. 12.15, as an introduction to Amos 9.11–12, speaks of the Lord's "returning" (ἐπιστρέφω) to the Gentile nations once he has punished them to reestablish them and to "build" (οἰκοδομέω) them into the midst of "my people" (τοῦ λαοῦ μου) if they "turn"/"return" (ἐπιστρέφω) to the Lord and swear by his name. Amos 9.11–12 speaks of the restoration of the Davidic dynasty as in "ancient days" (ἡμέραι τοῦ αἰῶνος, verse 11), and says that it will include all the nations, upon whom the Lord's name is called, seeking the Lord through that restored rule in Israel. The MT, unlike the LXX, expresses this inclusion as Israel "possessing" the nations, a clear reference back to the promises to David such as Ps. 2. 8. Isa. 45.21 speaks of the

---

[32] We should note how the expression in 13.48b depicting the numbers of Gentiles who do "believe" ("as many as were appointed/set in the way [τεταγμένοι] for eternal life") reflects the "predetermined plan and foreknowledge of God" (2.23; cf. 13.36) or "script" we have been tracing.

Lord doing in the final days of salvation that which he declared
"from the beginning" (ἀπ' ἀρχῆς/αἰῶνος), namely that all
nations "shall turn (ἐπιστρέφω) to me and be saved (σῴζω) from
the end of the earth" (ἀπ' ἐσχάτου τῆς γῆς). Moreover, this
final salvation of the nations is introduced by the Lord's
"anointed" (ὁ χριστός μου), Cyrus, returning (ἐπιστρέφω) the
captive Israelites (αἰχμαλωσία τοῦ λαοῦ; cf. Lk. 4.18: αἰχ-
μάλωτοις ἄφεσις) and building (οἰκοδομέω) the city all for the
glory of Israel and their God, Israel's "Savior." It is not certain
what time framework "from the beginning" in Isa. 45.21 or
"from of old" in the Acts 15.18 citation is referring to. In any
case, the will or plan of the Lord to include the Gentiles in the
final salvation conceived as the restored and eschatological
rule of the line of David is certain "from of old" (cf. Acts
15.21). Therefore, James concludes, it is not necessary for
Gentiles turning to (ἐπιστρέφω) God to become members of
Israel through adherence to Torah. At least in its formal or
structural aspects, James' view is "in harmony" with Paul's
construal of the "plan of God."

9 ACTS 26.1–23

Before Israel's "king" and his "excellency Festus" (26.2, 25; cf.
Lk. 1.3; 21.12b) Paul gives his autobiographical defense of the
accusations brought by Jews from Jerusalem. In this his final
speech Paul sums up his entire calling in terms of his original
call as well as the response to it by the people of Israel. In both
respects, the eschatological mission of the Servant of Isaiah has
been determinative.

(1) The call

Paul introduces his call by stressing his background as an
ardent Pharisee that has continued up to that very moment
(26.4–11). Though he changed from a rabid persecutor of "the
name of Jesus of Nazareth" to an obedient servant of that
Jesus, he has remained throughout devoted to the "hope of the
promise made by God to our ancestors" in solidarity with all

the twelve tribes as they like Paul worship (λατρεύω) night and day in the Temple (verses 6–7; and also like Hanna, Lk. 2.36–38). It is because of his zeal for this hope, Paul claims, that he is being accused by Jews (verse 7b).

1. In 26.8 Paul specifies this hope as hinging on "whether (εἰ) God raises the dead." But Paul has not previously in Acts been charged by Jews with propounding a belief in resurrection, nor has his advocacy of the name of Jesus been tainted with the accusation that Paul believes this Jesus to have been raised up. Rather, the accusations against Paul are parallel to those against Jesus in Luke – against Moses (God/Law/Temple), the people (agitation, false teaching), and Caesar (another king Jesus). The overall sentiment that unites these "three" and provokes the nearly successful "lynching" in the Temple is that Paul "is teaching apostasy from/forsaking of Moses to all the Jews among the nations, namely, that they should not circumcise their children nor follow the customs" (21.21; cf. 26.3; 28.17). Thus Paul is not defending himself against the specific charge that he believes in resurrection in general or that Jesus has been raised.

2. When Paul is placed by the Roman tribune before the Sanhedrin to answer the accusations brought by the raging crowds (23.1–9), he takes advantage of the mixed group of Sadducees and Pharisees and pits the former against that which he and the other Pharisees have in common, namely the hope of resurrection from the dead ("concerning hope in the resurrection of the dead I myself am being judged," 23.6). In other words, Paul realizes that the essence of the matter against him is the *interpretation of Scripture* with regard to *God's eschatological reign* and that in this regard he is much closer to his Pharisee brethren in teaching Moses and all the prophets than the Sadducees could ever be. Thus his appeal to the resurrection is not just a strategic maneuver to "save his skin" – although it has that temporary effect – nor is it a "trick" to make it appear that his view of the hope is no different than that of the Pharisees. And certainly it is not an attempt to single out the most or even the only critical element that effects the forgiveness/ release of sins. Rather, Paul knows that, as the

critical *pivot* of the interpretation of eschatological hope *in Scripture*, resurrection of the dead is also the *point of departure* in presenting the fulfilled "plan of God" that effects release in the final reign of God.

As we saw in his argument from Scripture in his seminal "word of exhortation" accompanying the "reading of the law and the prophets" in Pisidian Antioch (13.15–16), it is the resurrection hope that makes possible the fulfillment of the eschatological reign of God promised through the line of David. Appeal to the resurrection hope, then, in chapter 23 is an appeal to Scripture for the adjudication of the charges against him. Certainly this is the way this appeal functions in his next defense before Felix in 24.10b–21 as he prefaces his "hope in the resurrection of the just and unjust" by appealing to "everything written according to the law and the prophets" (24.14–15) and concludes by repeating 23.6b. Again in his defense in chapter 26 Paul climaxes his appeal to resurrection (26.8) by "appealing" to Agrippa's "belief in the prophets" (verse 27) and summarizes his total presentation with "nothing other than what the prophets and Moses said would come to pass" (26.22b).

3. A light (φῶς) brighter than the sun "shines," and from that light a voice tells Paul to "stand upon your feet" in order that he might be a "servant" (ὑπηρέτης) and "witness" (μάρτυς) of all that Paul is seeing now in/from the "Lord Jesus" and "of the things in which I will appear to you" (26.16). Paul is to be "sent to the people (λαός) and the nations" (ἔθνη) in order that their eyes might open and they might turn (ἐπιστρέφω) from darkness (σκότος) to light (φῶς) and from the authority of Satan to God so that they might receive release of sins (26.18). But this "seeing" and "turning" is accomplished only as Paul is "rescued from the people and the nations" (verse 17a)! What Paul is "seeing" on the Damascus road is a Jesus who is being persecuted by Paul, and what the people of Israel and the nations will "see" when they "turn" is a Jesus suffering in solidarity with a persecuted Paul (cf. 4.23–31). Paul's witness as a servant is thus focused on a suffering Jesus Messiah. Many of the images used in this

description reflect the vocabulary and substance of the calls to Ezekiel and Jeremiah.[33] But it is particularly the call of the Servant in Isa. 42.1–6 and 49.1–7 that is reflected in Paul's mission of shedding light on those who are in darkness, whether the blind of Israel like Paul himself[34] who go from darkness to light (Isa. 42.7; 50.10; cf. 42.16; 49.9) or the nations who through the suffering witness will receive the light of salvation (Acts 26.23; 13.47; Isa. 42.6; 49.6; 50.10; 51.4–5; 53.11; cf. 45.7; 49.9). Paul's "seeing" and "turning" thus becomes the most potent example of one who, though waiting earnestly for the hope of the twelve tribes, had to be released[35] from the vantage point of Satan in order to "worship the Lord your God" and to "serve (λατρεύω) him only" (Lk. 4.8; Acts 26.7; cf. Acts 24.11, 14–15, 17).

(2) Israel's response to the call

Paul continues his defense by linking the response of Israel and the nations (26.19–23) to his call to serve the hope of Israel (verses 4–18). It is because of his repeated proclamation of the necessity to "change their point of view/repent" and to "turn to God" and demonstrate this changed perspective that the Jews have seized Paul and are trying to kill him (verses 19–20). The reason for their volcanic reaction is stated succinctly in Paul's summary of the heart of his/God's (and the narrator's) point of view which he has been expounding as the "script" of the Scriptures (the prophets and Moses, verse 22b): "whether (εἰ) there is to be a suffering Messiah (εἰ παθητός ὁ Χρίστος) and whether (εἰ), being the first of the resurrection of the dead, he [the Christ] is to proclaim light to the people (λαός) and to the nations" (verse 23). The indirect question points to the heart of the questions, the great debates from Scripture that Paul has been carrying on with his fellow Israelites in

---

[33] Cf. Jer. 1.5,8; Ezek. 2.1.
[34] Cf. "Bar-Jesus" (Acts 13.6–12) and Lk. 11.17–23, 33–36; on "conversion," see, e.g., J. Dupont ("Conversion in the Acts of the Apostles," in *The Salvation of the Gentiles* [New York, 1979], pp. 61–84).
[35] Acts 22.16: "Arise, be baptized, and wash away your sins."

their synagogues throughout his calling, as our narrator has been at pains to illuminate. It is this three-pronged center of all the Scriptures that constitutes the "plan of God" for salvation, as we have seen, for example, in Acts 13, and is Jesus' own summary of his entire role in fulfilling Israel's Scriptures for salvation (Lk. 24.44–49) as announced in advance by Simeon and foreshadowed in Jesus' synagogue "debate" at Nazareth.

1. Throughout all his journeys from Damascus to Jerusalem and Judea as well as among the nations (verse 20), Paul has been contending that Israel's Messiah is a *suffering* Messiah and that as raised from the dead Jesus *is* that Messiah. In that argument from Scripture, as we have seen in Pisidian Antioch, the resurrection of Jesus is the decisive pivot which unites both the suffering/death of Jesus as Messiah and Jesus Messiah's proclamation through continued suffering in his witnesses to Israel and the nations. In Paul's "first" journey of chapters 13 and 14 our narrator has Paul, on his return to every city, summarize to the new *disciples* the hostility and persecution meted out to him and his cohorts from Jews in those same cities, as "it is a divine necessity (δεῖ) that we enter into the Kingdom/Reign of God through (διά) many afflictions (θλῖψις)" (14.22) (cf. Pisidian Antioch, 13.14–52; Iconium, 14.1–5; and Lystra, 14.8–20).

2. From the apostolic assembly to Paul's final journey to Jerusalem announced in Ephesus (19.21), the narrator focuses on Paul's "arguing (διαλέγομαι) from the Scriptures" in the synagogues from one city to the next. Similarly to chapter 13, the first appearance in a synagogue, in Thessalonica (17.1–9), sets the agenda for the subsequent debates: "arguing with them from the Scriptures for three weeks, opening (διανοίγω) them up and demonstrating that it was necessary (ἔδει) for the Christ to suffer and rise from the dead and that this Jesus whom I proclaim to you *is* that Christ" (διαλέγομαι: 17.2; 17.17 [Athens]; 18.5–6 [Corinth]; 18.19 [Ephesus]; 19.8–9 [Ephesus, second visit]; διακατελέγχομαι: 18.28 ["utterly confute," of Apollos in Corinth]; cf. already in Damascus, συγχύνω ["confound"], 9.22; συζητέω ["dispute"], 9.29 in

Jerusalem).[36] The point of view of this "new hermeneutic" is so diametrically opposed to the reading in the synagogue (cf. Lk. 4.16–30) that it requires a special "opening" (διανοίγω), as the Emmaus disciples had to discover and as Jesus had repeated for the apostles and gathered disciples back in Jerusalem as well (Lk. 24.32, 45). It is once again not surprising that Paul's teaching is described as "turning the world upside down," "saying that there is another king, Jesus" (17.6b–7), and that as in Damascus, Paul and cohorts have to be slipped out of Thessalonica, at *night* because of the enraged Jews (17.10; cf. 9.25). In Corinth the third prong becomes explicit when Paul, amid reviling, declares that he is innocent in proclaiming that "the Christ is Jesus" (18.5b): "from now on I shall go to the Gentiles" (18.6), while in Ephesus his arguing in the synagogue is about "the things concerning the Reign/Kingdom of God" (19.8).

3. Because of the "plots of the Jews" in Greece (20.3) and the fury against Paul in Ephesus, Paul bypasses the latter on his way to Jerusalem and meets with the Ephesian elders in Miletus (19.8–9, 23–41; 20.16, 17–38). Similar to *Jesus at the passion meal* before he suffers in Jerusalem, Paul gives encouragement to the leaders of the church before he suffers in Jerusalem, even as he announces that some from their rank will "rise up" to pervert the rest of the disciples (Lk. 22.21–22; Acts 20.30). What may appear, *prima facie*, incongruous with the lengthy and vivid depiction of the riot in 19.23–41 is that Paul describes his whole period of "serving (δουλεύω) with humiliation (ταπεινοφροσύνη) and tears and trials" in Asia as a persecution, *not* from the fanatics of the Artemis temple, but from "the plots of the Jews" (20.19b). But the narrator has already developed this "plot," as we have seen, through the skein of outrage expressed in one synagogue after another, and Paul declares that the "Holy Spirit has been testifying to him in every city (κατὰ πόλιν) that bonds and afflictions (θλίψεις)

---

[36] Beroea (Acts 17.10–15) is the one exception; for the plot of Acts and role of the suffering Messiah in the theology of Luke–Acts, see my forthcoming *The Christ Must Suffer*, vol. II of my *Ancient Narrative Hermeneutics and Ideological Construal of the Gospels: Toward a Postcritical, Historical-Critical "Theology" of the Ancient Narrative Luke–Acts.*

await" him in Jerusalem (20.23; cf. 14.22). Later the narrator will tell us that it was Jews from *Asia* who fomented the crowds' rage at the Temple, crying out, "this is the man who is teaching folk everywhere against the people, the law, and this place" (21.27–28). Paul again articulates why this is so. Despite the crushing pressure of opposition, he has – in his preaching of "the Kingdom" and "of change of mind toward God to both Jews and Greeks" (20.21, 25; cf. 19.8) – "*not shrunk back* from declaring the *whole plan of God*" (ἡ βουλή τοῦ Θεοῦ, 20.27; cf. verses 20–21). It is in response to this plan that Paul is innocent of the charges (blood) against him by all the Jews (verse 26). Therefore since they will no longer "see his face" (verses 25, 38), they must be all the more diligent to understand the "price" entailed in "caring for" and "exhorting" this whole script or plan of God for the church which God "purchased through/by means of (διά) the blood of God's Own (Beloved/Son)" (verses 27–28; cf. verse 31: "admonishing with tears"). It is for the great cost of this plan of God that Paul will have to pay with his life (verses 23–25).

Acts 26.22–23 thus climaxes Paul's defense by encapsulating his call and Israel's response to it. It is the raised up, crucified-suffering Messiah who proclaims the light of the saving release of sin through Paul's and his companions' suffering to both the people and the nations. Once again it is the proclamation of the light of this salvation to Israel and the nations through the solidarity of the messengers-servants with the Servant who suffers that constitutes the eschatological vision of Deutero-Isaiah in 49.1–6 and 52.13–53.12 in particular. In Acts, it is Paul's mission, our narrator tells us, that climaxes the risen Servant's "witness to the ends of the earth" (Lk. 24.44–49; Acts 1.8).

CONCLUSION

We can now sum up "the plan of God" for Luke's "second" volume. The rejection/suffering/death of Messiah Jesus, his raising up to the "throne" of God, and his preaching of this light to Israel and the nations constitute the three "necessary" components of God's saving action, the three moments of the *script* of all the Scriptures. Jesus' resurrection or enthronement forms the hinge which unites the suffering-crucified one to the suffering-exalted one who preaches through his suffering apostles-witnesses to the ends of the earth. This pivotal fulfillment is emphasized in the mission and defense speeches as *the point of departure* in arguing that the promise or hope of the twelve tribes in the eschatological reign of God through the line of David has indeed been fulfilled through the *crucified, suffering Messiah who is Jesus* and who brings the life of the final *release of sins* to Israel and the nations. In this argument from Scripture David is the premier prototype of Jesus' resurrection/ exaltation as a suffering servant of the Psalms who was delivered from the death of his enemies and perpetual abandonment to Hades. It is, however, the suffering or death of Jesus that is the fulfillment of Scripture tied most closely to "the plan of God" which results in the release of sins (ἄφεσις ἁμαρτιῶν). In this argument it is Moses the rejected ruler and deliverer who preeminently prefigures the death of the "prophet like" him. However, both "David" and "Moses" and both the death and the resurrection of the Messiah are *inseparably* combined in *one* plan or "script"-ural necessity in fulfilling the divine saving act for Israel and the nations in Jesus, the beloved and chosen suffering Servant of God.

We have seen, therefore, that Luke configures the death of Jesus as an atoning event through the interweaving of the stories of Israel's rejection of their Messiah and of God's overarching purpose for this rejection in God's plan (βουλή) for all humanity. The two "plots" have been fully integrated through the repeated emphasis on the scriptural "necessity" of the Messiah's suffering as the God-ordained means by which Israel's history of unrelenting sin is brought to a decisive "end" (τέλος) for the saving benefit of the whole world. In the Acts this suffering of Messiah is not transmuted into a theology of glory or triumph over Israel's rejection but, on the contrary, *Israel's* Messiah continues to suffer in order that the "plan of God" may become effective for Israel and *through* Israel for the nations. By using the notion of a transcendent "will" of (a) deity so common among Hellenistic historiographers, Luke comprehends the whole of Israel's history to create a uniform, consistent interpretation of the developing messianic "sect"/"way" in the eschatological fulfillment of this history. Particularly in the speeches of Acts this "βουλή" is highlighted to show how the twelve apostles (like Peter), the Hellenists (like Philip), and the obdurate, but Torah-abiding, zealous Israel which opposes "Messiah" Jesus (like Paul) all "converge" in a larger "script"-ural will of God. By such a *tour de force* Luke offers a theodicy of God's "Way" with the world.

CHAPTER 10

Luke's social location of Paul: cultural anthropology and the status of Paul in Acts

Jerome H. Neyrey

1.0 INTRODUCTION. FOCUS AND HYPOTHESIS

When scholars study the relationship of Luke's description of Paul to that found in Paul's authentic letters, they tend to work out of either a strictly historical or an ideological framework.[1] Is Acts a reliable source for the history of Paul's life and times? Is Acts the "synthesis" of the conflict between conservative Jewish Christianity and liberal Pauline thought? More recently, scholars have examined the literary structure of Acts with attention to the parallels between Jesus and Paul (Luke and Acts) and Peter and Paul (Acts).[2] Thus a shift is occurring in the study of Acts, with more attention given to the perspective of the author and his rhetorical agenda.[3] This chapter belongs in the latter.

Historical questions about the veracity of Luke's portrait of Paul are important and valid. But I focus here on the social

---

[1] P. Vielhauer, "On the 'Paulinism' of Acts," *Studies in Luke–Acts*, ed. L. Keck and J. L. Martyn (New York, 1966), pp. 33–48; C. Burchard, "Paulus in der Apostelgeschichte," *TLZ* 100 (1975), 881–895; J. Roloff, "Die Paulus-Darstellung des Lukas," *EvT* 39 (1979), 510–531.

[2] See C. H. Talbert, *Literary Patterns: Theological Themes and the Genre of Luke–Acts*, SBLMS 20 (Missoula, 1974); A. J. Mattill, "The Paul–Jesus Parallels and the Purpose of Luke–Acts: H. H. Evans Reconsidered," *NovT* 17 (1975), 15–45; and Walter Radl, *Paulus und Jesus in lukanischen Doppelwerk: Untersuchungen zu Parallel-motiven im Lukasevangelium und der Apostelgeschichte* (Frankfurt, 1975).

[3] Jacob Jervell, *Luke and the People of God* (Minneapolis, 1972), pp. 153–183 and his *The Unknown Paul* (Minneapolis, 1984), pp. 52–67 and 68–76; William R. Long, "The *Paulusbild* in the Trial of Paul in Acts," *SBLASP* (1983), 87–105; and Robert L. Brawley, "Paul in Acts: Aspects of Structure and Characterization," *SBLASP* (1988), 90–105. See especially Earl Richard, "Luke – Writer, Theologian, Historian: Research and Orientation of the 1970s," *BTB* 13 (1983), 3–15.

status which the author of Acts attributes to Paul. Where did
Luke imagine Paul fitted into the highly stratified society of his
world?[4] Where did he wish to locate him? I suggest that Luke
portrays Paul in the company of the elite of his world, acting
comfortably in the role of a citizen trained for public duties.[5]
In terms of his social status, Paul appears as a retainer to the
elites of Jerusalem and as a person who can speak eloquently to
Greek philosophers, Roman proconsuls, and Jewish kings. He
enjoys the patronage of elites. He resides, moreover, in many of
the most honorable cities of the Empire, which suggests a high
level of sophistication for him.[6]

Thus I am bringing to the study of Acts questions treated
more appropriately in cultural anthropology and social
description.[7] How does one discern Paul's status?[8] What does
this mean in the cultural world of Luke? What value is given in
terms of honor to Paul's social location or to the cities which he
either visits or in which he resides? Such social and cultural
questions require historical scholars to supplement their traditional methods of inquiry and bibliography. This chapter will
use the work of Gerhard Lenski to map out the levels of social

---

[4] On the social location of the author of Acts, see Vernon Robbins, "The Social
Location of the Implied Author of Luke–Acts," *The Social World of Luke–Acts: Models
for Interpretation*, ed. Jerome H. Neyrey (Peabody, MA, 1991), pp. 305–332; see also
Richard L. Rohrbaugh, "Methodological Considerations in the Debate over the
Social Class Status of Early Christians," *JAAR* 52 (1984), 519–546.

[5] In a recent study, John C. Lentz (*Luke's Portrait of Paul* [Cambridge, 1993]) has put
forward basically the same thesis as I am advancing here. The two studies, however,
are worlds apart in terms of the manner in which they describe social status (i.e. the
formal use of social science models) and in the choice of items in the text of Acts
which might illustrate high status. This is not to disparage Lentz's study, but to
indicate that this social science analysis finds support from more historical studies
such as his.

[6] Paul's own letters indicate that he visited noble cities such as Corinth (1 Cor. 1.1),
Ephesus (1 Cor. 15.32; 16.8), Philippi (Phil. 1.1), and Rome (Rom. 1.7). But from
these documents we never learn anything about the city, whether it has temples,
fountains, schools of philosophy, and the like; nor does Paul comment about the
status of the city, calling it either "no mean city" or "leading city of the district," as
he does in regard to Tarsus and Philippi respectively. Luke would seem more
interested in the honor rating of these cities, as part of his rhetorical agenda.

[7] See J. H. Neyrey (ed.), *The Social World of Luke–Acts: Models for Interpretation*
(Peabody, MA, 1991). For the letters of Paul, see W. A. Meeks, *The First Urban
Christians: The Social World of the Apostle Paul* (New Haven, 1983).

[8] See R. F. Hock, "Paul's Tentmaking and the Problem of his Social Class," *JBL* 97
(1978), 55–64.

stratification common to the type of society to which Paul belonged.[9] In addition to this, considerations of honor, especially as this relates to cities and citizenship, will be employed from the field of classical studies and cultural anthropology with a view to locating Paul in an honorable environment.[10] New questions warrant new methods of investigation, and the materials used here are increasingly being employed by traditional scholarly investigation.

2.0 PROSOPOGRAPHY AND SOCIAL STRATIFICATION

Gerd Theissen and Wayne Meeks have each attempted to describe the social composition of Pauline urban groups.[11] Theissen's interest lies in the social description of the Corinthian congregation, namely its composition of mostly "lower classes" with some "upper class" people. He basically performs a prosopographical analysis both of the persons named in 1 Corinthians and of the offices mentioned. He concludes that "the majority of the Corinthians known to us by name probably enjoyed high social status."[12] His study employs little in terms of formal sociological modeling to differentiate various strata both among the upper and lower classes. And it is no fault of his that we learn nothing about Paul's own status.

Meeks, on the other hand, attempted to describe "the social level of Pauline Christians" using more explicit measurements

---

[9] Gerhard Lenski, *Power and Privilege: A Theory of Social Stratification* (Chapel Hill, 1984).

[10] Basic expositions of the cultural meaning of honor are: J. G. Peristiany, *Honour and Shame: The Values of Mediterranean Society* (Chicago, 1966); D. D. Gilmore, *Honor and Shame and the Unity of the Mediterranean*, Special Publication of the American Anthropological Association no. 22 (Washington, DC, 1986); adaptations of this material for biblical studies are found in Bruce J. Malina, *New Testament World: Insights from Anthropology*, rev. ed. (Louisville, 1993), pp. 28–62, and Bruce J. Malina and J. H. Neyrey, "Honor and Shame in Luke–Acts: Pivotal Values of the Mediterranean World," in *The Social World of Luke–Acts: Models for Interpretation*, ed. J. H. Neyrey (Peabody, MA, 1991), pp. 25–65.

[11] Gerd Theissen, "Soziale Schichtung in der korinthischen Gemeinde: ein Beitrag zur Soziologie des hellenistischen Urchristentum," *ZNW* 65 (1974), 232–272, translated and reprinted in his *The Social Setting of Pauline Christianity* (Philadelphia, 1982), and Meeks, *The First Urban Christians*, pp. 52–73.

[12] Theissen, *The Social Setting of Pauline Christianity*, p. 95.

of social stratification. Noting that "class" is an inappropriate category for close description of ancient populations, he suggests that we examine references to the Roman "orders" and inquire about what constitutes "status."[13] He then presents a prosopographical survey of named figures in both the Pauline letters and the Acts of the Apostles.[14]

Theissen, Meeks, and others[15] have pioneered new scholarly approaches to social description. But their particular studies are limited to strictly historical issues[16] and tend to focus on the data in the letters of Paul. The guiding issue behind most of these studies has been the question of whether the early Christians belonged to upper or lower classes.[17] Rarely does a scholar engaged in this sort of study ask about the rhetorical strategy of the author of Acts, i.e. whether he consciously attempts to portray Paul and the people in his documents as belonging to a more respectable social stratum. The rhetorical importance of names, offices and labels is outside the concerns of social description. Prosopography, moreover, has its limits.[18] Nor is social description always possible or adequate without more formal appreciation of social theory. Thus, this chapter

---

[13] Meeks, *First Urban Christians*, pp. 53–55. In a subsequent study, Meeks enumerates observable indices of status: "Some of the indices of higher status were these: Roman citizenship, especially in the early years of the empire, when it was rare; citizenship in the local polis, compared with resident aliens; among the citizens, the decurions or city councillors of smaller cities; wealth, more and more, preferably inherited rather than worked for, and invested in land rather than trade; family and origin: the older the better, the closer to Rome the better, Greek better than "barbarian"; military office or the status of veteran in a colony; freedom by birth" (Wayne A. Meeks, *The Moral World of the First Christians* [Philadelphia, 1986], p. 34).

[14] Meeks, *First Urban Christians*, pp. 55–73.

[15] See E. A. Judge, "The Early Christians as a Scholastic Community," *JRH* 1 (1960), 4–15, 125–137, and "The Social Identity of the First Christians: A Question of Method in Religious History," *JRH* 11 (1980), 201–217.

[16] For example, Erastus "the city treasurer" (Rom. 16.23) has been interpreted both as a slave (see Meeks, *First Urban Christians*, p. 58) and as a citizen who was performing an office which was part of the municipal *cursus honorum* (see Theissen, *The Social Setting of Pauline Christianity*, pp. 76–83).

[17] See A. Deissmann, *Light from the Ancient East* (Grand Rapids, 1965), p. 144; and E. A. Judge, *The Social Pattern of Early Christian Groups in the First Century* (London, 1960).

[18] See Thomas F. Carney, "Prosopography: Pitfalls and Payoffs," *Phoenix* 27 (1973), 156–179.

asks a set of questions and employs a method different from investigations which were either strictly historical inquiry or rigorous social description.

This study, moreover, even though it will employ concepts and methods from cultural anthropology, aims at interpretation, not simply history or description.[19] It also considers the rhetoric of Luke's social location of Paul. It is my hypothesis that Luke has positioned Paul in the retainer level of the social strata common in ancient cities. As such, Luke portrays him in the employ of upper-strata elites; he states that Paul was educated to perform as a citizen at home in both the public courts and the halls of political power. Luke consciously presents him as an urbane person, at home in the great cities of the Empire, the client of elites, and a very honorable person. This sort of information simply cannot be gleaned from Paul's letters and would appear to be at variance with the presentation of himself in those documents. But such seems to be the Lucan rhetorical aim in his presentation of Paul's social location.

3.0 SOCIAL LOCATION: TOWARD A USEFUL MODEL

Many recent scholars have begun to use the work of Gerhard Lenski[20] as a useful tool for gaining a sense of the radical stratification of the social world of antiquity.[21] The part of Lenski's work pertinent to this chapter is the description of advanced agrarian societies, which adequately describes at a

---

[19] For recent descriptions of social status in antiquity adapted for New Testament readers, see Meeks, *The Moral World of the First Christians*, pp. 32–38, and Lentz, *Luke's Portrait of Paul*, pp. 7–22.

[20] G. Lenski and J. Lenski, *Human Societies: An Introduction to Macrosociology* (New York, 1974), and G. Lenski, *Power and Privilege*.

[21] See A. J. Saldarini, *Pharisees, Scribes, and Sadducees in Palestinian Society: A Sociological Approach* (Wilmington, 1988), pp. 35–49; D. A. Fiensy, *The Social History of Palestine in the Herodian Period* (Lewiston, 1991), pp. 155–176; D. C. Duling, "Matthew's Plurisignificant 'Son of David' in Social Science Perspective: Kinship, Kingship, Magic, and Miracle," *BTB* 22 (1992), 99–116, and his *The New Testament: Proclamation and Parenesis, Myth and History*, 3rd ed. (New York, 1994), pp. 49–50, 55–58, 141–142; and R. L. Rohrbaugh, "The Social Location of the Marcan Audience," *BTB* 23 (1993), 114–127.

macro level the Roman Empire of the time of both Paul and Luke. It was characterized, he argues, by "marked social inequality . . . pronounced differences in power, privilege and honor" associated with mature agrarian societies.[22] Thus Lenski sets out to describe nine levels of social status, beginning with the imperial and urban elite at the top of the pyramid and concluding with artisans, untouchables, and expendables at the bottom.

Lenski's description of social stratification involves another model, the pre-industrial city, which has been adequately described for New Testament readers by Richard Rohrbaugh.[23] The importance of Rohrbaugh's studies lies in their appreciation of the fact that the elites lived safely and elegantly in cities and that they were assisted by a retainer class which served their interests. Yet the bulk of the city's population consisted of merchants and artisans, some of whom were well off, but most of whom lived at a subsistence level, at best. This model of the ancient city presupposes that the bulk of the total population dwelt in villages and lived as subsistence peasant farmers (90 percent), while the remaining 10 percent (elites, their retainers, merchants, and artisans) lived in cities. Acts describes Paul as an urban person, who, while he may travel through the countryside (16.1–7), lodges in cities and deals with all the levels of the ancient stratified city, especially the elites.

Briefly, then, how does Lenski describe the social stratification of an advanced agrarian society?

(1) Ruler

At the top is the ruler,[24] who might have been a Seleucid or Ptolemy, but in Luke's world was the Roman Emperor, Caesar. He enjoyed vast wealth and power; Roman armies

---

[22] Lenski, *Power and Privilege*, p. 210.

[23] R. L. Rohrbaugh, "The Pre-Industrial City in Luke–Acts," in *The Social World of Luke–Acts: Models for Interpretation*, ed. Jerome H. Neyrey (Peabody, MA, 1991), pp. 125–150, and "The City in the Second Testament," *BTB* 21 (1991), 67–75.

[24] Lenski, *Power and Privilege*, pp. 210–219.

pillaged the East in their conquest,[25] and all that wealth and newly acquired lands made Caesar the ultimate elite figure in the world. There were, of course, numerous client kings in the East who held their positions through imperial patronage.

(2) Governing class

This small majority[26] of aristocrats[27] served as the officers and advisors of the ruler.[28] They might be civic as well as military figures. Most held their appointments directly from the ruler.[29] They tended to have vast grants of land, which supported their elite lifestyle and facilitated the discharge of their civic responsibilities. Lenski estimates that as a group they received at least a quarter of the national income, and together with the ruler, they acquired not less than half of the wealth gained from the land or commerce.

[25] J. H. Kautsky, *The Politics of Aristocratic Empires* (Chapel Hill, 1982), pp. 51–56 and 65–66.

[26] Lenski, *Power and Privilege*, pp. 219–230. The Roman governing stratum was extremely small, as Ramsey MacMullen points out: "The senatorial stratum amounted to something like two-thousandths of one percent . . . *Equites* probably totalled less than a tenth of one percent. Senators had to have property worth 250,000 times the day's wage of a laborer; *equites* qualified for their rank by less than half of that estate. In Italy, at its richest moment, in its second largest city (Padua), the *equites* constituted no more than one percent of the inhabitants; in poorer regions of the empire and in the rural population of every region, *equites* were of course much scarcer" (pp. 88–89 in his *Roman Social Relations* [New Haven, 1984]). Comparably, the local aristocracy in the cities of the East would be quite small, perhaps only 1 percent of the population.

[27] MacMullen, *Roman Social Relations*, pp. 89–90, writes of the local aristocracies: "Between the top and bottom, taking into account in a single glance the entire empire, a range of intermediate wealth made up the aristocracy of small cities. In a given city, however, the aristocracy nevertheless stood upon the summit of a very steep social pyramid." On aristocrats, see Kautsky, *The Politics of Aristocratic Empires*, pp. 89–98, and Reinhard Bendix, *Kings or People: Power and the Mandate to Rule* (Berkeley, 1978), p. 106.

[28] Fiensy, *The Social History of Palestine in the Herodian Period*, pp. 160–161, offers a further definition of this stratum. One can distinguish between the ruler and his circle of elites and another group of lay aristocrats: "They are called 'elders' (*presbuteroi*) (Mk. 15.1, Acts 4.5), 'leaders' (*proestotes*) (*V* 194), 'first men' (*protoi*) (*V* 9, 185), Mk. 6.21, 'notables' (*gnorimoi*) (*B* 2.410, 318), 'powerful ones' (*dynatoi*) (*B* 2.316, 411), 'those first in rank (*time*) and birth (*genos*) (*A* 20.123), and 'honored men' (Yoma 6:4)."

[29] On the Herodian aristocracy in the first century, see Fiensy, *The Social History of Palestine in the Herodian Period*, pp. 157–161.

(3) Retainer class

The governing class maintained in its service "a small army of officials, professional soldiers, household servants and personal retainers."[30] They mediated relationships between the governing elites and the common people.[31] If the governing class was small (1–2 percent), its retainers constituted another 5 percent of the population.

(4) Merchants

Although this society was basically agrarian and wealth came from land and farming, there was a modest amount of trade and commerce. Merchants[32] could be quite wealthy, especially those dealing with luxury goods,[33] but generally the majority were poor. Wealthy entrepreneurs were not despised, since elites used them to increase their own wealth,[34] whereas smaller-scale merchants were held in contempt.

(5) Priests

In the Greco-Roman world there were many famous temples and shrines, frequently associated with important cities. These "political" structures were maintained by a priestly class,[35] whose food, clothing, shelter, etc. were provided by taxes from the land or benefactions from the elite. Its buildings were often richly endowed and served frequently as repositories of wealth. Priests could perform the role of clerk and diplomat, depending on their literacy and social standing.

(6) Peasants

The subsistence farmers who worked the land and produced

---

[30] Lenski, *Power and Privilege*, p. 243; his full treatment is found on pp. 243–248.
[31] Saldarini, *Pharisees, Scribes, and Sadducees*, pp. 87–88, 92–94, 137–143 and 155–167.
[32] Lenski, *Power and Privilege*, pp. 248–256.   [33] Ibid., p. 253.
[34] The attitude of Cicero (*De Officiis* 1.42.151) is typical in this regard.
[35] Lenski, *Power and Privilege*, pp. 256–266; see also Bruce J. Malina, "'Religion' in the World of Paul: A Preliminary Sketch," *BTB* 16 (1986), 92–101.

the agricultural surplus constituted the bulk of the population.[36]

(7) Artisans

Because they had no land and thus no status or means of making advantageous marriages, the artisans of the city are ranked below peasants.[37] In most agrarian societies, this stratum was recruited from the ranks of landless peasants, either dispossessed or non-inheriting ones. Their ranks were continually replenished from migrants from the countryside. While the urban population represented 5–10 percent of the total population of the Empire, the artisan class constituted about half of that.[38]

(8) Unclean, degraded and expendables

At the very bottom of the social scale were the untouchables, who lived just outside the city. Below them were the expendables, such as petty criminals, outlaws, beggars, itinerant workers, and those who lived by charity or their wits.[39]

The value of this model lies in its accurate description of the world of urban elites and non-elites, as well as the differences between urban and rural populations in antiquity.

When we survey the data in Acts about the people with whom Paul has contact, we can begin to discern a definite pattern in the Lucan rhetoric which portrays Paul exclusively

---

[36] Lenski, *Power and Privilege*, pp. 266–278; D. E. Oakman, *Jesus and the Economic Questions of his Day* (Lewiston, 1986), pp. 100–102, and his "The Countryside in Luke–Acts," in *The Social World of Luke–Acts: Models for Interpretation*, ed. Jerome H. Neyrey (Peabody, MS, 1991), pp. 152–164. D. Fiensy (*The Social History of Palestine in the Herodian Period*, p. 157) calls attention to the "the essential bifurcation of peasants society into aristocrats and peasant." This allows us to appreciate the ancient distinction between urban and rural populations, with the attendant snobbery by urban peoples toward the rural, peasant peoples (Fiensy, pp. 168–169). Thus it matters greatly whether Luke presents Paul as just another "uneducated, common man" from the countryside like Peter and John (Acts 4.13) or as an urban dweller in major cities of the Empire.

[37] Lenski, *Power and Privilege*, pp. 278–280.   [38] Ibid., p. 279.

[39] Ibid., pp. 281–284.

as an urban person of the "retainer" class, who has access to rich merchants, members of the retainer stratum, and even the governing class. Let us use Lenski's model as a template for assessing Luke's social location of Paul according to Acts.

4.0 READING THE STATUS OF PAUL IN ACTS ACCORDING TO THE LENSKI MODEL

(1) Ruler

Although the narrative never tells us whether Paul ever had his requested audience with the Roman Emperor, he did "appeal to Caesar" (25.11, 21; 26.32). An angelic messenger told Paul in a dream, "You must stand before Caesar" (27.24); and in the Lucan schema of prophecy-fulfillment, a reader might be expected to imagine that the prophetic Word of the Lord was fulfilled. At least on the narrative level, Paul is a suitable person to appear before the Emperor.

In regard to client kings, when Ananias is instructed to attend to Paul upon his arrival in Damascus, the appearing Lord says of Paul, "He is my chosen instrument to carry my name before the Gentiles and kings and the sons of Israel" (9.15). This prophetic remark is amply fulfilled by Paul's appearance before King Agrippa and his queen, Bernice. Although in the presence of the Roman governor Festus, Paul addresses his remarks directly to the monarch: "I think myself fortunate that it is before you, King Agrippa, I am to make my defense today" (26.2,19). Having heard Paul, the King declared him innocent (26.32). Although Agrippa is clearly a client king of the Roman Emperor, the narrative accords him the status of a ruler in his own right.

(2) Governing class

It will be important to distinguish as best we can between three distinct groups with whom Paul is associated: (a) the governing Jewish elite classes in Jerusalem, (b) the Roman authorities (consuls, proconsuls, governors, tribunes), and (c) the leading citizens of various Greek cities. When Luke introduces Saul, he is a retainer of the governing class in Jerusalem. Paul himself goes to the "high priest" for letters authorizing him to act (9.1–2), apparently a publicly known fact "as the high priest and the whole council of elders bear me witness" (22.5). He persecutes the Way "with the authority and commission of the chief priests" (26.12). Luke, then, portrays Paul as a retainer of the governing class in Jerusalem, who acts as their agent, with their authority, and with official documents from them to legitimate his activities and to support his claims. It is, moreover, no minor item that Paul later appears before the elites of Jerusalem, "the chief priests and all the council" (22.30). Among them Luke lists representatives of the governing elite of Jerusalem: chief priests (23.1–5; 24.1), aristocratic Sadducees (23.6), and elders (24.1). Luke would have us believe that he is no stranger to this group.

The first Roman member of the governing class before whom Paul appears is Sergius Paulus, "proconsul and man of intelligence" (13.7). This person of very high status summoned Paul and sought to hear the Word of God. The narrative says that Sergius "believed" (13.12), suggesting that Paul found favor while speaking before this elite person. In Corinth Paul was dragged before Gallio, proconsul of Achaia, in circumstances less than favorable (18.12). Although dismissed by Gallio, Paul was a significant enough person to warrant the attention of the highest governing official in the area.

His stay with the two Judean governors, Felix and Festus, was more auspicious. Felix was informed that Paul was a Roman citizen and so deserved special protection from assassination (23.26–33). He had "a rather accurate knowledge of the Way" (24.22) and so deferred judgment until another official, Lysias the tribune, arrived (24.22). Yet Felix kept Paul in custody for two years, and on occasion heard Paul "argue about justice and self-control and future judgment" (24.25), topics hotly debated by the major philosophical schools of the

Stoics and Epicureans.[40] Paul then pleaded his case before Festus, the new governor (25.6–12), and was given a full, formal hearing (26.1–32). Although the narrative indicates that Paul remained in prison (24.27), he nevertheless had occasional access to the highest governing authorities in the province and engaged at least one of them regularly in formal conversation.

As regards others, Luke narrates that on one occasion Paul was the guest of a person whom we have reason to evaluate as a member of the governing or elite class. After his shipwreck, "the leading man of the island," Publius, offers Paul hospitality (28.7) and even seeks his influence to cure his ailing father (28.8–9). And he remarks that at Thessalonika, Paul was persuasive to a great number of Greeks and "not a few of the leading women" (γυναικῶν τε τῶν πρώτων, 17:4). This cryptic remark does not allow much elaboration, for no details whatsoever are given us; it may be a parallel to Lk. 8.2–3.

(3) Retainer class

Both the retainer and the merchant class contain higher- and lower-ranking retainers, as well as richer and poorer merchants. We take this into account as we investigate the persons with whom Paul typically had social relations.

In recent publications, A. Saldarini has argued persuasively that the Pharisees of Judea in the time period described by the Gospels and the letters of Paul were themselves members of the retainer class who served the needs and interests of the governing elite.[41] Paul, at least, appears in Acts as a literate person, even a scribe. He claims formal training as an educated and so literate Pharisee, under a famous teacher, Gamaliel (22.3). As noted above, he acts as agent for the Jerusalem elite, function-

---

[40] See J. H. Neyrey, "Acts 17, Epicureans, and Theodicy: A Study in Stereotypes," in *Greeks, Romans, and Christians*, ed. D. Balch, E. Ferguson, and W. Meeks (Minneapolis, 1990), pp. 118–134.

[41] A. J. Saldarini, *Pharisees, Scribes and Sadducees*, pp. 277–297, and "The Social Class of the Pharisees in Mark," in *The Social World of Formative Christianity and Judaism* (Philadelphia, 1988), pp. 69–77.

ing not only as "ambassador" with letters of authorization, but possibly also as "bailiff." When he enters synagogues in the cities of Asia Minor, he is regarded as a literate person, with the ability to discourse on the Scriptures and exhort the group (13.15–16; 14.1).

Luke portrays Paul as sufficiently literate and rhetorically eloquent to engage both Stoics and Epicureans in a formal discourse on the Areopagus in Athens (17.16–31). His discourse contains a description of the Stoic deity in terms of the topos on "providence."[42] Excluding Cynics, it seems safe to suggest that philosophers in the Greco-Roman world themselves belonged to the retainer class, serving as advisors and teachers to the elites. Luke would have us think of Paul as being a worthy member of this retainer class and as someone to whom they would listen.

When Paul begins his public career at Antioch, he is mentioned in the company of four other persons, some of whom probably belong to the retainer class. Barnabas, a native of Cyprus and a Levite, owned property (4.36–37), which he sold and the proceeds of which he donated to the Jerusalem church. He later acts as the trusted agent of the Jerusalem church to the new foundation of disciples at Antioch (11.22–26), and as their agent to convey funds to the Jerusalem church during famine (11.29–30). These are not the actions of a mere artisan, but of a person of some wealth and standing. Although we are ignorant of the status of "Simeon who is called Niger and Lucius of Cyrene," we are on safer ground concerning "Manaen, a member of the court of Herod the tetrarch" (13.1). This translation of σύντροπος may be too strong, for it may more modestly mean that Manaen was "reared together with" Herod in the royal residences.[43] Perhaps not himself a member of the governing class, he was likely a retainer in the royal household.

In Philippi, Paul ran afoul of certain persons in the city, who first haled him before the city leaders (ἄρχοντας, 16.19), and

---

[42] See J. H. Neyrey, "Acts 17, Epicureans, and Theodicy," pp. 124–126.
[43] LSJ, p. 1728.

then before the civic "magistrates" (στρατηγοί). These persons function as the military and civic officials charged with the order of the city (Herodotus 5.38). They in turn can employ the services of "police" (ῥαβδούχοι), that is, those who "carry the rod," namely lictors who carry the *fasces*. The "magistrates" have authority to arrest Paul, chastise him, and then release him. As the narrative unfolds, they simply expel Paul from the city as a troublemaker, but Paul demands of them much more. Humiliated and shamed as a Roman citizen (16.37), he demands from these public officials a formal public apology. Luke does not claim that Paul associated with these "magistrates," but rather that he recognized their social status as members of the retainer class responsible for public order and public reputation. They in turn are made to recognize Paul's own status (citizen) and offer a public acknowledgment of Paul's honorable position.

(4) Merchants

The most notable merchant with whom Paul has social contact appears to be Lydia of Philippi. On the Sabbath, Paul approached a sacred grove where devout women gathered ("there was a place of prayer") and attracted the attention of Lydia, "from the city of Thyatira, a seller of purple goods" (16.14). Wayne Meeks cites three things which indicate that she was no minor merchant, but enjoyed some wealth and status.[44] "Purple goods" (πορφυρόπωλις) may mean that she engaged in the dyeing of these goods or the sale of the dyed item. Either way, purple was a luxury item and was bought and worn by the elite.[45] Second, she prevails upon Paul and

---

[44] Meeks, *First Urban Christians*, p. 62.

[45] See F. W. Danker ("Purple," *ABD* v. 557–560), who indicates that fine purple clothing, of course, was a luxury item of the rich; he notes too that inexpensive mineral and vegetable dyes were also used to produce approximations. He concludes that "it is not possible to determine that Lydia limited her sale to luxury items or to a specific clientele," p. 558. G. H. R. Horsley, *New Documents Illustrating Early Christianity* (Macquarie University, 1982), 2.26–28, notes that the name "Lydia" suggests a person of servile status, who drew her name from her place of origin. He hints, moreover, that she may well have been of "Caesar's household"

associates to accept hospitality in her house (16.15), which does not appear to be a small shop on a narrow street with meager living quarters behind or above it. Finally, her name, occupation, and origin suggest that she belongs to the Greek-speaking merchants who have settled alongside Italian, agrarian colonists. These clues do not allow us to designate her a "rich" merchant, yet she acts as a kind of patron to Paul.

(5) Priests

The priests most frequently associated with Paul in the early part of his career were the elite high priests of Jerusalem, whom I located above in the *governing class*. Priests in other cities also had dealings with Paul. During the riot at Ephesus, "some of the Asiarchs ('Ασιαρχῶν), who were friends of his (φίλοι)," sent messengers to him to prevent his engagement in the riot (19.31). According to L. Taylor, "Asiarchs were the foremost men of the province of Asia, chosen from the wealthiest and the most aristocratic inhabitants of the province."[46] As leaders of a religio-political organization, they promoted the cult of the reigning Emperor and with him the goddess Roma.[47] The "Asiarchs" mentioned by Luke are said to be "friends" of Paul, which term can readily bear the meaning of patron.[48]

From a historical perspective one must wonder how aristocrats dedicated to the promotion of the cult of the Emperor

(Phil. 4.22), an ex-slave working in Philippi in an industry over which emperors from the time of Nero exercised an imperial monopoly (see Eusebius, *HE* 7.32.2–3).

[46] L. R. Taylor, "Note XXII: The Asiarchs," in *The Beginnings of Christianity*, ed. K. Lake and H. J. Cadbury (Grand Rapids, 1979), vol. II, pp. 256–262. Yet there continues to be a critical debate over whether an Asiarch was also an ἀρχιερεύς; see R. A. Kearsley, "Asiarchs, Archiereis, and the Archiereia of Asia," *GRBS* 27 (1986); 183–192 and his "Asiarchs," *ABD* 1.495–497.

[47] Whether an Asiarch was necessarily a high priest is controversial; but as Kearsley notes ("Asiarchs," p. 496), they were highly prominent people: Roman citizens, members of important families, benefactors of the city, supporters of the Roman rulers, and honored by the city as patron-benefactors. They clearly belong to the ruling elite.

[48] Examples of clients being called "friends" of kings and the aristocracy include: John 19.12; Josephus, *Ant.* 12.134 and 298; Philo, *Flac.* 40; 1 Macc. 2.18; 3.38 and 10.65. See also E. Bammel, "*Philos tou Kaisaros*," *TZ* 77 (1952), 205–210 and P. A. Brunt, "'Amicitia' in the Late Roman Republic," *Proceedings of the Cambridge Philological Society* 191 (1965), 1–20.

could possibly be interested in Paul and his monotheism. Yet Luke's rhetorical strategy concerning Paul's social location indicates that they were his "friends" and patrons. Moreover, if Luke's own portrayal of these figures as leading aristocrats is correct, then they hardly belong in the *priestly* class, but should be ranked higher in the *governing class*.

Luke narrates that after Paul's healing of a crippled man at Lystra, the populace acclaimed Barnabas "Zeus" and Paul "Hermes," because he was the chief spokesman (14.11–12). At this point, "the priest of Zeus," whose temple was in front of the city, came forward with oxen and garlands to honor Paul and Barnabas (14.13). This priest quite accurately fits Lenski's description of a person in charge of the sacred rites at a local shrine. Paul forestalled the reverence offered by this priest, but the incident is noteworthy for two reasons. Paul was in contact with this class of person. More importantly, he was honored as a deity by them (see also 28.6).

(6) Artisans

When Paul arrived in Corinth, he "found" a Jew named Aquila and his wife Priscilla. "Because he was of the same trade he stayed with them" (18.2–3). They are tentmakers, or workers in leather; and so they are clearly artisans. We cannot tell whether they were well-off or penurious artisans. This association was entirely natural: Paul found people of his own ethnos (Jews), who plied his trade, and who presumably spoke his language. We may assume that Aquila and Priscilla did not live in the exclusive part of the city reserved for elites, but in one of the many artisan neighborhoods. A certain Crispus lived in that quarter as well. He was the "ruler of the synagogue" (ἀρχισυνάγωγος), and became a believer as well (18.8). Crispus, because of his social position, is probably to be considered an artisan of some means and status.

Although Paul was on good terms with the artisans mentioned above, he becomes the dedicated enemy of Demetrius the silversmith at Ephesus. The latter "brought no little business to the craftsmen," and was able to persuade this group of artisans to riot against Paul (19.23–27). They are persuaded to bring their grievances before the civic magistrates (19.38). The narrative does not indicate that Paul resided in the quarter of the city where Demetrius and his artisan associates worked or that he had any social relations with them.

Luke comments once more about Paul's association with artisans in the story of his final visit to Troas. Paul and his Christian disciples are apparently meeting in an artisan's rooms in an insula. The young boy Eutychus falls from the window on the third story (τριστέγου, 20.9). We are hardly to imagine a multi-storied house of an aristocrat, for which three stories would be most unusual. Rather, this appears to be an insula, a residence of poor artisans.

Placing Lenski's model as a template over the social relationship in Acts, we gain a sense of the author's rhetorical strategy. Luke claims that Paul was at home with the elites of his world. He depicts him as sufficiently educated to engage in philosophical discourse and as trained in forensic rhetoric so as to make numerous public speeches,[49] which is one of the duties of a citizen. Paul is clearly the retainer of the elites of Jerusalem and privy to their circle. In his own right, he is a worthy person suited to discourse with Roman proconsuls and client kings. His patrons are said to be Asiarchs, elites of Ephesus, and well-to-do merchants (i.e. Lydia at Philippi). In short, Paul is a very honorable person of relatively high social status, who associates with the elites of his world and is trained to perform suitably at that level of society.

5.0 THE URBAN AND URBANE PAUL

One's status and honor were related to one's place of origin. Jesus was dismissed by Nathanael simply because he came from the village of Nazareth (John 1.46), whereas Paul claimed honorable status because he was from Tarsus, "no mean city" (Acts 21.39). We investigate now the honor rating of the

---

49 J. H. Neyrey, "The Forensic Defense Speech and Paul's Trial Speeches in Acts 22–26: Form and Function," in *Luke–Acts: New Perspectives from the Society of Biblical Literature Seminar*, ed. C. H. Talbert (New York, 1984), pp. 210–224.

various cities which, according to Acts, Paul either visited or in which he resided.[50] As R. Rohrbaugh has shown, there is considerable confusion in Luke–Acts over what is a village, a town, and a city.[51] He quotes Pausanias on what the ancients considered a "city," which native description will serve us well in evaluating the cities of Paul's labor and residence:

> if indeed one can give the name of city to those who possess no public buildings, no gymnasium, no theatre, no market-place, no water descending to a fountain, but live in bare shelters just like mountain huts on the edges of ravines. (10.4.1)

Pausanias points to the public arenas where honorable males speak, act, see, and are seen. Such places denote a vibrant civic life and a sophisticated cultural ambiance. They are the natural places of urban elites.[52] Such buildings, monuments and temples might take up 35–50 percent of the area of a walled city.[53] Apart from death, the worst punishment that could be meted out to a Roman citizen was banishment from Rome to some obscure island or region.

5.1 HONOR RATING OF CITIES

Several sets of evidence help us to appreciate the honor rating of the cities in Acts which Paul visits.[54] First, the author himself comments on the status of the various cities: for example,

[50] See W. Ramsey, *St. Paul the Traveller and the Roman Citizen*, 7th ed. (London, 1903), and *The Cities of St. Paul* (London, 1907); see also A. H. M. Jones, *The Greek City from Alexander to Justinian* (Oxford, 1940); David Magie, *Roman Rule in Asia Minor* (Princeton, 1950); and S. E. Johnson, *Paul the Apostle and His Cities* (Wilmington, 1987).

[51] R. L. Rohrbaugh, "The Pre-Industrial City in Luke–Acts," *The Social World of Luke–Acts*, pp. 125–127.

[52] Ibid., pp. 133–136.

[53] R. Stark, "Antioch as the Social Situation for Matthew's Gospel," in *Social History of the Matthean Community*, ed. D. Balch (Minneapolis, 1991), p. 192.

[54] One author of ancient progymnasmata, Menander Rhetor, has left explicit rules for the "praise of a city" (*Menander Rhetor* [trans. D. A. Russell and Nigel Wilson (Oxford, 1981)], pp. 33–75). Examples of this praise of cities can be found in the two speeches of Dio Chrysostom on Tarsus, especially *Or.* 33.17–18, 21. Unfortunately, Luke has given very few details about the various cities of Paul to test whether he was familiar with such encomia. Many of Dio Chrysostom's orations are directed toward cities such as Tarsus and Alexandria, and so offer valuable data on their reputations and how public speakers praised them.

"Tarsus, no mean city" (21.39) and Philippi, "the leading city of the district of Macedonia" (16.12). Second, other cities were well known as major centers of learning and commerce, such as Antioch, Ephesus, and Tarsus. Finally, there are archaeological data on these and other cities, indicating that they, too, had public buildings, gymnasia, theaters, market-places, etc. Specific information may or may not have been available to general readers of Acts, but the author presumes some common lore or fame for various cities mentioned.[55]

In terms of the honor one derived from being born and raised in a certain city, I cite the rules from the προγυμνάσματα of Menander Rhetor for composing an encomium on a city. These rules were commonplaces in antiquity, and all who learned to write Greek were schooled in these exercises. They represent, then, general cultural expectations from the Hellenistic world. The very first thing an author should note when composing an encomium on someone is the honor which accrues from being born in an honorable city (or country). Because of its relevance for this chapter, I cite Menander in full:

If the *city* has no distinction, you must inquire whether his *nation* as a whole is considered brave and valiant, or is devoted to literature or the possession of virtues, like the Greek race, or again is distinguished for law, like the Italian, or is courageous, like the Gauls or Paeonians. You must take a few features from the nation . . . arguing that it is inevitable that a man from such a [city or] nation should have such characteristics, and that he stands out among all his praiseworthy compatriots.[56]

Thus it was "inevitable" that a person from such an honorable city would have its honorable characteristics.

Moreover, in terms of the honor rating of cities, it is helpful

---

[55] Further investigation needs to be done in the Lucan shift of focus from Jesus, peasant of the countryside to the early church, artisans of the urban world. See H. M. Coon, "Lucan Perspectives and the City," *Missiology* 13 (1985), 415–418. The change of social location in Luke–Acts has been investigated in terms of a shift from the political-religious institution of the Temple to the kinship institution of the family; see J. H. Elliott, "Temple versus Household in Luke–Acts: A Contrast in Social Institutions," in *The Social World of Luke–Acts: Models for Interpretation*, ed. Jerome H. Neyrey (Peabody, MA, 1991), pp. 211–240.

[56] Menander Rhetor, *Treatise* II 369.17–370.10.

to note the intense "vanity and rivalry of cities in the matter of rank and titles."[57] Cities in Asia Minor regularly made honor claims to titles such as "metropolis," "First and Greatest," "autonomous," "Warden of the (Imperial) Temple," "Inviolable," "Friend of Rome," and the like.[58] According to Dio Chrysostom, Nicea and Nicomedia "contended for primacy" (πρωτείων; *Or.* 38.24). Nicea, moreover, was rightly flattered to be known as

noble and worthy of renown . . . both as to its power and grandeur, for it is inferior to no city of distinction anywhere, whether in nobility of lineage or in composition of population, comprising as it does, the most illustrious families, not small groups of sorry specimens who came together from this place and from that, but the leaders among both Greeks and Macedonians, and, what is most significant, having had as founders both heroes and gods. (Dio Chrysostom, *Or.* 39.1)

Ephesus and Smyrna engaged in rivalry to be called "the First and Greatest Metropolis of Asia."[59] Miletus was known as "First Settled city of Ionia, Metropolis of Many Great cities in Pontus and Egypt and in Many Places of the Inhabited World."[60] The titles mattered to the ancients, for they drew part of their personal honor from the honor of the renowned city in which they lived. And they were highly jealous of sharing this honor with a neighboring city (see Dio Chrysostom, *Or.* 38.39).

The scope of this chapter does not allow us to investigate thoroughly all of the cities of Paul's sojourns and travels.[61] I examine four of them in the light of Pausanias' remarks about

---

[57] David Magie, *Roman Rule in Asia Minor* (2 vols., Princeton, 1950), vol. II, p. 1496, n. 17.

[58] Athenaeus contains an excellent illustration of this: "Athenaeus speaks of Rome as 'the populace of the world,' and says that one would not shoot wide of the mark if he called the city of Rome an epitome of the civilized world; so true is it that one may see at a glance all the cities of the world settled there. Most of them he details with their individual traits, such as the 'golden' city of Alexandria, the 'beautiful' city of Antioch, the 'very lovely' city of Nicomedia, and beyond and above these, 'the most radiant of all the towns that Zeus created'" (*Deipnosophistae* 1.20b).

[59] See Magie, *Roman Rule in Asia Minor*, vol. II, p. 636.

[60] Ibid., pp. 636 and 1496, n. 19.

[61] See Ramsey, *The Cities of St. Paul*; Johnson, *Paul the Apostle and his Cities*; J. McRay, *Archeology and the New Testament* (Grand Rapids, 1991), pp. 225–350; and Meeks, *First Urban Christians*, pp. 9–16, 40–50.

what constitutes an honorable city in the popular mind. Since Tarsus is the place of Paul's birth[62] and Luke claims that it is "no mean city," it is a fitting place to begin.

5.1.1 Tarsus

Climaxing a long and glorious history, Tarsus became the capital of the Roman province of Cilicia after its conquest by Pompey. Cicero, when proconsul of the province, resided there (*Att.* 5.20.3; *Fam.* 2.17.1).[63] Augustus favored Tarsus[64] by exempting it from taxes and fostered its development as a center of philosophy and rhetoric. In his speeches to Tarsus, Dio Chrysostom[65] spoke of its rank as a "metropolis" from the start and as "the greatest of all the cities of Cilicia" (33.17; 34.7),[66] and Strabo praised it as a premier center of learning:

The people of Tarsus have devoted themselves so eagerly, not only to philosophy, but also to the whole round of education in general, that they have surpassed Athens, Alexandria, and any other place that can be named where there have been schools and lectures of philosophers. (*Geog.* 14.5.13; see also 14.5.15)

From excavations at Tarsus, we know that it enjoyed the typical theater, gymnasia, market-places, fountains, and the like.[67] Apollonius of Tyana found the city more concerned with luxuries than learning, and so left it (*Vita* 1.7). But he attests to its wealth, and so its prestige and honor.

---

[62] Acts 22.3; see W. C. van Unnik, *Tarsus or Jerusalem? The City of Paul's Youth* (London, 1962), pp. 6–14; for a revisionist point of view, see Martin Hengel, *The Pre-Christian Paul* (Philadelphia, 1991) pp. 18–39.

[63] For a convenient history of Tarsus, see W. Ruge, "Tarsos," *PW* 2.4 (1932), 2413–2439.

[64] See Dio Chrysostom, *Or.* 34.7 and 25.

[65] Dio's two encomia to Tarsus (*Or.* 33 and 34) are valuable sources of what was considered praiseworthy by the ancients; on these orations, see C. B. Welles, "Hellenistic Tarsus," *Mélanges de l'Université Saint Joseph* 38 (1962), 62–75.

[66] It was also known as νεωκόρος or "Warden of the (imperial) Temple" (Magie, *Roman Rule in Asia Minor*, vol. I, p. 637). On its acclamation as a "metropolis," see Strabo, *Geog.* 14.5.13.

[67] Dio Chrysostom (*Or.* 33.18) seems to be describing the public buildings of Tarsus when he mentions the praise of a city for its "rivers and baths and fountains and porticoes and a multitude of houses and a wide extent of space." See F. F. Bruce, *Paul: Apostle of the Heart Set Free* (Grand Rapids, 1977), pp. 32–36.

5.1.2 Antioch

Josephus called Antioch the third city of the empire, after Rome and Alexandria: "a city which, for extent and opulence, unquestionably ranks third among the cities of the Roman world" (*Wars* 3.29).[68] It was truly famous for its elegance ("Antioch the Great,"[69] "the Beautiful"[70]), its size,[71] wealth, and importance.[72] From coins, we know that Antioch called itself "Antioch, metropolis, sacred, and inviolable, and autonomous, and sovereign, and capital of the East."[73] Its population has been estimated as between 200,000 and 400,000.[74] With the Roman conquest, it maintained its importance as a major city, becoming the capital of Roman Syria.[75] As befits a major city, it was encircled with great walls;[76] it enjoyed the typical public buildings of a noble city, namely a great colonnaded street, circus, theater, forum, agora, palace, baths, and the like.[77]

---

[68] Strabo remarked, "Antiocheia is the metropolis (μετρόπολις) of Syria. It does not fall much short, either in power or in size, of Seleuceia-on-the-Tigris or Alexandria in Egypt" (16.2.5).

[69] Philostratus, *Vita Apol.* 1.16.

[70] Athenaeus, *Deipnosophistae* 1.20b; Libanius, *Q.* 31.9; see B. M. Metzger, "Antioch-on-the-Orontes," *BA* 11 (1948), 72.

[71] Libanius remarked, "There is no city in the world in which big size has been united in equal measure with such beautiful situation" (*Or.* xi.196).

[72] J. Malalas, *The Chronicle*, as cited in George Haddad, "Aspects of Social Life in Antioch in the Hellenistic-Roman Period" (unpublished diss., University of Chicago, 1949), pp. 20–30.

[73] See E. T. Newell, "The Pre-Imperial Coinage of Roman Antioch," *Num. Chron.* 19 (1919), 69–113; see also Malalas, *The Chronicle*, as cited in Haddad, "Aspects of Social Life," p. 16. Strabo also reports that Antioch was rightly called a "metropolis" (*Geog.* 16.2.5).

[74] See C. Kraeling, "The Jewish Community at Antioch," *JBL* 51 (1932), 130–160.

[75] See A. H. M. Jones, *The Cities of the Eastern Roman Provinces*, 2nd ed. (Oxford, 1971), pp. 241–242.

[76] Strabo says, "Antiocheia is . . . a Tetrapolis, since it consists of four parts; and each of the four settlements is fortified both by a common wall and by a wall of its own" (*Geog.* 16.2.4).

[77] For a thorough survey of the public buildings erected in Antioch during the Augustan Empire, see G. Downey, *A History of Antioch in Syria from Seleucus to the Arab Conquest* (Princeton, 1961), pp. 169–184; see also his *Ancient Antioch* (Princeton, 1963), pp. 75–77, 81–84.

5.1.3 Ephesus

Strabo called this city the largest commercial center in Asia Minor west of the Taurus (*Geog.* 641). From archaeological investigation, we know that it had extensive public buildings: the great temple of Artemis (Acts 19.24, 27–28)[78] and a splendid theater (Acts 19.29), as well as several market-places, a number of gymnasia, and many fountains.[79] Since Augustus, it enjoyed the honor of being the capital of the Roman province of Asia, and was acclaimed as "First and Greatest Metropolis of Asia." When Ephesus was praised by Strabo, he followed the conventions of the encomium and lauded the city for its famous temple, its environment and harbor, and finally the famous men from it.[80] In a recent article, Peter Lampe has argued that Luke, at least, was quite familiar with the social and topographical features of Ephesus.[81]

5.1.4 Corinth

This famous and wealthy[82] city was refounded as a Roman colony under Julius Caesar in 44 BCE. It enjoyed considerable imperial patronage, first under Augustus and then under Tiberias, when a vast public building program was accomplished. As a result, Corinth was a truly honorable city, with extensive walls (Strabo, *Geog.* 8.6.21), numerous rings and fountains, an upper and a lower market-place, theater,

---

[78] Antipater of Sidon ranked the temple of Artemis over all the other honorable wonders of the ancient world: "I have set eyes on the wall of lofty Babylon on which is a road for chariots, and the statue of Zeus by the Alpheus, and the hanging gardens and the colossus of the Sun, and the huge labor of the high pyramids, and the vast tomb of Mausolus; but when I saw the house of Artemis that mounted to the clouds,those other marvels lost their brilliancy, and I said, 'Lo, apart from Olympus, the Sun never looked on anything so grand'" (*The Greek Anthology* 9.58); see also Strabo, *Geog.* 14.1.22.

[79] Richard Oster, "Ephesus," *ABD* II.542–548.   [80] Strabo, *Geog.* 14.1.22–25.

[81] Peter Lampe, "Acta 19 im Spiegel der ephesischen Inschriften," *BZ* 36 (1992), 59–76.

[82] Strabo repeatedly calls attention to its great wealth (*Geog.* 8.6.20), which in antiquity was also a claim to great honor.

temples,[83] fountains, monuments, baths and the like (Pausanias 2.2.6–3.6).[84] It hosted the Isthmian games, the second most prestigious Panhellenic games.[85]

From our investigation of these four cities and from other data in Acts, we can discern how Luke portrays Paul as traveling to and residing in provincial capitals, "no mean cities."[86] Tarsus, Antioch, Ephesus, and Corinth were wealthy cities, which enjoyed considerable imperial patronage, and which were for the most part centers of learning. Thus Paul is presented as a citizen of the world,[87] at home in the important cities of the Empire. Given the known data about the public buildings in these cities, we are led by Luke to envision Paul under the stoa in the market-places, at the theater, and in the various public arenas of the city. Luke tells us that in Corinth Paul "argued in the hall (σχολῇ) of Tyrannus" (Acts 19.9), a recognized place for educated disputation.[88] Luke's positioning of Paul in most of the major cities of the Empire constitutes a rhetorical strategy that would have his readers accept Paul as a sophisticated person, at home in all parts of the Hellenistic world and truly an honorable person. Honorable people come from and reside in honorable cities.

5.1.5 Parts of the city

More specifically, in what part of the city does Luke present Paul residing when he arrives or stays? We know from studies of ancient and pre-industrial cities that they were divided into numerous neighborhoods: a central part for the few elites and

[83] Especially the elegant art work in the temple of Dionysus: see Strabo, *Geog.* 8.6.23.

[84] See J. Murphy-O'Connor, *St. Paul's Corinth* (Wilmington, 1983) pp. 25–26, and "The Corinth that Saint Paul Saw," *BA* 47 (1984), 147–159; J. Wiseman, "Corinth and Rome I: 228 BC–AD 267," *ANRW* VII.1, pp. 438–548.

[85] See O. Broneer, "The Apostle Paul and the Isthmian Games," in *The Biblical Archaeologist Reader*, ed. D. N. Freedman and E. F. Campbell (New York, 1970), pp. 393–428.

[86] See J. L. Kelso, "Key Cities in Paul's Missionary Program," *BS* 79 (1922), 481–486; Conn, "Lucan Perspectives and the Cities," pp. 409–28.

[87] See A. J. Malherbe, "'Not in a Corner': Early Christian Apologetic in Acts 26.26," *SecCent* 5 (1985), 193–210.

[88] See S. K. Stowers, "Social Status: Public Speaking and Private Teaching: The Circumstances of Paul's Preaching Activity," *NovT* 26 (1984), 60–63.

their retainers and the periphery for the many poor artisans. Thus it matters in what part of the city persons are found and where they belong.[89]

Only three times are we told about Paul's place of residence. Lydia, the dealer in purple clothing, invites Paul to "my house" (16.15). Our problem lies in knowing whether Lydia is a wealthy merchant or an average artisan. At a minimum, she appears to be a person of *some* means, not the typical struggling artisan; this will reflect on where she lives in Philippi. At Corinth Paul stayed with the artisans Aquila and Prisca (18.2–3), presumably in the artisan part of the city, and even there, one for workers in leather. Finally, Paul was the guest of Publius, "the chief man of the island" of Malta (28.7). He is presumably a landed aristocrat with a fine house. On balance, Paul seems to find patronage in honorable residences, even the homes of wealthy persons. But we note quickly that he never resides long in the houses of members of the elite.

Although we know that Paul enters synagogues,[90] Luke presents him in other public places. At Athens, he is frequently found in the market-place (ἀγορᾷ, 17.17); the only other reference to a market-place is that of Philippi, where Paul faces the city magistrates (16.19). Then Luke reports that some philosophers brought Paul to the Areopagus, the site of the council of Athenian elders, who were wealthy oligarchs (19.19).[91] Paul is warned not to enter the theater at Ephesus (19.31), a place frequented by elites and non-elites alike. Finally, at Lystra he seems to be standing before the local temple outside the city (14.13), but it is difficult to determine whether this temple was as famous as the great temple of Artemis at Ephesus (19.27). At a minimum, Luke portrays Paul as a typical male of consider-

[89] See Rohrbaugh, "The Pre-Industrial City in Luke–Acts," pp. 134–136, 144–145. See Wayne A. Meeks, "Saint Paul of the Cities," in *Civitas: Religious Interpretation of the City* (Atlanta, 1986), p. 20.

[90] See Acts 13.14; 14.1; 17.1; 18.19; it is very difficult to determine whether any of these synagogues were in elite or wealthy parts of the city. We do not know whether they were actual buildings dedicated to this purpose or whether the Jewish worshipers gathered in the house of a patron. If the latter, then this person had *some* means, namely a residence large enough to host a sizeable body of people and sufficient wealth to act as a patron.

[91] See H. M. Martin, "Areopagus," *ABD* 1.371.

able social status: he regularly appears in public space; he frequently performs traditional elite male tasks such as arguing, debating and speaking boldly in public. Luke would have us think of him as a person at home in places reserved for elites.

6.0 PAUL, THE ROMAN CITIZEN

In a world of elaborate social hierarchy, it is no minor thing that Luke claims for Paul that he is both a citizen of Tarsus, no mean city (Acts 21.29), and a citizen of Rome (16.37; 22.27–28).[92] As we noted in regard to Paul the urban person, if one's prestige and standing are determined by the city of one's birth, all the more is it related to being a citizen of that city, and especially a Roman citizen. Such an honor was particularly rare among the population of the eastern Mediterranean in this period, and so, as F. F. Bruce remarked, "the few Roman citizens, whether Greek or Jews by birth, would constitute a social elite."[93]

When Paul's citizenship is discussed, scholars have tended to ask strictly historical questions,[94] such as, "If he was born a

[92] Among the standard works on Roman citizenship, see A. N. Sherwin-White, *The Roman Citizenship* (Oxford, 1937) and his *Roman Society and Roman Law in the New Testament* (Grand Rapids,1978), pp. 144–193; and F. Schulz, "Roman Registers of Births and Birth Certificates," *JRS* 32 (1942), 78–91, and 33 (1943), 55–64. On dual citizenship, see H. W. Tajra, *The Trial of Paul*, WUNT 35 (Tübingen, 1989), pp. 76–89.

[93] Bruce, *Paul: Apostle of the Heart Set Free*, p. 38. The remarks of Ramsay (*St. Paul the Traveller and the Roman Citizen*, pp. 30–31) remain valid: "According to the law of his country, he was first of all a Roman citizen. That character superseded all others before the law and in the general opinion of society; and placed him amid the aristocracy of any provincial town. In the first century, when the citizenship was still jealously guarded, the *civitas* may be taken as a proof that his family was one of distinction and at least moderate wealth. It also implies that there was in the surroundings amid which he grew up, a certain amount of friendliness to the Imperial government (for the new citizens in general, and the Jewish citizens in particular, were warm partisans of their protector, the new Imperial regime), and also of pride in a possession that ensured distinction and rank and general respect in Tarsus. As a Roman, Paul had a *nomen* and *praenomen*, probably taken from the Roman officer who gave his family *civitas*."

[94] The most recent challenger to the Lucan attestation of Paul's Roman citizenship is Wolfgang Stegemann, "War der Apostel Paulus ein römischer Bürger?," *ZNW* 78 (1987), 200–229. As arguments against the historicity of Luke's claim, he cites: (1)

citizen [Acts 22.28], how did his father gain the honor?" and "How could he prove his citizenship? Did he carry a *libellus* recording the honor?"[95] There simply are no data for answering these questions; and in this inquiry, we focus on the social status Luke claims for Paul, not the historical verifiability of his claims. More importantly for us are questions touching the "rights and duties" of citizens and the social position implied by citizenship.

Although Sherwin-White regularly speaks of the duties and privileges (*munera et honores*) of citizenship,[96] these are not clearly spelled out in his study. In terms of rights and privileges, Paul only claims Roman citizenship in forensic contexts: when beaten by the magistrates in Philippi (16.37), when threatened with scourging by the Roman tribune (22.25–27), and when demanding a trial before Caesar (25.10–11, 21; 26.32). Thus we infer that one of the rights Paul claimed was that of "a fair public trial for a citizen accused of any crime, exemption from certain ignominious forms of punishment, and protection from summary execution."[97] Acts says nothing more about the rights of a citizen, but from other studies we may infer that some citizens were exempt from certain taxes.[98]

What, then, of the duties? This involves some knowledge of what citizenship meant and how it was acquired. Since, in all probability, Paul's father or ancestor purchased this rare status,[99] we are allowed to imagine a person of considerable

Paul's low social class and Jewish background (2) Paul's silence on this point in his letters, and (3) the apologetic nature of Lucan composition in the parts of Acts where citizenship is affirmed.

[95] See Sherwin-White, *Roman Society and Roman Law in the New Testament*, p. 147.

[96] Ibid., pp. 144–147; at various places in his study, Claude Nicolet (*The World of the Citizen in Republican Rome* [Berkeley, 1980]) discusses the rights and duties of citizens. Their duties were their duties as soldiers and as munificent benefactors and their rights were basically civic and juridical safeguards and exemption from taxation. See Cicero, *De Off.* 1.17.53.

[97] Bruce, *Paul: Apostle of the Heart Set Free*, p. 39. See Stegemann, "War der Apostel Paulus ein römischer Bürger?," pp. 222–224.

[98] Sherwin-White, *Roman Society and Roman Law in the New Testament*, p. 147.

[99] Ibid., pp. 154–155. The Roman tribune who arrested Paul in Acts 22.28 remarks that he paid a considerable sum (πολλοῦ κεφαλαίου) for his citizenship; see J. H. Moulton and G. Milligan, *The Vocabulary of the Greek Testament* (Grand Rapids, 1974), p. 342. In a later study, Sherwin-White ("The Roman Citizenship: A Survey of its Development into a World Franchise," *ANRW* I.2:23–58) indicates how Rome

influence and wealth able to pay the right bribe to the right official. Such a well-placed person would have had civic obligations to act as patron and benefactor to his city, support its public buildings, and provide for certain of its feasts. None of this is even hinted at in Acts, but Luke surely appreciates the snobbery index that Roman citizenship brings.

The recent study by John Lentz examines the social significance of Paul's "appeal to Caesar" in Acts 25.11, 21 and 26.32. In keeping with the thrust of his study, Lentz argues that on the rhetorical level, whatever the historical situation might have been, such an appeal is best understood as Luke's claim for Paul's high social status.[100] He builds his argument on the following observations: (a) only a very small fraction of cases ever came before the Emperor (p. 144); (b) the various laws concerning trials favored those of high social status (p. 144); (c) Paul's appeal to Caesar is not a legal protest against the abusive authority of a local magistrate, which is the normal rationale for a change of jurisdiction (p. 146); and (d) numerous historical examples of change of jurisdiction all involve persons of high rank and status (pp. 148–149). Thus Lentz concludes that an appeal to Caesar or to higher legal authority was common for persons of "high social status and reputation, or personal ties to the emperor."[101]

7.0 CONCLUSIONS AND FURTHER CONVERSATION

I have used several models from the social sciences to give as much precision as possible to the Lucan presentation of Paul's status and social location. Both Lenski's model of the stratification of ancient agrarian societies and the perspective of honor articulated in cultural anthropology have served to give reliability to the intuitive perception that Luke perceives and presents Paul as a person of considerable honor and social status.

This brief chapter is but a voice in a chorus, a part of a

---

bestowed citizenship on provinces both west and east as a mode of building and confirming its imperial conquests.

[100] J. C. Lentz, *Luke's Portrait of Paul*, pp. 139–153.   [101] Ibid., p. 151.

conversation. It supplements Lentz's recent monograph on the status attributed to Paul by his presentation in terms of the classical virtues of antiquity.[102] If it adds anything to the conversation about Acts, two important questions then surface. First, how historically accurate is Luke's portrait of Paul? In addition to study of the differences between the chronology of Paul's letters and that of Acts and between the theology of his letters and that of his speeches in Acts, we should further investigate the social level of Paul as claimed or implied in his letters and that articulated by the author of Acts.

Second, whatever the historical reality, further inquiry should be made concerning the rhetorical strategy in the presentation of Paul, both in his own letters and in Luke's portrait of him. It is part of Paul's own rhetorical strategy to present himself as weak in public speaking and lacking in rhetoric (1 Cor. 1.17; 2.1–5), whereas we have seen that it is characteristic of the Lucan rhetorical argument to present Paul as forensically adept. In his own letters, Paul calls attention to his lack of honor (1 Cor. 4.8–13; 2 Cor. 4.7–12; 11.21–33).[103] In contrast, Luke calls attention at every turn to Paul's honorable status in terms of the cities where he lives, his associates and "friends," his citizenship, and the like. Much remains to be done, therefore, in terms of the rhetorical strategy of each author. Nevertheless, this chapter has advanced the conversation on the portrait of Paul in Acts by its careful use of reliable models for the recovery and articulation of Paul's social status and location.

---

[102] See ibid., pp. 14 and 62–104.

[103] See John T. Fitzgerald, *Cracks in the Earthen Vessel: An Examination of the Catalogues of Hardships in the Corinthian Correspondence*, SBLDS 99 (Atlanta, 1988).

PART III

Issues of literary criticism

Internal repetition in Luke–Acts: contemporary narratology and Lucan historiography

Joel B. Green

I INTRODUCTION

In her 1984 essay, "Jesus–Paul, Peter–Paul, and Jesus–Peter Parallelisms in Luke–Acts: A History of Reader Response," Susan Marie Praeder surveyed the cataloging and analysis of parallelisms in Luke–Acts from the nineteenth century to 1983.[1] In particular, she noted how different approaches to Lucan studies – tendency criticism (Schneckenburger, Bauer, Schwegler, Zeller), radical criticism (Bauer), literary criticism (Morgenthaler), typological criticism (Goulder), and redaction criticism (Talbert, Mattill, O'Toole, Radl, Muhlack) – have produced lists of alleged parallelisms that continue to share a significant degree of overlap, even if these data have then been subjected to disparate interpretations. Noting that parallelisms have been understood, for example, "as proof of literary sequences and structures, lack of historicity, and certain theological concerns," she maintains nonetheless that, "although interpretations of the parallelisms have tended to be relatively short-lived, the proposed parallelisms lend some con-

---

[1] Susan Marie Praeder, "Jesus–Paul, Peter–Paul, and Jesus–Peter Parallelisms in Luke–Acts: A History of Reader Response," in *Society of Biblical Literature 1984 Seminar Papers*, ed. Kent Harold Richards (Chico, 1984), pp. 23–39. Monograph-length studies of the parallelisms in Luke–Acts include Walter Radl, *Paulus und Jesus im lukanischen Doppelwerk: Untersuchungen zu Parallelmotiven im Lukasevangelium und in der Apostlegeschichte*, EH 23: Theologie 49 (Frankfurt-on-Main, 1975); Gudrun Muhlack, *Die Parallelen im Lukasevangelium und in der Apostelgeschichte*, TW 8 (Frankfurt-on-Main, 1979). The important work of G. W. Trompf, which locates Luke's narration of "the reenactment of significant events" in the context of Hellenistic historiography, escaped Praeder's scrutiny (*The Idea of Historical Recurrence in Western Thought: From Antiquity to the Reformation* [Berkeley, 1979] esp. pp. 116–178).

tinuity to the history of interpretation."[2] At the same time, she cautions against what we might call parallelomania – i.e. the undisciplined ransacking of Luke–Acts for recurring patterns of narration – and urges readers (1) to be more forthcoming regarding their criteria for locating parallelisms and (2) not to confuse their findings with authorial intent. In their words of caution, some redaction critics have gone much further, querying whether such "correspondences" or "parallel structures" have much relevance at all for attempts at discerning the theology of the Evangelist.[3] After all, in whose mind do these phenomena occur – Luke's or the modern reader's?

Against the backdrop of such concerns, we will argue that, from the standpoint of our reading of the narrative of Luke–Acts, authorial intentions are less material than are the manifold interpretive responses supported by the narrative itself. What is more, we will attempt to add to Praeder's list of possible approaches to the parallelisms of Luke–Acts a narratological reading that takes seriously the historiographical motivation of Luke–Acts.[4]

2 INITIAL QUESTIONS

Our interpretive agenda builds on a number of critical assumptions about Luke–Acts. Some of these need to be stated and developed.

2.1 The unity of Luke–Acts

As the recent, collaborative effort of M. C. Parsons and R. I. Pervo has suggested, the existence of parallels does not itself prove compositional unity.[5] If one understands the Acts of the

---

[2] Praeder, "Parallelisms," p. 38.
[3] See, e.g., R. Maddox, *The Purpose of Luke–Acts*, SNTW (Edinburgh, 1982), pp. 79–80; Joseph A. Fitzmyer, *The Gospel according to Luke* (2 vols., AB28–28a, Garden City, 1981/1985), vol. I, pp. 96–97.
[4] Hence, unless the connection to authorial intentionality is specifically made, by "Luke" we refer to the narrator of Luke–Acts.
[5] M. C. Parsons and R. I. Pervo, *Rethinking the Unity of Luke and Acts* (Minneapolis, 1993), pp. 57–59.

Apostles as a sequel to the Gospel of Luke, rather than viewing the two as a single, continuous work, one can account easily enough for the parallelisms observed by Luke's readers. Hence, although we argue elsewhere for the compositional unity of Luke's two volumes,[6] this is not a necessary assumption in this context. Instead, we will hope to show that the Lucan parallelisms are narratologically motivated, so as to tie the Acts of the Apostles into the story line of the Gospel of Luke.

2.2 The genre of Luke–Acts

We have already identified Luke's work within the genre of ancient historiography, reflecting the broad consensus that has developed in this century following the work of H. J. Cadbury.[7] Those who support alternative classifications – especially Greco-Roman biography,[8] the novel,[9] and the "scientific tradition" of technical writing[10] – maximize the formal discrepancies between Luke's preface and those of Hellenistic historiography or argue that Acts is not reliable as historiography. As for the latter argument, two points are worth reflection. First, an attempt to present material in the generic framework of historiography is not the same thing as a guarantee of historical veracity; choice of genre and quality of performance are separate issues. Second, Acts has too often been and unfortunately continues in some quarters to be evaluated as historiography on the basis of modernist, positivistic canons – i.e. on the basis of criteria that have themselves

---

[6] See J. B. Green, *The Gospel of Luke*, NICNT (Grand Rapids, forthcoming).

[7] Especially Henry J. Cadbury, "Commentary on the Preface of Luke," in *The Beginnings of Christianity, Part One: The Acts of the Apostles*, ed. F. J. Foakes Jackson and Kirsopp Lake, vol. II: *Prolegomena-II: Criticism* (Grand Rapids, MI: Baker, n.d.), pp. 489–510, "The Knowledge Claimed in Luke's Preface," *Expositor* 8, 24 (1922), 401–420 and "'We' and 'I' Passages in Luke–Acts," *NTS* 3 (1956–1957), 128–32.

[8] See, e.g., Charles H. Talbert, *Literary Patterns, Theological Themes and the Genre of Luke–Acts*, SBLMS 20 (Missoula, 1974).

[9] See esp. R. I. Pervo, *Profit with Delight: The Literary Genre of the Acts of the Apostles* (Philadelphia, 1987).

[10] Loveday C. A. Alexander, *The Preface to Luke's Gospel: Literary Convention and Social Context in Luke 1.1–4 and Acts 1.1*, SNTSMS 78 (Cambridge, 1993); Loveday C. A. Alexander, "Luke's Preface in the Context of Greek Preface-Writing," *NovT* 28 (1986), 48–74.

become problematic[11] and are in any case anachronistic with reference to Luke as historiographer.

As for the former, Luke's prefaces share many properties with their counterparts in Josephus' *Against Apion* (1.1.1–5; 2.1.1–2), as has often been noted. Moreover, Luke's two volumes evince a number of other attributes common in Greco-Roman historiography – for example a genealogical record (Lk. 3.23–28); the use of meal scenes as occasions for instruction (as in Greco-Roman symposia); travel narratives; speeches; letters; and dramatic episodes, such as Jesus' rejection at Nazareth (4.16–30) and Paul's stormy voyage and shipwreck (Acts 27.1–28.14).[12] Further, in characterizing his work as a narrative (διήγησις), Luke qualifies his project as a long narrative of many events, for which the chief prototypes were the historiographical writings of Herodotus and Thucydides.[13]

That Luke–Acts does not match in every detail the formal features of Hellenistic historiography presents no immediate problem, for Luke has been influenced as well by Israelite and Jewish historiography, especially with respect to the use of historical sequences to shape a narrative theology. On the other hand, what is evident is that the Third Evangelist has been influenced by an array of Greco-Roman literary forms – especially those related to the biographical genre – even if other formal features and above all the theocentric focus of his narrative preclude identification of Luke–Acts as "biography."[14]

---

[11] Cf. now, e.g., M. Krieger (ed.), *The Aims of Representation: Subject/Text/History* (Palo Alto, 1993); Hayden White, *The Content of the Form: Narrative Discourse and Historical Representation* (Baltimore, 1987); and B. Stock, *Listening for the Text: On the Uses of the Past* (Baltimore, 1990).

[12] D. E. Aune, *The New Testament in its Literary Environment*, LEC (Philadelphia, 1987), pp. 120–131.

[13] Cf. Hermogenes, *Progymnasta* 2; Lucian, *How to Write History* 55: "For all the body of the history is simply a long narrative" (διήγησις μακρά).

[14] The theocentric focus of the Lucan narrative (on which see below) raises serious questions against the recent analysis of Richard A. Burridge, which wrongly identifies Jesus as the primary actor of the Third Gospel and so classifies the Gospel as a biography (*What are the Gospels? A Comparison with Graeco-Roman Biography*, SNTSMS 70 [Cambridge, 1992]). In fact, Jesus, who acts as directed by God and empowered by the Holy Spirit, serves God's aim; Luke's two volumes are funda-

In any case, our primary aim in this regard is not to settle the question of the genre of Luke–Acts or of Acts, but to show that the repetition of significant events in narrative representation is understandable and well within the bounds of what one would expect of someone engaged in a historiographical enterprise.

2.3 The purpose of Luke–Acts and the purpose of God

Luke's agenda as set forward in Luke 1.4 foregrounds the desired effect on his narratee, Theophilus: "that you may know the truth concerning the things about which you heard." Ἀσφάλεια appears in the emphatic position of this opening period, and it has been easy to find here an emphasis on Luke's affirmation of the historical veracity of his narrative,[15] or even to argue that Luke thus sees himself as providing a historical foundation for the Christian message.[16] In fact, Luke's narrative combines events and kerygmatic interpretation as proclamation, and his terminology here suggests "the convincing nature of his presentation"[17] or "the certainty of these things."[18] So, while the Christian message is inseparably tied to the historical events related to its origins and progression, and Luke must therefore necessarily be concerned with "what happened,"[19] it is the question of interpretation that is vital for

mentally driven by the purpose of God. Burridge also presumes discontinuity at the generic level between the Third Gospel and the Acts of the Apostles.

For the recent identification of Luke–Acts within the genre of historiography, see also Aune, *Literary Environment*, pp. 77–157; D. L. Balch, "The Genre of Luke–Acts: Individual Biography, Adventure Novel, or Political History?," *SWJT* 33 (1990), 5–19; G. L. Sterling, *History and Self-Definition: Josephos, Luke–Acts and Apologetic Historiography*, NovTSup 64 (Leiden, 1992).

[15] Cf., e.g., W. C. van Unnik, "Remarks on the Purpose of Luke's Historical Writing," in *Sparsa Collecta: The Collected Writings of W. C. van Unnik*, vol. 1, NovTSup 29 (Leiden, 1973), pp. 6–15; A. Plummer, *The Gospel according to S. Luke*, ICC (Edinburgh, 1901), p. 5.

[16] See, e.g., Hans Conzelmann, *The Theology of St. Luke* (London, 1960; reprinted London, 1982), p. 11.

[17] Cf. Xenophon, *Memorabilia* 4.6.15; Colin Brown, "ἀσφάλεια," *NIDNTT* 1:663.

[18] Cf. Acts 2.36; 25.26.

[19] See the use of ἀσφαλής in Acts 21.34; 22.30 to signify "the facts" in a case. Cf. R. Trigg, "'Tales Artfully Spun'," in *The Bible as Rhetoric: Studies in Biblical Persuasion and Credibility*, ed. Martin Warner, WSPL (London, 1990), pp. 117–132.

him. For our understanding of Luke, the chief question is not,
"How can the past be accurately captured?" or "What
methods will allow the recovery of what actually happened?,"
for, as is increasingly acknowledged, historiography is always
teleological. It imposes significance on the past already by its
choice of events to record and to order as well as by its inherent
efforts to postulate for those events an end and/or origin. The
emphasis thus shifts from *validation* to *signification*,[20] so the issue
is, "How is the past being represented?" Luke's concern with
truth, then, resides above all in his interpretation of the past
and the desired effect of his narration is that others will find
this narration "convincing."

In other words, Luke's purpose is hermeneutical. He is not
hoping to prove that something happened, but rather to communicate what these events signify. The dominant interpretive
framework is established already in Lk. 1.1, in the phrase with
which Luke modifies "events": "that have been fulfilled
among us." In this way, the narrator indicates a key assumption, that the events about to be narrated are incomplete in
themselves; they must be understood in relation to a wider
interpretive framework. What is this framework for Luke? On
the one hand, the Septuagintal "feel" of Lk. 1.5–2.52, together
with the many echoes of the LXX in the Lucan birth narrative,[21] suggest immediately that this wider framework is the
Scriptures of Israel. On the other, as an exploration of the
Lucan writings makes clear, the Scriptures themselves are
subject at the interpretive level and give expression to something prior – namely God's purpose. Luke is concerned above
all to demonstrate that the events he has narrated continue as
its fulfillment the story of the realization of God's redemptive
aim.

---

[20] Similarly, R. H. Stein, *Luke*, NAC 24 (Nashville, 1992), p. 66. See H. White, "The
Value of Narrativity in the Representation of Reality," *CI* 7 (1980–1981), 5–27;
H. White, "The Narratization of Real Events," *CI* 7 (1980–1981), 793–798;
H. White, "The Question of Narrative in Contemporary Historical Theory,"
HT 23 (1984), 1–33; M. A. Fitzsimmons et al. (eds.), *The Development of Historiogra-
phy* (Harrisburg, 1954).
[21] See J. B. Green, "The Problem of a Beginning: Israel's Scriptures in Luke 1–2,"
BBR 4 (1994), 61–86.

Luke's interest in the controlling theme of God's purpose has been increasingly recognized.[22] For the pervasiveness of this theme in Acts (which embraces above all the motifs of the centrality of Jesus' death and exaltation, together with the extension of salvation in all its fullness to all people), one may point especially to the activity of the Holy Spirit, who guides and empowers the early missionary community;[23] to the employment of the Scriptures, both to communicate the continuity between God's activity vis-à-vis Israel and the coming of Jesus and to inscribe the life and ministry of the community of believers in God's project;[24] to the vocabulary of divine necessity (for example βουλή, βούλομαι, δεῖ, θέλημα, θέλω, ὁρίζω, πληρόω, and προφήτης); and, as the often-documented correspondence between Jesus in Luke and community leadership in Acts indicates, to the emphatic continuity Luke understands to exist between Jesus, who embodied God's purpose, and the early church of Acts.

3 HISTORICAL REENACTMENT IN LUKE–ACTS

An often-neglected entry-point into the discussion of parallelism within Luke–Acts is the parallel phenomenon that exists between Luke–Acts and the LXX. That is, internal repetition in Luke–Acts should be understood alongside its counterpart,

---

[22] See C. H. Cosgrove, "The Divine ΔΕΙ in Luke–Acts: Investigations into the Lucan Understanding of God's Providence," *NovT* 26 (1984), 168–190; G. P. V. du Plooy, "The Narrative Act in Luke–Acts from the Perspective of God's Design," Th.D. diss., University of Stellenbosch, 1986; J. T. Squires, *The Plan of God in Luke–Acts*, SNTSMS 76 (Cambridge, 1993); J. B. Green, *The Theology of the Gospel of Luke*, NTT (Cambridge, 1995), chap. 2.

[23] Some thirty years ago, G. W. H. Lampe argued that, in Luke's understanding, the activity of the Spirit united Luke–Acts with the Scriptures and the ministry of Jesus with that of his followers ("The Holy Spirit in the Writings of St. Luke," in *Studies in the Gospels: Essays in Memory of R. H. Lightfoot*, ed. Dennis E. Nineham [Oxford, 1955], pp. 159–200). Cf. V. C. Pfitzner, "'Pneumatic' Apostleship? Apostle and Spirit in the Acts of the Apostles," in *Wort in der Zeit: Neutestamentliche Studien: Festgabe für Karl Heinrich Rengstorf zum 75. Geburtstag*, ed. W. Haubeck and M. Bachmann (Leiden, 1980), pp. 210–235.

[24] Cf. J. A. Sanders, "Isaiah in Luke," *Int* 36 (1982), 144–155; B. J. Koet, *Five Studies on Interpretation of Scripture in Luke–Acts*, SNTA 14 (Louvain, 1989); R. G. Hall, *Revealed Histories: Techniques for Ancient Jewish and Christian Historiography*, JSPSS 6 (Sheffield, 1991), chap. 12.

external repetition, with both subsumed under the larger hermeneutical category of intertextuality.[25] An emphasis of this nature proceeds from the perspective that, in his composition of Luke–Acts, the Third Evangelist has created a text which is itself an interplay of other texts, "a system of references," "a node within a network"[26] – with some reverberations premeditated, others perhaps less so. Luke's account consequently participates in a discourse situation in which reverberations of other material, both internal and external to his narrative, encourage interpretive possibilities.

Of course, attention to intertextuality does not require that we postulate for Luke laborious, point-for-point retelling of an earlier story. Instead, we may grow to appreciate how he meditated on that earlier material and shaped it to his own ends, all the while building on the story of the covenanting God who intervenes on behalf of humanity to accomplish his gracious aim. Vis-à-vis the intertextual reverberations of the Lucan narrative with the LXX (i.e. external repetition), Luke inscribes himself in scriptural tradition, showing his debt to this previous story, and inviting his auditors to hear in this story the resounding continuation of that story. Vis-à-vis intertextual reverberations within Luke–Acts (i.e. internal repetition), Luke shows the great extent to which the story of the early church is inscribed into the story of Jesus, all as the continuation of the divine story of redemption.

3.1 The LXX as pre-text

We may illustrate briefly the phenomenon of external repetition by drawing attention to three examples of Luke's

---

[25] On the importance of repetition in narrative study, see esp. G. Genette, *Narrative Discourse: An Essay in Method* (Ithaca, 1980), chap. 3; and the helpful summary comments in M. Bal, *Narratology: Introduction to the Theory of Narrative* (Toronto, 1985), pp. 77–79. On intertextuality, see J. Still and M. Worton, "Introduction," in *Intertextuality: Theories and Practices*, ed. M. Worton and J. Still (Manchester, 1990), pp. 1–44; W. Vorster, "Intertextuality and Redaktionsgeschichte," in *Intertexuality in Biblical Writing: Essays in Honour of Bas van Iersel*, ed. S. Draisma (Kampen, 1989), pp. 15–26; J. Culler, *The Pursuit of Signs: Semiotics, Literature, Deconstruction* (London, 1981), chap. 5; L. Hutcheon, *A Poetics of Postmodernism: History, Theory, Fiction* (London, 1988), pp. 80, 120–140.

[26] M. Foucault, *The Archaeology of Knowledge*, WM (London, 1972), p. 23.

use of the LXX as pre-text. First, as we have demonstrated elsewhere, Luke 1–2 draws extensively on Genesis 11–21 as pre-text or subtext.[27] His interest in the Abraham story is immediately signaled by his reference to "our ancestor" "Abraham" and concern with the "covenant" in Lk. 1.55,73. One may also point to the correspondence between Gen. 16.7–13; 17.1–21; 18.1–15 and Lk. 1.11–20, 26–37; 2.9–12, all scenes of annunciation whose parallels exceed in detail even those expected within the birth announcement-type scene. Moreover, outside these more explicit points of contact, over twenty other parallels encourage our reading of the Lucan birth narrative as a case of historical reenactment. For example:

Lk. 1.6: ἦσαν δὲ δίκαιοι ἀμφότεροι ἐναντίον τοῦ θεοῦ, πορευόμενοι ἐν πάσαις ταῖς ἐντολαῖς καὶ δικαιώμασιν τοῦ κυρίου ἄμεμπτοι.

Gen. 17.1: καὶ ὤφθη κύριος . . . καὶ εἶπεν . . . ἐγώ εἰμι ὁ Θεός σου, εὐαρέστει[28] ἐναντίον ἐμοῦ καὶ γίνου ἄμεμπτος . . .

Lk. 1.7: καὶ ἀμφότεροι προβεβηκότες ἐν ταῖς ἡμέραις αὐτῶν ἦσαν.

Lk. 1.18: ἐγὼ γάρ εἰμι πρεσβύτης καὶ ἡ γυνή μου προβεβηκυῖα ἐν ταῖς ἡμέραις αὐτῆς.

Gen. 18.11–12: Ἀβρααμ δὲ καὶ Σαρρα πρεσβύτεροι προβεβηκότες ἡμερῶν . . . ὁ δὲ κύριός μου πρεσβύτερος.[29]

Luke 1.37: ὅτι οὐκ ἀδυνατήσει παρὰ τοῦ Θεοῦ πᾶν ῥῆμα.

Gen. 18.44: μὴ ἀδυνατεῖ [MT: פלא] παρὰ τῷ Θεῷ ῥῆμα.

Luke's hermeneutical procedure here is not typological; he can move back and forth between characters, so as to suggest how, for example, Abraham is like Zechariah, but so is Mary like Abraham. Nor does the Evangelist make use of "fulfillment" language to characterize his understanding of the

---

[27] Green, "Problem of a Beginning"; cf. N. A. Dahl, "The Story of Abraham in Luke–Acts," in *Jesus in the Memory of the Early Church* (Minneapolis, 1976), pp. 66–86.

[28] That is, "walk pleasingly" – cf. W. Foester, "εὐάρεστος, εὐαρεστέω," *TDNT* 1:456–457; as elsewhere in the LXX, the hithpael of הלך has been transformed from an action into a quality.

[29] Note that both narrators provide a report of their characters' advanced age, followed by a character who advances this theme in response to the divine promise of a son.

relationship between these parallel events. Rather, Luke has provided us with evidence of his own reflection on Abraham material, and reflection on the accounts of the births of John and Jesus in light of the Genesis narrative. This external repetition manifests Luke's desire to fix his narrative within the history of the interaction of God and Abraham, locating the present story in the ancient story of God's covenant relationship with Abraham.

A second example may be summarized. As Gerhard Lohfink has established, Luke's account of the ascension in Acts 1.9–11 is fully at home among the Greco-Roman and Jewish traditions of assumption and heavenly journeys.[30] But the importance of this observation should not blind us to the particularly impressive correspondences between this scene and the Elijah–Elisha narrative. Like Luke–Acts, the Elijah–Elisha narrative is carefully balanced, with the ascension at its mid-point. Moreover, there are literary allusions in Acts 1.9–11 back to 2 Kgs. 2.9–15, the juxtaposition of which suggests an analogous relationship between Elisha's receiving Elijah's "spirit" and mission, and Jesus' promise to his followers of the outpouring of the Spirit and charge to carry on his mission. In fact, Acts 1.1–11 builds on an Elijah-typology already present in Lk. 9.51–56 (cf. ἀναλαμβάνω in 2 Kgs. 2.9, 11, where "being taken up" includes no hint of "death").[31] Though one may discern typological elements here, again the complexity of Luke's Elijah-portrayal[32] resists simple categorization.

---

30 G. Lohfink, *Die Himmelfahrt Jesu: Untersuchungen zu den Himmelfahrts- und Erhöhungstexten bei Lukas*, SANT 26 (Münich, 1971); cf. P. Palatty, "The Ascension of Christ in Luke–Acts," *BibBh* 12 (1986), 107–117, 166–181; M. Dean-Otting, *Heavenly Journeys: A Study of the Motif in Hellenistic Jewish Literature*, JU 8 (Frankfurt-on-Main, 1984); M. Himmelfarb, *Ascent to Heaven in Jewish and Christian Apocalypses* (Oxford, 1993).

31 See T. L. Brodie, "Luke–Acts as an Imitation and Emulation of the Elijah–Elisha Narrative," in *New Views on Luke and Acts*, ed. E. Richard (Collegeville, 1990), pp. 78–85, 172–174; J. G. Davies, "The Prefigurement of the Ascension in the Third Gospel," *JTS* 6 (1955), 229–233; J. G. Davies, *He Ascended into Heaven: A Study in the History of Doctrine* (London, 1958), p. 186.

32 See J. A. Fitzmyer, "The Lucan Picture of John the Baptist as Precursor of the Lord," in *Luke the Theologian: Aspects of His Teaching* (New York, 1989), pp. 86–116 (96–99); D. L. Bock, "Elijah and Elisha," in *Dictionary of Jesus and the Gospels*, ed. J. B. Green and S. McKnight (Downers Grove, 1992), pp. 203–206 (204–205).

Finally, brief mention may be made of the parallels resident in Acts 10 between the story of Jonah and the Cornelius narrative.[33] We note the following: (1) continuity of location, Joppa (Jonah 1.3; Acts 9.43), to which God directs his messengers; (2) God's intervention to overcome the messengers' reluctance, together with the symbolically important use of the number 3 (Jonah 1.17; Acts 10.16); (3) the divine commission to "arise . . . and go" (Jonah 3.2; Acts 10.20) in order to deliver the message to the Gentiles; (4) a report of the Gentiles' faith (Jonah 3.5; Acts 10.43) and being forgiven; (5) a subsequent, hostile response (Jonah 4.1; Acts 10.14; 11.2); and (6) God's rejoinder to human animosity (Jonah 4.2–11; Acts 11.17–18; cf. 15.13–21). According to R. Wall, this instance of intertextuality inscribes the Cornelius narrative into scriptural tradition in order to highlight the message that Jonah's God (who extends grace even to the Gentiles) is Peter's God:

> Against this scripture-scape, the 'theo-logic' of the Gentile mission is painted by Luke: the Cornelius conversion is legitimized as the continuation of God's merciful work at Nineveh, Simon-Peter is the bar Jonah who is called by his ancestor's God to convert the Gentiles, and the people of God should do nothing but praise God and say, 'God has granted the Gentiles repentance unto life'. (Acts 11.18)[34]

3.2 Intertextuality within Luke–Acts

The Cornelius narrative contains reverberations of the Jonah story, but is also caught up in an intertextual web with other material in Luke–Acts. On the one hand, we may note the fact that Luke has narrated a series of episodes characterized by "complementary visions" – for example Zechariah/Mary (Lk. 1.8–56), Saul/Ananias (Acts 9.1–19), and Cornelius/Peter (Acts 10).[35] These are "complementary" since, in each case, visionary experiences are juxtaposed, with the successful

---

[33] See R. W. Wall, "Peter, 'Son' of Jonah: The Conversion of Cornelius in the Context of Canon," in R. W. Wall and E. E. Lemcio, *The New Testament as Canon: A Reader in Canonical Criticism*, JSNTSS 76 (Sheffield, 1992), pp. 129–140; C. S. C. Williams, *A Commentary on the Acts of the Apostles*, BNTC (London, 1957), pp. 152–153.

[34] Wall, "Peter, 'Son' of Jonah," p. 140.

[35] See Green, "Problem of a Beginning," pp. 80–81.

completion of the one act of God through a human agent related to the faithful response of the other. The points of contact between the stories of Zechariah and Cornelius are remarkable:

Lk. 1:5–13, 29, 39, 41	Acts 10.1–4, 17, 23
. . . there was a priest named Zechariah, who belonged to the priestly order of Abijah . . .	. . . there was a man named Cornelius, a centurion of the Italian cohort.
Both [he and his wife] were righteous before God, living blamelessly according to all the commandments and regulations of the Lord . . .	He was a devout man who feared God with all his household; he gave alms generously to the people and prayed constantly to God . . .
Once when he was serving as a priest . . . there appeared to him an angel of the Lord . . . when Zechariah saw him, he was terrified; and fear overwhelmed him.	One afternoon . . . he had a vision in which he clearly saw an angel coming in He stared at him in terror
But the angel said to him, "Do not be afraid, Zechariah, for your prayer has been heard . . ."	The angel answered, "Your prayers and your alms have ascended as a memorial before God . . ."

The circumstances and characters have changed, of course, but this does not mask the close correspondence of these two episodes at the narrative level. Recurrence in this case highlights the continuing intervention of the God who is graciously working out his salvific will. Luke underscores his understanding that historical events have proceeded under divine guidance and themselves served an underlying aim – namely God's salvific purpose. But this "working out" of the divine will is not a *fait accompli* in the narrow sense; God reveals his objective, according to Luke, but the Evangelist also shows in this pattern that the divine project of necessity involves the collusion of human agents, helpers of the divine aim.

This is one example among many[36] of Luke's organizing his

---

[36] See Trompf, *Historical Recurrence*, chap. 3; and the catalog in Praeder, "Parallelisms," pp. 24–29, 34–37.

material so that the contours and event-complexes of historical reenactment serve his larger purpose of speaking of the communication and realization of God's purpose behind and within human history. Luke has accomplished this end at the intertextual level in a multi-faceted way – by inscribing the story of Jesus and the early church into the story of Israel, by inscribing the story of the early church into the story of Jesus, and by repeatedly emphasizing the purpose of God which gives meaning to and, indeed, makes possible this continuing story of redemption.

3.3 Rhetorical overcoding and parody

In his evaluation of *The Role of the Reader*, Umberto Eco makes two observations of immediate consequence to the array of data under investigation here.[37] First, he observes that in the reading process, readers cultivate readerly competence allowing them to recognize the use of what have become stock expressions or conventional patterns whose meaning overflows denotative interpretation. Such expressions and patterns he describes as "overcoded" – i.e. they are meaningful as a consequence of their wider associations. The expression "once upon a time" is overcoded with nuances that suggest a fictional story taking place in an indefinite and non-historical era, for example. Similarly, Lk. 1.1–4 and Acts 1.1–2 are overcoded by their association with the primary and recapitulatory preface forms known to us from Hellenistic historiography.[38]

As a particular case of overcoding, Eco also mentions "inferences by intertextual frames," noting that "no text is read independently of the reader's experience of other texts."[39] On the basis of what we have seen thus far, we may posit that the sort of knowledge Luke assumes of his audience[40] includes some intimacy with the LXX, so that they will hear in his own

---

[37] U. Eco, *The Role of the Reader: Explorations in the Semiotics of Texts*, AS (Bloomington, 1979), pp. 19–22.

[38] See D. W. Palmer, "The Literary Background of Acts 1.1–14," *NTS* 33 (1987), 427–438 (427–428).

[39] Eco, *Role of the Reader*, p. 21.   [40] I.e. "model reader" or "implied reader."

writing echoes of Septuagintal texts and narrative schemes. At the same time, we may observe that Luke himself cultivates in his audience an ever-expanding knowledge base, so that interpretive linkages are generated within his two-volume work.

For example, we may note the complex of echoes in the following material related to the Holy Spirit:

Isa. 32.15: ἐπέλθῃ ἐφ᾽ ὑμᾶς πνεῦμα ἀφ᾽ ὑψηλοῦ

Lk. 1.35: πνεῦμα ἅγιον ἐπελεύσεται ἐπὶ σὲ καὶ δύναμις ὑψίστου ἐπισκιάσει σοι·διὸ καὶ τὸ γεννώμενον

Lk. 4.14: ὑπέστρεψεν ὁ Ἰησοῦς ἐν τῇ δυνάμει τοῦ πνεύματος εἰς τὴν Γαλιλαίαν

Lk. 24.49: ἕως οὗ ενδύσησθε ἐξ ὕψους δύναμιν

Acts 1.8: ἀλλὰ λήμψεσθε δύναμιν ἐπελθόντος τοῦ ἁγίου πνεύματος ἐφ᾽ ὑμᾶς καὶ ἔσεσθέ μου μάρτυρες ἔν . . .

Note in particular the repetition of "come upon," "Holy Spirit," "power," and the formula: activity of the Spirit followed by its consequences. The Isaianic text is set within a co-text dealing with the arrival of the age of peace. This is well-suited to the present intertextual reverberation between Luke's two volumes, and presages the eschatological import of Jesus' birth and mission, together with the continuation of that mission among Jesus' followers. The birth of Jesus and the birth of the church are thus brought into the closest relationship, for both serve the same divine purpose and proceed under the empowerment of the same Spirit. Elsewhere, too, Luke holds in tandem "Spirit" and "power" (cf. already Lk. 1.15–17), and, especially in Acts 1.8, shows that these are the muscle and drive behind the activity of "witnesses."

Reference to Eco underscores our understanding that the identification of "parallelisms" in Luke–Acts is not simply an issue of what Luke-as-author intended. The question of intentionality cannot be prejudged or, for that matter, engaged by way of certifying the presence or absence of specific cases of alleged parallelism. The issue, rather, is whether the narrative of Luke–Acts, understood within its own world of presuppositions, supports the identification of parallelisms.

It must be admitted, however, that points of similarity do not tell the whole story, for repeatedly the resonances to which we have drawn attention also aim in a different direction. These historical recurrences and narrative patterns can also be described as parodic – that is, they parody the history they also reenact. By "parody" we mean "repetition with critical distance that allows ironic signalling of difference at the very heart of similarity."[41] For example, with reference to the Abrahamic material noted above, the need for eschatological consummation of God's covenant with Abraham is unanticipated in Genesis, but history – at least as Luke understands it – had shown that Abraham had not (yet) been made the progenitor of many nations. The achievement of this divine promise would require activity that both recalled that covenant-making and also gathered up its possibilities in divine consummation. In the case of Zechariah and Cornelius, also noted above, it is surely of consequence that both are represented by Luke as persons of impeccable piety, but Cornelius is a Gentile while Zechariah is an Israelite priest! Luke's presentation of God's aim to embrace all peoples in his salvific project is thus emphasized by this "ironic signalling of difference at the very heart of similarity."[42] In this way, Luke shapes the story, transforming it and shedding fresh interpretive light on it.

4 NARRATOLOGY AND HISTORIOGRAPHY

The forms of intertextuality to which we have drawn attention are capable of analysis along a number of lines. By way of drawing together our understanding of the Third Evangelist as one who has employed narrativity in the representation of reality we may finally direct our attention to the characterization of writing history as shaping the past.

At the outset we should observe that Luke is well within the tradition of Hellenistic (and, we may add, Hebraic) historiography in his representation of patterns of recurrence. As

---

[41] Hutcheon, *Poetics*, p. 26.

[42] Note that this has been prepared for already by characterization in Luke: cf. the pronounced differences between the presentation of Zechariah (1.5–11) and Mary (1.26–27); J. B. Green, "The Social Status of Mary in Luke 1.5–2.52: A Plea for Methodological Integration," *Bib* 73 (1992), 457–471.

Trompf noted, Luke (along with other historians) reflected in his writing "a general apprehension of the human past as an arena in which certain types of situations, problems, characters, and styles make their reappearances."[43] Hence, our concern is not whether historiographers employed such devices as parallel patterns and repetition in their work, but rather how these might be understood as integral to the task of Luke the historian.

Perhaps it is too simplistic simply to suggest that this way of putting things represents reality as Luke understood it. Nevertheless, it is worth noting that, in the latter decades of this century, the positivist segregation of "what actually happened" and "what was perceived to have taken place" has become obscured. A historian like Luke, engaged in the historiographical task, commits to writing what has already been interpreted by others to him and his own perception of those interpreted events, and in doing so produces a text that is itself susceptible of interpretation. This text is, then, a cultural product which participates in and parades (one or more) interpretive agenda(s).

On the one hand, we are drawing attention to the reality long observed by ethnographers that antedating any "official" record of a community's past by an (outside) historian is a community-determined choice of retrospection. Significance is already attributed to events by political decisions implicitly and explicitly made about what will be remembered and how. In her examination of how institutions remember and forget, Mary Douglas observes,

When we look closely at the construction of past time, we find the process has very little to do with the past at all and everything to do with the present. Institutions create shadowed places in which nothing can be seen and no questions asked. They make other areas show finely discriminated detail, which is closely scrutinized and ordered.[44]

---

[43] Trompf, *Historical Recurrence*, p. 315; see esp. Trompf's chaps. 1–2, where he traces in Polybius cyclical and alternating ideas whereby the historian was able to provide predictive counsel on human affairs.

[44] M. Douglas, *How Institutions Think*, The Frank W. Abrams Lectures (Syracuse, 1986), pp. 69–70.

On the other hand, the writing of history is itself a relational event, so that "events" are already and always represented in their relation to the interpreter. To put it differently, the mimetic task does not find its reference so much in "historical fact" as in perception. As a consequence, the textual product of the writing of history – i.e. the utilization of narrativity in the representation of reality – "surpasses itself as a set of real events and is realized as a structure of meaning."[45]

It will not do to ask in a simplistic way, then, whether narrative representations of parallelism in Luke depict reality as it actually happened. Of course Luke–Acts (and with it, all historiography) is a "fiction" in the sense of "something made or shaped" (*fingere*); perhaps, though, it is better to classify Luke-Acts (and with it, all historiography) as "partial" – and that in a dual sense, incomplete and partisan. To put it another way, perhaps it is not so simplistic after all to say that, in his representation of historical recurrence, the Third Evangelist was representing reality as he understood it. In doing so, he shaped events to a teleological end, underscoring their standing in the divine purpose, in this way legitimating (his depiction of) "the events that have been fulfilled among us" together with the community he represents.

---

[45] Stock, *Listening for the Text*, p. 108. Cf. W. Iser, *The Fictive and the Imaginary: Charting Literary Anthropology* (Baltimore, 1993); J. Clifford and G. E. Marcus (eds.), *Writing as Culture: The Poetics and Politics of Ethnography* (Berkeley, 1986); C. Geertz, *Works and Lives: The Anthropologist as Author* (Stanford, 1988).

CHAPTER 12

Luke's characterizing use of the Old Testament in the Book of Acts

Bill T. Arnold

Luke's adroitness as a *littérateur* has become a dominant theme in recent studies. As non-biblical literary criticism continues to inform the work of biblical scholarship, scholars working on Luke–Acts have begun to explore the masterful way in which Luke has framed the Gospel and the history of the early church. This chapter will join the discussion by analyzing one aspect of Luke's literary artistry; namely his characterizing point of view in quoting or referring to the Old Testament in the Acts of the Apostles.

Luke's use of the Old Testament has attracted considerable attention in recent studies. In particular, Joseph A. Fitzmyer has demonstrated convincingly that Luke sought to shape the account of Jesus and the early church in a fashion that imitated Old Testament historiography.[1] Luke's Old Testament quotations come from the Pentateuch, the Psalms, and seven of the prophets. Surprisingly he rarely quotes the historical books directly, though his dependence on certain passages from these books is apparent (see below). Luke has so shaped his story in the manner of Old Testament language, themes, etc., that he appears to have intended consciously to write biblical history. He has imitated Septuagintal Greek, used Old Testament themes and models, and simulated biblical historiography with a high degree of literary sophistication.[2]

Of course, the view that Luke–Acts is in some way a continu-

---

[1] J. A. Fitzmyer, "The Use of the Old Testament in Luke–Acts," *SBL 1992 Seminar Papers*, ed. Eugene H. Lovering, Jr. #31 (Atlanta, 1992), p. 525.

[2] B. S. Rosner, "Acts and Biblical History," in *The Book of Acts in its Ancient Literary Setting*, vol. 1, ed. B. Winter and A. D. Clarke (Grand Rapids, 1993), pp. 65–82.

ation of the biblical tradition (especially the Deuteronomist) is not new. But the details of that relationship have taken many forms.[3] Is Luke dependent upon the Old Testament only for literary style, or also structure and organization? Or is the dependence only a theological one and not necessarily literary in nature? Recently, biblical scholars have emphasized the hermeneutical category of *intertextuality* in analyzing Luke's use of the Old Testament. This approach explores Luke's uses of repetition to produce a text that is itself an interplay of other texts, creating a system of references. These interplays may reverberate with other texts within the work ("internal repetition"), or they may echo extrinsic materials ("external repetition").[4] Clearly, the external reverberations of Luke–Acts demonstrate Luke's indebtedness to the Old Testament story of God's redemption of his covenant people and the conviction that his narrative is, in fact, a continuation of that salvation history.

It is also possible to investigate Luke's use of the Old Testament in terms of the Hellenistic literary practice known as *imitatio*.[5] This method was one of the basic elements of rhetorical training and method from Plato and Aristotle to Quintilian, about AD 95. Far from a rare or specialized practice, imitation of previous works appears to have been common from about 100 BC to AD 100. As T. L. Brodie puts it, during this period "the literary world was largely concerned with reshaping the great texts of the past."[6] Brodie has suggested

---

[3] The debate may be traced back to C. C. Torrey's suggestions that Luke's work should be compared to the Chronicler's (*The Composition and Date of Acts*, HTS 1 (Cambridge,MA, 1916]). For a brief survey of the issues and bibliography, see M. C. Parsons and R. I. Pervo, *Rethinking the Unity of Luke and Acts* (Minneapolis, 1992), pp. 33–35.

[4] For brief discussion of intertextuality and examples of both "internal" and "external" repetition, see now J. B. Green, "Internal Repetition in Luke–Acts: Contemporary Narratology and Lucan Historiography," pp. 283–299 in this volume.

[5] See particularly T. L. Brodie, "Greco-Roman Imitation of Texts as a Partial Guide to Luke's Use of Sources," in *Luke–Acts: New Perspectives from the Society of Biblical Literature Seminar*, ed. C. H. Talbert (New York, 1984), pp. 17–46; J. Drury, *Tradition and Design in Luke's Gospel* (Atlanta, 1976); and Rosner, "Acts and Biblical History," pp. 71–75.

[6] T. L. Brodie, "Towards Unravelling Luke's Use of the Old Testament: Luke 7.11–17 as an *Imitatio* of 1 Kings 17.17–24," *NTS* 32 (1986), 247–267.

that Luke's foundational Old Testament model was the Elijah–Elisha narrative, though he appears to have adapted Chronicles and Ezra–Nehemiah as a skeletal base for the early sections of his Gospel.[7] This approach has proved helpful in analyzing Luke's surface-level structure, his purpose for writing and his method of interpreting the events he describes in light of Old Testament texts. Indeed it accords well with his stated purpose (Lk. 1.3–4).

In this chapter, I will suggest a different level of Luke's treatment of the Old Testament in Acts. Besides his use of *imitatio* in which he consciously shapes his narrative in Old Testament garb and uses many direct quotations of Old Testament texts in the speeches of Acts, there are also numerous subtle quotations used in characterizing his speakers. Luke uses Old Testament quotations in the speeches of his leading characters (Peter, Stephen and Paul) to express his point of view about those characters. This chapter will not attempt to deal with Luke's perspective on other characters who appear in the narrative, since their speech contains no words from the Old Testament. We are interested in how Luke used the Old Testament quotes for characterizing the main players in the narratives of Acts. After a general survey of the technique used for expressing the narrator's point of view, I will proceed by listing and discussing several quotations in Acts.

A "POINT OF VIEW" AS A MEANS OF INVESTIGATING LUKE'S USES OF THE OLD TESTAMENT

One of the most important contributions of narratology for biblical scholarship has been the emphasis on techniques for expressing "point of view" as a means of characterizing the

---

[7] T. L. Brodie, "Luke–Acts as an Imitation and Emulation of the Elijah–Elisha Narrative," in *New Views on Luke and Acts*, ed. Earl Richard (Collegeville, MN, 1990), pp. 78–85, 172–174; T. L. Brodie, "Towards Unraveling the Rhetorical Imitation of Sources in Acts: 2 Kings 5 as One Component of Acts 8,9–40," *Biblica* 67 (1986), 41–67; and C. A. Evans, "Luke's Use of the Elijah/Elisha Narratives and the Ethic of Election," *JBL* 106 (1987), 75–83.

main players.[8] Literary critics use the expression "point of view" broadly to designate the perspective from which the story is told. Determining the perspective of a character may be critical for understanding the point of view of the narrator, and therefore may be the first step in discovering the meaning of the story.

Biblical scholarship is dependent on the theoretical ground-breaking studies of modern structural semiotics, which attempts to describe the types of communicative processes as part of the phenomenon of human culture. Specifically, the work of Boris Uspensky has been influential on biblical studies in isolating the ways in which the text indicates point of view.[9] Uspensky has differentiated four levels of point of view as a means of extracting from the surface structure of the text certain indicators of its compositional structure. The more obvious the surface structure, by which is meant the linguistic structure, the more confidently we may analyze the poetic or compositional structure.

Before applying these concepts to the Old Testament quotations in Acts, I briefly summarize here Uspensky's four planes for expressing point of view.[10]

1 The "ideological" plane

Uspensky calls this the most basic aspect of point of view.[11] This is the point of view assumed in evaluating and perceiving

---

8 For a survey of the recent literary approaches to Acts, see F. S. Spencer, "Acts and Modern Literary Approaches," in *The Book of Acts in its Ancient Literary Setting, vol. 1*, ed. B. Winter and A. D. Clarke (Grand Rapids, 1993), pp. 381–414.

9 *A Poetics of Composition: The Structure of the Artistic Text and Typology of a Compositional Form*, trans. V. Zavarin and S. Wittig (Berkeley, 1973). Though Uspensky was a literary theoretician bred in the climate of modern Russian structural semiotics, his work has had an important impact on biblical narratology. For a limited example, see R. Alter, *The Art of Biblical Narrative* (New York, 1981); A. Berlin, *Poetics and Interpretation of Biblical Narrative* (Sheffield, 1983); M. Sternberg, *The Poetics of Biblical Narrative: Ideological Literature and the Drama of Reading* (Bloomington, IN, 1987).

10 Some of these correspond roughly to the work of S. B. Chatman (*Story and Discourse: Narrative Structure in Fiction and Film* [Ithaca, NY, 1978]), pp. 151–153, who has isolated three ways in which the term "point of view" can be applied: the *perceptual* (perspective on the events of the narrative), the *conceptual* (perspective of attitudes or concepts) and *interest* (perspective of someone's benefit or disadvantage).

11 Uspensky, *Poetics*, pp. 8–16.

ideologically the world being described. This point of view may be concealed, be openly acknowledged, or lie somewhere between these two extremes. It may occur as evaluative statements which connote the ideological position of the author or characters. It may belong to the author himself or herself, or to one of the characters. This point of view is the system of ideas that shape the work and comprise the "deep compositional structure, as opposed to the surface compositional structure which may be traced on the psychological, spatio-temporal, or phraseological levels."[12] Typically, the ideological viewpoint in the Bible is that of the narrator.

Uspensky emphasized that the manifestations of the ideological viewpoint are less accessible to formal study than those of the other levels. But commonly, the ideological point of view is expressed through the speech characteristics of the characters.[13] This observation leads us to the next plane for expressing one's point of view.

2 The "phraseological" plane

Uspensky also calls this the "plane of speech characteristics."[14] This technique is especially apparent in those cases where the author uses different diction to describe different characters, or where reported speech is used. Though there are numerous ways in which the phraseological viewpoint may be used, one of the simplest, and the one most pertinent to this study, is when the author makes use of someone else's speech, either as a narrator or as an author using reported speech. This surface level technique refers to the linguistic features in discourse that reveal whose point of view is expressed. It is possible for the authorial viewpoint to shift, or for the author's point of view to conflict with that of his or her character.

3 The "spatial and temporal" planes

This level refers to the author's location in time and space to the narrative. The author may be relating the events of the

[12] Ibid., p. 8.   [13] Ibid., pp. 13–15.
[14] Ibid., p. 17, and see pp. 17–56 for his complete treatment.

narrative as they occur, or long afterwards. He or she may be closely attached to a particular character, in which case the events are related as that character saw them. Or the author may jump from one character to another, or assume any number of spatial points of view. Though this plane for expressing authorial viewpoint is not particularly related to our investigation of Luke's use of the Old Testament, it holds interesting potential for Lucan studies because of the famous "we-passages" of Acts.

4 The "psychological" plane

This refers to cases where the authorial viewpoint relies on an individual consciousness (or perception). This point of view may be either "subjective" (i.e. it is dependent on some individual perception or psychological point of view) or "objective" (i.e. facts are presented rather than impressions). In the case of the objective viewpoint, the author relies on his or her own point of view and not on the point of view of the character. Again, this holds interesting potential for studies on the Book of Acts, though the psychological plane is not the focus of this chapter.

The first two of these (ideological and phraseological) are of most interest in our investigation of Luke's use of the Old Testament, as is true of most of biblical narrative. Though a story may be told through narration alone, it is the nature of biblical narrative to prefer direct discourse whenever possible.[15] The phraseological plane is the most dramatic way of expressing the character's ideological and sometimes psychological points of view. The author's or character's point of view may be expressed on more than one level at the same time.

Each of Luke's quotations from the Old Testament discussed below is, by definition, an example of his use of the phraseological point of view. We are interested to demonstrate, not only *how* he used the Old Testament, but *why* he quoted it as he did, and to examine his ideological viewpoint where possible. Thus

---

[15] Berlin, *Poetics*, pp. 64–65.

for our purposes, it is important to understand the relationship between the ideological and phraseological planes. Strictly linguistic means of expressing viewpoint often characterize the person who uses the stylistic feature. In this way, the world view of the character (or author) may be defined, and his or her ideological point of view is thus revealed through stylistic analysis of speech. Thus, it is possible for the first two planes to work together in this way; the phraseological plane revealing the ideological. Frequently, a definite ideological position is expressed on the phraseological plane.[16]

B CHARACTERIZING QUOTES FROM THE OLD TESTAMENT IN THE BOOK OF ACTS

Luke's quotations of the Old Testament in Acts occur in concentration in the speeches of Peter in chapters 1–4, the speech of Stephen in chapter 7, and the speech of Paul in chapter 13.[17] His well-known summary statements and narrative accounts rarely contain allusions to the Old Testament. Fitzmyer avers:

These speeches were either missionary discourses, intended to stir up belief among Jews in Jesus as the Messiah and in his role in salvation history, or a polemical, apologetic discourse, in which Stephen is portrayed indicting the Jews for their disbelief . . . As Paul and his companion Barnabas turn in their missionary work to evangelize the Gentiles [Acts 13], Luke never again uses Old Testament quotations in his narrative of Pauline evangelistic activity, save [in] isolated instances . . . Thus chap. 13 serves not only as the turning point in Luke's story of Paul's ministry, but also in Luke's own appeal to the Old Testament in Acts. The "word of God" had to be addressed first to the Jewish people, and in addressing it to them Luke makes Peter and Paul appeal to their Scriptures to bolster up the Christian message, the story of whose spread to the end of the earth is the message of Acts itself.[18]

---

[16] Uspensky, *Poetics*, p. 15.
[17] Fitzmyer, "The Use of the Old Testament," p. 531.
[18] Ibid., "The Use of the Old Testament," p. 536.

Luke explicitly introduces forty-five quotations of the Old Testament with expressions such as "this is what was spoken through the prophet Joel" (Acts 2.16) or "as it is written" (Acts 7.42). Fitzmyer has divided these into three categories.[19] First, there are seventeen examples in which Luke has quoted the LXX verbatim. Then, there are twenty-two cases in which Luke cites the Old Testament text in a manner close to the LXX but not verbatim. Finally, Luke has quoted the Old Testament six times in Greek that is not close to the LXX. In this last category, Fitzmyer concedes that it is impossible to determine whether Luke has conflated, quoted from memory or quoted from a different Greek version.[20]

These Old Testament quotations introduced with specific introductory formulae are examples of phraseological point of view expressed through the direct discourse of the character.[21] These are the obvious cases in which Luke's point of view is expressed in the speaker's use of the Old Testament. The speaker has appealed to the Old Testament as an authoritative source to validate and substantiate his position. In these cases, the phraseological and the ideological planes are coalescing, resulting in authorial approval of the speaker's position. Luke places his speakers (Peter, Stephen, and Paul) clearly

---

[19] See ibid., pp. 533–535 for what follows. The subjectivity of categorizing and listing such quotations may be demonstrated by a comparison of Fitzmyer's list to the earlier one compiled by W. K. L. Clarke ("The Use of the Septuagint in Acts," in *The Beginnings of Christianity: Part I: The Acts of the Apostles*, ed. F. J. F. Jackson and K. Lake [London, 1922], pp. 85–93). For the text form of Luke's quotations, see T. Holtz, *Untersuchungen über die Zitate bei Lukas* (Berlin, 1968); H. Ringgren, "Luke's Use of the Old Testament," *HTR* 79 (1986), 227–235; and C. K. Barrett, "Luke/Acts," in *It Is Written: Scripture Citing Scripture*, ed. D. A. Carson and H. G. M. Williamson, Lindars Festschrift (Cambridge, 1988), pp. 231–244.

[20] I am not optimistic about the prospects of resolving the problem of Luke's specific sources for the Old Testament quotations. Even if his Old Testament citations were uniformly LXX based, this would not account for the possibility of assimilation to the LXX during the traditioning process. Furthermore, Luke's natural language was probably a Jewish or Semitic Greek, and he appears to have had the "skill to write what looks like a deliberate LXX style" (Nigel Turner, *A Grammar of New Testament Greek*, vol. IV, *Style* [Edinburgh, 1976], pp. 56–57). As was discussed years ago, a few of the references that diverge from the LXX may have come from an independent knowledge of the Hebrew and others may be accounted for as free quotations from memory (Clarke, "The Use of the Septuagint in Acts," pp. 97–98). All things considered, a solution is hopelessly beyond our grasp.

[21] Uspensky, *Poetics*, p. 44.

within the mainstream of salvation history by using these quotations.

But, as Uspensky points out, these are only the obvious types of phraseological expression. In addition to these quotations introduced specifically by Luke or his characters, Luke has also made frequent references to, and used occasional quotes from, Old Testament passages, which are not specifically introduced *as Old Testament quotations*. It is in such subtle quotation that Luke has artfully used the Old Testament to express his ideological point of view. These quotations from the Old Testament reveal the narrator's viewpoint on the phraseological plane. But they are less intrusive since they are not introduced by any set formula. These are the cases where Luke (or his speaker) has adapted Old Testament speech in order to evaluate. Hence, the phraseological and ideological planes have once again coalesced.[22]

1 Acts 2.30–31

In Peter's speech, lodged between two direct quotations from the LXX (2.25–28 and 2.34–35), Luke records allusions to two psalms, both of which build on an important theological Davidic tradition in 2 Sam. 7.12–13. As elsewhere in Peter's sermon (see also the famous quotation from the LXX in 2.17–21), he has quoted the Old Testament in order to substantiate his position that Jesus is the Messiah and the fulfillment of Old Testament prophecy. But the words of Acts 2.30–31 are not taken directly from the Old Testament. Instead, several LXX terms have become the words of Peter.

---

[22] I have collected here the quotations, or sometimes near quotations, from the Old Testament, which are not included in Fitzmyer's list because they are not specifically introduced as quotations. There are numerous other places in Acts where Luke may make a general allusion to the Old Testament without actually quoting. For example, in Acts 2.24, when Luke uses ὠδῖνας τοῦ θανάτου for "the agony of death," he has come very close to quoting the LXX of 2 Sam. 22.6; Ps. 18.4 and 116.3. However, this may not have been an actual quotation from the Old Testament expression. Luke may have been using a common stock expression, or perhaps an archaizing phrase from synagogal, Palestinian Greek. When combined with Fitzmyer's list, the list presented here makes up a catalog of Luke's quotes of the Old Testament in the Book of Acts.

Because David was a prophet, Peter announces, "God had sworn with an oath to him" that he would "put one of his descendants on his throne" (quoting Ps. 132.11).[23]

As with all of the quotations and allusions to the Old Testament in Peter's speech, this reveals his ideological viewpoint through phraseological means. In other words, in his appeal to his audience, Peter has adopted an Old Testament world view. He wants his believers to equate his viewpoint with that of Yahweh himself, who assured David that there would always be a son of David on the throne of Israel (and with Joel, who predicted this outpouring of the Spirit, 2.17–21; and with David, who foretold Jesus' resurrection, 2.25–28). Peter thus shifted his speech to Old Testament words in order to shift his viewpoint (or that of his listeners) to the divine world view.

Luke includes the Old Testament quotations in Peter's speech as a characterizing technique. He preserves the phraseological *specifica* because it also reveals his (the narrator's) ideological point of view. Since he believes Peter was right to quote the Old Testament for support, and since he approves Peter's alignment with the Old Testament prophecies and their interpretation, Luke includes the quotations as a means of sanctioning Peter as a leading character, and demonstrating his place in the story of salvation begun in the Old Testament.

2 Acts 3.13

After the healing of the lame man at the gate called Beautiful, Peter addressed those who witnessed the event and referred to the God of the patriarchs. His reference to "the God of Abraham, Isaac, and Jacob, the God of our fathers" is, of course, common in the Old Testament (Exod. 3.6,15). But its use here is an indication of an ideological scene shift in the narrative. Verse 11 is in the narrator's voice describing the action objectively: "While he [the healed man] clung to Peter

---

[23] Acts 2.31 may actually be an introduced quotation, taking the ὅτι as introducing direct discourse, in which case, this verse should be added to Fitzmyer's list (see NRSV).

and John, all the people ran together to them in the portico
called Solomon's Portico, utterly astonished." The actions of
the healed man and the people are described impartially. The
inner life of the people is mentioned in passing; "they were
utterly astonished." Verse 12 begins with the adverbial, participial phrase using ἰδὼν, "When Peter saw it," to indicate a
shift in point of view.[24] Peter's words to the crowd reveal his
perceptions of them as people who marveled at the miracle,
who "stare at us." Peter's perception is that they believe that
he and John healed the man by their own power.

But Peter's use of the quote at the beginning of verse 13
dramatically calls the crowd to look beyond Peter and John
to the God of the Old Testament. He has evaluated their
viewpoint and condemned it as inadequate. Moreover,
Luke's inclusion of this quotation characterizes Peter as a
speaker standing within the Old Testament tradition. If,
indeed, this quote called Exod. 3.6 and 15 to the minds of
Luke's readers, Peter became like Moses returning to the
enslaved Israelites in Egypt in the name of the God of the
patriarchs in order to lead them out of their bondage. So
Peter is presenting the Good News of Jesus to the enslaved
Jews in the name of that same patriarchal God. Peter also
turns this quotation into a powerful messianic claim. This
very God of the Old Testament patriarchs "has glorified his
servant Jesus." Though these words are not a quotation, they
seem to be drawing on Isa. 52.13.

3 Acts 4.24

Acts 4.25–26 has a direct quote from the LXX of Ps. 2.1–2
introduced as the words of David, and therefore included in
Fitzmyer's list. But the phrase in 4.24, "who made the heaven
and the earth, the sea, and everything in them," is also taken
from the Old Testament, and may actually reveal more
about Luke's uses of such quotations than the one of 4.25–26.

---

[24] For the scenic, almost film-like quality of biblical narrative and the ways in which
scenes may shift, see Berlin, *Poetics*, p. 45 and Alter, *Biblical Narrative*, p. 63.

This phrase from the Decalogue and a psalm of praise (Exod. 20.11; Ps. 146.6) occurs on the lips of Peter, John, and their companions while praying, after Peter and John had been released.

Together these quotations from the Old Testament reveal through phraseological details the ideological viewpoint of this early Christian group. Their perception of God (4.24) and the world around them (4.25–26) is expressed through the quotes in their prayer, which Luke records as a means of characterizing them and approving their world view. Hence, in Luke's use of the Old Testament quotations, the phraseological and ideological planes have coalesced again.

4 Acts 7.3

With this verse, we begin a discussion of Stephen's use of the Old Testament in the longest of the speeches of Acts (7.2–53). Perhaps more than in any other speech in Acts, the Old Testament plays a particularly dominant role here, and this is not surprising since he was speaking before the Sanhedrin. His goal is to tie Israel's past to the Jewish present; to link the persistent rejection of God's leadership during the Old Testament period with the first-century rejection of Jesus. His many quotations from and allusions to the Old Testament appeal to the very source of Jewish authority in order to make his argument irrefutable. But Luke is also characterizing Stephen by recording numerous LXX passages verbatim. Direct speech is the preferred means of characterization in biblical narrative because direct speech is the "most dramatic way of conveying the characters' internal psychological and ideological points of view."[25] Luke has included the Old Testament quotations and allusions in this lengthy speech partly as a means of representing Stephen as someone who stands well within the Old Testament traditions.

The first quote (Acts 7.3) is taken verbatim from Gen. 12.1: "'Leave your country and your relatives and go to the land

---

[25] Berlin, *Poetics*, pp. 64–65.

that I will show you.'"[26] This quote interrupts Stephen's
narration of the life of Abram. But the interruption is an
important one and anticipates the method Stephen will use in
the speech to condemn his audience. The words from Genesis
are the famous words of God himself, commanding Abram to
leave Ur of the Chaldees. As the *ipsissima verba* of God, the
command is clearly the plan of God for Abram's future and for
that of his descendants. But, as Stephen's speech unfolds, it
becomes clear that Abram's descendants would eventually
reject God's plan. This initial quote, then, is intended to
present the divine viewpoint; with his own words of command,
God initiated his covenant plan for his people.

5 *Acts 7.5*

The expression in 7.5b, "to give it to him as his possession and
to his descendants after him," has affinities with many passages
in Genesis dealing with the patriarchal land promise.[27]
Especially familiar in these passages is the recurring quote from
God to Abraham (and once to Jacob) that God will give
(always δίδωμι) the land to him and to his seed after him.
Twice the expression "as a(n eternal) possession" is used (Gen.
17.8 and 48.4). These appear to be stock expressions used in
Genesis to recount God's faithfulness to Abram and Jacob, and
to emphasize the centrality of the land promise to the patriarchal covenant (see especially Gen. 15.18 and 17.7–8). This is
the first step in the story of Israel's *Heilsgeschichte* as Stephen
relates it. Again, the words of God's promise are emphasized
because the plan of salvation for Israel was God's plan. Luke
uses the Old Testament quotes to characterize Stephen as one
who accurately represents God's plan.

---

[26] The quote differs from the LXX only in omitting the expression καὶ ἐκ τοῦ οἴκου
τοῦ πατρός σου.

[27] Specifically the following phrases are in view: τῷ σπέρματί σου δώσω τὴν γῆν ταύτην
(12.7); πᾶσαν τὴν γῆν, ἣν σὺ ὁρᾷς σοὶ δώσω αὐτὴν καὶ τῷ σπέρματί σου (13.15); τῷ
σπέρματί σου δώσω τὴν γῆν ταύτην (15.18); καὶ δώσω σοι καὶ τῷ σπέρματί σου μετὰ
σὲ τὴν γῆν . . . εἰς κατάσχεσιν αἰώνιον (17.8); σοὶ δώσω τὴν γῆν ταύτην καὶ τῷ
σπέρματί σου (24.7); καὶ δώσω σοι τὴν γῆν ταύτην, καὶ τῷ σπέρματί σου μετὰ σὲ, εἰς
κατάσχεσιν αἰώνιον (said to Jacob, 48.4).

6 *Acts 7.10–11*

These verses appear to be a conflation of quotes from the Joseph story, particularly Gen. 41.37–44. The Old Testament narrative has been summarized by selecting key words instead of quoting any single continuous passage. Stephen's speech is laden in these two verses with allusions to the Old Testament narrative. As before, it is the actions and words of God that are so quoted: God granted favor before Pharaoh; made Joseph governor of Egypt and over Pharaoh's household; and sent a famine throughout the land.

7 *Acts 7.18*

The statement that "another king who had not known Joseph ruled over Egypt" is dependent on the LXX of Exod. 1. 8. Though these are not the words of God or a direct action of God, it is clearly a turning point in the Old Testament narrative. The reason for including such verbal *specifica* here is less obvious than in other examples in Acts. The phraseological perspective is probably meant to mark the accuracy of the account.

8 *Acts 7.27–28*

The Hebrew slave's comment to Moses is taken directly from the LXX of Exod. 2.14: "Who made you a ruler and a judge over us? Do you want to kill me as you killed the Egyptian yesterday?"

Interestingly, the entire narrative described in this paragraph (Acts 7.23–29) is from Exod. 2. But this is the only direct quote.[28] The overarching purpose of Stephen's speech is to condemn the spirit of rejection prevalent among his Jewish audience. The direct Old Testament quote is used here because Stephen, as speaker (and in this case, Luke as hidden

---

[28] The quote from Exod. 2.13–14 is not included in Fitzmyer's list because it is not introduced by Luke with an introductory formula.

author), is shifting his point of view through the use of phraseological *specifica*. The quote becomes a phraseological means of highlighting the ideological point of view: a perspective that condemns the Israelites for rejecting God's messenger. This forcefully condemns Stephen's listeners for also rejecting God's messenger, Jesus, as becomes clear in 7.35.

9 *Acts 7.30–34*

Stephen continues his discourse on Moses in 7.30–34, where he describes Moses' encounter with God at the burning bush. The paragraph begins with several words that appear to rely on the text of Exod. 3.1,2, though it does not appear to be a direct quote from the LXX. The words "an angel appeared to him" are all identical to the LXX, though the order has been changed. The reference to the "flame of a burning bush" uses the same vocabulary as the LXX, though the specific forms are altered considerably. Again, as we saw above for Acts 7.10–11, Stephen's speech here is clearly dependent on a specific Old Testament passage and the vocabulary reflects that relationship.

But beginning in verse 32, Stephen's speech quotes selected portions of the LXX of Exod. 3.4–10 with little, and in some cases no, alteration. Interestingly, it is the speech of God that has been excerpted most faithfully. The divine identification, "I am the God of your ancestors, the God of Abraham, Isaac, and Jacob," appears to have been taken directly from the LXX of Exod. 3.6, though there are a number of rather minor changes. The verb εἰμί is omitted, "father" is made plural, and θεός is made articular and is used only once to introduce all three patriarchs, not repeated before each name as in the LXX. But these are all insignificant variants, and the phrase is clearly dependent upon the Exodus passage.

Then verses 33 and 34 are taken directly from selected phrases in the LXX of Exod. 3.5–10. To be sure, there are subtle changes. For example, the LXX's use of the imperatival infinitive (λῦσαι), "Loose your sandals," has been changed to the simple imperative in Acts 7.33 (λῦσον). In one case, the vocabulary has been altered to emphasize the point of the Old Testament text. The rather generic term κραυγή (which in NT times has a wide semantic field, "shout, outcry, clamor," etc.) is replaced with the more specific στεναγμός, "groaning, sigh." But by and large, Acts 7.33 and 34 are taken directly from the LXX of Exod. 3.5–10.

Perhaps the most enlightening way in which the Old Testament is used in these verses is the way Stephen's speech summarizes the reactions and speeches of Moses, but highlights divine speech. The Old Testament narrative has been reviewed succinctly, except where God speaks to Moses from the bush. Even here, much of the LXX is omitted. But that which is included reveals the purpose of the Old Testament quotation. God's voice is used to emphasize the truth that Moses had been God's chosen instrument of salvation, sent to the Israelites in Egypt to deliver them from their bondage. This purpose climaxes at the end of verse 34 when Stephen juxtaposes two phrases from Exod. 3.8 and 3.10: "I have come down to rescue them. Come now, I will send you to Egypt." These two sentences are separated by much more material in the LXX version. But Stephen is emphasizing the unity of God's purpose and Moses' mission. Moses was God's own servant for the role of savior.

In this speech, the Old Testament has been used artfully to express the point of view, both of the speaker and the narrator. Luke's ideological point of view has coalesced with Stephen's and been expressed on the phraseological plane by quoting the Old Testament. He approves of the ideas expressed, especially since the ideas are those of God himself. Here, Luke's character has actually assumed the divine point of view in opposition to his audience.

10 Acts 7.35

The point of Stephen's speech becomes clear with this verse. The quote from Exod. 2.14 used already in Acts 7.27 is repeated here: "Who made you a ruler and a judge?" Stephen's point is contained in the emphatic "It was this Moses whom they rejected," the very one whom "God now sent as both ruler and liberator." The quote is repeated to express the point of view of both character and narrator, again both phraseologically and ideologically. The speech is flatly condemning the rejection of Moses as the very one prepared and sent forth by God to bring salvation. The speech of God quoted in the previous paragraph (Acts 7.33–34) expresses the approving point of view. Moses was God's man for God's mission. Now the speech of the Hebrew slave is used to disapprove of the Israelite rejection of God's plan for salvation. Again, Old Testament quotations are being used to express the ideological point of view. And of course, the implication is that history has repeated itself. God's appointed servant has once again been rejected by the ones he came to save.

11 Acts 7.37

The quote in this verse from Deut. 18.15 carries a clear messianic message that would not have been lost on Stephen's listeners. The words of Moses are quoted by Stephen in one of the strongest messianic verses of the Old Testament: " God will raise up a prophet for you like me from your brothers." The quote is taken directly from the LXX with minor modifications. The pronouns are made plural and the word order is changed. The word order of the LXX follows strictly that of the MT.

This quote anticipates Stephen's main indictment, which does not come until verse 51. The words of Moses foretelling the coming of the Messiah subtly assume his (Moses') point of view, in adumbrating the coming of the Christ. But on Stephen's lips, they imply also that the Christ has appeared. Rejecting Jesus in Stephen's day was paramount to rejecting Moses in Old Testament times. The narrator and character points of view have merged with Moses, and once again affirmed ideologically the validity of Christ and his mission; all through phraseological uses of the Old Testament point of view.

12 Acts 7.40

The archetypal example of rejecting God's ways and plans is now quoted by Stephen. The Golden Calf episode epitomizes the Israelite refusal to follow the Lord's will, equaled only by the subsequent failure at Kadesh-Barnea (Num. 14.1–4). The words are taken almost verbatim from Exod. 32.1 (and repeated again in Aaron's pathetic defense in Exod. 32.23). The point of view adopted is again an ideological use of the phraseological plane. The words of the Israelites are equated with those who would reject the work of God in Christ, and therefore the ideological point of view is made poignantly through the Old Testament quotation. The words of Jeremiah are also used by Stephen to condemn the Israelite actions in Acts 7.42b,43, a quote included in Fitzmyer's list.

13 Acts 7.51

Stephen's speech is so full of Old Testament allusions that very often the line between direct quotation from the Old Testament and subtle allusion is difficult to maintain. Acts 7.9 contains several words possibly coming directly from the LXX and others that are slightly altered for context. For example, in describing the inner life of Joseph's brothers, Luke uses the verb "to be jealous" (ζηλόω) in the form of an aorist participle as a coordinate circumstance, but the Old Testament form is an aorist indicative in Gen. 37.11. Likewise, in describing Jacob's instructions to his sons to go down to Egypt to acquire food during the famine, Stephen's speech uses the same vocabulary, though certainly not a direct quote (ἀκούω and σῖτος, Acts 7.12, and see Gen. 42.2). So Stephen is characterized as having a specific text of the Old Testament in view as he speaks. This could be illustrated numerous times for Stephen's speech.

The most striking examples of this use of the Old Testament are found here at the conclusion of Stephen's speech, where he indicts his listeners most emphatically. Acts 7.49–50 is a quote taken from the LXX of Isa. 66.1–2, and introduced as direct speech. But the point of Stephen's speech becomes clear with the first word of verse 51: σκληροτράχηλοι, "Stiff-necked people!". This term occurs only here in the New Testament. Its use in the LXX is so developed that it is possible to trace the origin of the word to its usage there.[29] Though its appearance in Acts 7.51 is not a direct quote from the Old Testament, it seems to have clear reference to Exod. 33.3 and 5, where the term is used in divine speech to describe the rebellious Israelites.[30]

In point of fact, 7.51 serves as a climax to Stephen's speech. The verse contains three indictments of his audience:

(1) "You stiff-necked people,"
(2) "uncircumcised in heart and ears,"
(3) "you are forever opposing the Holy Spirit . . ."

It appears that each element of this tripartite indictment is *conceptually* dependent on the Old Testament, if not phraseologically. We have already seen how the term "stiff-necked people" is rooted in the exodus narrative. The concept of the uncircumcised heart is, of course, well known from Jer. 6.10 and 9.26, and the vocabulary is at least similar to the LXX of those verses. The charge of opposing the work of the Holy Spirit is less obviously related to the Old Testament, but is probably dependent lexicographically on Isa. 63.10. The very phrase used there (τὸ πνεῦμα τὸ ἅγιον) is rare enough in the Old Testament that the connection with the variation in the dative case used in Acts 7.51 may be affirmed with relative confidence. The concluding phrase of Acts 7.51 ties all these Old Testament phrases of condemnation directly to Stephen's audience: "just as your ancestors used to do." With this phrase, Stephen has equated the rebelliousness of the Old Testament Israelites, condemned so roundly by these same Old Testament expressions, with his first-century Jewish listeners.[31]

---

[29] K. L. and M. A. Schmidt, *TDNT* v, p. 1029.

[30] The occurrence of σκληροτράχηλος here also parallels the MT of Exod. 32.9, though the verse has been omitted in the LXX, possibly on the basis of homoiarchton (verses 9 and 10 beginning with the same consonant).

[31] The opening of the next verse of Stephen's indictment (Acts 7.52) may also be a subtle reference to 2 Chr. 36.16, though the phraseological connections are much less obvious.

Of course, the point of Stephen's speech is that the rejection and crucifixion of Jesus is the historical climax of Israel's rejection of God's leadership. The rejection of Joseph, Moses, and the prophets has now culminated in the denial of the Messiah. So Stephen's speech uses the Old Testament to tie current events of the Gospel (and in the next chapter, the death of Stephen himself) to God's saving history in the past.

14 Acts 13.22

On his first missionary journey, Paul spoke in the synagogue one Sabbath day at Antioch in Pisidia. He addresses his listeners as "Israelites" and brothers, who are "descendants of Abraham's family" (13.16 and 26). In such a context, we should not be surprised to find Paul's speech loaded with Old Testament allusions. Indeed, from the beginning of Luke's presentation of this Pauline sermon, it is clear that several Old Testament passages are in view. But with the exception of 13.22, direct quotes are avoided until Paul comes to his conclusion that Jesus' life, death, and resurrection are the fulfillment of the Old Testament promises to the Jews' ancestors (13.33). After this point, there are several other direct quotations, all of which were included in Fitzmyer's list.

Our brief quote in Acts 13.22 combines a rare quote from the historical narratives of the Old Testament with a psalm. Paul (and Luke) expressed God's point of view by quoting his evaluation of King David: "I have found David" (Ps. 89.20) to be "a man after my [LXX his] heart" (1 Sam. 13.14). By using the phraseological *specifica* of God himself, the speaker has revealed his ideological point of view. This was logical preparation for the next verse, which declares that Jesus is a Savior brought from this man's posterity.

15 Acts 14.15

In Lystra of Lycaonia, while Paul was preaching, he commanded a man crippled from birth to stand up on his feet (Acts 14.8–10). When the man was healed, the crowds assumed that

Barnabas was Zeus and Paul Hermes, and with the help of a
local priest of Zeus, they prepared to make sacrifices to them as
local expressions of the Greek deities (14.11–13).[32]

There is no mention of a Jewish synagogue in Lystra, and we
may assume that Paul and Barnabas were dealing with an audience of polytheists. In order to stop the misunderstanding and
teach the Lystrans about the Gospel, they began a mini-sermon
(14.15–17). The sermon was apparently cut short by the crowd,
which proceeded to stone Paul and leave him for dead (14.19).
Thus the sermon never even defines the Gospel of Jesus Christ,
because Paul was laying the foundations of monotheism and
attempting to correct the theological distortions of his audience.[33] The Old Testament quote in verse 15 is a conflation
from Exod. 20.11 and Ps. 146.6, and is nearly identical to the
quotation found in Acts 4.24 discussed above. Paul attempts to
introduce the Lystrans to "the living God," who is defined with
the relative clause "who made the heaven and the earth, the
sea, and everything in them." The line is identical to Ps. 146.6,
except that the aorist substantival participle (ποιήσαντα) has
been changed to an indicative here. This is, of course, among
the highest expressions of monotheism found in the Old Testament. Unlike the famous Shema of Deut. 6.4, this quote is particularly appropriate for Paul's pagan audience at Lystra since
it does not center on the distinctive Israelite covenant name for
God, Yahweh. Paul's point of view is expressed with these
specific words from the Old Testament, which substantiate his
position. The quote is again ideological, since it also presents
the narrator's approving point of view.

CONCLUSION

Scholars working on these quotations of the Old Testament

---

[32] Local tradition of Phrygia–Lycaonia preserved an ancient legend that Zeus and
Hermes descended to earth in human form. They had been rejected by the
populace, which consequently suffered a severe flood. (The account is given in
Ovid's *Metamorphoses* 8.626ff.) It seems likely that the Lycaonians wanted to prevent
another such disaster.

[33] A more complete example of how Paul addressed strictly pagan audiences is found
in the Areopagus speech (Acts 17.24–28). There also, Paul began with the crea-
torship of God as the foundation for monotheism.

often assume a "proof-from-prophecy argument" in Luke's two-volume work, not unlike the method one would expect from Matthew.[34] But this perspective may limit too narrowly his uses of the Old Testament in the speeches.[35] Along with Luke's view of the past in general, his quotations establish continuity and cohesion between past and present. As a hermeneutical technique, he finds testimony in the Old Testament to the significance and meaning of the events he describes.

We have seen specifically that Luke uses these phraseological techniques to characterize his main characters, especially Peter and Stephen. His purpose goes beyond the assessment of previous scholarship, which concluded that he used the Old Testament in chapters 1–13 because the Gospel was proclaimed first to the Jews. This is a purely *historical* explanation for a *literary* phenomenon. Though Luke's presentation of the early stages of the fledgling church is essentially accurate and historical, the Book of Acts is nonetheless a literary achievement.[36] His quotations from the Old Testament serve an

---

[34] For example, Fitzmyer, "The Use of the Old Testament," p. 537; and see D. L. Bock's proposal to use the expression "proclamation from prophecy and pattern" to strike a balance between "proof from prophecy" and a denial of the presence of a promise-fulfillment motif altogether (*Proclamation from Prophecy and Pattern: Lucan Old Testament Christology*, JSNTSSup 12 [Sheffield, 1987], pp. 13–53, 155–279).

[35] C. H. Talbert, "Promise and Fulfillment in Lucan Theology," in *Luke–Acts: New Perspectives from the Society of Biblical Literature*, ed. C. H. Talbert (New York, 1984), pp. 91–103; and M. L. Soards, *The Speeches in Acts: Their Content, Context, and Concerns* (Louisville, 1994), pp. 200–203.

[36] The reliability of the speeches of Acts remains a moot issue. Ancient historians did not generally engage in the free invention of speeches, as illustrated by the highly rhetorical writer Livy, whose sources may be checked in places where he draws on a speech by Polybius. Even Livy seems to have reproduced the speech content of his sources. Thucydides appears to have established the method of Greek historiographers when he remarked that he had endeavored "to give the general purport of what was actually said" (*History of the Peloponnesian War* [1.22.1]). Of course this comment has been subjected to endless scholarly debate and is open to other interpretations. Yet it is clear that ancient historians recorded speech, not as a transcript, but in a way that was *faithful* to the alleged situation and speaker (Conrad Gempf, "Public Speaking and Published Accounts," in *The Book of Acts in its Ancient Literary Setting*, vol. I, ed. B. Winter and A. D. Clarke [Grand Rapids, 1993], pp. 259–269 and 298–303). See also pp. 3–32 above in this volume.

The Greco-Roman method may well illustrate the procedure employed by Luke. It seems likely that Luke has faithfully represented the source content of the speeches in view of the fact that there was no convention among ancient historians

important literary function in Luke's presentation, just as the Old Testament played an important historical role in the preaching of the early church.

Luke is faithfully continuing the tradition of the earliest Christian sermons by quoting the Old Testament in his literary work. His quotations construct a carefully framed theological function because they express his ideological viewpoint, albeit in a phraseological manner. We have seen that a narrator's point of view is often most effectively communicated through the use of both ideas and phrases.

Luke desired to fit the history of the young church into the total panoramic schema of God's redemptive history. Because of this perspective, his use of *imitatio* served him well, as Brodie, Fitzmyer, and others have demonstrated. But beyond this creative use of the Old Testament, Luke has also quoted it frequently to express his viewpoint ideologically. He has portrayed his leading characters as the servants of God akin to the saints of old. Peter, Stephen and Paul use the words of Moses, David, even God himself. Luke approves of these characters and believes that their speeches and actions are part of a larger redemptive history with roots in the patriarchal beginnings of ancient Israel.

Luke's use of the Old Testament is most effective where he reports the words of characters speaking to hostile, or at least non-receptive, Jewish audiences. This is especially apparent in Stephen's speech in chapter 7. The rejection of Jesus (and eventually Stephen) is tantamount to the rejection experienced by Joseph, Moses, and the prophets. But the use of the Old Testament to indict the Jewish opponents of the Gospel is also clear in Peter's initial address to the multitudes at Pentecost (Acts 2.13), his appearance before the Sanhedrin (Acts 4.1–3), and Paul's speech at the synagogue at Antioch in Pisidia (Acts

---

freeing them to create speeches. See Ben Witherington, III, *The Book of Acts in its First Century Setting*, vol. VII (Grand Rapids, forthcoming); F. F. Bruce, "The Speeches in Acts – Thirty Years After," in *Reconciliation and Hope*, ed. R. Banks (Exeter, 1974), pp. 53–68; S. E. Porter, "Thucydides 1.22.1 and Speeches in Acts: Is There a Thucydidean View?," *NovT* 32 (1990), 121–142; and J. B. Polhill, *Acts*, NAC 26 (Nashville, 1992), pp. 44–47.

13.45,50).[37] Luke sees a parallel between the rejection of the Christian Gospel and the rejection of God and his leadership during the Old Testament period. His frequent use of the Old Testament on the lips of his characters expresses this viewpoint phraseologically.

In the Acts of the Apostles, the first Christians stand squarely in the Old Testament tradition. By preserving the Old Testament quotations in their speeches, Luke also stands in that tradition of faith. Theologically, we may speak in terms of Luke's understanding of *Heilsgeschichte*. Through his phraseological use of Old Testament expressions, Luke makes Peter, Stephen, Paul (and himself as hidden narrator) ideological extensions of the Old Testament story, participating in and continuing that salvation history.[38] Luke's skillful use of Old Testament quotations reveals not only the missionary purpose of the apostolic speeches historically, but also the polemical and theological purpose of the Book of Acts literarily.

---

[37] Paul's speech in Lystra of Lycaonia (Acts 14.15–17) is an exception since he was not dealing with a Jewish audience in this context.

[38] Jervell even states that Luke *intends* to write salvation history, which is to say that "Luke obviously has the idea that he is contributing to the Scriptures" (Jacob Jervell, "The Future of the Past: Luke's Vision of Salvation History and its Bearing on his Writing of History," pp. 104–126 in this volume).

CHAPTER 13

Editing the Good News: some synoptic lessons for the study of Acts

Ben Witherington, III

Perhaps it is a result of the canonical division of Luke–Acts, or perhaps it has been caused by the over-compartmentalization of NT studies in the guild, but whatever the cause, the study of Luke's use of sources in Acts has tended to be treated differently than his use of sources in his Gospel, especially in regard to the speeches in Acts.[1] This, I am convinced, is a mistake, for several good reasons.

First, the prologue to the Gospel (Lk. 1.1–4) and the first verse of Acts (1.1) make rather clear that the author considers the book we call Acts as the continuation of, or second volume of, his narrative.[2] Second, the detailed study of R. C. Tannehill has shown that a good case can be made for the general *narrative* unity of Luke–Acts.[3] Third, C. H. Talbert has shown

---

[1] It is not convincing to argue that because Luke seems to have no literary predecessors in composing a history of the early church, he also did not have sources, both written and oral, for Acts comparable to his sources for the Gospel material. *Contra* C. K. Barrett, *Luke the Historian in Recent Study* (Philadelphia: Fortress, 1970), pp. 21ff. For Luke, who sees the story of both Jesus and of his successors as part of the sacred story of salvation history, it is likely that he sought out, investigated, and sifted sources for both volumes in a similar manner.

[2] I offer an extended defense of this conclusion in my forthcoming commentary on the Acts of the Apostles for Eerdmans.

[3] See R. C. Tannehill, *The Narrative Unity of Luke–Acts: A Literary Interpretation* (2 vols., Philadelphia: Fortress, 1986,1990). This raises interesting questions about treating Luke's Gospel as a separate *genre* of literature from that of Acts. I am persuaded that Luke and Acts share the same genre – that of historical monograph in the Hellenized Jewish mold. It is, of course, true that the Gospel focuses predominantly on a central figure, Jesus, whereas Acts has no such singular focus, and that Acts has more speech material than the Gospel, but neither of these facts requires us to distinguish between the two volumes as far as genre or editorial technique is concerned. Biographical elements, passages, and even focus were not uncommon in some Hellenistic historical monographs about kings and the major events in which they participated. See A.

that the two volumes have certain structural similarities, for instance paradigmatic speeches in Luke 4 and Acts 2 presage the drama that follows.[4] Fourth, D. Juel has shown that even beyond the level of literary patterns, there is a thematic unity between Luke and Acts.[5] Fifth, G. Lüdemann has argued persuasively that a comparison of Acts with some material in Paul's letters (for example Acts 18 and 1 and 2 Corinthians), makes clear that Luke is most definitely drawing on various traditions in Acts, as he did in his first volume.[6] The uniformity of style in much of Acts does not count against such a conclusion, as one can equally well point to the similarity of style of the Gospel of Luke and Acts, and no one is arguing against the idea of extensive use of sources in the Third Gospel.[7]

In other words, there are a variety of reasons for thinking that Luke's purposes and *modus operandi* are one and the same, or closely compatible, in the two volumes. It thus seems very likely that the way Luke handled his source material in his first volume ought to provide us with *some* clues about how he

Momigliano, *The Development of Greek Biography* (Cambridge University Press, Harvard, MA, 1971), pp. 62ff. I would argue that one must pay strict attention to Lk. 1.1–4, where we are *not* told that Luke will recite a *bios*, but rather that he will narrate "the things which have happened among us." In other words the focus will be on events and actions rather than on personality *per se*, a description which suits Acts as well as, if not better than, the Gospel. See C. K. Barrett, "The Third Gospel as a Preface to Acts? Some Reflections," in *The Four Gospels 1992: Festschrift F. Neirynck*, ed. F. Van Segbroeck et al. (Louvain: Louvain University Press, 1992), pp. 1451–1466. Luke–Acts is about the actions of God through Jesus, the Holy Spirit, and the proclamation of the Word, all of which bring salvation to both Jew and Gentile in fulfillment of the promises of Scripture. I will deal with this matter at much greater length in my forthcoming Acts commentary.

4 See C. Talbert, *Literary Patterns, Theological Themes, and the Genre of Luke–Acts* (Missoula: Scholars Press, 1974). These sorts of parallels can be overpressed. Cf. the critique of Talbert's study in J. Fitzmyer, *The Gospel according to Luke I–IX* (Garden City: Doubleday), pp. 96–97.

5 D. Juel, *Luke–Acts: The Promise of History* (Atlanta: John Knox, 1983).

6 G. Lüdemann, *Early Christianity according to the Traditions in Acts* (Minneapolis: Fortress, 1989), pp. 9ff.

7 The Lucan vocabulary in the Gospel involves 2,055 words, of which 971 are *hapax legomena* and 352 are *dis legomena*, while in Acts there are 2,038 words, of which 943 are *hapax legomena* and 335 are *dis legomena*. There are at least 151 characteristic phrases in Luke's Gospel that are either never found in the other Gospels or are found twice as often in Luke. On all this see J. A. Fitzmyer, *The Gospel according to Luke 1–9* (Garden City: Doubleday, 1981), p. 109. It is interesting that 90 percent of his vocabulary is found in the LXX, and his use of it most resembles 2 Maccabees.

handled his oral and/or written sources in Acts, even though we have little and in some cases no access to those Acts sources now. I submit that a study of how Luke handles Mark, and to a lesser degree Q, should give us some basic clues about the character, style, and tendencies of his editorial work in general. This will provide us with a type of external check on our hypotheses about the sources and sorts of material we find in Acts.[8]

I LUKE'S HANDLING OF MARK

It will be worth while to be clear about the facts first. If one counts verses, out of a total of 661 verses in Mark, 350, or about 55 percent, appear in some form in Luke. If we count words the statistics are a bit different. Luke has 7,036 of Mark's 8,485 words. If we analyze the 55 percent Luke takes over from Mark, even on a conservative word count Luke reproduces about 53 percent of Mark's exact words, which is 2 percent more than Matthew does with the same material. One must say on this basis alone that there is a continuing and concerted effort on the part of Luke to reproduce the majority of the substance of the source material he takes over. Even more telling is the fact that when Luke is presenting sayings material that he found in Mark the "words of Jesus are hardly altered at all."[9] This is sometimes put down to the great reverence for the

[8] I am assuming, with the vast majority of scholars, the usual solution to the synoptic problem with Luke using Mark, and some form of Q. I will not be examining the L material since we have no external means of checking how Luke handles it, whereas at least with the Q material we can compare the use of the data in Matthew, even though we have no Q document to consult. I am by no means the first to pursue this sort of investigation. A. Von Harnack in his landmark work entitled *Luke the Physician: The Author of the Third Gospel and the Acts of the Apostles*, trans. J. R. Wilkinson (London: Williams and Norgate, 1911), pp. 87ff. showed that an examination of the way Luke uses Mark and Q reflects a conservative style of editing. J. Dupont was later to stress in *The Sources of Acts* (London: Darton, Longman, 1964), p. 84, n. 26: "Despite the numerous revisions made by Luke, the style, syntax, and vocabulary of Mark recur everywhere in the sections which the third Gospel owed to the second." By contrast, the "we" sections in Acts, as both Harnack and Dupont noted, are replete with Lucan vocabulary and reflect his style. I would suggest that it is in the latter material that we see what Luke's style looks like when he is not drawing on sources other than his own notes.
[9] K. F. Nickle, *The Synoptic Gospels: An Introduction* (Atlanta: John Knox, 1980), p. 131.

sayings of Jesus in the early church, but it is at least arguable that it may simply reflect reverence for the teachings of his protagonist in the drama, a reverence he might also show for the teachings of Peter, James, or Paul in Acts.

Another way to state this matter is that "Luke has not exercised . . . linguistic renovation of the tradition in a comparable way throughout the whole of the material: in the narrative material, especially in the introduction to the pericopes, the Lucan linguistic peculiarities are four times as frequent as in the sayings of Jesus."[10] If Luke operated in a similar manner in Acts we might expect: (1) that some at least of the speech material of Peter, James, Paul, or Stephen might be handled more conservatively than some of the narrative material; (2) we would look for Luke's hand especially in the verses opening and closing pericopes, and perhaps especially in summary statements (for example Acts 2.42–47; 4.32–36). In any case we would get no encouragement from Luke's handling of sayings material in Mark for the supposition that Luke simply composed speeches or sayings for important Christian figures in Acts, though he likely edited or summarized them using some of his own favorite and more universally recognizable vocabulary.

This matter needs to be pursued a bit further by considering *what sort* of stylistic improvements Luke tends to make on his Marcan source. It is widely recognized that Luke wrote the best Greek in the NT (with the possible exception of the author of Hebrews). He writes in good Greek, and in some places seems to imitate the style of the LXX (for example in Luke 1–2), while at other points he displays a knowledge of rhetoric.[11]

[10] W. G. Kümmel, *Introduction to the New Testament* (London: SCM, 1975), p. 138.

[11] L. Alexander, "Luke's Preface in the Context of Greek Preface-Writing," *Nov. Test.* 28 (1) (1986), 48–74, has made a case for Luke's style being neither highbrow nor lowbrow, but rather *Fachprosa*, or to put it another way, *Zwischenprosa*. Whatever the merits of this argument in regard to Luke's prologue, I do not think the argument works with some of the speech material in Acts, in particular with some of the defense speeches, which show clear signs of good forensic rhetorical prose. See J. Neyrey, "The Forensic Defense Speech and Paul's Trial Speeches in Acts 22–26: Form and Function," in *Luke–Acts: New Perspectives from the Society of Biblical Literature Seminar*, ed. C. A. Talbert (New York: Crossroad, 1984), pp. 210–224, and

In handling Mark, Luke tends to eliminate foreign words that his audience was unlikely to know (for example Semitic words or phrases like Ταλιθα κουμ [Mark 5.41; cf. Lk. 8.54]), or replace colloquial terms with more generally familiar ones (κράβαττος in Mark 2.4 becomes in Lk. 5.19 κλινίδιον; "rabbi" in Mark 9.5; 10.51 becomes "master" in Lk. 9.33). Luke also tends to replace Mark's often abrupt adverbial connectives with smoother transitions (for example the omnipresent "immediately": Mark 1.12, "The Spirit immediately drove him out"; Lk. 4.1, "And Jesus, full of the Holy Spirit, returned").

Another good example of stylistic improvement is the handling of tenses. Of 151 examples of the historic present tense in Mark, only one survives in Luke, and furthermore Luke regularly changes Mark's use of the imperfect tense to the more literarily correct aorist.[12] Luke also regularly abbreviates the Marcan account (cf. Mark 4.1–9 to Lk. 8.4–8). Most of these sorts of changes do not affect the essential substance or thrust of the narrative in a significant way, and we may expect that Luke felt free to make these sorts of changes with the sources he used in Acts as well, so the document would have a more uniform and acceptable Greek style. This matter, however, needs to be approached with some caution, as there are some reasons to think that in Acts we may have a first and less stylisticly refined edition, while in the canonical form of Luke's Gospel we may have a second edition.[13]

Much more important is the evidence of theologically, ethically, or socially tendentious editing of the Marcan source by Luke. For example, Luke regularly eliminates Mark's references to Jesus' emotions (cf. pity in Mark 1.41 to Lk. 5.13; grief and anger in Mark 3.5 to Lk. 6.10). Luke also tempers the

---

B. W. Winter, "The Importance of the *Captatio Benevolentiae* in the Speeches of Tertullus and Paul in Acts 24.1–21," *JTS* NS 42 (1991), 505–531. Even if we argue that this is merely a matter of the form and style of a source used, it likely presupposes that Luke recognized a rhetorically effective speech or tradition when he saw one.

[12] See Nickle, *The Synoptic Gospels*, p. 132.

[13] See now J. B. Polhill, *Acts* (Nashville: Broadman, 1992), pp. 41ff., although I myself am not persuaded by the Proto-Luke hypothesis.

harshness of the portrayal of the disciples that is found in Mark. While in Mark 14.37–41 the disciples are caught sleeping in the garden of Gethsemane three times, Luke reduces this to one, and adds that they slept "for sorrow" (Lk. 22.45), something one would never have guessed from Mark's account. Or again in the stilling of the storm episode, Luke omits the rebuking tone of the cry for help by the disciples to Jesus found in Mark (cf. Mark 4.38 to Lk. 8.24). Yet it is also true that in Luke the cost of discipleship exceeds the Marcan cost (cf. Lk. 9.23, daily cross bearing, to Mark 8.34; cf. also Lk. 9.62; Lk. 18.18–30; 14.26).

The apologetic tendencies in Luke's editing of Mark show up not only in the treatment of the disciples but also in the treatment of other major positive figures in the narrative – such as Jesus or Jesus' family. For example, in Luke's handling of the Marcan material about Jesus' family in 3.19b–21,31–35, Luke omits the harsh verse 21, and softens the contrast found in Mark 3.31–35 between Jesus' physical family and the family of faith. While Mark dramatizes the difference by saying "And looking around on those who sat about him, he said, 'Here are my mother and brothers. Whoever does the will of God . . .,'" Luke in 8.19–21 simply has "But he said to them 'My mother and brothers are those who hear . . .," which could include the Holy Family. Or again Luke leaves out altogether a potentially offensive saying like Mark 13.32, though he includes other Marcan eschatological sayings about the second coming (cf. Mark 14.62 to Lk. 22.69).

Luke also, alone among the Synoptic Evangelists, often calls Jesus ὁ κύριος in his narrative introductions and conclusions to pericopes but not in the dialogue in the text itself (cf. Lk. 7.13; 10.1,41; 22.61 and the parallels).[14] This shows a sensitivity on Luke's part to avoid historical anachronism, while at the same time affirming his faith in Jesus as Lord in the narrative framework of the material.

On the social front Jesus is more emphatic in Luke than in

---

[14] The use of the vocative κύριε to address Jesus may be no more than a polite form of address (cf. Lk. 5.8), *pace* W. G. Kümmel, *Introduction to the New Testament*, p. 139.

Mark in expressing his love for the poor and oppressed and sinful, both men and women, including Jews, Samaritans, and Gentiles (cf. Lk. 5.1–2; 5.8; 7.12–15; 7.36ff.; 8.1–3; 10.38ff.; 15.1ff.; 17.11ff.; 18.9ff.; 19.1ff.; 23.27ff.). This is accompanied by an equally strong critique of the wealthy, and of Mammon as unrighteous in itself (cf. Lk. 6.25–26; 12.15ff.; 16.9,11, 19ff.). While Mark 10.21–23 certainly provides a strong critique of the wealthy, money is not said to be in itself "unrighteous" or unclean; indeed, the "Render unto Caesar" saying (Mark 12.13–17) may suggest that Jesus sees it as a normal and natural means of paying debts. In any case, Luke's handling of his Marcan material on these matters (cf. Lk. 20.20–26) comports with what one finds in Luke's form of Q as well where we have a blessing on the poor and those now hungering (Lk. 6.20ff.), compared to Matthew's poor in spirit.

The above has a direct bearing on our analysis of Acts because there too we find the intensification of discipleship demands (Acts 4.32–5.11); a stress on compassion for the poor (Acts 6; 9.36ff.); on the demonically oppressed and possessed (Acts 8.4–8; 16.16ff.); and of course on women (cf. Acts 9.36–40; 12.12–17; 16.12–15; 18.24–26; 21.8–9).[15] The thematic similarity and at points even unity of the two works is certainly a strong reason for thinking that when Luke did tendentious and not merely stylistic editing, he proceeded in the same manner in both volumes. Indeed, one may argue that since Acts is about more current events to which there were presumably more living eyewitnesses, there was *less* need for embellishment or amplification in the narrative and speech material in Acts than in the Gospels.[16]

That Luke has an interest in placing his source material in a broader historical framework is clear enough not only from the synchronisms in Lk. 2.1–2; 3.1–2, but also from the reference to

[15] On all of this see my *Women in the Earliest Churches* (Cambridge: Cambridge University Press, 1988), pp. 143ff. Luke's editorial tendencies were distinct and clear enough to some early Christian scribes who tried to reverse their thrust. See my "The Anti-Feminist Tendencies of the Western Text of Acts," *JBL* 103 (1984), 82–84.

[16] This is not to deny that Luke made the material his own in terms of style, and that he edited it according to his own purposes.

the Caesars and other known Roman officials (cf. Acts 11.28; 18.2; 18.12ff.). Here is yet another editorial technique that is carried over from one volume to the next in Luke–Acts, and reveals a consistent editorial agenda and approach. In some respects this places Luke in the same realm as the political historiography of a Thucydides or a Polybius, but Luke's focus is on a particular religious and social movement within the larger body politic, and the larger political affairs are only brought in as they have a bearing on the growth and development of the Christian movement.[17]

Luke's attitude toward editing a source like Mark is also shown in the fact that, unlike Matthew, who tends to group similar sorts of material together (for example a group of parables, a group of miracles), Luke seems to have used Mark as his basic source providing the outline of the progression of the Gospel story, and into that outline he seems to have integrated blocks of Q and special L material. The Marcan blocks of material are basically found in Lk. 3.1–6.19; 8.4–9.50; and 18.15–24.11, while the Q material is found in two major blocks Lk. 6.20–8.3 and 9.51–18.14, with special L material largely found before these blocks in Luke 1–2, or after them in the passion and resurrection narratives, though there is likely some L material in 9.51–18.14 as well. What this tells us about Luke is that he respects his sources to a significant degree and by and large does not try to pull them apart, but rather integrates them in large blocks into his Marcan outline. This technique reveals to us someone who is more a creative editor than author, more reviser than originator of his material.

---

17 See especially D. P. Moessner, "Re-reading Talbert's Luke: The *Bios* of 'Balance' or the 'Bias' of History?," in *Cadbury, Knox, and Talbert: American Contributions to the Study of Acts*, ed. M. C. Parsons and J. B. Tyson (Atlanta: Scholars Press, 1992), pp. 203–228. Moessner says that this chronicling of a religious movement makes Acts a new subspecies of the genre of ancient historiography. I tend to agree with this point, as well as his overall argument that Luke–Acts should be seen as two volumes of a single historical monograph. This means that the Gospel of Luke should not be seen as a straightforward *bios*, but rather as a sort of history writing that has a particular biographical interest in the part which one key figure plays in the larger drama of salvation history.

II LUKE'S HANDLING OF Q

If Luke's handling of Mark suggests an editor, who while certainly having his own agendas and style, nonetheless manifests a considerable degree of restraint in his handling of his sources and does not feel free to create narratives out of wholecloth,[18] this is all the more the case in his handling of Q, which is mainly a sayings source. Of course our observations about the Q material have a lesser degree of objectivity, since we have no Q document to which we may compare Luke's version of the shared material. Nevertheless, a series of examples reveal some interesting trends.

In the first place, Matthew seems to have been much more likely to reproduce the *content* of his source than Luke. Matthew takes over 90 percent of his Marcan source, while Luke takes over considerably less. It is not a surprise, then, that when we compare Luke's Q Sermon in 6.20–49 to Matt. 5–7 we find that Luke's only has 29 verses while Matthew's is over three times as long (111 verses).[19] Luke, however, seems to have had a greater tendency to preserve the *order* of his material in Q, just as he did with his Marcan source. In terms of wording of material retained, I see no good reason to prefer Luke's wording over Matthew's in the Q material as a *general* policy. As J. A. Fitzmyer says, Matthew is often more apt to preserve the original wording of a saying than Luke.[20] Each example should be judged on its own merits.[21] Nevertheless, neither Matthew nor Luke is simply cavalier in his handling of the Q material.

Let us consider first a few examples from the Sermon on the Mount that reveal something of Luke's editorial tendencies. In the Beatitudes we notice that the Lucan form in Lk. 6.20–21

---

[18] *Pace* J. Drury, *Tradition and Design in Luke's Gospel* (London: Darton, Longman, and Todd, 1976), pp. 82ff.

[19] There are a few verses of the Sermon that appear in some form elsewhere in Luke, particularly in his travel narrative in Luke 9–18.

[20] J. A. Fitzmyer, "The Priority of Mark and the 'Q' source in Luke," *Perspective* 11 (1970), 131–170, here p. 154.

[21] See my discussion of the character of Q in *Jesus the Sage* (Minneapolis: Fortress, 1994), chap. 5.

speaks of the poor rather than the poor in spirit, and the hungry rather than Matthew's those who hunger and thirst for righteousness. It has commonly been argued that the Lucan form is likely more original, but this conclusion is hardly certain, in view of the evidence elsewhere in both Luke and Acts of Luke's interest in the poor and dispossessed (see above). On the other hand, it seems likely that Luke preserves the more authentic form of the saying found in Lk. 6.22–23, in view of the reference there to the Son of Man and the fathers, neither of which are found in the Matthean parallel. Luke's editorial tendencies did not involve adding colloquial phrases of Jewish provenance, and there is no evidence of Luke ever adding the phrase Son of Man to his source(s).[22]

In Lk. 6.35 (Matt. 5.44–45) the results are mixed. On the one hand the phrase "sons of the most High" in Luke seems more likely to be original, in view of Matthew's interest in the title Father, but on the other hand the mention of rain falling on the just and unjust seems more likely to be of Palestinian provenance than "for he is kind to the ungrateful and selfish."[23]

In Lk. 6.36 we find "Be merciful, even as your Father is merciful," whereas the Matthean form speaks of being perfect, as the heavenly Father is perfect. There is evidence elsewhere in uniquely Lucan material (1.50; 10.37) that mercy is an especial concern of Luke. Therefore, it would seem best to say that Luke may be more likely to have modified his source at this point than Matthew (except for Matthew's addition of "heavenly": cf. Matt. 6.32). If we consider the two versions of the Lord's prayer found in Lk. 11.2b–4 and Matt. 6.9b–13, what we basically find is Luke's tendency to abbreviate without altering the content of what is said in any major way. The same could be said of the somewhat lengthy saying about anxiety (Lk. 12.22–31; Matt. 6.25–33). For example, in Lk. 12.31 Luke simply has "Seek his kingdom, and these things shall be yours as well." If the saying originally included the

22 See I. H. Marshall, *The Gospel of Luke* (Exeter: Paternoster, 1978), p. 253.
23 See ibid., p. 264.

word "first" and the clause "and his righteousness," Luke has basically presented an abbreviated version.[24] It is quite believable that Luke would leave out the word "first," because its inclusion would suggest that seeking all these other things is acceptable after seeking the kingdom, something which does not comport with his view of money (see above).[25] A further example of condensing one's source material, this time by conflation, can be found in Lk. 6.43–45 where Luke seems to combine the tradition found in Matt. 7.17 and 12.35 with the possible addition of a saying about figs and grapes.[26]

A good example of editing that fits the pattern of Luke's theological tendencies can be found in Lk. 11.11–13/Matt. 7.9–11. The saying closes with a reference to God's gifts: in Matthew to "good things," in Luke to the Holy Spirit. In view of the obvious interest in the Holy Spirit in both volumes of Luke's work (mentioned seventeen times in Luke and fifty-seven in Acts), and the evidence that he has introduced the Spirit three other times at the beginning of the travel account (10.21; 12.10, 12), it is likely he has done so here as well.[27]

Even slight editorial touches show the tendencies of Luke to make sayings sensible to a broader and more Gentile audience. For example, Luke's form of the brief analogy about building on solid or unsound foundations (Lk. 6.47–49/Matt. 7.24–27) leaves out the contrast between the *wise* and *foolish* man which is likely original, going back to Jewish sapiential discussions.[28] He also changes the contrast between building on rock and building on sand to building on rock and building without a foundation, and closes with the less Semitic phrasing "and the ruin of that house was great" (cf. Matthew's "and great was the fall of it"). It seems clear enough that Luke is concerned to

---

[24] Although the Matthean version might suggest that the issue was a matter of priorities, not an exclusive concern for the kingdom.

[25] Nor does it appear to comport with what is likely the original text of Lk. 10.41–42. See my discussion in *Women in the Ministry of Jesus* (Cambridge: Cambridge University Press, 1987), pp. 102–103.

[26] See J. D. Crossan, *Sayings Parallels* (Philadelphia: Fortress, 1986), p. 45.

[27] See Fitzmyer, *Luke I–IX*, pp. 227ff.

[28] See my discussion of Jesus' indebtedness to Jewish wisdom material in *Jesus the Sage*, chap. 4.

make his sources comprehensible to a broader audience that is not predominantly Jewish in character.[29]

There also seems to have been some attempt by Luke to make sayings less theologically confusing for a Gentile audience. For instance, in Lk. 12.4–5 Luke has a longer form of the fear saying also found in Matt. 10.28 and later in 2 Clement 5.4b. The Clement form of the saying follows the Matthean one and suggests that the phrase "rather fear him who can destroy both soul and body in hell" is original. Luke however has "fear him who, after he has killed the body, has power to throw you into hell. Yes, I tell you, fear him!" I would suggest that this change may have been made because in the Greco-Roman world the idea of having a physical body in Hades that could be destroyed *there* would seem nonsensical, as might also the idea of the annihilation of the soul.

Many more such examples can be produced that reveal that sometimes Luke's editing is a matter of style and simple abbreviation, sometimes it is a matter of modifying sayings so that they would make sense to his Gentile audience without drastic change in the material's substance, and finally sometimes we see evidence in the Q material of modifications made because of certain theological, ethical, or social themes Luke wishes to highlight. In none of these cases, however, do we have any clear evidence of Luke simply creating sayings or narratives *ex nihilo*. At the most one may suggest that Luke may have created some summaries as transitional material, but even then they were likely based on some traditions he had available to him (see, for example, Lk. 8.1–3).[30]

III A SYNOPTIC "PROBLEM" WITHIN ACTS ITSELF

It will be worth our while to reflect on what could be called a synoptic problem in Acts itself, for it shows Luke presenting

---

[29] It is not impossible that Luke–Acts was in fact written for Luke's Gentile patron, Theophilus, perhaps a new convert needing instruction, and not for a community at all.

[30] See my discussion of this pericope in "On the Road with Mary Magdalene, Joanna, Susanna, and other Disciples: Luke 8.1–3," *ZNW* 70 (3–4) (1979), 242–248.

essentially the same story to three different audiences and shows the kinds of changes that result from the change in audiences *within the narrative* of Acts itself. There are important lessons to be learned here about Luke as an editor, especially since this example involves both sayings and narrative material. I am, of course, referring to the three accounts of Paul's conversion, which are sometimes assumed to provide clear evidence of Luke's carelessness as an editor and lack of concern for historical precision.[31] Instead they show Luke's tendency to adapt his source material according to the audience being addressed, *without* drastically altering that source material. For the sake of clarity it is necessary that I present a synoptic parallel of the three accounts of this story.[32]

Acts 9.1ff.	Acts 22.1ff.	Acts 26.1ff.
third person	first person	first person
Luke's summary	in Hebrew/Aramaic	spoken by Paul
from talking with	Paul's Greek	to Festus – Luke
Paul	summary given to	present
	Luke?	
Saul to high priest	letters from high	authorization from
letters to synagogues	priest and council	chief priests (verse 10)
bring Christians	bring back	
back to Jerusalem	Christians to	
(verse 2)	Jerusalem for	
	punishment (verse 5)	
light from heaven	at noon, great light	midday, light from
flashed about him	from heaven shone	heaven shining
(verse 3)	about me (verse 6)	around me and with
		me (verse 13)

[31] And also is assumed to show Luke's ignorance of Paul's letters. For a recent attempt to argue that Luke's portrait of Paul is in significant disagreement with the image of Paul in the letters see John C. Lentz, *Luke's Portrait of Paul* (Cambridge: Cambridge University Press, 1993). While I would agree that Luke by and large tries to depict Paul as an honorable person of reasonably high status, I do not regard such a portrait as incompatible with what one finds in the letters. Paul's rhetoric about shame and being shamed in his letters must be taken in its proper rhetorical sense and context. See my *Conflict and Community in Corinth* (Grand Rapids: Eerdmans, 1994).

[32] It must be kept squarely in view that the first of these accounts is part of the Acts narrative, and the other two a use of the same material in speeches.

fell to ground, heard a voice saying (verse 4)	fell to ground, heard a voice (verse 7)	we all fell to ground, I heard voice *in Hebrew* (verse 14)
"Saul, Saul, why do you persecute me?"	same as Acts 9	same as Acts 9 "It hurts you to kick against the goads."
"Who are you, sir?". "I am Jesus, whom you are persecuting." (verses 4–5	same as Acts 9 "I am Jesus of Nazareth, whom . . ." (verses 7–8)	The Lord said : "I am Jesus whom you are pers." (verse 15)
"Rise, enter city. You will be told what to do" (verse 6)	"What shall I do, sir?" "Rise, go into Damascus. You'll be told all that is appointed for you to do." (verse 10)	"Rise, stand on your feet. I have appeared to you for this purpose, to appoint you to serve and bear witness to the things in which you have seen me and to those in which I'll appear to you. Delivering you from the people and from Gentiles to whom I send you, to open their eyes, for they might turn from darkness to light" (verses 16–18)
Men stood speechless, hearing voice, seeing no one (verse 7)	men saw light, did not hear voice of one speaking to me. (verse 9)	
Saul arises. Can see nothing. Three days without sight and food. Led by hand into Damascus (verses 8–9)	Paul cannot see because of brightness of light. Led by hand of companions into Damascus. (verse 11)	——
vision of Ananias (verses 10–16)	Ananias (no vision mentioned) "Brother Saul, receive your sight." (verse 13)	——

Ananias lays hands on Saul. "Jesus sent me that you may regain sight and be filled with the Holy Spirit." (verse 17)	"God of our fathers appointed you to know his will, and see the just one, and hear a voice from his mouth. You'll be a witness to all people of what you've seen and heard." (verse 14)	
something like scales fall from Saul's eyes; he regains sight and is baptized (verse 19)	"rise and be baptized, and wash away your sins, calling on his name." (verse 16)	—— (no mention of Ananias)
takes food and is strengthened (verse 19)	——	the above was a heavenly vision

We will start by discussing the differences in the accounts in Acts of Paul's conversion.[33] Some of the differences are likely due to the fact that these three accounts serve different purposes and may originally have been meant for different audiences, though now they are all part of Luke's account written for Theophilus.[34] In general I subscribe to the thesis of R. Maddox that the narrative in Acts 9 is presented as a conversion story while the other two accounts are presented as call narratives because by now the audience will be familiar with the story of how Paul became a Christian and will be more interested in the authenticity of his call to ministry and how he came to be the famous missionary.[35]

It is true enough that these accounts are *summaries* and Luke

---

[33] Some of this material appears in a somewhat different form in my *Paul's Narrative Thought World: The Tapestry of Tragedy and Triumph* (Louisville: Westminster/ J. Knox, 1994), pp. 218ff.

[34] For a fuller discussion of this material in comparison to what Paul says about himself see ibid., pp. 220–225. I agree with Neyrey, "The Forensic Defense Speech and Paul's Trial Speeches," pp. 210–224, that the speeches in Acts 22 and 26 reflect the proper rhetorical form of forensic defense speeches, and that this in part accounts for some of the differences between them and the account in Acts 9.

[35] R. Maddox, *The Purpose of Luke–Acts* (Edinburgh: T. & T. Clark, 1982), p. 74.

has written them up in his own style and way.[36] The accounts, especially in Acts 22 and 26, may be condensations from speeches made by Paul himself. Paul, or if it is a Lucan creation, Luke, would be presenting this story to two very different audiences here and wishing to convey some different aspects of the account to these two groups.

A further complicating factor is that Luke tells us that Paul spoke the speech we have in Acts 22 *not* in Greek but "in the Hebrew tongue," which likely means in Aramaic. We however have this speech in Luke's Greek translation and condensation. Furthermore, we are told in Acts 26.14 that Jesus spoke to Saul from heaven in Aramaic or Hebrew in the first place, but in all three accounts we only have a Greek version of his words.

One may suspect that Acts 22 is Luke's own composition and account of that encounter based on Paul's summary report to him.[37] One must bear in mind that we have no clear evidence that Luke could even understand Aramaic, as he always seems to use the LXX or some Greek version of the OT in his two-volume work.[38] Luke, of course, was not present on the Damascus road either, and so the account in Acts 9 is likewise secondhand, perhaps based on Paul's relating of the account to Luke. Taken at face value, the "we" in Acts 21.17ff. and Acts 27.1 suggests that Luke was present with Paul at the occasion of the relating of the conversion to Festus.

When one compares Acts 22 and 26, one will notice that while in Acts 26 Paul presents himself as a prophet called of God and speaks in a way that will make this clear to Festus and Agrippa, in Acts 22 he is trying to present himself as a good Jew, a former Pharisee, to his fellow Jews and accordingly as one who is faithful to the God of Abraham. All three of these accounts go immediately back to Luke, who wrote them up, but in the case of Acts 9 and 22 ultimately they may go back to

---

[36] See my discussion on pp. 23–32 above about the conventions in regard to the handling of speeches in Hellenistic historiography.

[37] I still believe that it is more likely than not that Luke was a sometime companion of Paul, and that the "we" sections of Acts derive from his own personal encounters. I do not think, however, that he reflects much if any knowledge of Paul's earlier letters. Cf. Polhill, *Acts*, pp. 50ff.

[38] See the chapter by B. T. Arnold in this volume.

Paul, while Acts 26 is Luke's own firsthand account in all likelihood.

One of the factors which must count in favor of seeing these as narratives of real events and real speeches is their obvious differences. If Luke had set out to compose on his own multiple accounts of Saul's conversion, we would have expected the narratives to be more similar than they are. The account in Acts 9 or Acts 22 cannot be based on the account in Acts 26, where Luke was present, because Acts 26 omits Ananias and his role altogether.

The three accounts in Acts 9, 22, and 26 agree in essentials but differ in some details, some of which are inconsequential, and some of which are quite important. The essentials on which all three accounts agree are as follows: (1) Saul was authorized by a or some priestly authorities in Jerusalem to do something against Christians, and as the story goes on it is implied that the authorization applied to Christians in Damascus; (2) while Saul was traveling to Damascus, he saw a light and heard a voice; (3) the voice said "Saul, Saul, why do you persecute me?"; (4) Saul answered "Who are you, sir?"; (5) the voice said 'I am Jesus, whom you are persecuting." In other words, all three accounts confirm that Saul had an encounter including a real communication from Jesus in the context of a bright light which turned Saul from an anti- to a pro-Christian person. At the very least, one may say that this distilled summary comports with what one finds in Paul's letters when the apostle speaks of or alludes to his conversion.[39]

There is also a stress that this encounter was not merely subjective, for it also affected those who were with Saul to some degree. In Luke's portrayal of these events, Saul's name does not change at the point of his conversion: rather when he begins to be the missionary to the Gentiles, he adopts a Greek name (Παῦλος: cf. Acts 13.9).[40] It would appear, especially in

---

[39] Notice that reducing these three accounts to the clear similarities includes both sayings and narrative material.

[40] This story may even suggest that Saul took the name in order to aid in the process of converting another Paul who was a Gentile and a proconsul on Cyprus, Sergius Paulus: cf. Acts 13.7.

view of the way Acts ends, that Luke's interest in Paul is not purely personal, but is chiefly because Paul is part of and a vital player in the growing early Christian movement. He is not trying to present an encomium or even simply an *apologia* for Paul in Acts, and thus there is no good reason to think that he has significantly recast the telling of the story of Paul's conversion.

When we turn to consider further differences in the three Acts accounts, we must be prepared to examine them very carefully. Certainly, ancient historians were not nearly so concerned as we are today about minute details.[41] Often they were satisfied with general rather than punctilious accuracy so long as they presented the substance and significance of a speech or event. It is thus wrong to press Luke to be precise at points where he intended only to give a summarized and generalized account. Luke clearly exercised a certain literary freedom with his material, arranging it so as to get across the point he desired. This is only what one would expect from people who grew up in an environment saturated with and enamored of rhetoric, where persuasion and not merely informing the audience was a major goal.[42]

An example of Luke's literary freedom may be found in the Acts 26 account where we have a sentence not found in the other two accounts – "It hurts you to kick against the goads." A goad was a wooden stick with metal spikes against which it was fruitless to kick since one would only hurt oneself. This expression was a *Greek*, not Jewish, idiom, and it meant "It is fruitless to struggle against God, or against one's destiny." This proverbial saying was one that an Agrippa or Festus would likely have understood and perhaps even have heard before, but it is hardly something one would expect to originate on the lips of Jesus in Aramaic. Paul, or Luke, inserts this line into the discourse to make clear that Jesus had indicated to Paul that he was struggling against God by persecuting Christians, and indeed against his own destiny. This phrase, which Jesus did

---

[41] See the chapters by C. K. Barrett and W. J. McCoy in this volume.

[42] See my discussion in *Conflict and Community in Corinth*, pp. 10ff.

not likely use when he spoke to Saul originally, indicated to the audience that Paul was pursuing his present mission because God had mandated him to do so.

Another piece of evidence of literary license is that when one compares Acts 22 and Acts 26 one notices that the commission that comes to Saul from Ananias' lips in Acts 22 comes directly from Jesus in Acts 26, where there is no mention of the intermediary Ananias. Thus we must conclude that in Acts 26 either Luke (or Paul?) has telescoped the account. This should not trouble us, since the commission that came to Saul was ultimately from Jesus even if it did actually come *through* Ananias. Ananias could be left out of the account in Acts 26 since the crucial point was that Paul was authorized by God to do what he was doing. The differences between the three accounts on this matter can be accounted for in terms of Paul's or Luke's editing of the account to suit the purpose and audience currently being addressed.

Another point of difference in the accounts is that we are told in Acts 26.14 "we fell to the ground," while in Acts 9 and 22 it is only Saul who falls to the ground while the others stand (cf. Acts 9.7). Here again Luke may be simply generalizing because Saul was not alone in this encounter. The others also saw and heard something. It is in any case unlikely that Saul knew the position of his companions at this juncture since we are told he was blinded by the light! The point, then, of saying "we" was to indicate that this experience involved more than one person and was not simply the product of Saul's overheated imagination.

The most difficult difference to account for in these three narratives is what seems to be a flat contradiction between Acts 9.7 and Acts 22.9. The former says "the men stood speechless hearing the voice but seeing no one," while the latter says "the men saw the light but did not hear the voice of the one speaking to me." Scholars have argued that here is clear evidence that Luke was not a careful editor of his material. There is, however, another possible explanation.

The verb ἀκούω with the genitive normally means that someone has heard the sound of something or someone, while this same verb with the accusative refers to both hearing and understanding something. This sort of distinction is clearly in evidence in classical Greek, and the only question is whether Luke might have used it here. If so, then the meaning of Acts 9.7 would be that Saul's companions, like Saul, heard the sound of the voice communicating to Saul, while in Acts 22.9 the point would be that unlike Saul, the companions did not hear intelligible words so as to understand what the voice was actually saying to Saul. In Acts 9.7 the text says that the companions saw *no one*, while in Acts 22.9 there is a stress that these men saw the light that accompanied Saul's personal encounter with Jesus.

Thus we can explain these differences in the two accounts as follows: (1) only Saul had a personal encounter with Jesus involving seeing someone and hearing distinct words; (2) his companions saw and heard the phenomena that accompanied this encounter but had no such encounter themselves. Notice that Acts 22.9 does not say that they did not hear the sound of the voice at all, but only that they did not hear "the voice of the one speaking *to me*."

One more difference is of note. Acts 9 says nothing about Saul as a missionary to the Gentiles, while Acts 22 and 26 stress this point. This is likely because Luke did not need to mention this matter in Acts 9 as it would be evident in what followed, while in Acts 22 and 26 Paul did have to mention this to his audiences to justify what he had been doing. Each of the narratives and speeches is shaped to serve different purposes, and this is the major reason for the variations in the accounts.

What is crucial about this discussion for our purposes is that these three accounts show both the limits and the license of Luke's editorial approach. Most of the basic story and the crucial sayings of Jesus are identical or nearly so in all three accounts, but variations occur because of the audience being addressed within the telling of the story in Acts, and because in the latter two accounts the material is being used rhetorically in speeches. I would suggest that even here Luke has been faithful to his stated intention in Lk. 1.1–4 to carefully consult and arrange source material, the arranging and editing sometimes being done according to Luke's theological, ethical, and social purposes.

L. T. Johnson helpfully sums up matters as follows:

Concerning Luke's use of sources and his historical reliability, therefore extreme positions should be avoided. It is true that we cannot, because of Luke's artistry, determine the extent or even the existence of written sources [in Acts]. But this does not imply that Luke did not make use of tradition, or that he made up events solely from his imagination. Likewise, because Luke selected and shaped his story does not mean that it is simply fiction. These are false alternatives. All historical writing, after all, demands a selection and creative shaping of materials . . . Narrative can be significantly shaped by an author's imagination and still report substantial historical information . . . Where we can check him on details, Luke's factual accuracy in the latter part of Acts is impressive.[43]

I would add to this that the same can be said for the first part of Acts as well, as C. Hemer and others have shown.[44]

IV LUKE AS AN EDITOR — FINAL REFLECTIONS

What have we learned from this all too brief survey of Luke's editorial work? Perhaps the first thing to be said is that he should be compared with other ancient historians and their methods. On these grounds, Luke appears to be rather more like a Thucydides or a Polybius, and the character of his work like what Lucian said *ought* to be the character of the work of one who seeks to do history writing, rather than say a Livy, for whom history writing seems often to have been an exercise in almost pure Roman propaganda, with little serious concern for historical accuracy.[45]

---

[43] L. T. Johnson, *The Acts of the Apostles* (Collegeville: Liturgical Press, 1992), pp. 7, 5.

[44] See C. J. Hemer, *The Book of Acts in the Setting of Hellenistic History* (Winona Lake: Eisebrauns, 1990), pp. 1ff.

[45] This sort of judgment could also be rendered even against the cynical and critical Tacitus. See K. Wellesley, "Can You Trust Tacitus?," *Greece and Rome* 1 (1951), 13–37. Especially telling is the comparison between Tacitus' version of a famous speech by Claudius and the actual record of the speech on the so-called Claudian tablet. There are notable differences between earlier Greek historiography and Roman historiography especially as it developed during the Empire. My strong impression is that Luke is much more like Polybius and Thucydides than the later

It is clear enough from the above that Luke used sources, and that he edited them in various ways and to various ends. He has an overarching concern in both his volumes to make his story comprehensible in clear Greek to what appears to be a largely Gentile audience, or at least one not familiar with various aspects of Palestinian Jewish culture and colloquialisms. This largely explains why Luke edits certain things out. On the addition side of the ledger, however, Luke's interest in the poor, oppressed, and dispossessed, in the work of the Holy Spirit, in the universal spread of the Gospel up and down the social scale (the primary focus of Luke) and from Jerusalem to Rome (the focus of Acts) affects time and again how he edits his sources. One clear guide to Luke's editorial approach would be to search out the major themes and motifs in Luke–Acts, and when a particular passage appears with such a theme or motif, ask whether it is likely to betray Luke's own hand and agendas.

There are further lessons to be learned from a careful study of how Luke edited Mark and Q. Such a study offers no encouragement for thinking that Luke likely created speeches out of wholecloth in his second volume, any more than he did so in his first. Indeed, there is evidence that he may have treated certain kinds of speech material, particularly Jesus' sayings, more conservatively than he did even the narrative material. Possibly, though we cannot prove this, he treated important early Christian speeches with like reverence, faithfully summarizing their contents, using some of his own style and vocabulary. The fact that the speeches in Acts betray some elements of Lucan style and various Lucan themes likely shows that Luke has made this source material his own, con-

---

Roman writers such as Livy or Tacitus. See C. W. Fornara, *The Nature of History in Ancient Greece and Rome* (Berkeley: University of California Press, 1983), pp. 47ff. on the differences between Greek and Roman historiography. The Roman was not surprisingly fixated on one city and its history, Rome. The chief problem with E. Plümacher's *Lukas als hellenistischer Schrifsteller: Studien zur Apostelgeschichte* (Göttingen: Vandenhoeck and Ruprecht, 1972) is that he makes the mistake of comparing Luke to two "historians" with whom Luke has little in common – Livy and Dionysius of Halicarnassus. The former has been widely recognized as one who did not do careful research (*historia*), and the latter strongly subsumes history writing under the umbrella of epideictic rhetoric.

forming it to the style and agendas of the rest of the work.[46] What it does not reveal is that he did not use sources. Luke was a good editor, and as such we would only expect him to strive for a uniform style and presentation throughout his work.

The Marcan and Q material in Luke also suggests that Luke is most creative in his summary statements, and in the introductory and concluding verses to a given pericope that he is editing.[47] He is not, however, reluctant to edit out even a great deal of important material such as in the Sermon on the Mount, probably in order to make room for the inclusion of a variety of other traditions.[48]

In the end, in view of the considerable evidence that Luke and Acts are two volumes of one work, the burden of proof must be on those who want to suggest that Luke chose to deal with his source material (or lack thereof) in Acts significantly differently than he did in his Gospel. Even the differences in his threefold telling of Paul's conversion do not suggest a careless approach to his source material, or a lack of concern for basic historical accuracy. On the contrary, Luke believed that he was faithfully and in an orderly fashion presenting not theologized history or historicized theology, but rather theological or salvation history – the story of God's saving acts in and through Christ and his followers by the power of the Holy Spirit and for the sake of all humankind.[49] This is history writing that has not only theological, ethical, and social

---

[46] See now M. L. Soards, *The Speeches in Acts* (Louisville: Westminster/John Knox Press, 1994).

[47] Lüdemann, *Early Christianity*, pp. 16–18, comes to a similar conclusion about the narrative framework surrounding various of the traditions included in Acts.

[48] See the remarks of a careful scholar – Hemer, *The Book of Acts*, pp. 78–79: "But there is a prima facie case for saying . . . that the 'speeches,' of Luke's Gospel in particular, are largely dependent on extant or inferable sources [i.e. Mark and Q]. There is editing; there is rearrangement – and that may hardly be surprising in an 'episodic' narrative – but the striking thing is the extent to which Luke uses sources almost verbatim. This poses many questions about historicity and about the speeches in Acts. It may be argued that the words of Jesus were unique . . . But the preservation of the spoken word was not alien to the ancient world. The phenomenon merits further consideration."

[49] On this last point see M. Hengel, *Acts and the History of Earliest Christianity* (Philadelphia: Fortress, 1979), pp. 40ff.; Maddox, *The Purpose of Luke–Acts*, pp. 16ff.

agendas but theological, ethical, and social substance. Martin
Hengel said it best some time ago:

We only do justice to the significance of Luke as the first theological
historian of Christianity if we take seriously his work as a source, i.e. if
we attempt to examine it critically, reconstructing the story which he
tells by adding and comparing other sources. The radical "redaction-
critical" approach so popular today, which sees Luke above all as a
freely inventive theologian, mistakes his real purpose, namely that as
a Christian historian he sets out to report the events of the past that
provided the foundation for the faith and its extension. He does not
set out primarily to present his own "theology."[50]

[50] Hengel, *Acts*, pp. 67–68.

CHAPTER 14

The means of absent ends

Wm. F. Brosend, II

> He lived there two whole years at his own expense
> and welcomed all who came to him, proclaiming the
> kingdom of God and teaching about the Lord Jesus
> Christ with all boldness and without hindrance.
>
> (Acts 28.30–31)

The end of the book of Acts poses a significant problem for the
reader. Or it poses no problem at all. G. W. Trompf began an
essay on the end of Acts by arguing, "The present conclusion to
the book of Acts calls for an explanation . . . A modern reader
would like to learn how long Paul dwelt in Rome, whether he
lived there for a considerable period, was tried, imprisoned or
acquitted, whether he died there of 'natural causes' or was put
to death, or whether he subsequently journeyed to other parts
of the Mediterranean world."[1] In a dissertation on the end of
Acts written four years earlier, however, C. B. Puskas, Jr.
maintained, "A majority of scholars regard the problem of an
abrupt ending as a superficial one since Acts 28 can be seen as
a deliberate and complete conclusion from a literary and
theological standpoint."[2] In a footnote to these words Puskas
concludes, "It seems to us that the continued appearance of the
abrupt ending question in contemporary commentaries is more
a result of the self-imposed obligation of modern commentators

---

[1] G. W. Trompf, "On Why Luke Declined to Recount the Death of Paul: Acts 27–28
and Beyond," in Charles H. Talbert (ed.), *Luke–Acts: New Perspectives from the Society
of Biblical Literature Seminar* (New York, 1984), p. 225.

[2] C. B. Puskas, Jr., "The Conclusion of Luke–Acts: An Investigation of the Literary
and Theological Significance of Acts 28:16–31," Ph.D. dissertation, St. Louis University, 1980, p. 15.

to discuss the historical preoccupations of earlier commentators, than it is a result of the inherent importance of the question itself."[3]

This chapter maintains that both Trompf and Puskas are correct: The end of Acts is abrupt, but the abruptness of the ending was intentional and purposeful. I shall consider the significance of the end of Acts for discussions of its purpose, genre and date, and give attention to the literary precedents for the abrupt ending of Acts. My thesis is that conclusions about the conclusion of Luke–Acts are formed by, and in turn inform, conclusions about the genre, purpose and date of Luke's work. I shall also explore the implications of regarding Acts 28.30–31 as the intentionally abrupt ending of *Luke–Acts*, a topic rarely discussed even by those who hold most fervently to the idea of Luke–Acts as a single, two-volume, work.[4] Finally, I want to consider the origin and nature of Acts' ending within the context of Luke–Acts as a whole, to suggest that the most obvious precedent is another famously incomplete New Testament document, the Gospel of Mark.

PURPOSE AND ENDING

Scholars' conclusions about the appropriateness or abruptness of Acts 28.30–31 interact with their conclusions about the purpose, genre, and dating of Acts. While this chapter will in no manner presume to account for the literature on these areas of Luke–Acts study, a few important and representative examples should illustrate the importance which views on the purpose, genre, and date of Acts have for our understanding of its conclusion, and vice versa. Luke himself addressed the issue of the purpose of his work, so it seems a good place to begin:

Since many have undertaken to set down an orderly account of the events that have been fulfilled among us, just as they were handed on to us by those who from the beginning were eyewitnesses and servants

---

[3] Ibid., n. 2.

[4] Tannehill, for example, only makes mention of Lk. 3.6 "all flesh shall see the salvation of God," in his discussion of the end of Acts, contrasting this promise at the beginning of Luke with the blindness of the Jews in Acts 28.26 (cf. Isa. 6.9–10; Mark

of the word, I too decided, after investigating everything carefully from the very first, to write an orderly account for you, most excellent Theophilus, so that you may know the truth concerning the things about which you have been instructed. (Lk. 1.1–4, NRSV)

In the first book, Theophilus, I wrote about all that Jesus did and taught from the beginning until the day when he was taken up to heaven, after giving instructions through the Holy Spirit to the apostles whom he had chosen. After his suffering he presented himself alive to them by many convincing proofs, appearing to them during forty days and speaking about the kingdom of God. (Acts 1.1–3, NRSV)

Something, of course, seems missing. How gladly we would receive a verse along the lines of, "And now, Theophilus, I shall write to you of . . . in order that you may understand . . ." But this Luke does not give us, and so leaves it to the reader to discern the purpose of the second volume.

On the surface the answer seems obvious – to continue his account of "the events that have been fulfilled among us." Yet to what end? "To the ends of the earth" (Acts 1.8) is the first reply. One clear purpose of Luke's second volume is to narrate the spread of the Gospel throughout the Roman world, even to the Imperial City itself. Not surprisingly H. Conzelmann, given his view of salvation history divided into three epochs (the time of Israel, the time of Jesus, and the time of the church), understands the purpose of Acts to be the narration of events in this third epoch, itself divided into two parts.[5] For Conzelmann the end of Acts is in no way problematic because the purpose of Acts, to narrate the bringing of the Gospel to the ends of the earth (here represented by Rome), has been fulfilled. Thus there is nothing left to tell. "The purpose of the book has been fully achieved; therefore we ought to reject all hypotheses which understand the book as incomplete or which declare the ending to be accidental."[6]

4.12 = Lk. 8.9). Robert C. Tannehill, *The Narrative Unity of Luke–Acts: A Literary Interpretation*, vol. II, *The Acts of the Apostles* (Minneapolis, 1990), pp. 344–357.

[5] H. Conzelmann, *Acts of the Apostles*, trans. J. Limburg et al., Hermenia Series (Philadelphia, 1987), pp. xlv–xlvii.

[6] Ibid., p. 228.

A second purpose for Acts is apologetic. So argues F. F. Bruce, among many others:

When we examine the way in which Luke develops his narrative, we can hardly fail to be struck by his apologetic emphasis, especially in his second volume. He is concerned to defend Christianity against the charges which were popularly brought against it in the second half of the first century. We must recognize that in the eyes of those who set some store by law and order in the Roman Empire Christianity started off with a serious handicap. Its Founder had admittedly been condemned to death by a Roman governor on a charge of sedition.[7]

This apologetic intent is carried consistently through the work, according to Bruce, and reaches its culmination in Acts 28:

During this period the gospel was proclaimed freely in Rome through the lips of its chief messenger. The apologetic value of this fact was considerable. It is unlikely, Luke means to suggest, that if the gospel were illegal and subversive propaganda, it could have been taught for two years in the heart of the empire without let or hindrance . . . On this triumphant note, then, Acts is brought to an end.[8]

Again we see a view of purpose (apologetics) shaping a reading of the end of Acts. This reading of the end of Acts is one with which E. Haenchen concurred:

In Rome Paul works "unhindered." With this Luke brings to its final destination . . . the effort to prove that the Roman government was favourably disposed to early Christianity and permitted its proclamation . . . For the event which alone would have given telling force to the thesis of the favourable disposition and tolerance of Rome, Paul's liberation, Luke evidently could not report.[9]

If the purpose of Acts was to give an account of earliest Christianity which depicted the nascent movement as acceptable to the Roman authorities, it would hardly do to depict the execution of its chief spokesperson by those same authorities.

---

[7] F. F. Bruce, *The Book of the Acts*, The New International Commentary on the New Testament (Grand Rapids, 1970), p. 20.

[8] Ibid., p. 535.

[9] E. Haenchen, *The Acts of the Apostles*, trans. and rev. R. McL. Wilson (Philadelphia, 1971), p. 731.

Acts ends where it does, according to this reading, for apologetic reasons.[10]

But what if the purpose of Acts is entirely different? What if Acts was written to inform and entertain the earliest believers, not to impress authorities? This is the reading of R. Pervo in *Profit with Delight*.[11] Here we move close to the next section, on genre, for Pervo rejects historical and apologetic models for reading Acts. Instead he argues for parallels among the earliest novels, such as Chariton's *Chaereas and Callirhoe* and the later Apocryphal Acts, such as the Acts of Paul. And here Pervo runs into difficulty, for if the purpose of Acts is to entertain and instruct, spellbinding and gruesome executions are the order of the day! Recall only the Acts of Peter, which recounts Peter's head-downward crucifixion (from which position he offers an extended sermon), or the Acts of Paul, which recounts his beheading (complete with spurting milk instead of blood) and his appearance, resurrected, before Caesar.[12] While our tastes may be repulsed rather than entertained by such grisly depictions, ancient audiences were apparently delighted. For Luke to skip an opportunity to delight his audience is problematic for Pervo's reading; in the next section we shall consider more significant problems relating to Pervo's generic claim.

We may note, then, the interplay between views of the purpose of Acts and views of its ending. If the goal of Acts is to show the proclamation of the Gospel in Rome, Paul's fate is not important. If the purpose is to show the acceptability of Christianity to the authorities, it is best to leave Paul's fate unresolved, "since everyone knew Paul was not released but executed."[13] If, on the other hand, the purpose of Acts is to

---

[10] So also H. J. Cadbury, who suggested three "objects" for Luke–Acts: presentation of the message to the children of Israel, delivery of the message to the Gentiles, and a depiction of the legal innocence of Christianity of the charges brought against it by its opponents. *The Making of Luke–Acts* (London: SPCK, 1958 reprint), pp. 299–316.

[11] R. I. Pervo, *Profit with Delight: The Literary Genre of the Acts of the Apostles* (Philadelphia, 1987).

[12] E. Hennecke, *New Testament Apocrypha*, ed. W. Schneemelcher, trans. and ed. R. McL. Wilson (Philadelphia, 1965), vol. II, pp. 318–321 (Peter's martyrdom), pp. 383–387 (Paul's martyrdom).

[13] Haenchen, *The Acts of the Apostles*, p. 732.

enlighten and entertain, the ending represents a missed opportunity.

GENRE AND ENDING

History, biography, or novel – which genre best describes the book of Acts? Admittedly there are other generic possibilities, but the goal of this chapter is to be suggestive, not exhaustive. And admittedly the question may be put another way – what is the genre of Luke–Acts? The recent work of Pervo and Parsons, however, shows the difficulty, if not impossibility, of finding a common genre for Luke's two volumes, and they have argued persuasively that it is also unnecessary to maintain that Luke and Acts share a common genre.[14] We may return then to the question of the prevailing generic model of Acts.

The section on purpose ended with Pervo, and now that he has been mentioned again in this section, let us consider his suggestion that the genre of Acts is that of the ancient romance novel.[15] In important ways the suggestion is intriguing: Ancient romantic tales were filled with adventure, danger, mistaken identity, travel, shipwreck, piracy, kidnaping, miraculous deliverance, false accusations, trials, and, above all else, sex and romance.[16] Many of these characteristics are found in Acts, although it is a little short on sex and romance! But in other ways Pervo's suggestion fails to convince: The absence of romance is a significant omission, and the shift in emphasis from one major character to another (Peter to Paul) in the second half of Acts has no parallel in the extant ancient

---

[14] M. C. Parsons and R. I. Pervo, *Rethinking the Unity of Luke and Acts* (Minneapolis, 1993), pp. 20–44.

[15] "The data base for comparison of Acts to works of history that are similar in shape, scope, style and purpose is rather limited. Historical monographs with convincing affinities to Acts are difficult to identify. Novels that bear likenesses to Acts are, on the other hand, abundant . . . When the content of Acts, with its high proportion of exciting episodes, legendary presentations, and brief speeches, is taken into account, the scale tilts even more sharply toward the historical novel" (*Profit with Delight*, p. 137).

[16] See T. Hägg, *The Novel in Antiquity* (Berkeley, 1983), pp. 5–80. Hägg sees the parallel as between the Apocryphal Acts and the ancient novel, not between canonical Acts (pp. 161–162).

novels. While Acts does indeed entertain and inform, the ancient novels offer a profit/delight ratio weighed much more in favor of delight than does Acts, and have few parallels to the lengthy, stylized and repetitive speeches of Acts.[17]

For the purpose of this chapter it is the abrupt ending of Acts that is most troubling, as alluded to above. Ancient novels tell the tale of a hero or heroine, often both, following them through adventure and misadventure until they are reunited, married, and "live happily ever after." Villains are captured and punished, oracles fulfilled, the virtuous rewarded. There are no loose ends.[18] Acts follows Paul (leaving Peter forgotten!) through thick and thin, recounting preachings, beatings, arrest, trials, voyage, shipwreck, and eventual arrival in Rome. And then stops. If the genre of Acts is that of the ancient romance novel, the end of Acts is unthinkable: There are no parallels to the ending.[19]

What about Acts as biography? Such generic possibility is especially congenial for one who seeks a common genre for Luke–Acts, the Gospels having much in common with various biographical essays.[20] The literature on this topic is enormous, but since I have chosen to focus on Acts alone, an important recent study by L. Alexander will prove sufficient for consideration within the limited interest of this section.[21] Alexander

---

[17] Pervo maintains that the novels "provide more convincing and useful parallels to the contents and literary function of the speeches in Acts than will histories" (*Profit with Delight*, p. 76). But he offers scarcely any examples, and does not address the much broader use of speeches in Acts in comparison to the novels.

[18] "In general, the romances achieve full closure." J. Lee Magness, *Sense and Absence*, Semeia Studies (Atlanta, 1986), p. 42. Magness then quotes Hägg's early study, *Narrative Technique in Ancient Greek Romances* (Stockholm, 1971): "'The straight-forward mode of narrative . . . a beginning *ab ovo*, a linear succession of events, and a definite end' (Hägg, p. 310)."

[19] A topic Pervo does not address.

[20] See D. E. Aune, *The New Testament in its Literary Environment*, Library of Early Christianity (Philadelphia, 1987), pp. 17–76. Aune, as we shall see, regards Luke–Acts as an example of ancient historiography.

[21] L. C. A. Alexander, "Acts and Ancient Intellectual Biography," in B. W. Winter and A. D. Clarke (eds.), *The Book of Acts in its Ancient Literary Setting*, vol. I, *Acts in its First Century Setting* (Grand Rapids, 1993), pp. 31–63; see also pp. 73–103 above on Acts I.

maintains, following C. Talbert,[22] that Diogenes Laertius' *Lives of the Philosophers* is instructive for discussion of the genre of Acts. She does not go as far as Talbert, however, holding that a comparison of Diogenes and Luke–Acts shows as many differences as similarities.[23] Instead Alexander suggests that one look to the "hellenistic biographical tradition" upon which Diogenes Laertius, and presumably Luke, drew. She concludes that a "hellenistic school tradition offers clear evidence of biographical interest clustering around three foci: chronology and succession, doxography and bibliography, and the paradigm of the sage."[24] She points particularly to the "influential paradigm of Socrates" as exerting "some influence on the structuring of Luke's Pauline narrative."[25] But generically this leaves Acts 1–8, 10–12 adrift. And despite Alexander's carefully crafted eight points of comparison (divine call, mission, daimonion, tribulations, persecution, trial, prison, and death) one must again note the obvious: Luke does not narrate Paul's death. To be sure, Xenophon's *Memorabilia* does not narrate Socrates' death either, but Alexander is referring to a Socratic paradigm in which the manner of Socrates' death was well attested. "The Socratic paradigm was, above all, a paradigm for facing death: in Seneca's words (*Ep.*104.22) Socrates 'will show you how to die if it be necessary.'"[26] Put more simply, a biography which fails to narrate the death of its subject was either written before that death occurred, or is incomplete. The question of the end of Acts and its date of composition is the topic of the next section, but first we should consider a third generic alternative, the historical monograph.

Sunday School shorthand taught that Acts differs from the Gospels and the epistles, and is referred to as a "history,"

---

[22] C. H. Talbert, *Literary Patterns, Theological Themes and the Genre of Luke–Acts*, SBLMS 20 (Missoula, 1974).

[23] "It may be seen from this analysis that even where there are parallels in content between Acts and the Lives of Diogenes Laertius, detailed examination at the level of narrative mode points up as many contrasts as similarities." Alexander, "Acts and Ancient Intellectual Biography," p. 47.

[24] Ibid., p. 56.   [25] Ibid., p. 57.   [26] Ibid., p. 62.

unique among the writings of the New Testament. Our teachers were not far wrong, according to much recent scholarship. David Aune considers Acts to be a type of "general history," and while his generic designation may be influenced by his stated desire to treat Luke–Acts as a single genre,[27] his position is eminently defensible. "Using his rhetorical skills, Luke adapted the genre of general history, one of the more eclectic genres of antiquity, as an appropriate literary vehicle for depicting the origins and development of Christianity."[28]

D. Palmer's perceptive essay on the genre of Acts supports, while focusing, Aune's position.[29] Examining the positions of Sallust, Polybius, and Cicero, all ante-dating Luke's work by at least a century, Palmer sees clear parallels in their theories of historical composition: brevity, historical conciseness, thematic focus, and concentration on one figure at a time, as well as the use of letters, speeches, and a prologue. Josephus provides a contemporary parallel which Palmer, following G. E. Sterling, refers to as "apologetic historiography."[30] Palmer concludes that "the combination of length, scope, focus and internal literary features indicates that Acts deserves consideration as a short historical monograph."[31]

It is a suggestion I find congenial when dealing with the problematic interaction of the end of Acts and its genre. A biography that fails to narrate the death of its subject is odd, as odd as a biography that only devotes about half its space to its subject. An ancient romantic novel without romance, and which misses an opportunity for a graphic and bloody conclusion, is doubly unusual. But a work of history, be it "general" or a "monograph," with clearly apologetic concerns, that concludes its account before narrating an apologetically

---

[27] See the criticism of Parsons and Pervo, *Rethinking the Unity of Luke and Acts*, pp. 13–16.

[28] Aune, *The New Testament in its Literary Environment*, p. 77.

[29] D. W. Palmer, "Acts and the Ancient Historical Monograph," in B. W. Winter and A. D. Clarke (eds.), *The Book of Acts in its Ancient Literary Setting*, vol. 1, *Acts in its First Century Setting* (Grand Rapids, 1993), pp. 1–29.

[30] Ibid., pp. 15–18.   [31] Ibid., p. 29.

problematic event makes good sense.[32] Palmer is correct: Acts does indeed merit consideration as a short (apologetic) historical monograph.

DATE AND ENDING

There is a very obvious possible explanation for Luke's ending Acts where he does: He had brought his account up to date. He could not give an account of the trial and release or execution of Paul because they had not yet happened. This was the conclusion of Harnack, among others, and a conclusion which has a number of variations: Luke intended a third volume, in which Paul's release and later activity were narrated (Ramsay); Luke died before he could complete his account; and the ever popular theory that Luke wrote an account of Paul's execution, but it was suppressed or lost.[33]

The most important proposal for dating Acts at or close to the period Luke refers to as "two whole years" (διετίαν ὅλην) comes from F. F. Bruce. Here ideas of purpose, genre and dating come together. Bruce suggests that Acts was written sometime before the Neronian persecutions of 64.

> If we can date Luke's History a little earlier than the persecution of 64, we find a reasonable life-setting for the work. Paul's arrival in Rome, his apostolic witness there for two years, the legal procedure occasioned by his appeal to Caesar, must have brought Christianity to the notice of the Roman middle classes . . . If Theophilus was a representative of the intelligent reading public (or rather listening public) of Rome, here was Luke's opportunity to provide such people with a more accurate account of the rise and progress of Christianity . . . and also to vindicate the innocence of Paul and other Christians in relation to Roman law.[34]

Acts was written, then, when "Christianity was suspect, but not yet proscribed." And while it was not strictly a legal brief

---

32 There are other reasons, apologetic but of a different kind, for failing to narrate Paul's death. See Tannehill, *The Narrative Unity of Luke–Acts*, vol. II, p. 356.

33 For a summary of the possibilities see, among others, Jackson and Lake, *The Beginnings of Christianity*, vol. IV, pp. 349–350 and Cadbury, *The Making of Luke–Acts*, pp. 321–324.

34 F. F. Bruce, *The Book of the Acts*, p. 23.

meant to be used at Paul's trial, "some of the material in it would have been useful for that purpose." For Bruce, then, Luke wrote of what he knew and of what would be of use to his audience, who he presumes already knew of Paul, if not yet of his fate.

The assumptions here, it seems to me, are enormous. If one accepts Marcan priority, and Luke's (not proto-Luke's!) use of Mark, and also accepts that Luke was composed prior to Acts, a date of 61–62 for Acts requires a date for Mark, even assuming a Roman provenance for the Second Gospel, of the mid to late 50s, a date that is prior to Peter's death, *contra* the assumption of Papias' testimony about the composition of Mark, where Mark's relation to Peter is described as past.[35] Even among those who are not compelled by Mark 13 to date the Second Gospel to the period of 68 CE or after, few hold for such an early date for Mark.[36] Which makes such an early date for Acts unlikely.

Moreover, this early dating for Acts, along with all the other conclusions about purpose and genre, still leaves the reader with the issue with which we began: What an odd way for Luke to end his account! Even if Luke ended because he had nothing more to tell, why so abruptly? Or was it abrupt?

LITERARY PRECEDENTS AND PARALLELS, OR THE AX OF MARK

In his important study on the ending of Mark, *Sense and Absence*, J. Lee Magness makes a strong case that Mark 16.8 is the original and intended ending of the Second Gospel.[37] Magness cites a number of parallels from antiquity, secular and scriptural,

---

[35] Eusebius, *Ecclesiastical History* 3.39.15.

[36] This is, however, the conclusion of Carson, Moo, and Morris, *An Introduction to the New Testament* (Grand Rapids, 1992), pp. 96–99, 190–194. They seem dependent on Bruce. But note Colin J. Hemer, *The Book of Acts in the Setting of Hellenistic History* (Winona Lake, IN, 1990): "Although Mark's Gospel need not be later than the early sixties, it would be rash and unnecessary to claim that it is any earlier" (p. 404).

[37] J. Lee Magness, *Sense and Absence*, Semeia Studies (Atlanta, 1986).

which share Mark's abrupt ending.[38] The parallels are important for the end of Acts as well. But perhaps more important are the conclusions that Magness, and others, draw about the nature of Mark's ending, because I believe it likely that the ending of Mark had an important impact on the end of Acts, or rather, the end of Luke–Acts.

Whatever the parallels, be they biblical, such as the end of Kings, with Jehoiachin under "house arrest" wearing his own clothes and dining regularly in the Babylonian king's presence (2 Kgs. 25.29–30), cited by Trompf as a "fascinating similarity" that most scholars have missed,[39] or the end of the *Iliad*, with Hektor buried but the war far from resolved, ancient literatures are replete with endings which moderns find incomplete or insufficient. Setting aside the hubris of assuming that our notions of adequate endings are the only ones that matter, what is the significance of such endings for the reader? And assuming Luke–Acts to be a two-volume work, what should we make of the fact that Acts 28.30–31 is the conclusion of Luke and Acts? I propose to consider these issues by considering the ending of Luke–Acts in light of the ending of the Gospel of Mark, the only precedent which we may claim with confidence Luke was acquainted with.

No matter what one makes of the foreshadowing, hints, clues, and echoes found in Mark 16.1–8,[40] and no matter how one feels about the final γάρ, Mark 16.8 is an abrupt way to end the Gospel. Along with Magness, Fowler, Tolbert, and other literary and reader-response critics I am convinced that it is an intentional abruptness, an ending that, while it may not make sense, can be made sense of, which is precisely our task as readers.

Tolbert has shown that Mark's ending is previewed in the two stories of Jesus found in Mark 4 and Mark 12, passages she

---

[38] Among the important precedents and parallels of "suspended endings" cited by Magness are Homer's *Iliad* and *Odyssey*, Philostratus' *Life of Apollonius*; the story of Jephthah (Judges 11.29–40); the end of 2 Kings; Jonah; many of the parables of Jesus, most famously the "Lost Son" of Lk. 15.11–32; and many of the miracle stories in Mark. *Sense and Absence*, pp. 25–105.

[39] Trompf, "On Why Luke Declined to Recount the Death of Paul," p. 227.

[40] See Magness, *Sense and Absence*, especially the conclusion, pp. 107–125.

treats as revealing "the fundamental typologies underlying the story."[41] The so-called parable of the Sower outlines the different types of response to Jesus in chapters 5–11, and the so-called parable of the Wicked Tenants outlines the reception and fate of Jesus at the hands of his opponents in chapters 12, 14, and 15. Most critics have noted the foreshadowing implicit in the transfiguration (Mark 9.2–13), the anointing at Bethany (Mark 14.3–9) and the figure of the young man who flees from the site of Jesus' arrest (Mark 14.51–52). Magness has shown that fear and silence is a typical Marcan response to manifestations of the miraculous.[42] Tolbert and Fowler have suggested that the silence of the women, and their (narrative) failure to do as commanded, places the burden on the reader to "go and tell."[43]

Much has also been made of the open-endedness of Mark's closing verses. Rather than closing off the reader's options, providing a conclusion that "rounds off" the reading experience, Mark steadfastly resists the reader's desire for closure. Magness maintains that the ending is suspended, not absent. "The suspended ending causes the reader to act on the ending. Our contention has been that readers would have been forced to fill in the suspended ending."[44] My contention is that much the same is true for the ending of Luke–Acts.

Luke ends where he does for reasons theological, not chronological, by narrative design, not by the accident of history. Robert Tannehill reminds us that the farewell speech to the Ephesian elders in Acts 20 both foreshadows and leaves little doubt as to Paul's fate, and that the whole of Acts 28.17–31 reaches back to important events in Acts and Luke.[45] But where Tannehill sees "appropriate closure through circularity and parallelism" I see a more provocative openness, an openness arguably modeled on that of Mark.

---

[41] M. A. Tolbert, *Sowing the Gospel* (Minneapolis, 1989), p. 129.
[42] Magness, *Sense and Absence*, p. 94.
[43] Tolbert, *Sowing the Gospel*, p. 297; R. M. Fowler, *Let the Reader Understand* (Minneapolis, 1991).
[44] Magness, *Sense and Absence*, p. 123.
[45] Tannehill, *The Narrative Unity of Luke–Acts*, vol. II, pp. 344–357.

But where does Mark's open ending point? Some have argued that it points to Galilee, which is where Matthew takes Jesus and the disciples, in response to Mark 16.7 (= Matt. 28.7). But the reader cannot go to Galilee. Where the reader can go is back to the Gospel, returning to the beginning of the text and reading again. "Thus the awkward γάρ at Mark 16.8, coupled with the ambiguous allusion to Galilee in 16.7, signals the reader to return to the beginning of the Gospel, to begin reading all over again."[46] It is in this sense that Mark 16.8 provides closure, closing in on itself and holding the reader within its text, seeking answers to the questions posed by the silence of the women.

Such a proposal is commonplace for Mark among reader-response critics. A mysterious, incomplete, abrupt, unsatisfying conclusion forces the reader back into the text seeking clues to resolution, seeking answers. But what happens when it is extended to Luke–Acts? Tannehill and Haenchen have rightly argued one reason why Luke chooses not to narrate Paul's death is in order not to highlight martyrdom.[47] These and other suggestions seem grounded in attempts to account for the absence of Paul's execution from Acts. But how shall we explain its absence from Luke–Acts?

Paul, for all his heroism, for all the focus upon him in Acts 13–28, is not the central character of Luke–Acts; Jesus is. At some point, in some way, Luke needs to return the reader's attention to his central character. Just as Mark returns his readers to Jesus' passion, teaching, and miracles by refusing to recount his resurrection, so Luke chooses to turn attention back to Jesus by refusing to recount Paul's execution. Paul's absent martyrdom may, at one level, turn the reader to Stephen (Acts 7), but finally it will return the reader to the passion of Jesus. And, as the absent ending of Mark's Gospel sends the reader back to the beginning of his text, so the absent ending of Acts sends the reader back to the beginning, that is, to the beginning of the Gospel of Luke.

46 Fowler, *Let the Reader Understand*, p. 262.
47 Tannehill, *The Narrative Unity of Luke–Acts*, vol. II, p. 356; Haenchen, *The Acts of the Apostles*, p. 732.

Luke's model for an abrupt ending which raises questions
and forces the reader back into the text for answers was the
Gospel of Mark. This contention argues circularly for Mark
16.8 and Acts 28.31 as original endings. Luke, far from seeking
to erase Mark's ending by superimposing his own (what
Fowler reads Matthew as doing), borrowed from Mark and
used a similarly abrupt ending for Luke–Acts. This ending
works differently for Luke, however, for in returning the reader
to the beginning of his work he also turns the reader away from
a focus on Paul to a focus on Jesus. In this way Luke's literary
strategy, borrowed from Mark, reminds the reader of "the
teaching about the Lord Jesus Christ" (Acts 28.31).

Stephen Moore points out that in Luke "a narrative line
snakes out in a great loop until its mouth closes around the
Gospel's opening sentence. This loop is threaded through the
Acts of the Apostles."[48] The wryly post-everything Professor
Moore conjures up the snake swallowing its tail, exactly the
image I believe that the endings of Luke–Acts and Mark
suggest. By intentionally offering the reader only the most
abrupt of endings, Mark and Luke force the reader back into
the text, looping either directly to the opening of the Gospels,
inserting tale into mouth, or snaking back through to the
beginning.

Mark, it has been suggested from time to time, had an ax
taken to his text, lopping off its ending. Or it was lost, or
misplaced, or he died before he could provide a proper conclusion, the same sort of arguments put forth to explain the abrupt
ending of Luke–Acts. However one may regard the end of
Mark, the end of Luke–Acts is strong testimony that Mark
16.8, in all its abruptness, was the ending known in Luke's day.
And, while the end of Luke's Gospel gives testimony that
Mark's ending begged for extension, the end of Luke–Acts
suggests that it begged for emulation.

[48] *Mark and Luke in Poststructuralist Perspective* (New Haven, 1992), p. 7.

Index of biblical references